Baseball's Two-Way Greats

ALSO BY CHRIS JENSEN

Baseball State by State: Major and Negro League Players, Ballparks, Museums and Historical Sites (McFarland, 2012)

Baseball's Two-Way Greats

*Pitching/Batting Stars
from Ruth and Rogan
to Ohtani*

C̲h̲r̲i̲s̲ J̲e̲n̲s̲e̲n̲

McFarland & Company, Inc., Publishers
Jefferson, North Carolina

LIBRARY OF CONGRESS CATALOGING-IN-PUBLICATION DATA

Names: Jensen, Chris, 1963– author.
Title: Baseball's two-way greats : pitching/batting stars from Ruth and Rogan to Oohtani / Chris Jensen.
Description: Jefferson, North Carolina : McFarland & Company, Inc., Publishers, 2025. | Includes bibliographical references and index.
Identifiers: LCCN 2024057193 | ISBN 9781476696225 (paperback : acid free paper)∞ | ISBN 9781476654959 (ebook)
Subjects: LCSH: Baseball players—United States—Biography. | Pitching (Baseball) | Batting (Baseball)
Classification: LCC GV865.A1 J663 2025 | DDC 796.357092/273—dc23/eng/20241208
LC record available at https://lccn.loc.gov/2024057193

ISBN (print) 978-1-4766-9622-5
ISBN (ebook) 978-1-4766-5495-9

© 2025 Chris Jensen. All rights reserved

No part of this book may be reproduced or transmitted in any form or by any means, electronic or mechanical, including photocopying or recording, or by any information storage and retrieval system, without permission in writing from the publisher.

Front cover images: (left to right) Babe Ruth, 1916 (Culver Pictures); Charles Wilber "Bullet" Rogan (National Baseball Hall of Fame and Museum, Cooperstown, New York); Shohei Ohtani, 2022 (Mogami Kariya)

Printed in the United States of America

McFarland & Company, Inc., Publishers
  Box 611, Jefferson, North Carolina 28640
    www.mcfarlandpub.com

Table of Contents

PREFACE	1
INTRODUCTION	3
1. The Uniqueness of Two-Way Players: A Closer Look at the Stats	9
2. John Montgomery Ward: Baseball's First Two-Way Star	18
3. 19th Century: An Evolving Game Forces Players to Adapt	30

George Bradley 31; *Charlie Buffinton* 33; *Jimmy "Nixey" Callahan* 34; *Bob Caruthers* 35; *Dave Foutz* 38; *Kid Gleason* 39; *Guy Hecker* 40; *Win Mercer* 42; *Tony Mullane* 44; *Charles "Old Hoss" Radbourn* 46; *Jack Stivetts* 48; *Adonis Terry* 49; *Jim Whitney* 52; *Additional Players of Note* 53

4. Deadball Era 1900–1919: Two-Way Play Slows Down	56

Ray Caldwell 58; *Doc Crandall* 61; *Harry Howell* 63; *Johnny Lush* 65; *Al Orth* 65; *Reb Russell* 67; *Jesse Tannehill* 69; *Doc White* 70; *Smoky Joe Wood* 73; *Additional Players of Note* 76

5. Babe Ruth: Baseball's Larger-Than-Life Legend	80
6. Bullet Rogan: The Negro Leagues' Greatest Triple Threat	98
7. Martín Dihigo: Black Baseball's Versatile and Underrated Star	111
8. The Negro Leagues: Teams Filled with Two-Way Players	120

Bernardo Baró 122; *James "Cool Papa" Bell* 122; *William Bell* 125; *Ramón Bragaña* 126; *George "Chippy" Britt* 127; *Barney "Brinquitos" Brown* 128; *Ray Brown* 128; *Harry Buckner* 130; *Bill Byrd* 130; *Tatica Campos* 131; *Walter "Rev" Cannady* 132; *Oscar Charleston* 133; *Phil Cockrell* 134; *Homer "Goose" Curry* 134; *Johnny Davis* 135; *Walter "Steel Arm" Davis* 135; *John Donaldson* 136; *Charles Earle* 137; *Isidro Fabré* 138; *Luther Farrell* 138; *Wilmer "Red" Fields* 139; *Andrew "Rube" Foster* 140; *Manuel "Cocaína" Garcia* 141; *Bill Gatewood* 142; *Willie "Three Finger" Gisentaner* 142; *Carl*

"Butch" Glass 143; *Bob "Schoolboy" Griffith* 143; *Lewis Hampton* 143; *Dave Hoskins* 144; *Jesse "Mountain" Hubbard* 144; *Wade Johnston* 145; *Harry Kenyon* 145; *Holsey "Script" Lee* 146; *Bill Lindsay* 146; *Verdell "Lefty" Mathis* 147; *Dan McClellan* 148; *Terris McDuffie* 149; *Henry McHenry* 149; *Hurley McNair* 150; *José Méndez* 150; *Eddie Miller* 152; *George Mitchell* 152; *José Muñoz* 153; *Luis Padrón* 153; *Tom Parker* 154; *Roy "Red" Parnell* 155; *Roy Partlow* 155; *Eustaquio Pedroso* 156; *Alonzo Perry* 157; *Willie Powell* 157; *Connie Rector* 157; *Ed Rile* 158; *Lázaro Salazar* 159; *Hilton Smith* 159; *Theolic Smith* 161; *Joe Strong* 161; *Ben Taylor* 162; *Cristóbal Torriente* 163; *Smokey Joe Williams* 164; *Nip Winters* 165

9. Ted "Double Duty" Radcliffe: Baseball's Greatest Catcher-Pitcher Combo — 167
10. Leon Day: More Than Just an Ace Pitcher — 178
11. Live Ball Era 1920–Present: Two-Way Play That Bucked the System — 186
    Clarence Mitchell 187; *Jack Bentley* 189; *Rube Bressler* 191; *George Sisler* 193; *Lefty O'Doul* 195; *Johnny Cooney* 196; *Bob Smith* 197; *Red Lucas* 198; *Ben Chapman* 199; *Bobby Reis* 200; *Bucky Walters* 201; *Lovill "Chubby" Dean* 203; *René Monteagudo* 203; *Max Macon* 204; *Johnny Lindell* 204; *Erv Dusak* 206; *Clint Hartung* 206; *Hal Jeffcoat* 207; *Dick Hall* 208; *Willie Smith* 209; *Mel Queen* 210; *Ron Mahay* 211; *Brooks Kieschnick* 211; *Rick Ankiel* 212; *Michael Lorenzen* 214; *Matt Bush* 215
12. Shohei Ohtani: On the Path to Baseball Immortality — 217
13. Pitchers at the Plate: Profiling the Best-Hitting Pitchers — 234

CHAPTER NOTES — 249
BIBLIOGRAPHY — 263
INDEX — 265

Preface

Shohei Ohtani's arrival in major league baseball in 2018 and his spectacular breakout season of 2021 led to lots of references and comparisons to Babe Ruth. No one alive had ever seen a two-way player perform such amazing feats game after game, but press reports seemed to give the impression that Ruth and Ohtani are the only two-way players in baseball history. I was well aware that a number of Negro League stars shined as two-way players, so I felt compelled to research and identify just how many two-way players there have been.

Once I started diving into the career stats, it quickly became apparent that two-way play was even more prevalent in the 19th century and in the Negro Leagues than I had thought. Also, Ruth was not the only two-way player in the Deadball Era. The Seamheads Negro League Database was used as the definitive source for career stats of the Negro Leaguers, and the continued development of that site has been a valuable resource for researchers like me. Baseball-Reference helped me identify and evaluate the rest of the major leaguers. Using the Statfinder query tool from Sports-Reference enabled me to determine which players stood out for their single-season and career two-way play.

The more I learned about the careers of Negro League stars Bullet Rogan, Leon Day, Martín Dihigo, and Ted "Double Duty" Radcliffe, the more intrigued I became. Was it possible the greatest two-way player in baseball history was not Babe Ruth or Ohtani? Now that was a research subject that interested me enough to want to write a book about it. I could find no other books that have been written about the history of two-way players, so I set out to write the definitive book about the subject.

My research for this book included a week digging through files at the Giamatti Research Center at the Baseball Hall of Fame in Cooperstown.

I took a closer look at 19th-century stars like John Montgomery Ward, Bob Caruthers, and Dave Foutz; evaluated the brief interludes of players like Johnny Lush and Willie Smith; and explored the generational excellence of the Bambino and the sustained two-way brilliance of numerous

Blackball stars. I pored over the ground-breaking work of Cuban baseball historians Peter Bjarkman and Jorge Figueredo, along with other researchers, to ensure Negro League players' time in the Latin leagues was given full consideration. Although Ohtani's baseball history is still being written, it was important to see how his first six seasons stacked up against the careers of other two-way stars.

I found myself comparing apples to oranges when trying to compare the careers of Negro League stars like Rogan, Day, Dihigo, and Radcliffe to major leaguers like Ruth and Ohtani. Same thing with trying to compare Ruth's brief stint as a two-way player (right before the Live Ball Era commenced) with what Ohtani is doing in today's modern game and to what John Montgomery Ward and many other two-way players did during the 19th century.

This book takes a chronological look at baseball's history of two-way players. The first chapter sets the stage by taking a closer look at the stats that define what constitutes a two-way player. I started with a reasonable standard—all players who pitched in at least 10 games and recorded more than 200 at-bats in a season—then looked at what happened when I adjusted the parameters up or down. The same players kept cropping up no matter how I sliced the data. Ultimately, I identified 133 two-way players who were worth mentioning in this book.

Separate chapters in this book are devoted to distinct periods, including the 19th century, Deadball Era, Negro Leagues, and Live Ball Era, with a final chapter on the 25 best-hitting pitchers as ranked by offensive wins above replacement (WAR). Interspersed are in-depth profiles of seven of the greatest two-way players: Ward, Ruth, Rogan, Dihigo, Radcliffe, Day, and Ohtani. I attempted to place each player's career in the proper context of the era they played in and share what their peers thought of their abilities, while doing my best to share relevant statistics across distinctly different eras. Many of these two-way players were good at pitching and batting at different points of their career, but not necessarily at the same time. Once baseball's Live Ball Era commenced in 1920, two-way play became a rarity and great two-way play even rarer. Blackball players, on the other hand, were forced to be versatile to enable their teams to navigate grueling schedules with thin benches. I identified 60 standout two-way players from the Negro Leagues whose accomplishments are covered in Chapter 8.

Baseball's rich history is filled with two-way players who shined when given a chance to showcase their all-around skills. Readers can draw their own conclusions about who was the greatest two-way player in baseball history, and we can all look forward to who might be coming next.

Introduction

When the Los Angeles Dodgers signed Shohei Ohtani to the largest contract in baseball history before the 2024 season—$700 million over 10 seasons, most of it deferred—the team did so because he possessed the most jaw-dropping combination of hitting and pitching talents anyone had ever seen. The Dodgers signed an ace pitcher and an all-star slugger in one bold move while only needing to fill one roster spot.

Ohtani's emergence has provided a teaching moment for some to point out his two-way accomplishments had been commonplace in the Negro Leagues. "It shines a very bright light on the history of the Negro Leagues and the immense talent that was in the Negro Leagues," said Bob Kendrick, president of the Negro Leagues Baseball Museum in Kansas City. "It's been refreshing for me to see this kid from Japan, to basically defy what skeptics probably thought."[1]

Awe-inspiring feats aside, it is difficult to compare what Ohtani is doing to what Black and Latino stars like Bullet Rogan, Martín Dihigo, Leon Day, Ted "Double Duty" Radcliffe and other Negro Leaguers did. When Rogan, Dihigo, and Day were not pitching, they played center field or some other position in the field. When Radcliffe was not pitching, he was playing the physically demanding position of catcher, which is how the "Double Duty" nickname originated. When Ohtani is not pitching, he serves as the designated hitter (DH), a non-fielding position that never existed in the Negro Leagues. It remains to be seen how much time, if any, Ohtani will spend playing in the field for the duration of his career, just as we are waiting to see if he can return and pitch effectively once he recovers from his second elbow surgery.

These are the conclusions I have reached after conducting the research for this book: John Ward was the best two-way player of the 19th century. Babe Ruth was the best two-way player in the segregated major leagues in the modern era, which covers after the American League was founded in 1901 up until Jackie Robinson broke the color barrier in 1947. Martín Dihigo was the best two-way player in the Latin leagues. Bullet Rogan was the best two-way player in the Negro Leagues. Shohei Ohtani is the best two-way player in the post-integration era (after 1947).

I will take it a step further and declare that Bullet Rogan is the best triple-threat player in baseball history. By triple threat, I mean the impact he had on games as a pitcher, batter, and fielder. Rogan was a one-man wrecking crew for more than two decades. When he wasn't pitching like Bob Gibson, he was playing center field, batting, and running the bases like Joe DiMaggio. Ruth was not a top-notch fielder or baserunner—especially as he aged and gained weight—and he only performed as a two-way player in two seasons. Ward had two distinct careers, first as a workhorse pitcher under now-archaic rules, and then as an everyday shortstop and batsman. More importantly, 19th-century baseball is far removed from the game played by Ruth and Ohtani. When Ward started his pitching career in 1878, pitchers were required to throw with an underhanded delivery and players didn't use gloves. Ohtani has solely been a designated hitter when not pitching, and he has been able to pitch less than half the time. Rogan played 150 to 200 games a year and when he was not pitching and batting cleanup, he was playing center field or some other position. He could steal a base, hit a home run, make a diving catch, and strike out the heart of the opponents' lineup, sometimes all in the same game. Ruth, Ward, and Ohtani never did that.

When comparing Ruth and Ohtani, one big distinction should be made—Ruth never aspired to be a two-way player. Ruth's manager on the Red Sox, Ed Barrow, feared he would be laughed out of the league if he allowed his best pitcher to play the field every day. As a result, he resisted the move despite overwhelming evidence Babe was the best slugger in the majors. Once the Bambino started hitting home runs and playing every day in the field, he did not want to pitch anymore. If the Yankees had wanted him to keep pitching and playing the outfield after they acquired him in 1920, he would have resisted that move.

It is difficult, if not impossible, to compare Ruth's production as a pitcher and hitter to Ohtani's production as a pitcher and hitter. The game of baseball evolved for almost a full century before Ohtani came on the scene, so the two stars played in vastly different eras. Through the 2023 season, Ohtani had appeared in 627 games as a designated hitter, a position not available to Ruth during his playing days. Ruth played in an era of segregation. He never had to compete against Black players, deal with jet lag from flying across the country, play on artificial turf, face a bullpen full of fireballers throwing 100-mph heat, survive three postseason rounds to get to the World Series, or outsmart a pitching staff armed with analytical data on how best to pitch to him.

Ohtani has had better access to year-round training facilities and equipment, better coaching, and first-class travel. He has taken advantage of medical advancements to have two elbow surgeries. Such an injury back in Ruth's era would have probably ended his career as a pitcher. Players today are better conditioned and overall better athletes. Almost every pitcher today throws harder than the fastest pitcher of Ruth's era. Ruth mainly faced fastballs and curveballs, along with the occasional knuckleball and screwball. Emery balls and spitballs were outlawed after 1920, and he did not have to hit sliders, sweepers, or any other pitch with much spin.

Baseball historian Bill James points out that pitchers were by far the most valuable players when the National League began in 1876, because the teams' top pitchers were pitching nearly every game. Pitchers were worth three times the value of position players back then, according to James.[2] Plus, most pitchers in those days were as proficient with the bat as any of the position players. When the mound got moved back to 60 feet, six inches in 1893, it made it physically impossible for pitchers to throw every day. By the time the 19th century came to a close, teams were using a full complement of pitchers and the value of pitchers more closely equaled that of position players. Ruth was smart enough to realize he could help his team a lot more by batting and playing the field every day rather than pitching every fourth or fifth day.

Players such as Smoky Joe Wood sometimes turned to position play and batting when they developed sore arms while pitching. Until the DH came along, all pitchers were in the lineup batting every time they took the mound—it was a regular part of the game for them. Managers could quickly spot the pitchers who were the best hitters. Before modern substitution rules were adopted in 1890, pitchers could only be taken out of the game due to injury. If you wanted to replace a pitcher for poor performance, you had to swap him with another position player, usually the right fielder.

Hall of Famer Stan Musial started out as a pitcher before switching to be an outfielder and first baseman. Hall of Fame relief pitcher Trevor Hoffman initially played shortstop before switching to the bullpen, while Hall of Fame pitcher Bob Lemon debuted in the majors as a third baseman before getting converted to the mound. As any MLB player would tell you, doing one thing like batting or pitching at a high level is incredibly hard. Most cannot fathom being able to do both at a high level.

Major League Baseball's recent recognition of seven Negro leagues as major leagues, while long overdue, does not immediately level the playing field when it comes to game stats. MLB is only embracing Negro League action from 1920 to 1948 as part of Major League Baseball's history. That leaves a lot of Black baseball pre–1920 to remain relegated to second-class status, not to mention all the barnstorming games against semipro teams that don't count in the official stats. The end result is a diminished level of recognition for Rogan, Day, Dihigo, Radcliffe, and many other Blackball stars. If Rogan could generate 9.8 WAR from a 1925 season in which he is credited with 25 pitching appearances and 145 at-bats, just imagine what his full-season stats would be like.

Major League Baseball's owners succeeded in keeping Rogan and other Negro League players from playing as equals with white players, which is ultimately a loss to everyone. MLB teams deprived themselves of the thrilling play and wide appeal that stars like Rogan and teams like the Monarchs proved every time they hit the road.

One of the foremost experts on the Negro Leagues, Larry Lester, was happy to share his thoughts with me on the subject of two-way players. "In my opinion the greatest two-way player is, without a doubt, Bullet Rogan. I would put Rogan over Leon Day and Martín Dihigo, because Day's primary role was as a pitcher, while Dihigo seldom pitched and is better known for his hitting and versatility in the field. Rogan was equally a threat on the mound and in the batter's box. There was no off-day when it came to showcasing his talents," he said.

Lester added, "We cannot compare Ohtani and Rogan, or Dihigo or Double Duty across generations. Ohtani has better trainers, eats better and has better post-game treatments. To Ohtani's detriment, he has to play on artificial turf, play in night games and occasionally fly coast to coast to play in a series. Rogan and Dihigo did not play on manicured fields and often traveled by bus or motorcade lacking A/C. Without a doubt Ohtani is a generational talent, but so was Rogan. Despite being shut down for pitching duty in 2024, Ohtani is pretty amazing. Today, I give the edge to Rogan, because he did double duty for a longer period of time."

When evaluating the career of Bullet Rogan, the most striking thing to me is the nine years of his prime that he lost while serving in the U.S. Army. He was a standout two-way player in the Army, but none of those hits, strikeouts, and wins are included in his career stats. Nine more years of top-notch performing in the Negro Leagues would have undoubtedly cemented his status as the greatest two-way player in baseball history.

My son, Brandon, was a two-way player in high school who played center field when he was not pitching. Then in his junior year, his coach decided he would only be a pitcher. That is the same story that has played out for thousands of baseball players in the high school and college ranks, including stars like Aaron Judge, Dave Winfield, Aaron Hicks, Nick Markakis, Josh Hamilton, John Olerud, and Ken Brett. Ohtani's greatness as a two-way player is already opening the door to more players being allowed to pursue their own two-way path in high school, college, and the minor leagues.

Introduction

A record eight two-way players were selected in the 2023 Major League Baseball draft, and some will be allowed to see how far they can go down that path. Florida's Jac Caglianone has been tearing it up in college as a starting pitcher and first baseman, so who knows if he can keep that going into the majors. He tied an NCAA record in 2024 by homering in nine straight games and was 5–1 on the mound with 63 strikeouts in 53 innings to go with a .412 average and 27 homers through most of the season. What major league team wouldn't want a player who can pitch a few innings here and there while also playing the field? That is the definition of a true utility player.

A new kind of two-way sensation is developing in the college ranks. Jurrangelo Cijntje, a native of Curaçao, is an ambidextrous pitcher for Mississippi State who throws equally well with either arm. Pat Venditte was a switch pitcher who pitched to a 4.73 ERA in 61 games across five seasons in the majors from 2015 to 2020. As a righty hurler, Venditte threw over the top at about 85 mph. He side-armed his lefty pitches in the low to mid 80s, but he never threw hard enough or had enough deception with either arm to be much of a weapon. Cijntje, on the other hand, tops out at 99 as a righty and 95 as a southpaw and had recorded 88 strikeouts in 66 innings through 12 starts in his sophomore season. Being able to throw heat like that with either arm positions Cijntje as a valuable two-way weapon out of the bullpen.

Baseball fans look forward to every time Ohtani takes the mound or steps up to the plate. They know they are witnessing something unique and special, a form of baseball artistry that might never get topped or duplicated. Now sit back and imagine yourself in the stands of Muehlebach Field in Kansas City as Bullet Rogan takes the mound to face Martín Dihigo, with the roles reversed in the bottom half of the inning. It would be every bit as exciting as it was to watch Ohtani pitch to Mike Trout in the 2023 World Baseball Classic. The Negro Leagues' greatest players regularly performed astonishing two-way feats on baseball diamonds across America, but they were forced to play in the shadows mostly beyond the witness of white society. That doesn't make their accomplishments any less worthy of recognition.

"For me, the excitement of Ohtani creates the exact opportunity we have today, to say, 'Nah, it's not just Ruth,'" said Kendrick. "Maybe this will put the spotlight on those legendary players that people did not know."[3]

Chapter 1

The Uniqueness of Two-Way Players

A Closer Look at the Stats

Shohei Ohtani and Babe Ruth are not the only major league players who have performed as two-way players across an entire season, but it's still an exclusive club. More Negro League players would be added to the list of two-way players if complete records of all their games were available, and if a large number of their games were not excluded from the count due to the level of competition they faced. Top Negro League players played upwards of 200 games a year, but their official stats reflect their performance in roughly a third of those games.

One of the best ways to compare the careers and individual seasons of two-way players is by looking at Wins Above Replacement or WAR. Babe Ruth, John Ward, Bullet Rogan, and Martín Dihigo are the only players who have generated at least 20 career WAR as both a pitcher and a batter. Dihigo accumulated more than half of his career WAR (35.8) in Latin leagues versus 29.3 WAR in Negro League action. Ohtani should soon join these four players in this exclusive club, assuming he is able to resume pitching at a high level—he was at 19.4 offensive WAR and 15.1 pitching WAR through the 2023 season.

Bob Caruthers, Ruth, and Ward are the only players in major league history to post at least 16.0 WAR as both a pitcher and a batter, according to Baseball-Reference. Lázaro Salazar joins Rogan and Dihigo as Negro Leaguers who have earned that distinction, according to Seamheads.

What follows is a look at the WAR totals for some of the most prolific two-way players in the major leagues (using data from Baseball-Reference) and the Negro Leagues (using data from Seamheads, the acknowledged authority in statistics for Black baseball).

Major League Player	Offensive WAR	Pitching WAR	Defensive WAR	Career WAR
Babe Ruth	154.5	20.4	-2.3	182.6
John Ward	29.7	28.1	10.4	62.3
Bob Caruthers	16.8	44.7	-3.8	59.5
Kid Gleason	12.3	33.0	-1.7	41.8
Smoky Joe Wood	12.0	29.6	-3.6	40.1
Guy Hecker	12.6	27.6	-3.2	37.3
Dave Foutz	12.4	22.7	-1.1	35.4
Shohei Ohtani	19.4	15.1	-5.6	34.7
Nixey Callahan	11.2	15.6	-4.1	24.9

Source: Baseball-Reference

Negro League Player	Offensive WAR	Pitching WAR	Defensive WAR	Career WAR
Martín Dihigo	28.8	33.7	3.8	65.8
Bullet Rogan	25.7	35.6	1.4	61.6
Ray Brown	6.7	37.5	-0.2	43.5
Eustaquio Pedroso	14.6	34.6	-4.8	42.5
Ben Taylor	31.5	2.8	5.4	36.0
Lázaro Salazar	16.5	16.7	1.6	33.6
Luis Padrón	12.3	12.0	0.8	24.0
Leon Day	3.8	19.3	0.3	23.5
Ed Rile	10.3	9.8	-0.8	18.0

Source: Seamheads

In 2021, Ohtani became the only player in modern major-league history (since 1901) to generate at least 4.0 WAR per 162 games batting and pitching in the same season—he did it again in 2023 and just missed in 2022. Using WAR per 162 games as a statistical comparison tool levels the playing field for Negro League players, who typically played seasons of 80–90 games. By including the Negro League players, we see that Bullet Rogan becomes the leader of the club with six qualifying seasons, as well as Ed Rile for one season. Dihigo accomplished this feat four straight years (1940–43), but that was for his play in the Mexican League. Going back to 19th-century play leads to the inclusion of one player: Bob Caruthers. Ruth did not come especially close to joining the club in his two primary seasons as a two-way player, 1918 and 1919. In 1918, he generated 5.91 offensive WAR per 162 games and 2.95 pitching WAR per 162. In 1919, he produced 9.74 offensive WAR per 162 but just 0.93 WAR with pitching. Here is a look at the full list of major league and Negro League seasons with at least 4.0 WAR per 162 games pitching and batting.

Chapter 1. The Uniqueness of Two-Way Players

Player	Season	Offensive WAR Per 162	Pitching WAR Per 162	Total WAR Per 162
Bullet Rogan	1925	4.05	13.80	17.85
Bullet Rogan	1922	7.69	7.89	15.58
Bullet Rogan	1923	5.12	10.45	15.57
Bob Caruthers	1886	5.01	8.85	13.86
Bob Caruthers	1887	4.34	7.98	12.32
Ed Rile	1927	6.05	5.56	11.61
Bullet Rogan	1924	5.94	5.53	11.47
Shohei Ohtani	2023	6.0	4.0	10.00
Shohei Ohtani	2021	4.8	4.1	8.90
Bullet Rogan	1921	4.77	4.09	8.86
Bullet Rogan	1928	4.45	4.25	8.70

Source: Seamheads, Baseball-Reference

According to research conducted through Stathead, there have been 45 instances when a major league player pitched in at least 10 games and recorded more than 200 plate appearances in a single season since 1900. If you include 19th-century games, then 336 player seasons meet these criteria.

Shohei Ohtani has the four most-recent seasons hitting these marks: 2023, 2022, 2021 and 2018. Out of these 45 seasons, Ohtani posted the three-highest home run totals of 46 (in 2021), 44 (in 2023) and 34 (in 2022), as well as the two-highest stolen base totals: 26 steals in 2021 and 20 steals in 2023.

Of the 336 seasons in which a major league player pitched in at least 10 games and recorded more than 200 plate appearances, 291 of them came during the 19th century. With a total of 2,007 players playing in one of the five officially recognized major leagues between 1876 and 1899, that means 14.5 percent of them met these criteria for being a two-way player. By comparison, Ohtani was the only MLB player out of 1,457 players to pitch at least 10 games and make 200 plate appearances in 2023.

After Babe Ruth reached this same threshold in 1918 and 1919 with the Red Sox, only Negro League players accomplished the feat from 1920 to 1930—17 seasons from 12 different players. Five of them were by Rogan. The only other Negro Leaguer with multiple seasons was Harry Kenyon in 1921 and 1925.

Here is the list of Negro League players who pitched in at least 10 games and recorded more than 200 plate appearances in a season:

Bullet Rogan: 1920, 1921, 1922, 1923, 1928
Ben Taylor: 1920

Jim Jeffries: 1920
John Donaldson: 1920
Isaac Lane: 1921
Harry Kenyon: 1921, 1925
Eustaquio Pedroso: 1922
Wade Johnston: 1922
Jesse Hubbard: 1927
Ed Rile: 1927
Ted Radcliffe: 1930
John Williams: 1930

After Radcliffe and Williams hit the threshold in the Negro National League in 1930, the next players to accomplish the feat were René Monteagudo with the Phillies in 1945 and Willie Smith with the Los Angeles Angels in 1964. Then there was a long wait until Ohtani came on the scene, with more spectacular seasons to come for him in the future.

A closer examination of the 45 player seasons with 10 games pitched and 200 plate appearances since 1900 reveals only 12 seasons of any distinction. Four were accomplished by Ohtani, four by Rogan, two by Ruth and the other two were produced by Negro Leaguers Rile (1927) and Radcliffe (1930).

Few baseball fans marveled at Monteagudo posting a 7.49 ERA in 45⅔ innings in 1945 to go with his .301 average from 35 stints in the outfield; or Art Hoelskoetter pitching to a 57 ERA+ from 12 appearances in 1906 to go with a .224 average and .238 OBP while splitting time at six positions in the field. Likewise with Negro Leaguer Isaac Lane's 1921 season with the Columbus Buckeyes, when he compiled a 5.80 ERA across 45 innings and batted .255 during short stints at third base and left field.

Including the 19th-century players, here are the best batting seasons recorded from the 336 two-way players, as ranked by adjusted OPS:

Player	*Season*	*OPS+*
Babe Ruth	1919	217
Bob Caruthers	1886	201
Bullet Rogan	1922	199
Ed Rile	1927	194
Babe Ruth	1918	192
Shohei Ohtani	2023	184
Bob Caruthers	1887	169
Guy Hecker	1886	161

Chapter 1. The Uniqueness of Two-Way Players

Player	Season	OPS+
Shohei Ohtani	2021	157
Shohei Ohtani	2018	151
Bullet Rogan	1923	150
Bullet Rogan	1928	149

Source: Stathead

Looking at players since 1871 who pitched in at least 10 games, had 200 or more plate appearances and generated WAR (wins above replacement) greater than 3.0 as a position player in a season, six players make the list for 10 seasons. An unexpected name rises to the top, but 19th-century pitchers accumulated a lot of WAR by pitching nearly every game.

Player	Season	Position Player WAR	Pitching WAR	Total WAR
Bob Caruthers	1886	3.9	7.6	11.5
Bob Caruthers	1887	3.9	6.8	10.7
Shohei Ohtani	2023	6.0	4.0	10.0
Babe Ruth	1919	9.1	0.8	9.9
Shohei Ohtani	2022	3.4	6.2	9.6
Bullet Rogan	1922	4.5	4.6	9.1
Shohei Ohtani	2021	4.9	4.1	9.0
Babe Ruth	1918	4.7	2.3	7.0
Ed Rile	1927	3.7	3.2	6.9
Ben Taylor	1920	3.1	0.6	3.7

Source: Stathead

John Ward's 1879 season should also be noted—he produced 9.2 total WAR that year with 7.3 WAR coming from pitching and 1.9 from being a position player. Bullet Rogan's best overall season was 1925 when he produced 9.8 total WAR (7.5 from pitching, 2.2 from batting and 0.1 WAR from fielding).

Changing the Stathead criteria to at least 50 career games in the outfield and 50 career games at pitcher since 1871, you get 91 players. Twenty-five of those are Negro League players, led by Rogan with a career adjusted OPS of 152 and Dihigo with a career adjusted OPS of 138.

Adjusting the criteria to only Negro League players playing at least 75 games in the outfield and 75 games at pitcher, nine players emerge: Rogan, Homer Curry, Luther Farrell, Ray Brown, Harry Kenyon, Barney Brown, Terris McDuffie, Willie Gisentaner, and Jim Jeffries.

Searching for players with 150 plate appearances and 10 pitching appearances in one major league season, up pops Hanser Alberto in 2022. The infielder pitched in 10 games (totaling 11 innings) for the Dodgers that season with 159 plate appearances. No one views him as a two-way player.

If you adjust Stathead criteria to 200 plate appearances and 15 pitching appearances, you wind up with 309 player seasons but just 33 of them since 1900. Twelve of these seasons were posted by Negro League players, four of them by Rogan.

Looking at which players have multiple seasons of at least 10 pitching appearances and 200 or more plate appearances, we find 73 players have two or more such seasons. The list is led by Guy Hecker, who posted nine consecutive seasons of 10 pitching games and at least 200 plate appearances from 1882 to 1890. Next is another 19th-century player, Tony Mullane, with eight seasons. Rogan produced five qualifying seasons, Ohtani has four (through 2023), and Harry Kenyon, Babe Ruth, Doc White, and Wyatt Lee each had two seasons. The other 67 players with multiple seasons of 10 pitching games and at least 200 plate appearances are all 19th-century players.

There are 22 players who have pitched at least 160 games and played at least 160 games in the field during their career, according to Baseball-Reference. Only one of them is a Negro League player: Bullet Rogan. A number of other Negro League players would undoubtedly meet those criteria, but not enough game stats have been verified yet to prove their accomplishment since barnstorming games are excluded.

Among those 22 players with at least 160 appearances on the mound and in the field, here are the pitching and batting leaders by WAR:

Player	Pitching WAR	Career WAR
Tony Mullane	61.0	66.6
Jim Whitney	47.5	56.0
Bucky Walters	46.5	53.5
Bob Caruthers	44.7	59.5
Jack Stivetts	40.3	48.5
Bullet Rogan	38.0	61.4

Source: Baseball-Reference

Player	Position Player WAR	Career WAR
Babe Ruth	162.2	182.6
John Ward	34.3	62.3
Bullet Rogan	23.4	61.4
Bob Caruthers	14.8	59.5

Player	Position Player WAR	Career WAR
Dave Foutz	12.8	35.4
Smoky Joe Wood	10.5	40.1

Source: Baseball-Reference

Since the American League was formed in 1901, there have been 27 player-seasons with at least 20 appearances on the mound and 20 appearances at a position other than pitcher. Ohtani (2021, 2022 and 2023) is the only player to do it three times—with designated hitter being considered a position for him—and he is the first player to accomplish this feat since Willie Smith in 1964. Babe Ruth and Johnny Cooney both accomplished it twice. Four players did it during the 1902 season: Nixey Callahan, Harry Howell, Jock Menefee and Doc White.

Taking a closer examination of Negro League players, Stathead comes up with 29 players who appeared in at least 100 games as pitcher with 400 career plate appearances and WAR over 1. The list is led by Hall of Famers Rogan, Ray Brown, and Hilton Smith, as well as Homer "Goose" Curry, Ed Rile, Lewis Hampton, Bill Byrd, and Luther Farrell. Among those players, here is the leaderboard for career offensive wins above replacement (which takes out the fielding value incorporated into WAR):

Player	oWAR
Bullet Rogan	22.5
Homer Curry	12.9
Ed Rile	11.1
Ray Brown	6.3
Luther Farrell	5.7

Source: Stathead

Much progress has been made over the last decade to compile statistics from the Negro Leagues and grant these players major league status, but much work is still to be done. If you go to Baseball-Reference and look at the career leaders for pitching WAR, Satchel Paige is the highest-ranked Negro League pitcher—he comes in at 124th place with 47.0 WAR, helped out by the 10.2 WAR he accumulated during six seasons pitching in Major League Baseball. Next highest is Hall of Famer Bill Foster in 131st place with 45.6 WAR and Bullet Rogan in 197th place with 38.0 WAR. Baseball-Reference only has stats for 214 pitching appearances for Rogan, while Seamheads shows him with 236 pitching appearances. He pitched in significantly more games than that, but barnstorming games against semipro and town teams are not included due to the level of competition they offered.

Below is a comparison between Ohtani's first full-time season as a two-way player in 2021 and Ruth's first two-way season in 1919. Bold text denotes they led the league that year.

	Ruth 1919 Season	**Ohtani 2021 Season**
At-bats	432	537
Runs	**103**	103
Hits	139	138
Doubles	34	26
Triples	12	**8**
Home Runs	**29**	46
RBI	**113**	100
Stolen Bases	7	26
Average	.322	.257
OBP	**.456**	.372
Slugging	**.657**	.592
OPS	**1.114**	.965
OPS+	**217**	157
Total Bases	**284**	318
Offensive WAR	**8.3**	4.8
Games in Field	116	7
Games Pitched	17	23
Innings Pitched	133⅓	130⅓
Complete Games	12	0
Shutouts	0	0
Won-Loss	9–5	9–2
W-L%	.643	.818
ERA	2.97	3.18
Strikeouts	30	156
WHIP	1.545	1.090
ERA+	102	141
Pitching WAR	0.8	4.1

Neither player led the league in a pitching category in those seasons, while Ohtani only led in triples in 2021. Ruth led the American League in nine hitting categories in 1919, but he was in his own universe with slugging at the beginning of the Live Ball Era. The biggest number that jumps out is Ruth played 116 games in the field that season, while Ohtani played seven games in the outfield in 2021 totaling eight innings and didn't have a ball hit to him.

During Ohtani's six years with the Angels, he recorded 148 OPS+ and 142 ERA+, meaning he was 48 percent better than the average batter and 42 percent better than the average pitcher. During Ruth's six years with the Red Sox, he produced 190 OPS+ and 125 ERA+, so he was more productive as a hitter and less productive as a pitcher compared to Ohtani's first six years.

As Ohtani's career plays out, baseball historians and analysts will continue digging into the numbers to see how he compares to those who went before him. However, Ohtani is a baseball unicorn who is writing a new chapter of history every year. We will have to wait until he retires to truly define his standing among baseball's greatest two-way players.

Chapter 2

John Montgomery Ward

Baseball's First Two-Way Star

John Montgomery Ward exploded onto the scene as baseball's first star player, displaying exceptional talents on and off the diamond that prepared him for an important role as an influential and trailblazing maverick. Small in stature like many of his peers—five-foot-seven and 145 pounds when he debuted[1]—he proved a polarizing and larger-than-life figure as his baseball career played out. He was the Forrest Gump of his time—always in the news doing something big. Maybe a better reference can be found in the Dos Equis beer commercials: John M. Ward was the most interesting man in the baseball world.

The Bellefonte, Pennsylvania, native spearheaded the formation of the first baseball players' union, which evolved briefly into its own league; became the youngest manager in MLB history, going on to serve as player-manager for 40 percent of the games in which he played; earned law and political science degrees and became a part-owner of a team during his playing career; married a starlet, who had the first World Series trophy named after her; umpired a game while still an active player, and won amateur golf championships in his post-baseball life. That is just some of the highlights.

Baseball in the 19th century was a game played by men who bounced regularly between pitching and playing the field. Few were individually or collectively better than Ward at the disparate skills of batting, pitching, fielding, and running the bases. However, his best skill was an innate ability to outsmart the other team, a grand chess master in a sport of checkers players. He emerged as the 19th-century version of Charlie Hustle, taking the extra base and ranging far to snag balls that seemed uncatchable. His controversial actions to secure a fairer system for players obscured the multi-faceted splendor of his talents.

Enrolled at Penn State's prep school at age 13, Ward joined the school's first baseball club in 1875 and was later expelled from the school for infractions that included stealing chickens.² Recovering from that setback, he had a successful stint pitching in 1877 for several independent teams and in the minors with the Philadelphia Athletics and Phillies.³

He faced his future career as a baseball player with trepidation, recognizing that he didn't have better options. As he said at the time, "I had but little confidence in my ability to succeed among such players as I imagined them to be. I had already seen that baseball was lucrative only to players of the first class, and I concluded if I could not get into that, I would quit altogether. I am free to confess that I was frightened."⁴

The National League was in its third year of existence in 1878 when an 18-year-old Ward made his debut as the youngest player in the league.⁵ He was thrown into the proverbial fire as the ace pitcher for the Providence Grays, a new franchise in its first year in the league. For a player who had already lost both parents by the age of 14, no challenge would prove too daunting.⁶

His major-league debut on the mound—which came on July 15, 1878—was inauspicious. A nervous Ward surrendered 11 hits, uncorked three wild pitches, and lost 13–9 to the Cincinnati Reds. It didn't help that Providence made 28 errors behind him.⁷ He went on to accomplish an impressive feat the next month on August 9, becoming the second pitcher to win two complete games on the same day, according to Baseball Almanac. He became the youngest hurler to hit a home run—at 18 years, six months, and 24 days—on September 27, 1878, until Scott Stratton edged him out by five days a decade later.⁸

Ward hurled 334 innings that season—236 more innings than anyone else on the team—and he ended up with six shutouts and a league-leading 1.51 ERA over 37 pitching appearances. Relying primarily on a baffling curveball that he had mastered as a teenager, Ward posted 22 wins, which accounted for two-thirds of the Grays' 33 wins over the 62-game regular season. His batting average was a paltry .196 with just 27 hits in 140 plate appearances. He played no other position but pitcher during his rookie season, but that would soon change.

The next season, 1879, Ward nearly doubled his pitching appearances to 70, pitching an astounding 587 innings (third highest in the National League) for the Grays as they won 59 games out of 85 to finish first in the National League. He led the league with 47 wins, 239 strikeouts, and .712 winning percentage. The *New York Clipper* newspaper described him as one of the "youngest and most promising players in the country" who ranked "second to none at his position."⁹ Ward had an unusual but effective pitching technique, in which he turned his back on the batter before quickly delivering the underhanded pitch.

The Grays deployed only one other pitcher that season—Bobby

Mathews threw 189 innings in 27 games. When Mathews was on the mound, Ward tried his hand at playing third base (16 games) and outfield (eight games), versatility that would prove handy as his career evolved. Ward batted a solid .286 (112 OPS+) with 104 hits. He was charged with 23 errors in the field, which was not bad considering gloves were not widely used until the 1890s. Ward posted a career high 9.2 WAR (wins above replacement) that season, combining 7.3 pitching WAR with 1.9 WAR as a position player.

The 1880 season was a pivotal one for Ward in many respects. He finished second in the NL with 595 innings pitched in 70 appearances and went 39–24 with a sparking 1.74 ERA and a league-high eight shutouts to seemingly solidify his status as the staff ace. Only two other players pitched for the Grays that season: third baseman George Bradley chipped in 196 innings in 28 appearances and outfielder Mike Dorgan pitched eight innings in one game.

Ward also went 18–13–1 as player-manager for the Grays at the ripe age of 20, although his "captaincy" of the team

JOHN M. WARD.
ALLEN & GINTER'S
RICHMOND. Cigarettes. VIRGINIA.

Baseball in the 19th century was filled with two-way players, but none were better at the combined skills of pitching, batting, fielding, and baserunning than John Montgomery Ward. He was also instrumental in forming the first baseball players' union (Library of Congress, Prints & Photographs Division, LC-DIG-bbc-0006f).

was not well-received by his fellow players. His batting average dropped to .228, while he mainly played third base (25 games) and some outfield (two games) when not on the mound. His 7.7 WAR for the season mostly came from pitching (6.7 WAR).

Ward made history by pitching baseball's second perfect game on June 17, 1880, just five days after Lee Richmond tossed the first one. The game was moved to the morning so it would not conflict with a regatta, clear proof baseball had not yet become America's national pastime. It would be the last perfect game pitched in the 19th century and the last one pitched in the National League for 84 years until Jim Bunning hurled one in 1964. Ward batted sixth in the lineup that day, collecting one single in four at-bats, and he registered six assists in the field.

At 20 years and 105 days old, Ward remains the youngest pitcher to throw a perfect game, two full years younger than Catfish Hunter was when he tossed his gem in 1968, according to Baseball Almanac. The pitching mound was only 45 feet from home plate in 1880, so Ward's feat cannot be viewed in the same light as the 22 perfect games that have followed. It should be pointed out that Ward had pitched the day before his big feat.

Despite the successful start to his pitching career with the Grays, Ward was miffed that he had to share the spotlight the next season with a 26-year-old rookie, Charles Radbourn. "Old Hoss" started one more game than Ward and his 325⅓ innings pitched were just shy of Ward's total of 330 innings. Radbourn's 25 victories were seven more than Ward, who went 18–18 and saw his ERA rise to 2.13. It was a year of adjustments, as pitchers had to start throwing from 50 feet away from home plate instead of 45 feet. Ward struggled to adapt, which hastened his transition to become a position player.

Ward pivoted by adding to his versatility, playing shortstop for the first time in 1881 (13 games altogether) to go with 40 games in the outfield and 39 games on the mound. His shortstop play dropped to four games in 1882, but he still patrolled the outfield for 49 games. His bat produced middling but similar results those two seasons—87 hits in each and averages of .244 and .245.

Ward's herculean effort on the mound on August 17, 1882, might have hastened his demise as a pitcher. On that day, he pitched the longest complete-game shutout in baseball history—18 innings—a feat later matched by Ed Summers in 1909 (although it ended in a tie), Walter Johnson in 1918, and Carl Hubbell in 1933. Ward got locked into a pitchers' duel with George "Stump" Wiedman of the Detroit Wolverines, who matched zeroes with him through 17 innings. Ward did double duty at the plate, collecting one hit in seven at-bats and registering five assists in the field. Then in the bottom of the 18th inning, Radbourn lifted a long fly ball over the fence in left field to give Ward the walk-off win.[10] Pitch counts were not kept from games back then, but it's safe to say no pitcher would be allowed to approach the number of pitches Ward threw that day at Providence's Messer Street Grounds.

Before the 1883 season, Ward was acquired by tobacco magnate John Day to join his newly formed team in New York in the National League, marking the first year for the franchise now known as the San Francisco Giants.[11] Ward was excited to be playing on a bigger stage in front of more fans, who loved cheering on their handsome "Johnny" with his elegant mustache. He would maneuver to play in New York City for the rest of his career, viewing it as the fitting place for someone as educated and well-connected as he.

Ward started off the 1883 season with a bang. With two outs in the bottom of the ninth in the second game of the season on May 2, Ward dashed around the bases for an inside-the-park home run—it was the first home run in the history of the New York franchise and the first one hit in the first version of the Polo Grounds in Central Park.[12] He pitched a complete game for the win.

He outdid himself the next day. On May 3, 1883, Ward made history by becoming the first major league player (let alone a pitcher) to slug two home runs in one game. He had entered the game to pitch in the third inning. Considering Ward hit a total of seven homers that season and 26 for his career, it was an unlikely feat. If that wasn't enough, Ward led his team to a 10–9 win that day by scoring the winning run from second base in the bottom of the ninth.

Ward won 16 games that season as the team's number-two pitcher and batted a middling .255 while playing 64 games in the field, mainly in the outfield. He led all NL hurlers with five home runs that season and finished fourth in the league with seven total homers. He was able to change his batting technique to boost his extra-base hits from 14 to 32, which raised his slugging from .299 to .395.

Ward's career underwent significant changes during the 1884 season, partly due to an injury to his right pitching arm. It was the first season pitchers were allowed to pitch overhand, a change that benefited those able to throw hard. Ward threw only 60⅔ innings in nine appearances that season, producing just three wins and a 3.41 ERA. Although he claimed the injury happened from a hustling slide on the bases, there is considerable evidence his arm was bothering him throughout the previous season.[13]

With his arm unable to hold up to the strain of overhand throwing, Ward switched to playing the outfield (59 games), where he taught himself to throw left-handed,[14] and second base (47 games), where he could still make the shorter throws right-handed. He also taught himself to bat left-handed, partly due to fear of the faster pitches he was starting to see in the batter's box.[15]

Ward might be the only Hall of Fame player who ever admitted to being scared of the ball, although it's not like he was able to defend himself with a helmet, or elbow and ankle guards like current players are allowed. As he wrote at the time, "I was hit so hard several times that I grew afraid of the ball."[16] To add insult to injury, players were not yet allowed to take first base when hit by a pitch.

Other major-league players have switched their batting side mid-career, but Negro Leaguer Larry Kimbrough is believed to be the only player besides Ward to evolve into being a switch-hitter and an ambidextrous thrower.[17] Tony Mullane evolved into an ambidextrous pitcher, but he was always a switch-hitter.

With his batting and fielding producing middling results, Ward found another way to impact the outcome of games—with his legs. Stolen bases were not compiled as a statistic until 1886, but Ward finished ninth in the NL with 98 runs scored in 1884, legged out eight triples, and was in the middle of every late-game rally. He scored 65 percent of the time he was on base that year, a figure that ranked fifth in the league.

Near the end of that season, Ward took over as captain of the Gothams for the final 16 games, an important role akin to that of a modern-day manager. At 24 years of age, he was as knowledgeable and strategically savvy as anyone else on the team, and his analytical and sharp mind was always several steps ahead of others. None of his teammates or peers were going to law school at night and in the offseason like the ambitious Ward, always looking to add another tool to his toolkit.

Relying on his charisma and law background, Ward was the driving force behind the formation of the Brotherhood of Professional Baseball Players with eight of his Giants teammates in 1885. In essence it was the first labor union for baseball players. The 25-year-old Ward, who was elected president of the Brotherhood, had long been irritated by the way the game's owners treated players, who had no bargaining power during contract negotiations due to baseball's reserve clause. Under Ward's leadership, the standard player's contract was revised to curtail some of the power wielded by owners, limiting their ability to cut salaries and discipline players.[18]

Switching full time to shortstop for the 1885 season, Ward took well to the new position, leading National League shortstops in putouts and double plays while becoming one of the first players to use a thin fielding glove. *Sporting Life* called attention to his knack for playing short, noting he was "as great at short field as he used to be in the pitcher's box. Ball playing comes as natural to him as eating does to other men."[19] His steady fielding sparked the Giants in 1885, although his .226 average proved a weak link in a lineup anchored by fellow future Hall of Famers Jim O'Rourke and Roger Connor. The Giants went 85–27 to finish 28 games ahead of third-place Philadelphia but two games behind the pennant-winning Chicago White Stockings.

Ward found new thunder in his bat in 1886, boosting his average to .273 and knocking in 81 runs for the Giants, who finished third that season. His 69 errors at short were mitigated by the many sparkling plays he made to snuff out rallies. His involvement in the Brotherhood paid off when he attended the National League meetings in the offseason as a representative of the players. With his pitching days behind him, Ward sided with many other players who felt baseball's rules favored the pitchers. Thanks to his input, the league raised the number of strikes needed for a strikeout from three to four, lowered the number of balls from seven to five for a walk, and ruled pitchers needed to keep at least one foot on the rubber while pitching.[20]

Baseball players' first union president was not shy about sharing his views on the unfairness of baseball's labor practices. One can only imagine the uproar if social media had existed back in 1887, when Ward contributed an article to *Lippincott's* magazine titled "Is the Base-Ball Player a Chattel?" In that article, he denounced the league as a monopoly, outlined the unfairness of the one-sided reserve clause as an *ex post facto* rule—showing off his command of legal terms—that shackled players to their clubs, and acted as an institution for evil, not good.[21]

It would take nearly a century for Ward to be proved right and for Marvin Miller to succeed where he had failed in abolishing baseball's reserve clause in 1974. Ward had established himself as a thorn in the side of baseball's authorities, and the powers that be would never forget his rebellious words and deeds.

Ward almost made history in another way in the spring of 1887. He urged his team to sign pitcher George Stovey and catcher Fleet Walker, who were both African American and playing in the International League for the Newark Little Giants. Entrenched prejudice proved to be a tough obstacle to overcome and the two were not signed.

If the MVP Award had been given out back in 1887, Ward would have been a leading candidate. That season he led the NL with 6.6 WAR—by far the highest position player WAR of his career—after batting a personal best .338 (fourth best) with 114 runs scored, 184 hits (second best) and a league-record 111 stolen bases (now tied for sixth most in MLB history). His play at shortstop that season is credited with a league-leading 2.7 dWAR and an RField value of +26 by Baseball-Reference.

By the time the 1888 season rolled around, professional baseball was caught in a topsy-turvy evolution. Fans were getting restless watching so many pitches thrown with so little result. That season, nearly 40 percent of the runs scored as a result of errors by the defense.[22] Ward's average plummeted from .338 to .251 as he experimented with switch-hitting, while his errors at shortstop rose from 61 to a league-high 86. He even found time to umpire a game on September 21, 1888, according to Retrosheet.

Ward found creative ways to serve as the sparkplug shortstop for the New York team, now known as the Giants. They would win the first of two consecutive World Championship series against the American Association pennant winners in 1888. Ward batted .379 and stole six bases in the 10-game series and perhaps took a turn hoisting the Dauvray Cup named after his new bride, actress and diva Helen Dauvray, who had pushed baseball to start the new tradition a year earlier.[23]

With his thrilling play, he had blossomed into a popular, nationally known icon even if he was no longer the highest-paid player in the league. He topped off his year by authoring an instructional book, *Base-Ball: How to Become a Player*—one of the earliest attempts to explain successful strategies and proper techniques for every position, along with a decent overview of the game's historical origins.

In his book, Ward demonstrated the high regard he held for the role of pitchers. "Of all the players on a base-ball nine, the pitcher is the one to whom attaches the greatest importance. He is the attacking force of the nine, the positive pole of the battery, the central figure, around which the others are grouped."[24] He wrote that pitchers needed to have the ability to throw with speed, endurance, courage, and self-control, while also showcasing a deceptive style of delivery.

After detailing the proper form and technique for batting—don't try to hit the ball too hard, he suggests—Ward the author shared a description that sounds more apropos for a youngster new to Little League. "But the most important attribute of all in the composition of a good batter is *courage*. In this term I include the self-control and the resolution by which a man will force himself to stand before the swiftest and wildest pitching without flinching, the fearlessness that can contemplate the probability of a blow from the ball without allowing the judgment to be affected. Out of ten poor batters, nine are so because they are afraid of being hit."[25]

Ward had a solid year in 1889, batting .299 with 62 stolen bases. He took 14 games off in the middle of the season, reportedly because of a sore arm, but it was actually to lay the foundation for a big move to come. With Ward setting the table, the Giants won the pennant with a record of 83-43-5. They faced Brooklyn in the first all–New York World Series, with Ward collecting 15 hits, scoring 10 runs, stealing 10 bases, and batting .417.

Down three games to two, Ward singled and stole two bases to get into position to score the tying run in the bottom of the ninth. He then drove in the winning run in the 11th inning as the Giants evened the Series and went on to sweep the next three games. John Thorn, Major League Baseball's official historian, described Ward's clutch heroics this way: "Long before Reggie Jackson, *he* was New York's Mr. October."[26] An article in the *New York Journal* stated, "(Ward) was, too, the hero of more close games that were won—pulled out of the fire by individual excellence, grit and ginger—than any other Giant, old or new."[27]

With the Brotherhood of Professional Baseball Players unable to make much headway in their dealings with obstinate owners, Ward rallied some of the game's biggest stars and formed the eight-team Players' National League of Professional Base Ball Clubs, which would compete against the National League and American Association in 1890. Gate receipts were to be shared equally among all teams, players were able to sign three-year contracts free of the reserve system and curiously, alcohol was prohibited. The league would be run by a Senate comprised of two representatives from each team.[28]

The Brooklyn Ward's Wonders was named after the team's popular shortstop, who made a dashing figure around the city. Ward served as the manager and the starting shortstop, guiding the upstart team to a second-place finish with a 76–56–1 record. He excelled at the plate that season, batting .335 with 188 hits and 63 stolen bases. He set career marks with 134 runs scored, 12 triples, .393 on base percentage, and .426 slugging, and he also led the league in putouts (303) and assists (450) by a shortstop.

As for the Players' League, it put competitive teams on the field but found itself outmaneuvered financially by the owners of the more established National League franchises.[29] The league folded after one year, although Ward was not done trying to make the system more favorable for players. His bold action did hasten the demise of the American Association, which lasted only one more year before folding as the National League expanded its hold on baseball.

For 1891, Ward moved on to Brooklyn's team in the NL, humbled by his failure with the Players' League but pleased that he could serve as manager with less interference. He batted .277 with 57 steals and 85 runs scored, but the team finished sixth in the eight-team league.

Brooklyn improved to third place with 95 wins in 1892, with Ward the skipper pushing his squad to steal 409 bases. Ward also made his final move on the diamond, as he would finish his career as a second baseman. He played a career-high 148 games in 1892, batting .265 with 109 runs scored and leading the league with 88 stolen bases—pretty good for a 32-year-old in his 15th season. He also set a major league record on June 10,

1892—since matched by nine other players—for most assists by a second baseman in a game with 12.

Ward's managerial style was never popular with players, who deemed him too autocratic and aloof. Consequently, his final two years were spent back with the New York Giants, for whom he had become a minority owner. He finished eighth in the NL with 129 runs scored in 1893 while batting a robust .328 with a career-high 193 hits, helped by the mound being moved back five feet. He played in 135 of the team's 136 games as the Giants limped to fifth place under his direction.

The 1894 Giants fell short by three games in Ward's final season. He scored 102 runs with a .266 average, but his adjusted OPS was down to 50 and his 66 errors were second-most in the league.

He announced his retirement in November 1894, which caused the *Clipper* to serenade him with this tribute: "How many enthusiasts are there who can recall the times when Ward has snatched a victory out of the fire, as it were, by bunting the ball, and beating it out at first. Then, with a daring steal and a great slide to second, had come home from that point of the diamond on almost any kind of hit."[30]

Ward contemplated purchasing majority own-

John Ward emerged as one of the greatest pitchers of the 19th century before carving out a second career as a shortstop that would lead him to the Hall of Fame. He is the only player in baseball history to record at least 2,000 hits and 150 pitching wins (Library of Congress, Prints & Photographs Division, LC-DIG-bbc-0293f).

ership of the Giants that year, since the team's owner, E.B. Talcott, wanted badly to sell. Ultimately, he chose to go all in with his law practice. However, he did succeed in getting the National League to release him from the reserve clause—the first player to earn that distinction. He would go on to stir up more trouble representing several players in their fights against the league.

In late 1911, he jumped at a chance to become president and part-owner of Boston's bottom-dwelling franchise in the National League. It did not go well and Ward did not last a full season before selling off his interest. Ward had made more enemies than friends in the game and his miserly, dispassionate approach to ownership—strange for a former player—was reminiscent of the owners he hated playing for during his career. A later front-office stint with a team in the upstart Federal League also went nowhere, as did an earlier attempt to become president of the National League.

Ward's 17-year career showcased his talent, versatility, and clever play. He was a true two-way player in six seasons—1879 to 1884—before ending his career solely as a position player. He demonstrated speed, skill, and cunning on the base paths, twice leading the National League in stolen bases. His 540 career steals rank 29th on the all-time list, even though stolen bases were not a recorded statistic for his first eight seasons. He played 826 games at short, 493 at second base, 214 in the outfield, and 46 at third base, while pitching in 293 games. His managerial record over some or all of seven seasons was 412–320, a stellar .563 winning percentage that ranks 30th all-time.

Ward's batting ability was inconsistent, but he had marvelous bat control and excelled at bunting and moving the runner over. He managed to lead the NL in singles in 1887 (the strange year when walks counted as hits) and 1890 and came in fourth in home runs in 1883 with seven. He finished in the top 10 in hits four times. When he retired, he ranked sixth in runs scored with 1,410 and eighth in RBI with 869. He finished with 2,107 hits and a .275 average, with an adjusted OPS of 92—eight percent below average. His batting average in World Series action was an impressive .400.

He ranks higher on the pitcher leaderboard, a testament to his mastery of the curveball and ability to outsmart batters. He still holds the all-time record for lowest career on-base percentage allowed by a pitcher at .254. His 2.10 career ERA ranks seventh all-time, just ahead of Christy Mathewson, who pitched nearly twice as many innings. His WHIP (walks and hits per inning pitched) of 1.0435 ranks sixth all-time, right behind Clayton Kershaw and Mariano Rivera. Ward's career record was 164–103 with 245 complete games and 24 shutouts in 2,469⅔ innings, checking in with an adjusted ERA of 119—19 percent above average.

Baseball in the 19th century was a different game, still evolving under the influence of pioneers like Ward. No one player has ever worn more hats during a season than the multi-talented John Montgomery Ward did during the 1880 and 1884 seasons, when he served as a pitcher, batter, outfielder, infielder, and manager. He excelled in all those roles, with a flair that resonated with adoring fans. Every time he hit adversity during his playing career, he just pivoted and showed his mastery of a new position. If he had umpired more than one game, he probably would have been great at that, too.

"Versatility was indeed more common in professional baseball's early years," explains Thorn, Major League Baseball's official historian. "But Ward was uncommonly proficient as a pitcher, as an infielder-outfielder and as an author."[31]

Whether it was competing in high-profile golf tournaments or playing baseball, Ward continually demonstrated that he was a winner. Ward's teams finished first three times (with two World Series titles) and finished second six times, and they finished with a winning record in 15 of his 17 seasons. Sportswriter Grantland Rice eulogized Ward as "the greatest competitor this country ever has known."[32]

When Ward was inducted into the Baseball Hall of Fame as a shortstop in 1964, his all-around skills were recognized as a pitching pioneer who turned to shortstop. His plaque also noted he "played an important part in establishing modern organized baseball."

Using the Win Shares method, Bill James identified Ward as the second-best pitcher-hitter combination of all time, noting that Ward "has career batting numbers similar to Maury Willis, pitching numbers similar to Addie Joss."[33] He ranks 70th all-time among shortstops, according to JAWS—the Jaffe WAR Score System developed by Jay Jaffe.

For John Montgomery Ward, being orphaned at age 14 did not define his life or limit his aspirations. He remains the only player in baseball history to record more than 2,000 hits and 150 pitching wins.

Chapter 3

19th Century

An Evolving Game Forces Players to Adapt

The sport of baseball grew so popular with the masses that by 1856 it was already being referred to as America's "national pastime."[1] Americans liked the rough and rowdy action punctuated with occasional wallops of the bat and dashing bare-handed catches.

One of the primary jobs of the pitcher was to frighten the batter—tossing underhanded until 1884—while catering to the batters' demands for high or low pitches. Batters tried their best to swat at pitches hurled at creative angles from pitchers dancing around the pitcher's box 45 or 50 feet away.

Runners strived to slide roughly and violently into any fielders that might be in their path. Fielding in those early years was a crapshoot. Some players were better than others at catching hot shots, deep drives, and sharp grounders with their bare hands, so expectations on fielding performance were low until gloves gained wide adoption by the mid–1890s.[2] If a player got banged up by a rough slide or threw his arm out with too many pitches, he played through it—no 15-day stints on the disabled list. A player who couldn't play due to injury often found himself suspended, so the owner didn't have to pay him for idleness.

Major League Baseball in the late 19th century was a frenetic game of shifting rules that changed on an annual basis. If too many players were drawing walks, then require nine balls to get a free pass. Here are some of the official rule changes that occurred in the National League (the first major league) between 1878 and 1893, as compiled by Baseball Almanac:

- 1878—The number of "called balls" became nine and all balls were either strikes, balls or fouls.
- 1879—Batters were only given three called strikes; base on balls reduced to seven "called balls."
- 1880—Pitchers allowed to throw sidearm; front of pitcher's box moved to 50 feet from center of home plate.

1882—Pitchers could deliver the ball from above their waist.
1883—Six "called balls" constituted a base on balls.
1884—Pitchers allowed to throw overhand.
1885—A portion of the bat could be flat on one side.
1886—Batters could no longer call for high or low pitches; four "called strikes" adopted for only that season.
1887—Bases on balls were recorded as hits, but only for that season. Pitcher had to keep back foot on the rear line of the pitcher's box (55.5 feet from middle of home plate).
1889—Four balls constituted a base on balls.
1893—Rubber pitching slab moved from 50 feet to 60 feet 6 inches from rear of home plate.

These rule changes, not surprisingly, greatly impacted player performance and stats. While pitchers could throw faster overhanded, it also meant they couldn't keep pitching every game due to the extra strain on arms and shoulders. Pitchers also lost the upper hand when they could no longer dance around a large pitcher's box before releasing the ball.

Teams in the 19th century required versatile players who could play multiple positions, because rosters were nothing like the 26-man teams that compete today. In fact, the reserve clause adopted by National League owners in 1879 mandated that each team could reserve and lock up a certain number of players. For the 1886 season, it was a dozen players, the next season it rose to 14 players—that is essentially what each active roster comprised. The 1876 Chicago White Stockings went through the entire season with just 11 players. All five of the team's pitchers also played in the field and three of the pitchers only threw in one game each. Managers (who were typically player-managers) in the 19th century did not have the luxury to look down at a deep bench and mix and match against the competition. Luckily, teams had one or two ace pitchers who could toss 400-plus innings and mitigate the need to carry additional pitchers.

Modern player substitution was adopted in 1890 but not used frequently by managers for many years. Up until then, pitchers could only be taken out of the game due to an injury or switched out with another position, often right field.[3]

What follows in this chapter is a closer look at thirteen 19th-century players who stood out for their exceptional two-way playing ability.

George Bradley

Two players named George Washington Bradley played in the majors. One was an outfielder who appeared in four games for the St. Louis Browns in 1946, while the other pitched the first no-hitter in the history of the National League. We shall delve into the exploits of the latter.

Nicknamed "Grin" for the ever-present smile he displayed on the mound—*The Sporting News* described it as a tantalizing smirk[4]—Bradley won 33 games in his rookie season with the St. Louis Brown Stockings in 1875 while batting .244 with 62 hits.

The Brown Stockings joined the new National League the next season, and Bradley threw his no-hitter against the Hartford Dark Blues on July 15. It marked his third shutout of Hartford in five days, and he would take a no-hitter and shutout into the ninth inning in his next start. He went on to surrender a double and a run, which broke his record streak of 37 consecutive shutout innings. It would remain the NL record until Christy Mathewson reached 39 innings in 1901.[5]

During the 1876 season, Bradley finished second in the league with 45 wins (tied for 12th all-time) and 63 complete games, and he led with a 1.23 ERA and 16 shutouts, generating 8.8 WAR from the mound. He started every one of the team's 64 games that season, pitching all but four innings. The 16 shutouts remain a major league record, matched by Pete Alexander in 1916. Low earned run averages in the early days of baseball were deceptive and often a function of lots of errors being committed by bare-handed fielders. Bradley gave up 229 runs in 1876 but only 78 were earned, leading to an adjusted ERA of 170.

In his book about the 1876 season, Neil McDonald wrote that Bradley excelled as a dual-threat hurler, combining the abilities of a "straight pitcher like Al Spalding, considered to be the best in the game, with the ingenuity of a breaking ball specialist like Candy Cummings, the consummate chucker of curves."[6]

Bradley lost 40 games pitching for a bad Troy Trojans team in 1879 despite a 2.85 ERA. He played sporadically in the field until seeing action in 57 games at third base (plus nine games at other positions) for the Providence Grays in 1880, to go with 196 innings pitched in 28 appearances. He and John Ward alternated between third base and the mound. Bradley led NL third basemen in assists that season and finished third in fielding percentage. On the mound he went 13–8 with a 1.38 ERA (second in the NL) but batted just .227 with 70 hits.

Signing to play for the Cincinnati Outlaw Reds of the Union Association in 1884—he led them with 25 wins in his last pitching stint—caused Bradley to be banned from playing the next season.

Playing for 10 teams in four leagues during his 11-year career, Bradley won 172 games in 347 appearances with a splendid 2.43 ERA (35th all-time). He is tied for eighth place in ERA among 19th-century pitchers (minimum 500 innings pitched). However, his batting never took off, as he posted a .229 average with 518 hits. He played 170 games at third base, 47 in the outfield, 33 at shortstop, and 19 elsewhere in the field. His career WAR of 22.3 came primarily from 21.6 WAR pitching.

Charlie Buffinton

Described by *The Sporting News* as "the Christy Mathewson of the 1880s,"[7] Charlie Buffinton deserves greater consideration for the Hall of Fame. He threw a drop-curve with a baffling delivery, winning 20 games seven times with a high of 48 wins in 1884 (fifth highest in history). His career mark was 233–152 across 11 seasons with a 2.96 ERA, and he ranks 70th all-time among starting pitchers, according to JAWS—the Jaffe WAR Score System developed by Jay Jaffe.

By his second season he was already appearing in 51 games in the outfield while making 43 pitching appearances, but his .238 batting mark was overshadowed by his 25 wins on the mound across 333 innings.

During Buffington's 1884 season with Boston, his 48 wins (tied for fifth best all-time) and 417 strikeouts (sixth best all-time) were both second in the National League, while his 2.17 ERA ranked seventh and his 63 complete games, eight shutouts, and 587 innings pitched all ranked third. He reeled off a 13-game winning streak that season and his 17 strikeouts on September 2, 1884, against Cleveland set a franchise record for a nine-inning game. It was also one of his best seasons with the bat, as his .267 average and 94 hits while playing 13 games in the outfield and 11 at first base helped Boston to a second-place finish. His 16.3 WAR that season ranks seventh all-time.

As sportswriter Tim Murnane once described, "...Buffinton had mastered a drop that fell into the hands of his catcher like a snowflake."[8]

On May 22, 1885, Buffinton became the second pitcher to accumulate five hits in a game. With an ailing pitching arm limiting him to 18 appearances in 1886, Buffinton played 19 games at first and nine in the outfield and recorded a strong .290 average. His arm rebounded and he won 20 games in four of the next five seasons, while his batting fluctuated from .181 to .273. On August 6 and 9, 1887, he pitched consecutive one-hitters for the Philadelphia Phillies.[9] That feat has been accomplished 10 other times in baseball history by nine different pitchers.

Jumping to the Philadelphia Athletics of the new Players' League started by John Ward in 1890, Buffinton ended up serving as player-manager in short order. He guided them to a fifth-place finish and pitched in with 19 wins.

Buffinton was released in the middle of the 1892 season at age 31 after refusing to take a pay cut for the Baltimore Orioles, who were on their way to a last-place finish.[10] His 4–8 record with 4.92 ERA (70 ERA+) showed his best days were behind him.

He wound up playing in 137 career games in the outfield and 68 games at first base, receiving poor marks for his fielding. Buffinton provided little with the bat in his 2,309 plate appearances, averaging .245 with 543 hits for an adjusted OPS of 71—29 percent below average.

His career WAR of 60.7, which came entirely from pitching, is tied with Andy Pettitte for 62nd place all-time and ahead of Hall of Famers such as Dizzy Dean, Herb Pennock, Jim Kaat, Burleigh Grimes, and Addie Joss, who all posted pitching WAR below 50.

Among 19th-century pitchers, Buffington ranks ninth in strikeouts with 1,700, 13th in shutouts with 30, 15th in wins, 16th in games started with 396, and 17th in complete games and innings pitched. "Buffington was one of the greatest pitchers of his day,"[11] commented John Morrill, his manager with Boston.

Jimmy "Nixey" Callahan

Jimmy Callahan pitched the first no-hitter in Chicago White Sox history on September 20, 1902, against the Detroit Tigers. For decades it was believed to be the first no-hitter in American League history, but research later revealed that distinction belongs to Pete Dowling.[12] Callahan would win one more game the next season and then be finished as a pitcher at age 29, falling one game shy of 100 career wins. "Nixey" was his childhood nickname; he mainly went by Jimmy during his playing career.[13]

Callahan's playing career bridged two centuries and lasted 13 seasons over a 20-year period, although he only pitched in eight seasons. After a nine-game, unsuccessful stint as a 20-year-old rookie with the Philadelphia Phillies in 1894, he blossomed as a two-way player in the minors for two seasons. That attracted the attention of the Chicago Colts, who liked his pitching and baserunning ability.[14] He would spend the rest of his career in Chicago with the Colts/Orphans and White Sox.

His best two-way season was 1897, when he batted .292 with 105 hits playing 50 games around the infield and 21 games in the outfield. On the mound that year he went 12–9 with a 4.03 ERA in 189⅔ innings (110 ERA+). He fell 67 at-bats shy of qualifying for the ERA and batting title.

Nixey made 684 appearances in the field, primarily in left field (373 games) and third base (110 games), to go with 195 pitching appearances. With a lifetime average of .273 and 901 hits (94 OPS+), his batting contributed nearly as much as his pitching. He generated 9.3 WAR as a position player and 15.6 WAR as a pitcher.

Combining with Clark Griffith, Callahan batted .331 and won 15 games to help lead the White Sox to the AL pennant in 1901. He later guided the team as player-manager during four seasons. His best year batting was 1903, when he hit .292 with 128 hits, 56 RBI, and an OPS+ of 117 while playing 102 games at third base.

Known as one of the fastest players in the league, Callahan possessed speed that was sometimes counterproductive. "Time after time, when a grounder was hit his way, Callahan darted at it with such terrific speed that he couldn't check himself over the ball, but overran, and the hit went on unhindered," John McGraw once remarked.[15]

Callahan's best year on the mound was 1898 for the Orphans, when he went 20–10 with a 2.46 ERA (fifth in the NL) in 274⅓ innings. His 2.42 ERA in 1901 ranked second in the American League. His approach was to pitch to contact, which meant he generated few strikeouts or walks. He posted five straight seasons with more than 200 innings pitched, recorded 169 complete games in 177 games started, and posted a career record of 99–73.

Nixey is the only pitcher to collect five hits in a game three times. He did it in 1897 and 1902 and then for the final time on May 8, 1903, which proved to be the last game he pitched in the majors.

He took off five years in the prime of his career to operate his own sandlot team, returning to the White Sox for the 1911 season at age 37. He batted .281 that season playing 114 games in the outfield while setting career marks with 131 hits, 60 RBI, and 45 stolen bases. Another strong year followed with a .272 average and 111 hits in 1912, as he guided the Sox to a fourth-place finish. He ended his career with 186 stolen bases and a managerial record of 394–458.

Bob Caruthers

Another player who deserves more consideration for the Hall of Fame is Bob Caruthers, whose nine-year career falls one year short of Hall qualifications. The Society for American Baseball Research named Caruthers as the top Overlooked 19th Century Baseball Legend for 2017,[16] while he ranks 73rd all-time among starting pitchers, according to JAWS (the Jaffe WAR Score System).

He posted a career record of 213–99 playing from 1884 to 1892 with a 2.83 ERA, 298 complete games, and six straight seasons with at least 300 innings pitched. He won 40 games in 1885 and 1889. However, he did rack up a lot of wins against weak teams in the American Association, which generally featured inferior competition compared to the National

League. Baseball-Reference lists his size as five-foot-seven, 138 pounds, but Caruthers' approach on the mound was to use deception rather than power,

Among 19th-century pitchers, the righty hurler ranks fourth in winning percentage (minimum 100 decisions) at .688, 17th in wins, 18th in shutouts with 24, and 21st in ERA (minimum 100 games). He won 191 games between 1885 and 1890. Pitching for the pennant-winning Browns in 1885, Caruthers led the league with 40 wins, .755 winning percentage, 2.07 ERA, and 160 ERA+, pitching 482⅓ innings across 53 complete-game starts. His winning percentage ranks eighth in baseball history.

As noted earlier in Chapter 1, Caruthers posted the two best Wins Above Replacement (WAR) totals in a season for a player who pitched at least 10 games, had 200 plate appearances, and position player WAR over 3.0. He recorded 11.5 WAR in 1886 and 10.7 WAR in 1887.

Parisian Bob—he picked up that nickname from negotiating a contract while vacationing in France—was a lefty beast swinging the bat those seasons. In 1886, he batted .334 (fourth in the league) and slugged .527 with 106 hits and led the American Association with .448 on-base percentage, .974 OPS, and adjusted OPS of 201. His eight homers tied for fourth in the league, and he played 43 games in the outfield and two at second base to go with 44 pitching appearances. His 30 regular-season wins were supplemented by two more wins for the champion St. Louis Browns in the 1886 World Series—the only time an American Association (AA) team defeated the National League pennant winner.

He followed that up in 1887 with a .357 average (5th in AA), .463 OBP (3rd best), .547 slugging (2nd), 1.010 OPS and 169 OPS+ (3rd), 130 hits, 102 runs, and 49 stolen bases, playing 54 games in the outfield and seven at first base. With 29 wins that season, Caruthers became the first player to win 20 games and steal 30 bases in the same season—only Adonis Terry has accomplished that feat since.

Over 10 seasons, Caruthers generated 14.8 WAR as a position player, batting .282 with 695 hits and 152 stolen bases, getting on base at a .391 clip and recording a 134 OPS+. He often batted leadoff or in the second spot in his four years with the St. Louis Browns.[17] He played more games in the outfield (366) than at pitcher (340), plus 22 more at first and second base. His batting stats took a downward turn once he could no longer call for his preferred low pitches and pitchers realized he struggled against most high pitches.

Playing against Brooklyn on August 16, 1886, Caruthers slugged two home runs and added a double and triple for 13 total bases—the only pitcher in American Association history with four extra base hits in a game. Only Babe Ruth and Snake Wiltse matched that feat in American

League history and no pitcher in the National League's long history has posted more than three extra-base hits in one game, according to Baseball Almanac. Caruthers narrowly missed a third home run in that game—getting thrown out at home in a close play trying to stretch a triple— which would have matched Guy Hecker's feat set the day before.[18]

On May 29, 1886, Caruthers accumulated five hits against the Philadelphia Athletics. He led the Browns to three straight American Association pennants from 1885 to 1887, pitching a one-hit shutout in game two of the 1886 World Championship series the Browns went on to win.[19] In 1889, he helped the Brooklyn Bridegrooms win their first pennant by posting a 40–11 record. Brooklyn moved to the National League the next year and again won the pennant behind Caruthers' 23 wins.

Back with the Browns again in 1892, Caruthers was washed up as a pitcher at age 28, so he played 122 games in the outfield and

Bob Caruthers won 30 games in 44 pitching appearances in 1886. That season, he batted .334 with 106 hits while playing 43 games in the outfield and two games at second base. Parisian Bob won 40 games for the second time with Brooklyn in 1889 (Library of Congress, Prints & Photographs Division, LC-DIG-bbc-0560f).

averaged a team-high .277 with 142 hits and 69 RBI. Extending his career in the minors as a first baseman, he batted .331 in 1894 and .321 in 1895. Throughout his career, Caruthers demonstrated his two-way ability to impact games. He was a true two-way player in seven of his 10 seasons. He ranks second all-time in pitching wins in American Association history with 175.

Dave Foutz

Dave Foutz turned into an effective two-way player because his bat proved too good to be kept out of the lineup on days he didn't pitch. Nicknamed "Scissors" due to his tall and lanky frame, he collected 1,253 hits with a .276 average while playing 596 games at first base, 320 games in the outfield and pitching 251 games from 1884 to 1896. His career WAR total of 35.4 included offensive WAR of 12.4.

He was already 27 years old when he struck out 13 batters during his major league debut with the St. Louis Browns on July 29, 1884.[20] Showing remarkable mastery of a curveball, he won 15 games with a 2.18 ERA that season.

Foutz teamed up with another emerging two-way star to lead the Browns to the American Association pennant in 1885. Bob Caruthers won 40 games and Foutz went 33–14 with a 2.63 ERA, with both players exceeding 400 innings pitched and 50 hits at the plate. Foutz accounted for two of the Browns' three victories in the championship series against the White Stockings that ended in a tie. Both players debuted in the majors in 1884 and played together for the next eight seasons. When one was pitching, the other was out in the outfield or first base, showcasing similar skills and posting nearly identical stats.

Foutz's best season was 1886 with the St. Louis Browns, when he pitched 504 innings and led the American Association with 41 wins, .719 winning percentage, and 2.11 ERA. His 11 shutouts that year were one behind leader Ed Morris and that total remains eight-best in baseball history. Playing 34 games in right field and 11 games at first base that year, he batted .280 and collected 116 hits and 59 RBI with an OPS+ of 111. The Browns won the pennant again and won the championship rematch with the White Stockings.

The next season his .357 average ranked sixth in the league, while his .508 slugging and .901 OPS ranked seventh. His 1887 season remains the only time a major league player has won 20 games as a pitcher and driven in 100 runs in the same season—Foutz won 25 games with 108 RBI. Unfortunately, he never recovered his top pitching form after a struck ball injured his thumb that season and he transitioned to become primarily a position player the rest of his career.[21]

From 1887 to 1890, Foutz topped 150 hits and ranked in the top five in RBI every season as he typically batted in the middle of the Brooklyn lineup. He batted over .300 three times, scored more than 100 runs twice and collected 308 extra-base hits. Also a good baserunner, he stole 280 bases with three straight seasons of at least 40 steals. His 147–66 career record generated a winning percentage of .690 that is tied with Whitey Ford for sixth all-time. Foutz was a true two-way player—playing at least 10 games at pitcher and in the field—in seven of his 13 seasons. Bill James ranks him as the fourth-best pitcher/hitter combination, right behind teammate Caruthers.[22]

He served as player-manager during his last four seasons in Brooklyn, finishing back of the pack every year but with a lifetime .507 winning percentage. A few months after his career ended following the 1896 season, Foutz died of an asthma attack at the age of 40.[23] Charles Byrne, Brooklyn Grooms club president, eulogized Foutz as a "quiet, honest, and conscientious man and one of the greatest ballplayers the country has produced."[24]

Dave Foutz recorded 25 pitching wins for the St. Louis Browns in 1887 while finishing sixth in the American Association with a .357 batting average. That season, Foutz played 50 games in the outfield and 15 games at first base in addition to 40 mound appearances (Library of Congress, Prints & Photographs Division, LC-DIG-bbc-0057f).

Kid Gleason

Most remember William "Kid" Gleason as the manager of the infamous Black Sox team of 1919, but that does disservice to his distinguished 22-year playing career that ended at age 46.

Gleason only pitched during his first eight seasons, not playing much in the field in those years, then transitioned to become one of the finest second basemen in the majors. Bill James ranked him number 72 all-time among second basemen.[25] His brother, Harry, also played five seasons in the majors.

Gleason had one outstanding season as a pitcher, 1890 for the Philadelphia Phillies, when he won 38 games (second in the NL) with a 2.63 ERA (fifth in NL) and finished third in complete games (54) and innings pitched (506). It was a strange year marked by the emergence of a third league, the Players' League, which watered down the talent pool. Although Gleason won at least 20 games the next three seasons, his numbers were otherwise pedestrian. He ended up going 138–131 over his pitching career with a 3.79 ERA, an ERA+ of 104.

Sold to the Baltimore Orioles in the middle of the 1894 season, Gleason batted .349 and pitched in with 15 wins to help spur the team to the pennant. He ended up appearing for six teams, spending 19 of his 22 seasons in the National League and is one of 31 Major League players to play in four different decades.[26]

He batted over .300 three times but his lifetime 78 OPS+ shows he made limited impact with the bat. His best year at the plate was 1897, when he averaged .317, stole 44 bases, and drove in 106 runs for the New York Giants. Gleason, who accumulated 329 stolen bases, 1,022 runs scored, and 1,946 hits, posted 12 straight seasons with at least 100 hits.

Gleason was considered a strong defender at second base, despite high error totals. He led the league in putouts and assists three times each. Kid helped his teams win with intangibles and hard-nosed play. After his playing career ended, Gleason spoke proudly of the methods he used to get an edge: "They can't bring back the old kind of game, not the way we played it.... I'd let them slide onto the bag, then kick them off the bag. That's the way we put them out."[27]

Despite being forever associated with the Black Sox scandal, Gleason remained beloved and admired throughout baseball. When he died in 1933 at the age of 67, the estimated crowd of 5,000 people included many baseball luminaries. Giants manager John McGraw summarized the thoughts of many by saying: "He was, without doubt, the gamest and most spirited ball player I ever saw and that doesn't except Ty Cobb. He was a great influence for good on any ball club, making up for his lack of stature, by his spirit and fight. He could lick his weight in wildcats and would prove it at the drop of a hat."[28]

Guy Hecker

Righty Guy Hecker, a fan favorite during his eight seasons with the Louisville Eclipse/Colonels, is one of the best pitchers in the history of the short-lived American Association (AA). He ranks third in AA wins with 173 and second in games started, complete games, and innings pitched. At six-feet tall and 190 pounds, his size was above average for the period, giving him an intimidation factor many of his peers did not possess. His pitching style evolved from power to finesse over the years.

During the sixth start of his rookie season in 1882, Hecker pitched the American Association's second no-hitter on September 19, eight days after teammate Tony Mullane pitched the first one. They were the first no-hitters tossed from the new 50-foot pitching distance.[29] Hecker would win six games in 13 appearances that year with a sparkling 1.30 ERA.

Hecker achieved the pitching Triple Crown in 1884 while going 52–20 with a 1.80 ERA and 385 strikeouts (seventh best all-time). He also produced a league-leading 72 complete games and 670⅔ innings pitched, which both rank third best in baseball history. The 52 wins are the third-highest figure in baseball history. That year he also hit .297 (third best on the team) with 94 hits and a 148 OPS+ for the Eclipse, who finished in third place. His total WAR of 17.8 that season is the fifth-highest mark all-time. Five of the top 11 seasons for WAR all happened in 1884, the first year pitchers were allowed to throw overhand.

In 1886, Guy Hecker became the first pitcher to hit three home runs in a game. He batted .297 in 1884, when he won the pitcher's Triple Crown with 52 wins, a 1.80 ERA, and 385 strikeouts (Library of Congress, Prints & Photographs Division, LC-DIG-bbc-0433f).

Two years later, Hecker led the American Association with a .341 average in 84 games (although it was not recognized at the time) and ended up second with a .402 on-base percentage. He remains the only pitcher to win a batting title. His pitching was still strong but not quite as dominant, with a 26–23 overall record despite reeling off 11 straight wins in the middle of the season.

On August 15, 1886, Hecker had himself an historic day at the plate, in the second game of a doubleheader against Baltimore. He smacked three inside-the-park home runs to go with three singles, reaching base on an error in another at-bat. It's unclear exactly how many runs he drove in, but it was at least six. He pitched a complete game four-hitter for the win. His seven runs scored remains the major-league record, while his 15 total bases set a major-league record that has since been surpassed many times—Shawn Green now holds that record with 19 total bases. Hecker produced the first three-homer game by a pitcher, a feat later matched by Jim Tobin in 1942, and it was the only three-homer game in American Association history.[30]

Hecker's historic day at the plate came in the midst of a torrid streak for him. He pitched in seven consecutive games between August 8 and August 22 and got 23 hits in 34 at-bats—a tidy .676 average. He scored a remarkable 63 runs as a pitcher that season in 49 games pitching, and he batted .376 as a pitcher in 1886 while batting .219 at other positions.[31]

Hecker's effectiveness as a pitcher waned after his first five seasons, a combination of the new pitching rules and lingering arm trouble. He started playing more games at first base, where he would end up playing 322 games. His .319 average in 1887 trailed only Pete Browning on the Louisville Colonels, and he was one of seven players on that team to register at least 40 steals.

The western Pennsylvania native was brought in as player-manager of the Allegheny City team in the National League for the 1890 season, which ended up as Hecker's last. He skippered the team to a last-place finish with a 23–113–2 record. He batted .226 and posted a 2–9 record with 5.11 ERA.

Hecker, who often batted in the top three spots of the lineup, ended his career with 812 hits, a .282 average, adjusted OPS of 117, and 123 stolen bases, to go with a pitching record of 175–146. Hecker and Babe Ruth remain the only major-league players to lead the league in earned run average and batting.

Win Mercer

Postseason glory proved elusive for George "Win" Mercer, who had the misfortune to play for second-division clubs in each of his nine

Chapter 3. 19th Century

seasons. That makes his nickname—Win was short for Winner—a tad ironic. His 132–164 career record as a right-handed pitcher is deceiving. He gave up a lot of hits—11.2 hits per nine innings over his career—but recorded a respectable ERA of 3.98, with adjusted ERA of 107.

Mercer won 25 games for the 1896 Washington Senators, reeling off nine consecutive wins at one point and accounting for nearly half the team's 58 wins that season. He produced his best pitching the next season with 21 wins and a 3.18 ERA while leading the NL in games started (43) and shutouts (3)—that generated ERA+ of 135. However, he batted just .244 that season in 156 plate appearances. In 1898, Mercer was replaced by Gus Weyhing as the Senators' ace, and he ended up playing 23 games at short, 19 games in the outfield and six games at third and second, batting a solid .321. He would bat between .294 and .300 each of the next three seasons.

He served as a utility player in the field, playing every position except catcher during his career. He ended up playing 90 games at third base, 76 games in the outfield, 39 games at shortstop, and 31 games at other positions. He set career highs with 112 hits, 73 runs scored, seven triples, and 35 RBI in 1899, but his pitching record was 7–14. He batted .285 with 506 hits and 87 OPS+ for his career, generating total WAR of 27.2.

When the Senators were disbanded after the 1899 season, Mercer landed with the New York Giants, who were three years away from entering a dominant stretch. He won 13 games in his lone season with the Giants, followed by a return engagement to the Senators' new franchise in the American League.

The handsome Mercer was a notorious favorite of the ladies, which reportedly caused a riot during one game. The Senators frequently held "Ladies Day" games when Mercer was pitching, with all women admitted for free. One such game was scheduled for September 13, 1897, with Mercer on the mound facing Cincinnati. After Mercer was ejected in the third inning by Umpire Bill Carpenter for arguing a call, it undoubtedly upset some of the women in the crowd who had come to watch him pitch. However, their displeasure with Carpenter—which led to a brief kerfuffle after the game—was the result of a call late in the game that went against the home team, according to the game report in *The Washington Times*. There was no riot, no damage to the field, and no police were called to restore order.[32]

On August 10, 1901, Mercer became the first American League pitcher to steal home in the modern era. He hit .353 that season as a pitcher (tops in the AL) and .300 overall. He played exclusively as a pitcher and did well in what ended up as his last season, 1902, winning 15 games with a 3.04 ERA for the seventh-place Detroit Tigers. With 282 hits allowed in 281⅔ innings, it was his only season without allowing significantly more hits than innings pitched.

Mercer was well-liked by fans and players, who were pleased when the Tigers announced he would serve as player-manager for the 1903 season. He had just completed an offseason barnstorming tour with a group of other MLB players when the 28-year-old shockingly took his own life on January 12, 1903, at the Occidental Hotel in San Francisco.[33] The circumstances surrounding his death were the subject of a book by Jimmy Keenan titled "The Life, Times, and Tragic Death of Pitcher Win Mercer." Mercer left behind a suicide note that warned of the evils of women and gambling, but many of his friends rejected the idea he would have committed suicide over money.[34]

Tony Mullane

Irish-born Tony Mullane made pitching history on two occasions in 1882. He became the first ambidextrous pitcher in major league history on July 18, and he pitched the first no-hitter in American Association history on September 11, against the Cincinnati Red Stockings.

A switch-hitter at the plate but a natural righty hurler, Mullane learned to be an ambidextrous pitcher while overcoming an arm injury. In that July 18 contest, he fell behind Baltimore and grew frustrated with the results he was getting ... so he whipped out his new secret weapon. As described in the *Baltimore Sun* game report: "Mullane, of the Eclipse club, changed hands in the fourth inning and pitched with his left" to get outs "in good style."[35]

Mullane switched back and forth the rest of the game, to good effect, although still in a losing effort. It was an innovative strategy at the time to recognize his best bet against lefty batters was to throw southpaw. The *Boston Herald* sang his praises as a pitcher, calling him "a most effective pitcher; his delivery is low and his command of the ball wonderful. He pitches with left or right arm equally well."[36] He did the southpaw switcheroo two more times in games on July 5, 1892, and July 14, 1893.[37]

One could see why Mullane's arm got sore. He won 30 games pitching 460⅓ innings and 51 complete games for Louisville during his first full season in 1882, leading the league in games started and strikeouts. He pitched 2,434 innings in the five seasons he played between 1882 and 1887, winning 30 games in each of those seasons while recording 266 complete games. If he had not been suspended for the 1885 season for trying to break his contract, Mullane would have most likely exceeded 300 wins for his career and been a shoo-in for the Hall of Fame. Playing in an era filled with contract disputes, the stubborn pitcher had more than his share.

As noted earlier in this chapter, Mullane's no-hitter preceded teammate Guy Hecker's by eight days. Five previous no-hitters in the National League had been tossed at the shorter distance of 45 feet. Mullane was not against raising his arm above his shoulder to get more power, which he learned was only illegal if the rule was enforced.

An exceptional athlete and good fielder, Mullane stole 112 bases and had three seasons with 20 or more steals. In 1883, he pitched in 53 of the 98 games for St. Louis. When he didn't pitch that season, he typically played the outfield (30 games) or sometimes the infield (five games).

Mullane is tied with Ferguson Jenkins for 29th place all-time in pitching wins with 284. Roger Clemens, Bobby Mathews, and Tommy John are the only hurlers with more wins who are not in the Hall of Fame. He is the all-time leader in pitching wins in American Association history with 202 and ranks seventh in wins during the 19th century. His 3.05 ERA and adjusted ERA of 117 show he was a top-notch pitcher. Bill James once ranked him as the number 82 pitcher all-time, ahead of two fellow 19th-century hurlers who are in the Hall of Fame: Pud Galvin and Mickey Welch.[38] He ranks 61st all-time among starting pitchers, according to JAWS (the Jaffe WAR Score System).

His batting marks were inconsistent, but he was good enough to see regular action around the infield and outfield. He played 154 games in the outfield, 52 at third base, 38 at first base, and 21 at shortstop or second. In addition to serving as staff ace for the 1884 Toledo Blue Stockings, Mullane finished second on the team with a .276 average and third with 97 hits. Another strong year at the plate was 1889 with Cincinnati, when he batted .296 with 58 hits.

Mullane's nicknames "Apollo in the Box" and "Count" referred to his good looks. His career mark of 343 wild pitches is 66 ahead of Nolan Ryan for the most all-time, and he also led the NL in walks three straight seasons.

Mullane's bloated ERA of 6.59 in his final season, 1894, can be attributed in part to his horrific start for the Baltimore Orioles on June 18 when he surrendered a major-league record 16 runs to Boston in the first inning. Manager Ned Hanlon left him in, perhaps because it was the first game of a doubleheader, and the final beating was 24–7. Baltimore traded him to Cleveland a month later for future Hall of Famer John Clarkson, and Mullane won one final game before getting released.

With no major-league teams interested in his services, Mullane hung around playing in the minors until 1902 at the age of 43, winning an additional 38 games. Playing 60 games at first base in 1895, he batted .320 with 114 hits while also winning 15 games on the mound for St. Paul in the Western League.

Charles "Old Hoss" Radbourn

Charles "Old Hoss" Radbourn has owned one of baseball's most enduring records for more than 140 years—most pitching wins in a single season. In 1884, he won an astounding 60 games for the Providence Grays, which topped his record of 48 wins from the previous season.

With the way starters are used these days, it's unlikely another pitcher will ever approach this record. His win total represented 71 percent of the Grays' wins that year as he led them to the pennant, and he pitched all 22 innings and went 3-0 in the World Championship series. Beginning August 7, Radbourn rattled off an 18-game winning streak (over a period of 31 days) and 26 out of 27, while the team enjoyed a 20-game winning streak to take over first place.

Not only did Old Hoss win the pitching Triple Crown that season, he set major-league marks that still stand for complete games (73) and innings pitched (678⅔). He completed every game he started. His 1.38 ERA is the fourth best all-time, his 11 shutouts are tied for fourth best, and his 441 strikeouts rank fifth all-time. The .833 winning percentage ranks seventh all-time, while the adjusted ERA of 205 ranks 10th. He led the National League that year in each of these categories. It was a strange year, the first year in which pitchers could throw overhand and with talent spread across a third league with the Union Association in existence for just that season. Other rules favored the pitcher, such as requiring six balls for a walk.

Radbourn was not even supposed to be the Grays' ace that season, but when Charlie Sweeney was kicked off the team in July it depleted the pitching depth. The temperamental Radbourn, who had maintained a jealous feud with Sweeney all season, agreed to pick up the slack and started 41 of the Grays' final 51 games.

Manager Frank Bancroft, who roomed with Radbourn on the road, remarked: "His showing was all the more remarkable and phenomenal when one knows that this great pitcher suffered untold agony in endeavoring to attain the goal for which he worked so hard and so pluckily. Morning after morning upon rising he would be unable to raise his arm high enough to use his hair brush. Instead of quitting he stuck all the harder to his task, going out to the ballpark hours before the rest of the team and beginning to warm up by throwing a few feet and increasing the distance until he could finally throw the ball from the outfield to home plate."[39]

Radbourn's 1884 win total remains in dispute. On July 28, Cyclone Miller started a game for the Grays and left after five innings with a 7–4 lead. He was followed by Radbourn, who closed out the victory with four shutout innings. Back in the 1880s, stats were not compiled in an organized or meaningful way. *The Sporting News* began publishing win-loss records for pitchers in 1888 and didn't expect it would catch on. Major League Baseball lists Radbourn with 59 wins, after retroactively applying a 1950 rule for assigning wins that is still in place today. SABR researchers and Baseball-Reference have determined that Radbourn should be credited with the win, by the standards of the 1880s, as the most effective pitcher in that July 28 game.[40] We will share their recognition of 60 wins for Old Hoss. One win doesn't change the all-time leaderboard, as John Clarkson is far back in second place with 53 wins.

Radbourn shouldered a heavy workload for three more seasons before slowing down starting in 1888. His 1.90 ERA during his first four seasons (1881–84) was best in the majors by a wide margin—Jim Whitney was next at 2.38. His 3.35 ERA over his last seven seasons was pedestrian compared to the other top pitchers. He varied his pitching style, keeping batters off-balance by effectively mixing pitches such as a masterful changeup and a sharp curve with a submarine ball. Radbourn was believed to be the first pitcher who developed a strategy of walking or pitching around the heavy hitters and then attacking the lightweight hitters in the batting order.[41]

Ted Sullivan, who had a distinguished career as a manager, league organizer, and scout, called Radbourn the greatest pitcher in baseball history: "From the time I met Rad, he was continually inventing a new delivery and trying to get it under control. He had a jump to a high fastball, an in-shoot to a lefthanded batter, a drop ball that he did not have to spit on, and a perplexing slow ball that has never since been duplicated on the ball field. When he let fly with the high fastball, he threw it so hard he actually leaped off the ground."[42]

Radbourn played 22 games in the field in 1884, spread across the infield and outfield, but he made minimal impact with the bat with 83 hits, .230 average, and 37 RBI. His best year at the plate was 1883, when he batted .283 with 108 hits, 59 runs scored, and 48 RBI while playing 15 games in the field. A capable fielder and batter, Radbourn didn't play much in the field because his talents were needed on the mound for nearly every game.

Playing right field, his walk-off home run to help John Ward win the 18-inning marathon on August 17, 1882, showed he was capable with the bat—it was his first career home run and his only homer of the season. It marked the first walk-off home run in a 1–0 game in major-league history. Just as clutch was his bare grab of a deep shot to right in the 15th inning with two outs and a man on third.[43]

Old Hoss had supplanted Ward as the staff ace in 1882, pitching 466 innings and collecting 33 wins (14 more than Ward). It was a precursor of more big things to come, but no one could have predicted 60 victories in a

114-game season. That is the equivalent of winning 85 games in a 162-game season.

On July 25, 1883, Radbourn pitched a no-hitter against the Cleveland Blues. He won 33 games with a 2.11 ERA during that 84-game season while also contributing 78 hits.

Radbourn saw his win total plummet to 28 in 1885 as the Grays fell to fourth place. His production never again approached his dream season, although he won at least 20 games in nine seasons. Jumping to Boston in the Players' League in 1890, Old Hoss produced his best season in five years with 27 wins and a .259 average. A final season with Cincinnati pushed him over 300 wins, and he finished his career with 310 wins (19th all-time) and a 2.68 ERA. He completed 488 of the 502 games he started and still holds the National League record for most career one-hitters with seven. He ranks 36th all-time among starting pitchers, according to JAWS (the Jaffe WAR Score System). Old Hoss was elected to the Baseball Hall of Fame in 1939.

Jack Stivetts

Impressing as a hard-throwing 21-year-old rookie in 1889, Jack Stivetts paced the American Association that season with a 2.25 ERA and 186 ERA+ (pitching significantly fewer innings than other top pitchers) while winning 12 games for the St. Louis Browns. He pitched four complete games that ended in a tie on the way to 18 complete games.

The next year his bat kicked in, and he clubbed seven home runs to finish third in the league—it was the most in a single season by a pitcher until Wes Ferrell hit nine in 1931. On June 10, 1890, Stivetts slugged two home runs including a game-winning grand slam and pitched a complete game to beat Toledo.[44] On the mound that year, he won 27 games and finished second with 289 strikeouts. His 259 strikeouts paced the league in 1891.

Nicknamed "Happy Jack" for his genial manner (when he wasn't drinking), Stivetts was a capable fielder who played all around the diamond during his 11-year career, seeing the most time in the outfield—141 games—in addition to 388 pitching appearances. At six-foot-two and approaching 200 pounds, he was an intimidating presence on the mound and at the plate and often batted in the middle of the lineup.

His career WAR of 48.5 came mostly from pitching his way to 203 victories, with six seasons of at least 20 wins and three straight seasons of 400 innings pitched. As an article in *Sporting Life* opined, Stivetts threw the baseball as fast as Amos "The Hoosier Thunderbolt" Rusie, hit the ball as "hard as any man in the league," and was versatile enough to play every position except catcher.[45]

His .305 average and 33 wins led the Browns to a second-place finish in 1891—he led the league with 232 walks and 259 strikeouts. He already had one foot out the door. He jumped to Boston in the National League the next year and helped guide them to the pennant by matching Kid Nichols with 35 wins.

On August 5, 1892, he single-handedly defeated the Brooklyn Bridegrooms 2–0 by smacking a two-run homer in the 12th inning. To top that the next day, he pitched a no-hit shutout against Brooklyn while mashing a double and a triple.[46]

Stivetts wasn't done with amazing feats that year. He started and won complete games in both ends of a doubleheader against Louisville on September 5—the first game lasted 11 innings. Then on October 15, he threw his second no-hitter of the season against the Senators in a game shortened to five innings, so it is not viewed as an official no-hitter.[47]

The 1892 season ended with a first-ever National League championship series, which gave Stivetts a chance to shine on the big stage. In the pitchers' duel of the decade, Happy Jack pitched Cy Young to a scoreless 11-inning draw in the first game. He won two later games as Boston swept the favored Cleveland Spiders, with Stivetts giving up just three earned runs in 29 innings in the series.

Preferring batting to pitching, Stivetts often pestered his skippers to keep him in the lineup. He batted .328 and slugged .533 with 64 RBI and a .902 OPS in 1894. Another highlight that season came when he belted a pinch-hit three-run homer on June 28, 1894, that tied the score in the ninth—it was the second pinch homer in the majors and Stivetts closed out the game on the mound to earn the win in the 10th inning.[48]

He upped his average to .347 in 1896. On June 12, 1896, he clubbed two homers while pitching a complete-game win. Three times during his career, Stivetts homered twice in a game while pitching.

The next season on a Boston team that had 10 players with a batting average over .300, Stivetts topped them all at .367. His 35th and final career home run came on June 9, 1898, a pinch-hit, walk-off to beat Cincinnati. He hit a total of three pinch-hit home runs. His career marks were .298 average, 593 hits, and OPS+ of 106, and he batted over .300 four times.

Adonis Terry

William "Adonis" Terry was an accomplished two-way player for the first half of his career, before he settled into a role mainly as a righty pitcher. Along the way, he threw two no-hitters and became the second player to win 20 games and steal 30 bases in the same season.

Terry was just 19 years old when he debuted with the Brooklyn Atlantics in 1884, winning 19 games but losing 35 for the ninth-place team. His 476 innings pitched over 56 pitching appearances that season were paired with 13 stints in the outfield, producing a .233 average. His fielding was a work in progress, as Terry committed 34 errors as a pitcher.

After a slow start to the 1885 season on the mound, Terry was shifted to become a starting outfielder, seeing action there in 47 games. However, he batted just .170 for Brooklyn to go with his 6–17 record.

Relying on a mix of the speediest fastballs and the slowest curves in the league, his pitching rounded into form during the 1886 season. On July 24, he no-hit the first-place St. Louis Browns 1–0, contributing a single and stolen base to help his cause. It represented one of Terry's five shutouts on the season, and he would go on to record 18 wins with a 3.09 ERA. His play during a 13-game stint at shortstop was another matter—he committed 20 errors in 80 chances.

Terry's batting took off in 1887, which led him to receive 49 starts in the outfield. He averaged .293 with 103 hits, 65 RBI, and 27 stolen bases, pitching in with a 16–16 record on the mound. Also in 1887, we find the first reference to the handsome Terry as "Adonis," as he was compared favorably to an actor portraying the Greek god in a Broadway show.[49]

In his fifth year with Brooklyn in 1888, Terry produced one of his finest years as a pitcher. His 13–8 record came in just 23 starts, but his 2.03 ERA and 1.087 WHIP were career-best figures and he led the American Association with 6.4 strikeouts per 9 innings. On May 27, 1888, Terry threw his second no-hitter against the Louisville Colonels. Then in his next start, he banged a game-winning single in the 13th inning.

The next season, Terry produced his first 20-win season and first .300 average as he led Brooklyn to the World Series. He won two games but lost three as the Bridegrooms fell to the Giants 6–3.

He won both games of a doubleheader for Brooklyn on August 20, 1890, and he finished fifth in the league in strikeouts. He ended up with 26 wins and 32 stolen bases that season, becoming the only player in National League or American League history to accomplish the feat—Bob Caruthers did it three years earlier in the American Association.

With a three-game lead in the division, the Bridegrooms played a pivotal tripleheader on September 1, 1890. Terry played left field in the first two games and then exhibited clutch pitching in the nightcap as Brooklyn swept all three to extend its lead to 5½ games. They would go on to win the pennant.[50]

An 1890 article in *Sporting Life* sang Terry's praises on the mound:

The 1889 Brooklyn Bridegrooms won the American Association pennant behind the play of two-way stars Dave Foutz, Bob Caruthers, and Adonis Terry. Foutz led the team with 113 RBI, Caruthers led the league with 40 wins, and Terry batted .300 with 22 wins. Seated in front for the team picture is Mickey Hughes. Second row, from left: George Pinkney, Caruthers, Hub Collins, Manager Bill McGunnigle, Thomas "Oyster" Burns, Bob Clark, and Tom Lovett. Back row, from left: Germany Smith, John Corkhill, Terry, Foutz, Darby O'Brien, Doc Bushong, and Joe Visner (Library of Congress, Prints & Photographs Division, LC-DIG-ppmsca-18409).

"Such competent judges as Tom Gunning, Jack Kerins and Harry Stovey say he throws the hardest ball to hit of any pitcher living. His outcurve is the sharpest and speediest ever seen.... Terry has great speed and excellent command of the ball."[51]

Terry had a chance to be a dual threat during the 1890 World Series against Louisville. He pitched a two-hit shutout to win game one, moved to right field for game two, pitched to a tie in game three, then shifted to left field for the next game. Playing center field in game five, Terry contributed a double in a winning effort—it was his only hit in 20 at-bats. He lost game six on the mound and the Series was postponed at 3-3-1 and never rescheduled.

Teams gave up on Terry too quickly. He won 18 games with a 2.57 ERA pitching for three teams in 1892, then won 21 games for the Chicago

Colts in 1895. He did produce some ugly games, such as the 1894 game when he surrendered 25 runs to Boston, or the July 13, 1896, game in which he served up four home runs to Ed Delahanty.[52]

For his career, Terry went 197–196 on the mound with a 3.74 ERA and 367 complete games (23rd most all-time). His 31.2 career WAR came mainly from pitching. His 216 games in the outfield plus 32 games in the infield generated -1.8 defensive WAR and just 1.6 offensive WAR. He collected 594 hits, stole 106 bases, and averaged .249 over 14 seasons. Using the Win Shares method, Bill James identified Terry as the 14th best pitcher-hitter combination of all time.[53]

Jim Whitney

Jim Whitney was an immediate success as a 23-year-old rookie with Boston in 1881. He won his pitching debut while collecting three hits. He led the National League that year in wins (31), games started (63), complete games (57), and innings pitched (552⅓) while finishing eighth in ERA at 2.48. He also paced the league with 33 losses as Boston finished sixth. Playing 15 games in center field and two at first base, his lefty bat contributed 72 hits that year with a .255 average.

The next season he led the team in average (.323) and slugging (.510) while winning 24 games on the mound. Then his 37 wins and league-record 345 strikeouts in 1883 to go with 115 hits and a .281 average led the Beaneaters to the NL pennant. In mid–September, Whitney pitched in three of the four games that Boston swept against the first-place White Stockings to open a division lead they would not relinquish.

Whitney produced a 107 ERA+ with 162 strikeouts in 1881—slightly above average—but he accumulated 7.8 pitching WAR largely due to his high total of innings pitched. Two years later, he more than doubled his strikeouts and posted an incredible 11.4 pitching WAR. Whitney didn't get significantly better at striking out batters, he merely benefited from a series of rule changes.

Several possible explanations exist for Whitney's nickname of "Grasshopper." It could have been related to his weird running gait, his oddly shaped head or more likely, a tribute to the distinctive hop he incorporated into his windup and delivery in the pitcher's box. His hopping delivery was once described as "doing a running high jump and a back handspring before sending the ball at the terrified batsman."[54]

Hall of Famer Jim O'Rourke paid him a high compliment: "There were no restrictions placed on (pitchers) as to delivery, and they could double up like a jack-knife and deliver the ball. That was the way Jim Whitney used to do, and he would let the ball go at terrific speed. It was a wonder that anyone was able to hit him at all. He was the swiftest pitcher I ever saw."[55]

On June 9, 1883, Whitney rapped out five hits and scored six runs while pitching Boston to a 30-8 win over Detroit—he played part of that game in center field. On the mound, he exhibited remarkable control. The 1883 season was the first of five consecutive seasons he would lead the league in bases on balls per nine innings; he would also lead in strikeout/walk ratio in four of the next five seasons.

A critical four-game series with the Chicago White Stockings from September 10-13, 1883, showed off Whitney's versatility and star power. He played center field in the third game and pitched complete games to win the other three while batting cleanup, as Boston swept the series to gain a foothold on the pennant. He surrendered 13 hits and two earned runs while striking out 19 in 27 innings against a stout White Stockings lineup anchored by King Kelly and Cap Anson.[56]

New rules were adopted by the National League for the 1887 season that forced pitchers to keep their back foot on the rear line of the pitcher's box. No more hopping for "Grasshopper" Whitney. He adapted and won 24 games that season and 18 the next before chronic illness began to sap his strength.

After batting .238 and winning just two games for the Philadelphia Athletics in 1890, Whitney was released in July. Ten months later, he would be dead at age 33 of tuberculosis. Some have speculated that being struck hard on the chest by a batted ball in 1888 led to his eventual demise.[57]

Whitney rode his lively fastball to win 191 games across 10 seasons with a 2.97 ERA. He recorded top 10 finishes five times in ERA, six times in wins, seven times in innings pitched, six times in strikeouts, eight times in games started, and seven times in complete games. His 377 complete games rank 22nd all-time and his 47.5 pitching WAR outpaces a number of Hall of Famers including Jack Morris, Lefty Gomez, Charles Bender, Jack Chesbro, and Bob Lemon.

In addition to 130 games played in the outfield, Whitney made 31 appearances at first base. He produced a respectable lifetime average of .261 with 559 hits and an OPS+ of 112. His WAR as a position player totaled 8.5. His 113 doubles are the most all-time by a pitcher.

Additional Players of Note

A few additional 19th-century players are noteworthy two-way players with some level of accomplishment. **Elmer Smith** led the American

Association with a 2.94 ERA in 1887 while winning 34 games. He won 22 games the next season before an arm injury curtailed his pitching career and he shifted to the outfield. He won 75 games in 149 pitching appearances. At the plate, he had seasons of .346, .357 and .362, and averaged .310 over a 14-year career with 1,456 hits and 233 steals.

Charlie Sweeney won 41 games pitching for the Providence Grays and St. Louis Maroons in 1884, while also playing 18 games in the outfield and first base and batting .307 with 104 hits. On June 7, 1884, he set a record with 19 strikeouts that was matched by Hugh Dailey a month later but not topped for 102 years. A sore arm limited him to 64 career pitching wins, and he collected just 224 hits over six seasons.

Cy Seymour led the National League in strikeouts as a southpaw hurler in 1897 and 1898 and he won 18 and 25 games in those seasons for the New York Giants. However, he also led the NL in walks three straight seasons and his control problems turned him from a part-time outfielder to a full-time outfielder. He totaled 1,333 games across 16 seasons in the outfield and collected 1,724 hits with a .303 average and 222 stolen bases. In 1905, he led the NL in nine batting categories including average (.377), slugging (.559), hits (219), doubles (40), triples (21), and RBI (121).

Hall of Famer **Mickey Welch** played 59 games in the outfield across six seasons in addition to making 565 pitching appearances. Thirty-eight of those outfield appearances came in 1883, when he served as a fourth outfielder for the New York Giants and batted .234 with 75 hits and pitched in with 25 wins as the staff ace.

George Van Haltren walked 16 batters in his major league debut on June 27, 1887—still a National League record—an inauspicious start that set him on the path to stardom as a batter. He won 13 games with a 3.52 ERA, four shutouts, and 24 complete games pitching 245⅔ innings for Chicago in 1888, while batting .283 with 90 hits from 57 outfield appearances. His next playing season was 1890, when he won 15 games and recorded 23 complete games while also playing 67 games in the outfield, three games at shortstop, and batting .335. He posted a career average of .316 with 2,544 hits, 583 stolen bases, 122 OPS+ and 41.3 WAR playing 1,833 games in the outfield. He won just 40 games from 93 pitching appearances that mainly came in his first three seasons.

Scott Stratton won 34 games and led the league in ERA in 1890, when he batted .323. He ended up playing 133 games in the outfield and 34 at first base while collecting 381 hits and averaging .274. He hit a career-high .360 in 1894. Stratton's pitching record was 97–114 with a 3.87 ERA. On May 29, 1886, the 18-year-old became the youngest pitcher to hit a home run. The next year he became the youngest pitcher to hit a grand slam.[58]

Billy Taylor had one exceptional two-way season in 1884 playing for two teams in two leagues. Starting off with the St. Louis Maroons in the Union Association, Taylor went 25–4 with a 1.68 ERA for a team that would go on to finish first with 94 wins. He also batted .366 for the Maroons with 68 hits while playing 14 games at first base and the outfield. Taylor jumped to the Philadelphia Athletics in July and pitched 260 more innings, winning 18 games with a 2.53 ERA and batting .252. He won just seven games in his other six seasons.

Al Maul won 84 games over 15 seasons, leading the NL with a 2.45 ERA in 1895 and winning 20 games in 1898. Maul batted .241 lifetime while playing 185 games in the outfield and 40 games at first base.

Other 19th-century players did a fair amount of two-way playing but didn't produce memorable results. **Ed Daily** won 66 games across 151 pitching appearances and played 497 games in the outfield with a .239 average. His best two-way season was 1890, when he won 18 games pitching 344⅔ innings for three different teams. Daily also collected 116 hits and 62 stolen bases that season playing 78 games in the outfield. **Charlie Ferguson** won at least 20 games in each of his four seasons, and he batted over .300 in two of them while playing 85 career games in the field. **Ed Crane** went 72–97 as a pitcher and averaged .238 with 335 lifetime hits. He played 145 games in the outfield and 46 games at catcher. Crane batted .285 with 122 hits in his rookie season, and he later won 18 games and led the American Association in ERA in 1891.

CHAPTER 4

Deadball Era 1900–1919
Two-Way Play Slows Down

The Deadball Era in baseball history started with the formation of the new American League in 1901 and lasted until 1919. Ban Johnson's boldness to break up the National League's monopoly and start the American League allowed baseball to flourish in more cities. He promised a cleaner game less polluted with rowdy players and unruly fans, which made baseball games more desirable for women and children to attend. Stars such as Walter Johnson, Nap Lajoie, Cy Young, and Joe McGinnity jumped to the new league and gave it credibility from the start.

Baseball in the 19th century lacked stability in franchises, leagues, and rules, which forced players to continually adapt new methods to gain competitive advantage. It was barely controlled chaos. The game grew up as a new century dawned. Bunts, stolen bases, and the hit-and-run play were all in vogue as small ball took hold and every game held the promise of turning into another pitchers' duel.

Changing the pitcher's mound from 50 feet to 60 feet, six inches in 1893—along with allowing overhand throwing in 1884—had a tremendous impact on the art of pitching. Workhorse aces could no longer pitch complete games day after day, pitching 500-plus innings a season. Pitchers who could excel throwing every three or four days became valuable commodities—especially if they had good control and didn't walk many batters. Franchises were less inclined to have those stars play the field in their off days. The best-hitting pitchers didn't stand out much, because most of the hitters were overshadowed by the guys on the mound.

Managers in the Deadball Era finally started taking advantage of modern substitution rules that had been around since 1890. No longer did they have to swap out a position player when they wanted to make a pitching change. Teams, who were more stabilized as franchises now, carried deeper rosters up to 25 players, which meant players could specialize in one position.

Chapter 4. Deadball Era 1900–1919

In 1902, the second year of the new American League, Socks Seybold led the league in home runs with six. Ty Cobb was not noted as a home run hitter, yet he led the AL with seven home runs in 1909. When Aaron Judge set the new AL record with 62 home runs in 2022, he hit more home runs in five separate months than Cobb did for all of 1909. It was a different game, for sure.

When the American League adopted the foul-strike rule in 1903—a rule enacted in the National League in 1901—it brought the game in alignment with rules that could carry forward without the need for major tinkering. With the first two foul balls counted as strikes, batters were no longer emboldened to keep fouling off pitches to frustrate and tire pitchers. Strikeouts rose sharply and teams looked for pitchers who could get outs without the ball being put in play.

New ballparks were built that were more conducive to watching a baseball game in comfort. Shiny concrete-and-steel ballparks began springing up, the first being Shibe Park in Philadelphia in 1909. Others soon followed and two of them remain in operation—Fenway Park, opened in Boston in 1912; and Wrigley Field, opened in Chicago in 1914 as Weeghman Park. With franchises stabilized in a dozen cities and without a new league being formed to stir up trouble every few years, players found themselves on the move less frequently. Their rights were still controlled by owners due to the reserve clause, but they were more apt to stay in one city and build a loyal following of fans.

The Deadball Era gets its name from the distinct lack of offense in the period as pitchers gained the upper hand. In 1894, the National League average for team batting was .309, followed by .296 the next year. That had dropped to .267 in 1901 and dropped further to .239 in 1908. The team average for earned run average went from 5.33 in 1894 to 2.35 in 1908. The adoption of the cork-centered baseball in 1911 did cause batting levels to rise to some degree, until pitchers discovered the advantages of scratching the ball.[1]

Home run totals in the National League went from 629 in 1894 (many of them of inside-the-park variety) and 352 in 1899 to 96 in 1902. In 1919, the last year of the Deadball Era, 207 home runs were hit among the National League's eight teams and 240 were hit among the American League's eight teams. By contrast, 5,868 home runs were hit by the 30 major-league teams in 2023.

It is important to note that pitchers' improved performance during this 20-year period was helped immeasurably by the fact the fielders behind them finally had functional gloves to use. No more attempting to snag a hot shot with your bare hand.

The spitball had a huge impact on the game throughout the Deadball

Era, along with the shine ball, the emery ball, and other custom-modified pitches learned on the sly. Lots of pitchers learned to throw balls loaded with slippery elm spittle or tobacco juice or some other foreign substance, which created challenges for batters and fielders. Only one or two balls would be used in the course of a game, which meant by the late innings batters could barely see the darkened ball as it whizzed by them. A partial ban on spitballs was adopted in 1920, with each team allowed to have two spitball practitioners. Spitball use was then banned before the next season, although 17 pitchers were allowed to continue throwing it until the end of their careers.

As the Deadball Era was winding down in the late 1910s, managers began using more players in a platoon situation and utilizing pinch hitters and pinch runners. Relief pitchers were starting to be deployed as weapons instead of for mop-up duty. However, before baseball could explode in popularity with the emergence of the Sultan of Swat, it needed to first survive the Black Sox Scandal of 1919, which exposed the still-seedy underbelly of the game.

"I say the dead ball should be brought back. It would give the fans a game that is decided inside the park, not outside it. The dead ball makes for exciting catches in the outfield, eyelash plays at third on triples when the ball and the runner arrive at the same time, and more base stealing, which was an exciting part of the game," commented Hall of Famer Ed Walsh in a 1957 interview in *The Sporting News*.[2]

Once Babe Ruth changed the game with his mammoth home-run blasts, there was no going back. What follows in this chapter is a closer look at nine Deadball Era players who excelled as two-way players.

Ray Caldwell

Despite his many accomplishments on the diamond and tantalizing brilliance as a pitcher, Ray Caldwell is most remembered for a singular episode—he was struck by lightning while on the pitcher's mound and lived to complete the game.

Caldwell debuted at age 22 with the New York Highlanders (often called the Americans by the press) in 1910. He threw right-handed but swung the bat from the left side. Armed with a top-notch curve and blazing fastball, Caldwell kept teasing with his talent while self-destructing with alcohol-related "outbreaks of misbehavior." Three failed marriages during his playing career exacerbated his stress, but he later embarked on a fourth, successful marriage at the age of 51.

His 14 wins from 41 pitching appearances in 1911 were supplemented by 11 games in the outfield and eight pinch-hitting opportunities. Caldwell batted .272 that year with 40 hits to demonstrate his two-way abilities. On July 12, 1911, he threw a complete-game three-hitter against the St. Louis Browns and helped his own cause with three hits to raise his average to .396.

An 8–16 record with a 4.47 ERA followed for the Highlanders in 1912, as Caldwell battled arm issues and the bottle. His erratic behavior caused him to quickly fall out of favor with Frank Chance, the Yankees' new manager for 1913, who debated converting him to outfielder.

A July 14 game against the St. Louis Browns demonstrated his high ceiling. Caldwell finished the game with five innings of shutout relief, and he belted two hits to boost his average to a league-leading .421. He would finish with a 2.41 ERA that season with 15 complete games while batting .289. Chance called on him 21 times as a pinch hitter. In addition to appearing 22 times as a pinch runner, Caldwell garnered 111 plate appearances as a pinch hitter over his career, batting .238 with two homers in those at-bats.

Caldwell took his pitching performance to another level in 1914, throwing shutouts in his first three starts. He went 18–9 with a 1.94 ERA (fourth in AL) and 22 complete games (third best) for the season, cementing his status as a star pitcher. Nicknamed "Slim" for his tall, slender build, it also was a fair description of batters' chances against his pitches.

It was reported that Washington's owner, Clark Griffith, was so enthralled with Caldwell that he offered future Hall of Famer Walter Johnson in trade. American League President Ban Johnson stepped in and advised the Yankees' new owner, Jacob Ruppert, that he would be foolish to accept such a deal due to Caldwell's unlimited potential. The deal didn't happen, nor did Branch Rickey of the St. Louis Browns get his hands on Caldwell like he wanted.[3]

Caldwell showed flashes of greatness the next season. On June 10, 1915, he belted a ninth-inning home run as a pinch hitter, then came back the next day and smacked a three-run, pinch-hit homer that proved the difference in a one-run game. Then to top it all off the next day, Caldwell homered for a third straight game, a three-run blast, while pitching a complete-game victory. He won 19 games while pitching 305 innings for the fifth-place Yankees in 1915. At the plate, he pinch-hit 35 times and batted .243 with a career-high four home runs and 27 runs scored.

Slim pitched 21 consecutive complete games for the Yankees across the 1915 and 1916 seasons, which is five shy of Jack Chesbro's team record. On July 3, 1916, Caldwell pitched a three-hit shutout over 11 innings to outduel Walter Johnson and the Senators 1–0. He would be suspended by Manager Bill Donovan later in the season when his drinking again got out of control. His performance on the field ebbed and flowed over the next few seasons, interspersed with suspensions for his transgressions. He played 19 games in the outfield in 1918 including 12 games in center field, and his bat still held strong with a .291 average.

Unable to depend on Caldwell, the Yankees traded him to the Red Sox in December 1918. He had produced a 96–99 record for the team over nine seasons. "Caldwell might have been the Mathewson of the Yankees, but he turned out to be the Bugs Raymond of the local Americans. His irregular habits destroyed his effectiveness," commented sportswriter Fred Lieb of *The Sun*.[4]

The Red Sox strangely had Caldwell room on the road with another player who liked the nightlife: Babe Ruth. The Babe, who was in the last year of his experiment with two-way playing, was evidently not the good influence Slim needed. Caldwell produced a 7–4 record with a 3.96 ERA before being released by the Sox in August.

Like a cat with nine lives, Caldwell was signed by the Cleveland Indians two weeks later. Tris Speaker, the Indians' player-manager, came up with a counterintuitive plan to keep his new pitcher productive. It was written into his contract that Caldwell had to get drunk after each game he pitched, and that he would be excused from reporting to the ballpark the next day while he slept off his hangover.[5]

Five days after signing with the Indians, Caldwell took the mound on August 24, 1919, for his first home appearance at League Park. Relying on a new spitball he learned from teammate Stan Coveleski, Caldwell mowed down Philadelphia's lineup through eight innings and

Ray Caldwell is shown here during the 1918 season with the New York Yankees. That year, he recorded a 3.06 ERA in 176⅔ innings on the mound while batting .291 from 19 games in the outfield (Library of Congress, Prints & Photographs Division, LC-DIG-ggbain-26800).

even contributed a single at the plate as ominous storm clouds appeared. Entering the ninth with a 2–1 lead and with the wind howling around him, he got two quick outs and was one out from victory. Then came the shock of his life ... literally.

A flash of lightning exploded into the middle of the field, causing players to dive to the ground as panicked cries enveloped the stadium. All except the pitcher, Caldwell, who was lying on his back on the mound and not moving—he had been struck directly by lightning. No one dared touch him, because his chest seemed to be smoldering.[6]

Caldwell was not dead, as feared, and his teammates were overjoyed to see him slowly regain consciousness. "It just felt like somebody came up with a board and hit me on top of the head and knocked me down," he told the *Cleveland Press* afterwards.[7]

Despite his near-death experience, Caldwell was primarily concerned with finishing the game, barking that "I have one more out to get."[8] His incredulous teammates went back to their positions and watched as Caldwell threw one more pitch to retire Joe Dugan on a groundout to third. Down to his last chance to stay in the majors, Caldwell had left it all on the field and defied death to deliver a complete-game victory.

A plaque on a brick wall along the third-base line at Cleveland's Progressive Field sums it up best: "Caldwell had perhaps the most electric debut in Cleveland Indians history."[9] Two weeks later, he pitched a no-hitter against his old team, the Yankees, on September 10. He ended up leading American League pitchers with a .309 batting average that season.

Caldwell was one of 17 pitchers who were exempted from the 1920 ban on spitballs. He would win 20 games for the first time that season to help lead the Indians to the pennant. He surrendered 286 hits in 237⅔ innings and had nothing left in the tank when the World Series got underway. He recorded only one out as the Game 3 starter, which would be his only appearance as the Indians won their first World Series.

He won six games the next year before Cleveland released him, giving him a career record of 134–120 with a 3.22 ERA. Slim hung around for 12 years pitching in the minors, collecting 141 more wins to give him 293 total wins as a professional pitcher. Caldwell could have been as great as any pitcher in baseball history, and on some days, he certainly was.

Doc Crandall

James "Doc" Crandall was deployed as an unusual weapon— as a relief specialist who led the National League in games finished five straight seasons with John McGraw's New York Giants. He made 168 relief appearances in 10 seasons compared to 134 starts, relying on a sharp curveball to snuff out rallies.

Crandall mostly started as a rookie, going 12–12 with a 2.93 ERA (83 ERA+) in 214⅔ innings for the Giants in 1908. He won six, 17, 15, and 13 games from 1909 to 1912 while finishing a total of 93 games and making 51 starts.

"Crandall is the Giants' ambulance corps…. He is first aid to the injured. He is the physician of the pitching emergency, and they sometimes call him old Doctor Crandall. He is without an equal as an extinguisher of batting rallies and run riots, or as a pinch hitter," wrote sportswriter Damon Runyon in 1911.[10]

Crandall's versatility was on display during the 1911 World Series. In Game 5, he came on as a pinch hitter and doubled in a run, scored a run, added a walk, and then closed out the game to get the win with three innings of scoreless relief.

"Crandall was one of the coolest pitchers I ever saw. He had no fear, no nerves," recalled McGraw.[11]

A strong batter, Doc made 120 appearances as a pinch hitter. His lifetime average of .285 with 123 RBI produced an OPS+ of 120, which is the highest in major league history for a player who played at least 75 percent of his games as pitcher. His .419 career slugging percentage as a pitcher is the second-best mark since 1900.

His best year at the plate was 1914, when he batted .309 with 86 hits and 41 RBI while playing 63 games at second base to go with 27 pitching appearances. He batted .342 and slugged .521 in 1910—both figures were higher than the league leader but not enough at-bats to qualify. Crandall compiled 253 career hits and got two triples in a game twice, on September 10, 1910, and again on April 15, 1911.

In 1913, he became the first major-league pitcher to make more than 30 relief appearances in a season, coming out of the bullpen 33 times in two stints for the Giants during the season. In a bizarre stretch of 13 days spent with the Cardinals that August, Crandall made only two pinch-hit appearances before getting sent back to New York. In 1914, he set a modern-era record by walking 27 times while in the game as a pitcher.

Crandall's best year pitching came in 1915 for the St. Louis Terriers in the Federal League. He won 21 games with a 2.59 ERA (123 ERA+) and 22 complete games making 33 starts and 18 relief appearances across 312⅔ innings (second-best in league). He finished his major-league career with a 102–62 record and a 2.92 ERA.

Although he threw his last pitch in the majors at age 30, Crandall was not done pitching. He went on to pitch 13 more seasons in the minors, mainly for the Los Angeles Angels, posting five seasons with 20 wins.

He had a no-hitter with two outs in the ninth inning broken up by his brother, Karl, on April 7, 1918.[12] Adding his 211 wins in the minors to his 102 major-league wins, Crandall finished with a total of 313 victories as a professional pitcher.

Harry Howell

Harry Howell's production as a pitcher improved greatly once he mastered the spitball, a pitch he learned from teammate Jack Chesbro in 1903.[13] One of the foremost practitioners of the spitball in the Deadball Era, Howell's 2.06 ERA during seven seasons with the St. Louis Browns remains the franchise record for what is now the Baltimore Orioles. He used to chew the soft bark from slippery elm trees, mix it with his saliva and then rub up the baseball with his disgusting concoction.[14]

Hall of Famer Eddie Collins weighed in on the frustration of facing Howell's spitball: "Howell used so much slippery elm we could see the foam on his lips and on hot days some of the boys thought he was about to go mad."[15] Howell's teammates were less than thrilled about fielding and throwing balls that were covered with his spittle.

Howell's lifetime winning percentage of .473 reflects more on the caliber of teams he played for than the quality of his pitching. The one exception was 1900, when he started 10 games and pitched 11 games out of the bullpen for the Brooklyn Superbas, who won the National League pennant that year.

"Handsome Harry," as he was known, saw his first action as a position player during the 1901 season. He appeared in nine games in the outfield and nine games around the infield, in addition to 37 pitching appearances. That extra action produced a weak .218 batting average. Taking the mound that season for John McGraw's Baltimore Orioles, Howell won 14 games but lost 21, recording a 3.67 ERA in 294⅔ innings.

His best two-year season came in 1902 for the Orioles. Howell batted .268 with 93 hits in 347 plate appearances while scoring and driving in 42 runs. His 11 triples tied for 10th in the AL, with two of them coming as a pitcher. He played all over the diamond including 26 games at second base, 18 in the outfield, 15 at third base, and 11 at shortstop. His 26 mound appearances produced a 9–15 record with 243 hits surrendered in 199 innings, relying on a middling fastball and curveball. He fell 90 at-bats short of qualifying for the ERA and batting crowns.

On April 23, 1903, he pitched a complete game to win the first game in New York Yankees history—the team was called the New York Highlanders then. Playing 14 games in the field that year, Howell batted .217 and contributed nine wins while figuring out how to make the spitball work in his favor. Perhaps if Howell had not been distracted by the multi-year effort to make him a two-way player, he might have fared better as a pitcher.

Howell's best stretch of pitching started when he joined the Browns for the 1904 season, stopped playing much in the field, and began throwing the spitter on almost every pitch. He won 13 games that year with a 2.19 ERA and 32 complete games. He would average 308 innings pitched with a 2.02 ERA from 1904 to 1908. He set career marks for wins (18), ERA (1.89), and innings pitched (324⅓) in 1908 for the Browns.

After throwing out his arm in the spring of 1909, Howell was forced to retire a year later when surgery didn't fix the problem. Hanging around the Browns as a pitching coach, Howell made the mistake of getting involved in an underhanded attempt to let Cleveland's beloved Nap Lajoie edge the despised Ty Cobb for the 1910 AL batting title. For the first time, the winner would receive a fancy Chalmers 30 Touring Car with 30-horsepower engine and retractable top. Positioned with a nine-point cushion in the race, Cobb decided to sit his last two games.[16]

In the season-ending doubleheader in St. Louis, Jack O'Connor, the Browns manager, had rookie third baseman Red Corriden play well back in left field so Lajoie could bunt his way on. It worked like a charm eight straight times, except his ninth at-bat was ruled an error after a wild throw. Howell barged into the press box and attempted to convince the official scorer to change the error to a hit, but not even a bribe of a new suit did the trick. O'Connor and Howell were summarily fired by the team and unofficially banned from major-league baseball for life. Cobb was ruled the official batting champ by AL President Ban Johnson after a scorekeeper determined he had been deprived of a hit from earlier in the season.[17]

Harry Chalmers wisely decided to give cars to both players and for the next four years, gave out Chalmers autos to the players voted by sportswriters as the best. The story picks up again in 1981, when *The Sporting News* realized Cobb's two-hit game on September 25 had been counted twice in his 1910 season stats. Although Baseball-Reference and other stats bureaus recognize Lajoie as the rightful 1910 batting champion with a .383 average, Major League Baseball and the Baseball Hall of Fame still recognize Cobb with 12 batting titles including 1910, when he "officially" batted .382.[18]

Suitably chastised and unable to play again in the majors, Howell played 89 games at second base for Louisville and St. Paul in the minors in 1911, batting .260 with 87 hits. Not only did Howell make his mark as a two-way player, he umpired five American League games between 1904 and 1907 while still an active player and then umpired another 85 Federal League games in 1915, according to Retrosheet.

Johnny Lush

Possessing either the best or worst name of any player in the Deadball Era—depending on your perspective—Johnny Lush was the youngest player in the National League when he debuted at age 18 in 1904. That year he played 62 games for the Philadelphia Phillies at first base, 33 in the outfield, seven at pitcher, and four as a pinch hitter. He batted .276 with 102 hits and 42 RBI but produced an 0–6 record on the mound.

Lush's fourth career win was a two-hit shutout on April 23, 1906. His fifth career win came eight days later and was a no-hitter against the Brooklyn Superbas. Then on May 30, he tossed a one-hit shutout for his eighth career win. After that five-week stretch of superb pitching, Lush had established a major-league record (he still holds) for taking the fewest career games to throw a no-hitter, one-hitter, and two-hitter. He also remains the youngest pitcher—at 20 years, 205 days—to throw a no-hitter in the modern era (after 1900).[19]

Lush's 1906 season is the last time a player pitched 200 innings in a season with 200 at-bats and at least 20 games at a position other than pitcher. That was his best season as a pitcher, as he went 18–15 for the Phillies with a 2.37 ERA in 281 innings—his adjusted ERA was 110. At the plate, he batted .264 in 212 at-bats for an adjusted OPS of 93. He made 22 appearances in the outfield and two at first base that year, along with a league-leading 15 pinch-hitting chances.

On August 6, 1908, Lush tossed his second no-hitter against Brooklyn. Since the game was shortened to six innings due to rain, it doesn't count as an official no-hitter.

The southpaw's brilliance on the mound would prove to be short-lived. He went 66–85 over seven seasons with the Phillies and Cardinals with a 2.65 ERA that was three percent below league average.

Lush twice finished in the top 10 in shutouts and games started, and he compiled 252 career hits with a 97 OPS+ while playing 72 games in the outfield, 64 at first base, and 181 on the mound. His career WAR was 9.6.

Al Orth

Blessed with a cool nickname that was a backhanded compliment, Al "The Curveless Wonder" Orth made a career out of silencing his doubters. With 204 wins over a 15-year career, Orth proved to be a durable and productive pitcher who was unable to lead any of his teams to a pennant.

During his pitching debut for the Philadelphia Phillies on August 15, 1895, Orth showed off his other skill—his bat. He doubled off the wall on the first pitch he saw in the majors.[20] He went 8–1 that season with nine complete games in 10 starts while batting .356.

His best year at the plate came in 1897, when he batted .329 with 50 hits while appearing in six games in the outfield. On October 13, 1898, Orth started, completed, and won both games of a doubleheader against Brooklyn (the second lasted five innings). That season he averaged .293 with a 115 OPS+.

Also known as "Smiling Al," Orth led the National League in winning percentage in 1899 (.824) after going 14–3 with a 2.49 ERA that season. He led the NL in shutouts (six), WHIP (1.001) and BB/9 (1.0) in 1901 while winning 20 games for the first time.

Throwing pitches that didn't curve or come in fast, Orth gave up 10.2 hits per nine innings across his first nine seasons and averaged 2.5 strikeouts per nine innings for his career. He later became one of the early adopters of the spitball when he joined the New York Highlanders in 1904, which helped improve all his pitching stats. He called the spitball "more effective than a curve" and featuring a "quicker break."[21]

Pitching for the Washington Senators in the 1903 season opener on April 22, Orth outdueled New York's Jack Chesbro 3–1 in what was the first game in history for the franchise now known as the New York Yankees.[22] On July 18, 1903, Orth collected six hits during a doubleheader including a run-scoring single to win the first game. He set a modern-era record with seven triples that season.

Orth saw his most action in the field in 1904, appearing in 20 games in the outfield and five as a pinch hitter. He batted .247 with 41 hits and recorded 11 wins for the Highlanders after coming over in a July trade.

Riding his new spitball, Orth won 18 games for the Highlanders in 1905 and then had a breakout season the next year. He led the American League with 27 wins, 36 complete games, 338⅔ innings, and 8.1 pitching WAR. However, the team fell three games short of the White Sox in second place.

Despite a 2.61 ERA (106 ERA+) in 1906, Orth led the league in losses with 21 as New York dropped to fifth place. That gave him the distinction of being the only pitcher in baseball history to lead his league in wins one season and in losses the next season.[23]

A 2–13 record in 1908 showed the end was near. He did lead AL pitchers in batting average in 1907 (.324) and 1908 (.290). Brought back for his bat to play a final season in 1909, Orth made 15 pinch-hitting appearances and played six games at second base, one at first base, and one three-inning stint on the mound.

For his career, he ended up playing 74 games in the field and batting .273 with 464 hits, 12 home runs, and 184 RBI. He batted over .300 five times and generated 8.3 offensive WAR. His pitching record was 204–189 with a 3.37 ERA (100 ERA+), with 43.8 WAR from pitching.

Reb Russell

Finding instant success as a rookie, southpaw Ewell "Reb" Russell's star shone bright before an arm injury cut short his pitching career. Undaunted, he returned to the majors as a slugging outfielder and found more short-lived success.

The Mississippi native grew up in Texas and was first spotted pitching in the Texas League by White Sox scout Harry Howell, himself a former two-way star.[24]

Russell combined good stuff and sharp control with moxie to win 22 games for the White Sox in his 1913 debut season. He led the American League with 52 pitching appearances including 36 starts and posted 26 complete games in a team-high and AL rookie record 316⅔ innings with an ERA of 1.90 (fourth in AL).

"That boy has everything," gushed Jimmy Callahan, his manager on the Sox. "He has speed, he has curves, he has control, he has nerve, he has strength. What more could I ask for?"[25]

At the plate, Russell demonstrated flashes of his two-way ability. His 20 hits in his rookie year included three triples and a home run. Reb's effectiveness on the mound seemed to wane the next season after an early-season collision. His 7–12 record with 2.90 ERA fell short of high expectations. He was given five pinch-hitting opportunities on the way to batting .266.

His pitching produced 44 wins over the next three years for the Sox, and his 1.95 ERA in 1917 ranked fifth in the league. He led the team in innings pitched (264⅓) and wins (18) in 1916. He continued to mix starts with frequent relief appearances, coming in from the bullpen 94 times over the course of his seven-year pitching career. On May 31, 1915, against Detroit, he started both games of a doubleheader.

On August 7, 1916, Russell stole home while in the game as the pitcher. It was his only stolen base that season and one of nine he collected during his career. Russell had reported to spring training in 1915 so out of shape he was almost cut by manager Pants Rowland, so this daring feat demonstrated he was once again able to impact the game with more than his arm.[26]

Russell's sole postseason appearance came in the 1917 World Series, when he got a start but was removed after failing to record an out. The White Sox won the Series, but Russell was a non-contributor. He served as a part-time starter the next season before getting released with a dead arm in 1919 at age 30.

Playing out the 1919 season as an outfielder for the Minneapolis Millers in the minors, Russell batted .267 with nine homers. When the Millers needed a fill-in outfielder the next year, Russell caught fire with the bat with a .339 average and 101 hits. With still no interest from a major-league team, he returned to bat .368 in 1921 with 33 homers, 132 RBI, and 202 hits. He chipped in with five appearances on the mound.

Off to a torrid start again with Minneapolis in 1922, he was signed by Pittsburgh and ended up playing 60 games in the outfield. He crushed the ball at a .368 clip, blasted 12 homers and eight triples, drove in 75 runs, and slugged .668 with an OPS+ of 176. His teammate, future Hall of Famer Max Carey, had 482 more plate appearances but drove in five fewer runs than Russell.

At age 34 in 1923, Russell played 76 games in the outfield and averaged .289 with 84 hits, nine homers, and 58 RBI. However, his playing time dwindled because he was a defensive liability in the field, and the Pirates released him at the end of the season.[27]

In his last season in the majors, Reb Russell batted .289 with 84 hits as an outfielder for the 1923 Pittsburgh Pirates. That closed out a career in which he also went 80–59 on the mound (Library of Congress, Prints & Photographs Division, LC-DIG-ggbain-36175).

If the designated hitter rule existed back then, Russell's major-league career might have extended for years. Instead, it was the end of the line for a player once considered one of the American League's best lefty pitchers alongside Babe Ruth. His career pitching mark was 80–59 with a 2.33 ERA, while he averaged .268 at the plate with a strong 105 OPS+.

Russell hung around to play seven more years in the minors, never failing to bat .300 and winning an American Association batting title with a .385 average in 1927. He averaged .330 with 1,365 hits and 183 homers in 12 minor-league seasons.

Jesse Tannehill

He debuted at age 19 for his hometown Cincinnati Reds in 1894, but southpaw pitcher Jesse Tannehill was not ready for prime time yet. After two 20-win seasons in the minors, he was acquired by the Pirates for the 1897 season. His pitching was spotty, 9–9 with a 4.25 ERA in 142 innings, but he also batted .266 with 49 hits playing 33 games in the outfield. The Pirates felt he had as much potential as an outfielder, and the switch-hitter would play 87 games there during his career along with 57 pinch-hitting opportunities.

At five-foot-eight and 150 pounds, Tannehill was not an intimidating presence on the mound, but he knew how to command his slow curve to baffle hitters and rarely issued walks. He emerged as a pitching star in 1898, when he won 25 games for the Pirates with a 2.95 ERA in 326⅔ innings. He played seven games in the outfield but talk of converting him to be a full-time outfielder had quieted.

His minor league manager, Jake Wells, remarked, "No matter how hard his delivery may be, he never loses his head. I like a pitcher who can take punishment and pull himself together at a critical moment. Then don't forget that Tannehill is a good batsman."[28]

He would go on to win 20 games in six out of eight seasons, including two years pitching for Boston in the American League. One of the years he didn't win 20 games, 1901, he led the NL with a 2.18 ERA to boost the Pirates to the pennant. He was a workhorse who completed at least 24 games in nine straight seasons. In 1902, he went 20–6 with a 1.95 ERA (third in NL) and didn't allow a home run in 231 innings while also appearing in 16 games in the outfield. He joined Jack Chesbro and Deacon Phillippe as 20-game winners on that team, which went 103–36–3 to win the pennant by an incredible 27½ games.

Despite the team's success, players in the Deadball Era were still easily tempted by offers of more money. Tannehill was among a group of Pirates who secretly negotiated to join the newly formed American League. Granted his release by the Pirates, he and teammate Jack Chesbro signed with the New York Highlanders as their new star pitchers.

Pitching in the first season for the franchise now known as the Yankees, Tannehill had his worst year yet with a 15–15 mark and 3.27 ERA. He butted heads with Manager Clark Griffith and battled a sore arm but also hated pitching at Hilltop Park. "A man would have to have a cast iron arm to pitch winning ball under these circumstances," he remarked.[29] In the offseason, he was traded to Boston, where he posted two 20-win seasons before a steady decline.

Tannehill's younger brother, Lee, played 10 years with the Chicago White Sox as an infielder. Pitching for the Boston Americans on August 17, 1904, Tannehill threw a no-hitter against the White Sox—the third in American League history—retiring his brother three times to record his 16th win of the season on the way to 21. He helped his cause with a hit, walk, and run scored. Ten days later, he would beat the Sox 2–1 and again retire his brother all three times. Tannehill would beat the White Sox four times in six tries that season, pitching two shutouts and six complete games. He gained bragging rights over Lee, who had one hit in 19 at-bats with five strikeouts facing his older brother.

Tannehill's best year at the plate was 1900, when he averaged .336 with 37 hits while winning 20 games on the mound. He led AL pitchers in batting average in 1900 and 1906. He once stole home while in the game as the pitcher and recorded 19 career steals. The switch-hitter pulled off the remarkable feat of hitting safely in the first 14 games he pitched in 1902, going 21 for 52.[30]

His career marks of .255 average, 89 OPS+, 55 doubles, and 23 triples were all decent for the Deadball Era, but Tannehill made his mark on the mound. He finished 197–117 with a 2.80 ERA and a .627 winning percentage across 15 seasons that ranks 67th all-time. His 1.55 BB/9 ranks 28th all-time. He posted six top-10 finishes in adjusted ERA including second in 1901 (150).

Doc White

In addition to standing out as a two-way baseball player, Guy "Doc" White was at times a dentist, violinist, newspaper columnist, umpire, music composer, physical education teacher, manager, pitching coach, basketball coach, and traveling evangelist. If there was a baseball player who could appreciate the concept of Aristotle's "The whole is more than the sum of its parts" philosophy, it was Doc White, the privileged son of a Washington, D.C., iron foundry magnate.

White debuted with the Philadelphia Phillies in 1901, serving notice of his ability with 14 wins, a 3.19 ERA, and 132 strikeouts. The rail-thin

Chapter 4. Deadball Era 1900–1919

Doc White had more success as a pitcher than as a batter during his 13-year career, hurling five consecutive shutouts in 1904. His best two-way season was 1909 with the Chicago White Sox, when he posted a 104 OPS+ playing 40 games in the outfield, to go with a 1.72 ERA in 24 mound appearances (Library of Congress, Prints & Photographs Division, LC-DIG-hec-02785).

six-foot-one, 150-pound lefty was an unlikely strikeout artist, but he mixed in a tantalizing drop ball and a sinker with hard, inside fastballs that kept batters off balance. He would later add a devastating spitball to his offering.

For the 1902 season, White chipped in 19 outfield appearances as his bat showed potential with a .263 average. On the mound, he went 16–20 for a seventh-place Phillies team but his ERA dropped to 2.53 and his 185 strikeouts in 306 innings were second-best in the league. Off the field, White completed a degree in dentistry from Georgetown University—where he had starred as a pitcher and outfielder—and opened up a dental practice he operated in the offseason.[31]

Jumping to the Chicago White Sox in the new American League for the 1903 season, White won 17 games in 300 innings while his 2.13 ERA ranked fourth in the AL. The Sox preferred he concentrate on pitching rather than be a two-way player or serve as a fill-in umpire as he had done for games in 1902 and 1903.

On September 12, 1904, Doc pitched the first of five consecutive shutouts with a 1-0 shutout of Cleveland. Four days later, he took a no-hitter into the ninth but settled for a one-hit shutout of the Browns. A two-hit shutout of the Tigers was followed by a four-hit shutout of the Athletics and then a three-hit shutout of the first-place Highlanders on September 30. White had just set a record that would stand for 64 years, when Don Drysdale of the Dodgers hurled six straight shutouts in 1968.

With the White Sox hovering in third place and his streak on the line, White agreed to start both games of a doubleheader on October 2. He quickly gave up a first-inning run in the opener to break his scoreless streak at 45 innings, but he went the whole way for the 7–1 win. Clearly exhausted, he was relieved after pitching five innings in the nightcap and lost 6–3. His 45-inning scoreless streak is now tied for eighth best since 1900. White's dominant stretch of pitching caused even his own manager, Fielder Jones, to argue that the spitball should be banned so batters had a fair chance.[32]

White would end that season with a 1.78 ERA (third in AL) and 138 ERA+, which was followed by a 1.76 ERA in 1905. The next season he led the league in ERA (1.52), ERA+ (167) and WHIP (0.903) while going 18–6 for the pennant-winning Sox. They won the World Series over their crosstown rival the Cubs as White closed out Game 5 with three relief innings and won the clinching Game 6.

Still a workhorse in 1907, he walked a minuscule 38 batters in 291 innings. He also completed 24 games on the way to a league-best 27 wins with a 2.26 ERA. White didn't know it at the time, but he set a record with 65⅓ consecutive innings without issuing a walk. That streak was broken on September 11, when he intentionally walked a batter, and it would remain the American League mark for 55 years.[33]

His weak .222 batting average in 1907 was actually his best mark in five years. His bat had largely been a non-factor to that point in his career, although he was asked to pinch-hit occasionally. With his pitching going strong and his bat mostly silent, no one was clamoring for White to be a two-way player.

Eighteen wins followed in 1908, but he had already been replaced as the Sox ace by Ed Walsh. When his pitching arm finally slowed down in 1909, White was deployed regularly in center field and saw outfield action in 40 games. That brought about career marks in plate appearances (328), runs (24), hits (45), triples (five), and on-base percentage (.347). He would play 14 games in the outfield the next season, but his average dropped to .198. For his career, White batted .217 with 278 hits.

On the mound, his 427 pitching appearances had generated 43.8 WAR. His record of 189–156 in 3,041 innings produced 262 complete games (67th all-time), 45 shutouts (29th all-time), and an ERA of 2.39 (27th all-time). He was a World Series champion, not to mention a celebrated music composer. He hooked up with famous writer Ring Lardner to compose "Little Puff of Smoke, Good Night," a southern croon that became a mini hit in 1910, plus another song in 1911 titled "Gee! It's A Wonderful Game" that played off his baseball experience.[34] Before White died in 1969, he was the last surviving member of the 1906 championship team.

Smoky Joe Wood

Smoky Joe Wood and Babe Ruth are the only two-way players during the Deadball Era to post WAR over 10 for both pitching and offensive output. Wood recorded 29.6 WAR pitching and 12.0 offensive WAR, while Ruth was in another stratosphere with WAR totals of 154.5 for offense and 20.4 for pitching. Both players, who were briefly teammates on the Red Sox in 1914–15, generated negative WAR for defensive contributions.

Wood emerged as one of the Deadball Era's best pitchers and then switched to the outfield when his arm broke down. That move extended his career another five years. Although Wood didn't really pitch and play the outfield at the same time, his career accomplishments are unique in that he generated multiple seasons of all-star production in both roles.

He started as an infielder in the minors before a shortage of pitchers forced him into action on the mound. Debuting with the Red Sox in 1908 at 18 years old, the hard-throwing righty exhibited rookie jitters with 16 walks in 22⅔ innings.

Wood battled some injuries the next two years but flashed moments of excellence. His 1.69 ERA ranked eighth in the American League in 1910, while his 145 strikeouts were sixth best.

His breakout campaign was 1911, when he won 23 games with a 2.02 ERA and struck out 231 (2nd in AL) in 275⅔ innings. For the second straight season, he batted .261. It was a precursor of bigger things to come.

Fenway Park opened in 1912, and the Red Sox had a new star pitcher to showcase. Wood produced one of the most sensational seasons on the mound in baseball history to lead the Sox to their first pennant in eight years. He won 34 games with just five losses and his adjusted OPS of 177 showed his performance was 77 percent above league average. He led the AL in wins, winning percentage (.877), complete games (35) and shutouts (10), while pitching 344 innings (3rd in AL) and finishing second in ERA (1.91) and strikeouts (258). It was his best year at the plate as well, with a .290 average, .348 on-base percentage, and 36 hits. His total WAR of 11.4 for the year trailed just Walter Johnson and Ed Walsh.

"Gee, that boy throws smoke," remarked Paul Shannon, a sportswriter for the *Boston Post*.[35] And so a memorable nickname was born.

On September 6, 1912, Fenway was packed with 35,000 fans who were there to see Smoky Joe face off against Walter "The Big Train" Johnson of the Washington Senators. So many fans were in attendance they were allowed to take up space along the left and right field foul lines. Johnson's American League record 16-game winning streak had just ended 11 days earlier and Wood was working on a 13-game winning streak himself. The overflow crowd of fans on the field before the game meant Wood barely had room to warm up.

The two aces battled to a scoreless standstill until the bottom of the sixth inning. Tris Speaker and Duffy Lewis of the Sox poked back-to-back fly balls into the crowd that was standing in foul territory. Both were inexplicably ruled as doubles, which allowed one run to score. It proved to be the only run of the game as Wood finished a six-hit shutout to record his 14th straight win. At that point of the season, Johnson was 29–11 but Wood was even better, with a 30–4 record.

"Can I throw harder than Joe Wood? Listen, Mister, no man alive can throw any harder than Smoky Joe Wood," Johnson proclaimed.[36]

Four days later, Wood beat the White Sox 5–4 for win number 15 and then tied Johnson on September with a 2–1 win over the St. Louis Browns. On September 20, Wood gave up five walks and six runs to lose 6–4 to the Tigers. Wood would remain tied at 16 consecutive wins with Johnson—they were later matched by Lefty Grove in 1931 and Schoolboy Rowe in 1934. Rube Marquard holds the major-league record with 19 consecutive wins in 1912.

"Perhaps Walter Johnson was faster than Wood. Perhaps Grove and Feller were. But Wood threw smoke, and in 1912 if there was a better pitcher than Wood in baseball, even Walter Johnson or Christy Mathewson, the difference was merely academic," write James T. Farrell in *My Baseball Diary*.[37]

Wood was pitching on fumes as the Red Sox faced off against John McGraw and the New York Giants in the 1912 World Series. Although he wasn't sharp, surrendering 11 runs and 27 hits in 22 innings, he won three games in four appearances including the decisive Game 8 to help the Sox win their second Series title. "I threw so hard I thought my arm would fly right off my body," Wood exclaimed shortly after striking out Art Fletcher and Doc Crandall to end the first game.[38]

Baseball's best pitcher was slowed by a thumb injury in 1913 and then appendicitis in 1914. His performance went from great to good, with 21 wins in 32 starts across the two seasons and ERA marks of 2.29 and 2.62. His pitching improved in 1915—he led the league with a 1.49 ERA and .750 winning percentage—but he was only able to complete 157⅓ innings. "After each game I pitched I'd have to lay off for a couple of weeks before

I could even lift my arm up," Wood confessed in *The Glory of Their Times*.[39]

"Joe Wood has not been right since he was operated on for appendicitis. At times, he has shown flashes of his former smoke, but it is uncertain what he can do," wrote the *Washington Post*.[40]

The Sox won the 1915 World Series over Philadelphia, but Smoky Joe didn't even appear in a game. He had thrown his last pitch for the Red Sox. Wood didn't want to take a pay cut, so he ended up sitting out the 1916 season in hopes his arm would recover. It didn't. A comeback with old friend and roommate Tris Speaker of Cleveland lasted just five games in 1917, as the smoke that arose from his pitching arm had vanished.

The baseball community was skeptical when Wood announced his intention to return for the 1918 season as an outfielder. He joined Cleveland's lineup and proceeded to quickly knock off the rust. Playing

Smoky Joe Wood produced one of the greatest pitching seasons in baseball history in 1912, going 34-5 with a 1.91 ERA for the Boston Red Sox. When his pitching career was cut short by an arm injury, Wood converted to play the outfield and bat over the last six years of his career. He recorded lifetime marks of 110 OPS+ and 146 ERA+ (Society for American Baseball Research-Rucker Archive).

95 games in the outfield, 19 at second base, and four at first base, Wood was the unofficial "comeback player of the year" with a .296 average (10th in AL), .356 OBP, 125 hits, five home runs (5th), 22 doubles (7th), and 66 RBI (3rd). His 120 OPS+ proved he was worthy of this new shot at baseball, and he was still just 28 years old.

Wood looked back on May 24, 1918, as the day he realized he could successfully make the transition from star pitcher to outfielder. That day—the longest game ever held at the Polo Grounds—he played all 19 innings in left field for the Indians and slugged a home run in the seventh inning and made a game-saving catch against the wall in the ninth inning. In the top of the 19th inning, he belted a pitch over the left-field wall for his second home run of the game, which proved the decisive run in a 3–2 victory.

"The season was pretty young yet and I hadn't been in the outfield very long. It was up to me to show (manager) Lee Fohl I could do the job. But from that day on he knew I could do it, and so did I. And the worst was finally over," Wood said.[41]

Although he batted a respectable .271 against right-handed pitchers for his career, Wood slugged .472 against southpaws with a .328 average. Recognizing those splits, the Indians platooned Wood in the outfield with lefty-swinging Elmer Smith the next three seasons. He batted .255, .270, and then an outstanding .366 in 1921, when he collected 71 hits, knocked in 60 runs, and slugged .562. He posted an OPS+ of 151 that season as the Indians finished in second place.

Wood had one more year left in his bat. Playing full time in right field in 1922, he averaged .297 with 150 hits, 33 doubles, eight triples, 92 RBI (10th in AL), and 74 runs scored in 505 plate appearances. His bat seemingly had many more hits left, but Wood decided to retire for family reasons and was hired to coach baseball at Yale. He left behind a remarkable record of two-way success.

"Joe Wood faced the most difficult task a player can be called upon to face and against all seemingly insurmountable handicaps he made good," commented F.C. Lane, editor of *Baseball Magazine*.[42]

Additional Players of Note

Seven additional Deadball Era players are noteworthy two-way players with some level of accomplishment.

Jack Coombs went 5–0 playing in three World Series. Nicknamed "Colby Jack" because he went to Colby College, Coombs played every position except catcher while leading Colby College to Maine collegiate championships and gaining notoriety on the track team as the fastest sprinter in New England.[43]

Signed to play with Connie Mack's Philadelphia Athletics, Coombs pitched in a memorable game during his rookie season on September 1, 1906. He and Joe Harris of the Boston Americans each went the whole way in a 24-inning marathon. Coombs scattered 15 hits and registered an AL-record 18 strikeouts to get the 4–1 win, while the hard-luck Harris struck out 14 and saw his record go to 2–18 with the loss. Their combined

Chapter 4. Deadball Era 1900–1919

total of 32 strikeouts is the most by two pitching opponents in an MLB game.

Coombs led the American League in wins in consecutive seasons: 1910 and 1911. He served as the ace of the 1910 Philadelphia Athletics, who won the pennant and the World Series that year under Mack's direction. Coombs went 31–9 with a 1.30 ERA (2nd in AL) in 353 innings and a league-best 13 shutouts, riding a scorching fastball and a sharp drop curve. The 13 shutouts remain the American League record and tied for third best in major-league history. In the months of July, August, and September, he won 18 out of 19 starts, then won three complete game starts in the 1910 World Series to lead the A's to the championship.

On August 4, 1910, Coombs and Ed Walsh each pitched 16 scoreless innings in a game called due to darkness. Coombs, who struck out 18 and surrendered just three hits, ranked it as his best-pitched game.[44] Colby Jack would record a 53-inning scoreless streak in September that season, which ranks fourth in baseball history behind Orel Hershiser, Don Drysdale, and Walter Johnson.

His record for the 1911 season was 28–12 but his ERA jumped to 3.53. However, his bat kicked in with a .319 average and 45 hits and he set a modern-era record for pitchers with 31 runs scored. Both his home runs that season came in extra innings and Mack called on him five times as a pinch hitter. A third 20-win season followed in 1912, but Coombs would not approach the same level of success on the mound despite 158 career wins. He made 62 career appearances in the outfield—47 of them came in 1908 to replace an injured Socks Seybold—but his lifetime marks of .235 average and 74 OPS+ demonstrate his lack of impact as a two-way player.

George Cunningham produced one two-way season of note out of his five-year career. In 1918, he pitched in 27 games and played 20 games in the outfield. Throwing 140 innings in 27 games (14 starts) that year, Cunningham won six, lost seven, and his 3.14 ERA was 16 percent below league average. At the plate he collected 25 hits and averaged .223. His lifetime mark was 16–25 with a 3.13 ERA and 47 career hits.

Otto Hess, who remains the only major-league player to be born in Switzerland, served in the U.S. Army during the Spanish-American War and World War I. He impressed with a 1.67 ERA pitching for Cleveland in 1904, then broke out with 20 wins in 1906 with a 1.83 ERA (sixth in AL). His six seasons on the mound after that were spotty. Appearing in 28 games in the outfield in 1905, Hess batted .254 with 44 hits to go with his 10–15 pitching record. He batted .216 lifetime (63 OPS+) while playing 51 games in the outfield, six at first base, and 198 on the mound. His career record was 70–90 with a 2.98 ERA.

Nap Lajoie, Cleveland's player-manager, once commented, "I don't believe there's a pitcher in either league who has greater natural ability than Hess."[45]

Wyatt Lee lasted just four years in the majors, 1901–1904. He played the outfield and pitched the first three seasons and was just a pitcher in his last season. As a 21-year-old rookie with the Washington Senators, he went 16–16 hurling 262 innings but allowed the most home runs in the American League. The lefty batted .256 with 33 hits from seven stints in the outfield. The 1902 season was his best at the plate, with 100 hits, .256 average, and 61 runs scored while playing 96 games in the outfield. Lee won just five games that year with a 5.05 ERA in 98 innings. His ERA improved greatly to 3.08 in 1903, still with the Senators, as he produced an 8–12 record on the mound. However, his bat slowed to a .208 average from 47 outfield appearances. A final season with Pittsburgh produced a 1–2 record with an ERA of 8.74.

John Menefee played most of his career in the 19th century, but his brief stretch as a two-player came mainly in the 1901 and 1902 seasons. Arm trouble and a 25-loss season in 1894 turned him into an outfielder in the minors. In 1901, Menefee went 8–12 with a 3.80 ERA for the Chicago Orphans, hurling 19 complete games. He also played 24 games in the outfield and three in the infield that season, batting .257 with 39 hits. The next year, he recorded 50 hits in 253 plate appearances for a .231 average. Nicknamed "Jock," he appeared in 23 games in the outfield and 18 games at first base while going 12–10 with a sparkling 2.42 ERA in 197⅓ innings for Chicago. On July 15, 1902, he became the first National League pitcher to steal home in the modern era. He started both games of a doubleheader on September 7, 1903, which ended his major-league career in a unique way.

Jack Taylor was the Deadball Era's greatest workhorse. The four-time 20-game winner completed 187 consecutive starts from June 20, 1901, to August 13, 1906, setting a major-league record that is unlikely to be broken.[46] Within that streak, Taylor made 15 relief appearances in which he finished the game. Adding those in gives Taylor a streak of 202 consecutive appearances without being relieved by another pitcher. His 39 consecutive complete games in 1904 (without any relief appearances in between) is considered the National League record.

Taylor had an incredible 1902 season on the mound for Chicago, which was essentially his only two-way season as a player. In addition to winning 23 games as the staff ace throwing 333⅔ innings, he recorded a minuscule 1.29 ERA to lead the league. That mark ranks as the 25th-lowest ERA in baseball history. He also led the NL in shutouts with eight and ERA+ at 206. Playing 12 games at third base, three in right field, two at first base and one at second base, Taylor batted .233 with 44 hits.

Taylor played four more games in the infield the next two years and that was it for his two-way play. His career marks of 236 hits and .222 average generated an OPS+ of 68. On September 24, 1904, he started and completed both games of a doubleheader for St. Louis, although he pitched just six innings in the nightcap. The Ohio native won 152 career games with a 2.65 ERA (115 ERA+) and recorded 279 complete games in 287 starts.

Bob Wicker produced just one notable two-way season. Playing for the Chicago Cubs in 1904, he went 17–9 with a 2.67 ERA in 229 innings. His 20 appearances in the outfield that season only generated 34 hits with a .219 average. He won 20 games for the Cubs in 1903—joining teammates Jack Taylor and Jake Weimer as 20-game winners—but he was exclusively a pitcher that season. On June 11, 1904, Wicker outpitched future Hall of Famer Joe McGinnity to win 1–0. He had a no-hitter through nine innings, then gave up a hard shot to third in the 10th inning that was ruled a hit. Wicker was otherwise unblemished through 12 innings to get the win. Newspaper reports disagree on whether a first-inning play was ruled a hit or an error, so Wicker may or may not have lost his no-hitter in extra innings.[47]

Wicker's 13–6 record in 1905 with a 2.02 ERA (third best in the NL) was offset by a putrid .139 batting average from three outfield appearances. Wicker's career record was 64–52 with a 2.73 ERA in 138 games pitched but he posted a .205 average at the plate. Traded to the Reds in June 1906, Wicker was not around to see the Cubs win a major-league record 116 games that season but lose in the World Series.

Chapter 5

Babe Ruth
Baseball's Larger-Than-Life Legend

Babe Ruth played baseball the way he lived his life—large and loud. He did everything to excess including the distance and frequency of the home runs he hit. While some of his slugging records have been broken by modern-era stars like Hank Aaron and Barry Bonds, no player can compare to how much better Ruth's slugging was compared to that of his peers. When Babe hit 60 home runs in 1927, that was more home runs than any other team hit in the American League that season. He was a mere mortal on the mound, but he morphed into the Greek god of thunder at the plate.

Ruthian legend has been passed on to successive generations of baseball fans. All the stories are entertaining. Some are even true. The Bambino was the Roarin' Twenties all by himself. He was a crude but authentic star, utterly without pretense, whether he was impulsively overeating, womanizing, butting heads with managers, or visiting kids in the children's hospital. The Xaverian Brothers who raised him not only saved him from an otherwise bleak childhood and nurtured his baseball talents, they brought out the best instincts of his kind heart.

The Babe had a short run as a two-way player. He spent the first four seasons in the majors as a full-time pitcher, opened eyes with two seasons as a two-way player with the Red Sox, and then spent the remaining 16 years of his career as a full-time outfielder and batter. Ruth was an outstanding southpaw pitcher, but his slugging was so stupendous that sportswriters ran out of adjectives and nicknames to describe his hard-to-believe feats. The Sultan of Swat, The Bambino, The Great Bambino, Big Bam, The Colossus of the Clout, The Prince of Pounders, and The Mauling Mastodon—each nickname conjured up an image of a mythical superhuman created in a laboratory. His teammates usually called him Jidge, a snappier version of George. No one had ever seen anything like the Babe at the plate, whether he was connecting for a spectacular dinger or corkscrewing his body into the ground after a big whiff.

Ruth used massive bats ranging from 44 to 54 ounces that were longer, thicker, and heavier than other players' bats. The Bambino swung from his heels with full force every time, which was not sustainable for someone who also had to take the mound and pitch.

"There was only one Babe Ruth. He went on the ball field like he was playing in a cow pasture, with cows for an audience. He never knew what fear or nervousness was. He played by instinct, sheer instinct," remarked pitcher Rube Bressler in *The Glory of Their Times*. "One of the greatest pitchers of all time, and then he became a great judge of a fly ball, never threw to the wrong base when he was playing the outfield, terrific arm, good base runner, could hit the ball twice as far as any other human being."[1]

Ruth appeared in 10 World Series, winning seven rings—three with the Red Sox and four with the Yankees. Before he became America's most famous and colorful athlete, he first had to survive the hard knocks of a rough-and-tumble childhood.

In 1902, seven-year-old George Ruth was dropped off at St. Mary's Industrial School for Boys in Baltimore by his father, George Herman Ruth, Sr. Ruth's father was busy running a saloon and his mother was often in poor health, so they allowed their mischievous boy to navigate life largely unsupervised. He already had his first taste of chewing tobacco and beer by age six and by all accounts refused to attend school. Ruth had little contact with his parents after landing at St. Mary's. His long-term stay at the Catholic institution run by the Xaverian Brothers began in 1904 and lasted until 1914. His parents later divorced when he was 11 years old and his mother, Katie, died in 1912 after battling chronic illness. Spending the majority of his childhood at St. Mary's not only helped Ruth develop his baseball ability, it smoothed over the many rough edges to his personality.

The unruly boy with the moon face, who was always big for his age, displayed his baseball prowess while playing multiple games a day, practically year-round. Brother Matthias Boutlier, the imposing six-foot-six Prefect of Discipline, turned into the father figure Ruth desperately needed. Brother Matthias ran the baseball leagues for St. Mary's and typically had Ruth play with boys three to four years older.

"It was at St. Mary's that I met and learned to love the greatest man I've ever known," Ruth said. He was referring to Brother Matthias, who would encourage and nurture his confidence and allow his athletic talent to shine through, while working with him to improve his fielding and batting. Ruth's pigeon-toed, minced-step style of walking and running was a carbon copy of Brother Matthias' gait, and he also mimicked his all-out style of hitting the baseball.[2]

Ruth shined as a catcher and hitter at St. Mary's and didn't pitch much until later in his time there. "As soon as I got out there I felt a strange relationship with the pitcher's mound. It was as if I'd been born out there. Pitching just felt like the most natural thing in the world. Striking out batters was easy," he said.[3]

The left-handed Ruth used to catch with a right-handed catcher's mitt and take the glove off and transfer the ball to his other hand to whip it down to second. Brother Matthias converted Ruth from a left-handed catcher into a multi-positional player who could play any position, which is how all the boys at St. Mary's were trained. "Brother Matthias had the right idea about training a baseball club. He made every boy on the team play every position in the game, including the bench.... So whatever I may have done at bat or on the mound or in the outfield or even on the bases, I owe directly to Brother Matthias," Ruth recalled.[4]

No matter where he played, Ruth stood out for his natural ability. "Sometimes I pitched. Sometimes I caught, and frequently I played the outfield and infield. It was all the same to me. All I wanted was to play. I didn't care much where," he said.[5]

Brother Gilbert Cairnes, the athletic director and baseball coach at Mount St. Joseph's College, was familiar with Ruth's exploits on the diamond. Brother Gilbert was instrumental in getting Ruth signed in February 1914 by Jack Dunn's Baltimore Orioles, then a double–A team in the International League.

The pride and joy of St. Mary's headed to Fayetteville, N.C., for his first taste of professional baseball life. Ruth told Dunn how he had played eight games to get ready for his spring training with the Orioles. "I pitched two full games. I caught two games, played shortstop two games, one game at first base. In the other game, I played the whole nine positions, one inning at each position. Brother Matthias told me to do that so that I would be ready for any place that you want me to play," Ruth said.[6] Dunn had the good sense to tell his coaches not to mess with Ruth's batting stance, since he could quickly tell the young lad from St. Mary's was a natural.

Shortly after arriving in training camp and witnessing Ruth's talent up close, Dunn wrote Brother Gilbert an enthusiastic letter, saying: "That fellow, Ruth, is the greatest young ball player who ever reported to a training camp. If he doesn't let success go to his head, he'll become the greatest ball player of all time."[7]

A plaque was erected in Fayetteville to mark Babe's first home run as a professional on March 7, 1914—it traveled an estimated 428 feet into a corn field. Less publicized was the fact Ruth pitched and played shortstop in that debut game. The game report in the *Baltimore Sun* noted that the youngster "has plenty of speed and can bat from either side of the plate."[8]

Facing the Phillies, who featured Sherry Magee and Hans Lobert, in a spring exhibition game, Ruth won a 4–3 complete game. He came back and pitched 3⅔ innings against them the next day, striking out five in a comeback win.

Early in camp Ruth picked up the nickname that would define his fame. His more seasoned teammates picked up on his youth and naivete and dubbed him Dunnie's Babe. The sportswriters who followed the team began referring to him as Babe Ruth and the rest is history. Ruth was relieved his new nickname didn't make fun of his outsized lips and olive complexion, as he hated the cruel and racist moniker that haunted his years at St. Mary's.

On May 24, 1914, Ruth pitched 3⅓ innings in relief in the first game of a doubleheader. He started the night cap on the mound and went 11 innings to get the win.

With the Orioles overshadowed by the Baltimore franchise in the upstart Federal League, Dunn found himself deep in debt. As Dunn prepared to hold a fire sale for his players, he knew Ruth's talent held the most appeal. Connie Mack and the A's were given the first crack at Ruth, but Mack didn't have the money to make a fair offer. After spending half a season with the Orioles and pitching to a 14-7 record, Ruth's contract was sold to the Boston Red Sox, along with Ernie Shore and Ben Egan, for $25,000—the actual amount remains in dispute. He made his major league debut with the Sox on July 11, 1914.

The Red Sox found room for Shore in their rotation but didn't have a need for the lefty Ruth, so they sent him down to the Providence Grays. Or perhaps the team's owner, Joe Lannin, who also co-owned the Grays, felt Ruth could make more of an impact in Providence. In any event, he went 9–3 on the mound and batted .300 as the Grays won the International League pennant. He hit his only minor league home run on September 5, 1914, in Toronto while also hurling a one-hit shutout. He beat his old team the Orioles twice. Ruth, still in his speedy phase, accumulated two doubles, one home run and 10 triples that year.

Ruth credited Grays manager Bill Donovan with teaching him a lot about pitching. "Bill convinced me that a real pitcher works as if he knows he has eight men behind him," Ruth said.[9]

The 1915 Red Sox squad featured a strong rotation headlined by southpaws Dutch Leonard and Ruth, combined with righties Rube Foster, Shore, and Smoky Joe Wood. On June 25, 1915, against the Yankees, Ruth pitched a complete game for the win while clubbing a three-run homer and a single. A month later on July 21, he homered and added two doubles and a single against the Browns while pitching into the ninth inning to earn his ninth win of the season.

The Sox held off the Tigers to win the American League pennant that year. Ruth finished 18–8 with a 2.44 ERA (114 ERA+). He completed 16 of 28 starts and his .692 winning percentage ranked fourth in the AL. He batted .315 and his four home runs led the Sox that year despite having only 92 at-bats. His .576 slugging percentage would have led the league by 85 points if he had enough at-bats.

His only appearance in the 1915 World Series was as a pinch hitter, as manager Bill Carrigan recognized the six-foot-two "Big Fella" was his best, most dangerous hitter.

With Ruth's apprenticeship on the mound completed, he emerged as the ace of the Red Sox staff in 1916 and as one of the best southpaw hurlers in baseball. Babe won 23 games and led the AL with a 1.75 ERA, 158 ERA+ and 40 games started. His league-high nine shutouts that season set an AL record that was later matched by Ron Guidry in 1978. He pitched 323⅓ innings (third best in AL) without allowing a single home run. His 8.8 pitching WAR ranked second in the league.

Despite his success as a pitcher, Ruth longed for the days when he was playing all over the diamond like he did at St. Mary's. He played in just 67 of Boston's 156 games in 1916, and he grew restless sitting on the bench. His batting suffered too, as he batted .272 with three home runs that season—pretty good for a pitcher but not up to Babe's standards. His three homers came during a four-game stretch in June.

Babe Ruth was one of the best southpaw pitchers in the game during his six seasons with the Boston Red Sox. He led the American League in ERA in 1916 while winning 23 games, and he still ranks in the top 20 in lifetime ERA and winning percentage. Babe performed his only significant two-way play during his last two seasons with the Sox, leading the league in home runs both years (National Baseball Hall of Fame and Museum, Cooperstown, N.Y.).

He homered and went 3-for-3 while pitching on June 9, then belted a three-run homer as a pinch hitter on June 12. He went deep again on June 13 while pitching and getting the win.

"At any rate, I would like to go through an entire season playing regularly every day, in some position like first base. There is no discounting the fact that a pitcher is handicapped by not taking his regular turn against the opposing twirlers. A man needs that steady training day in and day out to put a finish on his work," Ruth was quoted saying in the 1916 World Series program.[10]

Ruth started both games of a doubleheader on July 11, 1916, against the White Sox. He retired the only batter he faced in the opener and was relieved by Rube Foster, then pitched a complete game to win the nightcap. The whole episode was a bit of gamesmanship by the managers, as White Sox manager Pants Rowland also pulled his first-game starter Dave Danforth, a lefty, after one batter and replaced him with a righty.

Walter Johnson was viewed as the best pitcher in baseball in those days, and Ruth and Johnson started five games against each other in 1916. Ruth won four while Johnson won one. Ruth pitched a three-hit shutout to beat The Big Train 1–0 on June 1. Then he pitched a complete game, 13-inning shutout on August 15 to again beat Johnson 1–0. Ruth didn't help his cause by going 0-for-6 batting against the fireballer in those two games. Then again, his lifetime average of .299 as a pitcher was 45 points lower than his .344 average as a position player.

Ruth employed a simple strategy while on the mound, as recounted by Brother Gilbert. "I merely studied the position of the batter's feet, then looked at his grip on the bat to find out whether he was a choke hitter or a cow-tailer." Choke hitters would be pitched outside on the corners, while cow-tailers were buzzed inside with fastballs.[11]

The Red Sox won the 1916 World Series 4–1 over the Brooklyn Robins, with Ruth pitching all 14 innings to win Game 2 by a 2–1 score—it was his first Series appearance on the mound. The Robins' only run scored on a fluke inside-the-park home run in the first inning. Ruth allowed six hits and struck out four batters and didn't allow a hit after the eighth inning. At the plate, the player known in Boston as "The Colossus" went hitless in five plate appearances.

Ruth was not an overpowering pitcher who struck out a lot of batters—he averaged 3.6 strikeouts per nine innings for his career. He didn't try to fool batters with trick pitches. He threw a fastball, curveball, and changeup with excellent control and relied on the fielders behind him to handle balls that weren't squared up very often. The southpaw never tired as the game went on—accustomed to throwing year-round at St. Mary's—and batters did not find him easy to hit. Babe was also an excellent fielder during his pitching years, fielding grounders up the middle like the shortstop he used to be. He led AL pitchers in putouts in 1916 and 1918, and he finished second in assists as a pitcher in 1917.

For the first three years of his career when he was a full-time pitcher, Ruth was the best left-handed hurler in baseball. Walter Johnson and Pete Alexander were still ahead of him on a statistical basis, but both were righties. Ruth generated 17.8 pitching WAR from 1915 to 1917.

"If Babe Ruth ever gets a chance to perform as a regular, he will prove to be the most sensational player in the game," said Jack Dunn, touting the player he discovered in an interview during the 1917 season.[12]

On May 7, 1917, Ruth outdueled Walter Johnson again, pitching a two-hit shutout to win 1–0. Although Ruth would bat .325 for the season and lead the Sox with 162 OPS+, he hit just two home runs in 142 plate appearances.

On June 23, 1917, against the Washington Nationals, Ruth walked the first batter of the game, Ray Morgan, and then got ejected after arguing with home plate umpire Brick Owens and punching him. Ernie Shore relieved him and pitched a perfect game the rest of the way—after Morgan was erased trying to steal second. It was credited as a combined no-hitter, although Ruth certainly did not make a meaningful contribution. He was suspended 10 games and fined $100 for his behavior.

For the 1917 season, Ruth went 24–13 for the Red Sox with a 2.01 ERA (7th best) in 326⅓ innings and led the league with six shutouts and 35 complete games. His 6.5 pitching WAR ranked fifth in the league.

Ruth traveled to Hot Springs, Arkansas, each spring from 1915 to 1918 for spring training with the Red Sox. For someone who spent most of his childhood in the spartan and sheltered environment of a school for boys, Ruth found soaking in the warm baths to be a luxurious experience that was hard to top. Of course, Babe was just as fond of the casinos, brothels, horse races, and booze that were readily available there.

Babe's legend grew into another dimension as a result of two Ruthian home runs he launched during spring training games in March 1918, in Whittington Park in Hot Springs. With no other first basemen available for the game on March 17, Sox manager Ed Barrow positioned the 23-year-old Ruth at first base. It marked his first professional game action at a position other than pitcher. Everyone knew he could hit, but Ruth's player value to that point was tied to his exceptional pitching ability. Babe was about to change perceptions on the subject, which would lead to the most consequential position change in baseball history.

Seizing the moment, Ruth belted a homer deep to left-center field in the fourth inning that landed in a woodpile. Then in the sixth inning he uncorked a monstrous shot off Norman Plitt that sailed well beyond the fence and landed somewhere in the Arkansas Alligator Farm, a feat so impressive the opposing Dodgers rose to their feet and cheered. Newspaper reports all agreed it was the longest ball ever hit in the ballpark, with the *Boston Globe* noting "…the intrusion kicking up no end of commotion among 'the gators.'"[13]

That feat was noteworthy enough, but Ruth was ready with an encore a week later on March 24, playing right field in the lineup. Facing Al Mamaux of the Dodgers with the bases loaded in the third inning, Babe uncorked a tremendous drive that traveled the same path as his previous shot but went even farther.

"Before the echo of the crash had died away the horsehide had dropped somewhere in the vicinity of South Hot Springs…. The sphere cleared the fence by about 200 feet and dropped in the pond beside the Alligator Farm, while the spectators yelled with amazement," wrote Paul Shannon for the *Boston Post*.[14]

"Every ball player in the park said it was the longest drive they had ever seen … soaring over the street and a wide duck pond, finally finding a resting place in the Ozark Hills," read the report in the *Boston Globe*.[15]

The legend of The Big Bam grew with each prodigious blast, since no other player was hitting home runs with regularity in a sport still mired in the Deadball Era. In 2011, baseball historian Bill Jenkinson spearheaded an attempt to measure how far Ruth's two Hot Springs homers had traveled almost a century earlier. He concluded that Ruth had become the first documented slugger to blast a home run that was at least 500 feet. The fact he did it twice within a week in the same ballpark almost defies belief. At Jenkinson's urging, an historic plaque was installed next to the Alligator Farm that notes Babe Ruth hit a 573-foot home run there on March 17, 1918. The plaque's accuracy is questionable, but it rightly calls attention to a noteworthy achievement. The true distance of the March 17 home run proved hard to pin down and Babe's March 24 home run definitely traveled farther, but the sentiment is the same—Babe unleashed two impossibly long home runs in Hot Springs that cemented his fame.[16]

Despite Ruth's unmatched ability to slug baseballs, the Red Sox began the 1918 season with Ruth ensconced in the rotation. He got the Opening Day start on April 15, scattering four hits to the A's in a complete-game 7–1 victory. He helped his own cause with a single and drove in two runs while batting ninth.

Pitching against the Yankees on May 4 and with Yankees co-owner Jacob Ruppert looking on in amazement, Ruth crushed a long drive over the roof at the Polo Grounds for his first home run of the season. Babe seemed to rise to the occasion every time he played in New York. Sox outfielder Harry Hooper kept pleading with Barrow to insert Babe into the lineup every day, but Barrow responded, "I'd be the laughingstock of baseball if I changed the best lefthander in the game into an outfielder."[17]

Babe played his first game at first base on May 6, 1918. Barrow relented partly because starting first baseman Dick Hoblitzell had an injured hand and was slumping with a .102 average, and partly because the Bambino was mashing the ball better than anyone on the team with a .438 average. Batting sixth that day, Ruth had two hits including a home run and was back at first base the next day. Batting cleanup, he hit a monstrous home run off Walter Johnson that bounced over the right field wall and into a garden across the street. It was the first of only seven home runs hit at Griffith Stadium that season.

"As a rule, a pitcher at bat holds little interest for the fans, but when Babe Ruth steps up to the plate the crowd is disappointed if the Red Sox twirler doesn't hit the ball a mile," went one report of the star's appeal.[18]

After seeing Ruth homer in three straight games and with fans clamoring to see more of the Big Fella, Barrow knew he would be the laughingstock of baseball if he took him out of the lineup. Ruth was back at first base for the May 8 game, and he clubbed a double.

With Babe's turn in the rotation coming up the next day, Barrow decided he couldn't afford to lose Ruth's batting or his pitching. Ruth took the mound and batted cleanup for the May 9 tilt against the Nationals. He went 5-for-5 with three doubles, a triple, and single, raising his season average to .500 and his slugging to 1.031. He pitched a complete game, losing in the 10th inning to Walter Johnson. The next day Boston's slugging sensation was positioned in left field, where he would find himself regularly when not pitching.

Soon after, Babe spent a week in the hospital with the flu and acute edema, with rumors spreading that he was dying. He bounced back in true Bambino fashion. He pitched and hit a home run in his first full game back and proceeded to homer in four straight games. When his turn to pitch came up again, he told Barrow that he didn't want to keep pitching, that the strain of pitching and playing the field every day was too much. The two butted heads over the issue the rest of the season. "I like to pitch, but my main objection is that pitching keeps you out of so many games. I like to be in there every day. If I had my choice, I'd play first base. I don't think a man can pitch in his regular turn, and play some other position and keep the pace year after year. I can do it this season all right. I'm young and strong and don't mind the work, but I wouldn't guarantee to do it for many seasons," Ruth said.[19]

After making a relief appearance on June 7, Ruth's next 20 appearances came as a position player. On July 17, 1918, Babe pitched a shortened five-inning shutout against the Browns while contributing a double and single from the cleanup position, making him the only player in the modern era to hurl a complete-game shutout while batting fourth. It would be his last shutout as a pitcher. Shohei Ohtani has only pitched one shutout during his career to date, and he batted second in that game.

If the strain of a hospitalization and daily battles with his manager over his role were not stressful enough, Ruth got more bad news as the 1918 season drew to a close. He learned that his father had died after getting in a fight outside his saloon with a brother-in-law. Babe's parents had given up on him at an early age and shipped him to an institution that was akin to an orphanage, and now he truly was an orphan.

During the 1918 season, Babe played 59 games in the outfield and 13 games at first base while making 20 pitching appearances. He batted cleanup while pitching 11 times that season. His 7.0 total WAR ranked fourth in the league. He went 13–7 with a 2.22 ERA and 18 complete games in 19 starts and led the league with 11 home runs, .555 slugging, and .966 OPS despite just 317 at-bats. Actually, Ruth slugged 12 homers that season, but a walk-off homer he hit in the 10th inning on July 8, 1918, was counted as a triple because that's what was needed for the winning run to score from first base, according to rules in place then. So, Ruth really should be credited with 715 career home runs. Major League Baseball decided in 1969 to retroactively award Ruth (and 36 similar batters) with their lost home runs, but then reversed its decision to avoid messing with a long-cherished number.[20]

The Red Sox rode Ruth's sensational two-way play to a first-place finish and squared off against the Chicago Cubs in the 1918 World Series. Babe pitched a six-hit shutout to win Game One. Taking the mound for Game Four, Ruth held the Cubs scoreless for the first seven innings and collected a triple while batting sixth. He got the win as the Sox held on to win 3–2. Ruth ended up pitching 29⅓ consecutive scoreless innings across the 1916 and 1918 World Series, a record finally topped by Whitey Ford in 1961. Ruth called that his proudest achievement in baseball, ahead of all his home run records. What is incredible about that scoreless streak is that Ruth gave up a run in his first Series inning on the mound in 1916 and he gave up two runs in his last Series inning on the mound in 1918—in between were 29⅔ scoreless innings.

Only a few pitchers can compare to Ruth's record 0.87 ERA in 31 innings of World Series play. First Harry Brecheen (0.83 ERA between 1943 and 1946) and then Jack Billingham (0.36 ERA between 1972 and 1976) surpassed him, followed more recently by Madison Bumgarner, who recorded a 0.25 ERA in 36 innings across three World Series for the Giants in 2010, 2012, and 2014.

With a salary of $10,000 for the 1919 season, Ruth felt he was extremely underpaid after Barrow turned him into a full-time outfielder while still expecting him to pitch frequently. As Ruth told reporters, "I'll win more games playing every day in the outfield than I will pitching every fourth day."[21] It was another bone of contention between the Sox and their star slugger, who caused ongoing headaches with his lifestyle choices and unwillingness to follow curfew. Sox owner Harry Frazee began giving serious consideration to trading Babe and was well aware the Yankees were interested.

"I still remember when the Babe was switched from pitching to become an outfielder. I finally convinced Ed Barrow to play him out there to get his bat in the lineup every day. That was in 1919, and I was the team captain by then.... Well, Ruth might have been a natural as a pitcher and as a hitter, but he sure wasn't a born outfielder," said Hooper.[22]

Ruth hit a mammoth blast on April 5, 1919, against the Giants during a spring training game in Tampa that went out of the ballpark and traveled an estimated 587 feet, making it the longest home run of Babe's career.[23]

Babe ended up playing 111 games in the outfield, five games at first base and pitching 17 times for 133 innings in 1919. He batted cleanup in 13 of his pitching starts that season. After making nine starts on the mound in May and June, he made just six the rest of the season as his outfield play picked up. His pitching record was 9–5 with a 2.97 ERA (102 ERA+) and 12 complete games for the sixth-place Sox.

Ruth led the American League in offensive WAR (8.3), on-base percentage (.456), slugging (.657), OPS (1.114), runs (103), total bases (284), RBI (113), OPS+ (217), and extra-base hits (75) while setting a league record with 29 home runs.

Two of Ruth's best seasons for triples were 1918 and 1919, the years he was a full-time, two-way player. He had 11 triples in only 95 games in 1918 and 12 triples the next season. He only topped those totals twice: 16 triples in 1921 and 13 triples in 1923.

Ruth hit 29 of the 33 homers for the Sox in 1919—Hooper hit three homers, Stuffy McInnis hit one and no one else on the Sox hit any. In fact, Ruth had as many grand-slam homers that season (four) as the rest of the team had total home runs.

Although the Sox were out of the pennant race at an early date, fans kept coming to see Babe attempt to surpass Buck Freeman's record of 25 home runs in a season, set in 1899. Ruth hit his 26th off Herb Thormahlen to set the new mark on September 8, 1919.

The Black Sox Scandal that arose from the 1919 World Series put the game of baseball on its heels. Luckily, baseball's biggest star would soon take his slugging skills to New York to save the national pastime and restore fans' faith in the game of baseball. Baseball's Live Ball Era launched in style.

Ruth's trade from the Red Sox to the Yankees on December 26, 1919, for $100,000 remains the boldest, most one-sided trade in major league history. "While Ruth, without question, is the greatest hitter that the game has ever seen, he is likewise one of the most selfish and inconsiderate men that have ever worn a baseball uniform," said Frazee, as he tried to justify the shocking move.[24]

Babe had always thrived playing in New York and still only 25 years old, he was ready to take off. Moving from Fenway Park's dimensions (380 feet to deep right and 302 feet along the foul line) to the Polo Grounds (258 feet in right) also helped his home run production. "He was the right man, in the right place, at the right time," remarked Ford Frick, future commissioner of baseball.[25]

Unshackled from the demands of being a two-way player, Ruth played all over the outfield in 1920 with 84 games in right field, 32 games in left field, and 25 games in center field. The Bambino set a record with 12 home runs in May, then matched it by slugging 12 more homers in June. In his first season with the Yankees, Babe shattered the American League record for home runs with 54, beating his record from the previous year by 25. He set the new record when he hit his 30th homer on July 19 in just the 87th game of the season. The Sultan of Swat hit 14.6 percent of all the home runs hit in the American League that year.

Babe had significantly more extra-base hits (99) than singles (73) that season, which is how he ended up with a batting mark of .376/.532/.847, with career highs in OPS (1.379) and OPS+ (255). It represented the best slugging mark of his career and his second highest on-base percentage. The .847 slugging would stand as the major league record until Barry Bonds slugged .863 in 2001.

The Yankees had not appeared in a World Series during their 17-year history before Ruth joined the team in 1920. They would appear in seven World Series in his first 13 years with the club, winning four championships.

"Ruth's homers are the longest that I have ever seen. Others hit home runs, too, but we must wait for them to drop before we are sure of them. When Ruth's hits leave the bat, there is no doubt of their mileage," said Connie Mack.[26]

As Babe's illustrious career with the Yankees played out, the team occasionally summoned Brother Matthias to New York to help them straighten out their wayward star. Babe knew if baseball didn't work out, he could just as easily be back at St. Mary's working in the tailor shop.

On June 10, 1921, Ruth blasted his 120th career homer to pass Gavvy Cravath for most homers post-1900. Three days later, he started the game on the mound and pitched the first five innings before moving to center field. He got the win despite walking seven batters and helped his cause by slugging two homers.

Babe made history on July 18, 1921, when he hit home run number 139 to pass 19th-century star Roger Connor for the all-time home run record. He broke the record in typical Bambino fashion, crushing an eighth-inning pitch from Detroit's Bert Cole to the deepest part of Navin Field—it officially traveled 560 feet. His 36th homer of the season raised his slugging percentage to .849.[27]

"Babe Ruth could hit a ball so hard, and so far, that it was sometimes impossible to believe your eyes. We used to absolutely marvel at his hits. Tremendous wallops. You can't imagine the balls he hit. And before that he was a great pitcher, too. Really great," exclaimed Sam Jones, who was Ruth's teammate on the Red Sox for four years and on the Yankees for five years.[28]

On June 13, 1921, Ruth did something that wouldn't be done again until Michael Lorenzen accomplished it on September 4, 2019: win a game as pitcher, hit a homer, and play center field in the same contest.

Babe set another new single-season record for home runs in 1921 with 59. However, he was battling an infected elbow as the World Series against the Giants got underway. He appeared in just six of the eight games and made the last out of the 1921 Series, hitting a weak grounder to first base as a pinch hitter as the Yankees lost 1–0.

When Babe Ruth joined the New York Yankees for the 1920 season after a trade, he transitioned to become a full-time outfielder and batter and stopped pitching. He set new records with 54 and 59 home runs his first two seasons with the Bronx Bombers and went on to become the greatest slugger in baseball history (Library of Congress, Prints & Photographs Division, LC-DIG-ggbain-30907).

After the season concluded, scientists at Columbia University undertook the task of dissecting Ruth's athletic and psychological abilities to determine how he managed to be so much better at hitting than other players. Their research revealed Babe's eyes were 12 percent faster than the average man, his reaction time was 10 percent faster, and his intelligence was 10 percent above normal. Overall, Ruth was 90 percent efficient compared to the human average of 60 percent. The scientists also noted Ruth would perform even better if he didn't keep holding his breath while hitting.[29]

Ruth was suspended for the first six weeks of the 1922 season for going on an unsanctioned offseason barnstorming tour. The Bambino batted just .315 with 35 homers in 110 games that year, although he still led the league with a 182 OPS+. When the Yankees met the Giants in an all–New York World Series that year, Manager Miller Huggins kept the Babe in the third spot in the lineup despite his struggles. He batted a weak .118 as the Yankees lost the Series 4–1.

The House That Ruth Built was opened in 1923 so Jake Ruppert, the owner of the Yankees, could properly monetize the iconic cash cow who kept bashing baseballs over the fence. Babe prepared for the first game in Yankee Stadium history by wolfing down several hot dogs right before he took the field. Fittingly, the Sultan of Swat hit the first home run at the new ballpark, smacking a three-run blast off Howard Ehmke of the Red Sox on Opening Day, April 18, 1923, which proved to be the winning runs. "A white streak left Babe Ruth's 53-ounce bludgeon in the third inning of yesterday's opening game at the Yankee Stadium," wrote Grantland Rice for the *New York Tribune*.[30]

Ruth narrowly missed the Triple Crown in 1923 while leading the Yankees to a third straight pennant. He led the league with 41 homers and 130 RBI while finishing second with a .393 average. He also led the league that year with 151 runs, 170 walks, .545 slugging, 239 OPS+ and 12.3 offensive WAR, and he won his only MVP Award that year. Babe batted .368 with three homers as the Yankees defeated the Giants in the 1923 World Series.

Babe won his only batting crown with a .378 average in 1924, registering 200 hits for the third time. He missed the first two months of the next season after undergoing surgery for an intestinal abscess—the bellyache heard around the world—caused in part by too much booze and his horrible diet. His numbers for the 1925 season—.290 average with just 25 homers and 67 RBI—were well below his standard. In the offseason, Babe hit the gym and got back in shape while losing more than 40 pounds. Returning to form, he led the league in home runs the next six seasons.

Ruth slugged three home runs in Game Four of the 1926 World Series against the Cardinals. It was his first time hitting three homers in a game, and the Yankees eventually lost the Series 4–3.

In 1927, Babe became the first player to reach 60 home runs, which would stand as the single-season record until Roger Maris hit 61 in 1961. The '27 Yankees are often considered the greatest team in baseball history, as they cruised to a record of 110–44–1, won the American League by 19 games, and swept the World Series over the Phillies. Ruth's 165 RBI were topped by teammate Lou Gehrig's 173 and the Bronx Bombers averaged .307 as a team.

With the Bambino bashing 54 homers and slugging .709, the Yankees won a third straight pennant in 1928. Ruth blasted three home runs in Game Four of the 1928 World Series to lead the Yankees to a four-game sweep of the Cardinals. He collected 10 hits and batted .625 to win his third championship with the Yankees.

Babe pitched a complete-game 9–3 win over the Red Sox on September 28, 1930, his first time on the mound in nine years. The crowd of 12,000 was "visibly and audibly impressed" by Ruth's mound performance, wrote the *New York Times*.[31]

Ruth hit his 500th career homer on August 11, 1929, and his 600th homer followed on August 21, 1931. He had been the first player to hit the 200-homer, 300-homer, and 400-homer mark.

The inaugural All-Star Game was played at Comiskey Park in 1933 as part of the Chicago World's Fair. Babe did the honors of hitting the first home run with a two-run shot to right field in the third inning and later added a single. He preserved the American League's 4–2 margin of victory by catching a fly ball against the right-center field fence in the top of the eighth inning.

The Yankees used Babe as a gate attraction for their last home game of the season on October 1, 1933, having him start the game on the mound against the Red Sox. He shut out the Sox for the first five innings and hit a home run in the fifth inning to give the Yanks a 6–0 lead. Ruth faltered and gave up five runs but hung on to pitch a complete game for the 6–5 win. He gave up 12 hits and walked three batters without a strikeout. It was an amazing performance considering he had not pitched regularly in 15 years and his catcher, Joe Glenn, was impressed. "He pitched better than a lot of guys who were pitching in the major leagues," Glenn said.[32]

"I lost eight pounds in that game. No regular pitching for me. The outfield has it licked. About one game a month is all I want to pitch. I've got a sore arm and a headache," Ruth said afterwards.[33]

Home run number 700 came in his last season with the Yankees on July 13, 1934, a two-run shot to deep right off Tommy Bridges of the Tigers at Navin Field. At that time, Lou Gehrig was in second place with 323 career homers. Babe hit his 659th and last homer as a Yankee on September 29, 1934, against Syd Cohen of the Senators.

Babe signed with the Boston Braves for the 1935 season, hoping to impress them enough to be named manager. He was crushed to learn the Braves had acquired him as a drawing card and were not interested in giving him a chance to manage.

The end of his playing career came awkwardly and abruptly, but not before Ruth shined for one last big moment. Red Lucas served up Babe Ruth's 712th home run on May 25, 1935. Before the game his fellow Pirates pitchers had assured him the Babe was done and incapable of causing damage. "Never mind him being through. I'm the guy pitching to him, and he might start again," Lucas said.[34]

In that same game, Ruth later hit two more homers and a single off Guy Bush, which ended up being the final hits of his career. His last home run cleared the right field roofline and went out of the ballpark at an estimated distance of over 500 feet and is the longest home run ever hit at Forbes Field. Babe's six RBI that day were one short of his career high, which he had accomplished four times. Ruth was hitless in his last nine at-bats, with his last game coming on May 30, 1935. He ended the season with a .181 average in 28 games.

Babe made his final appearance at Yankee Stadium on June 13, 1948, to help the team celebrate the 25th anniversary of The House That Ruth Built and see his number three jersey retired. Babe leaned on a bat he borrowed from Bob Feller and said, "I am proud I hit the first home run here in 1923. God knows who will hit the last one. It is great to see the men from twenty-five years ago back here today and it makes me feel proud to be with them."[35]

Ruth would die two months later of cancer at 53 years of age. Like a head of state, Ruth's body and coffin were displayed in Yankee Stadium so a nation of fans could come by and pay their respects. His monument at the Gate of Heaven Cemetery in Hawthorne, N.Y., reads: "May the Divine Spirit which animated Babe Ruth to win the crucial game of Life inspire the youth of America."

Ruth's teammate on the Red Sox, Harry Hooper, had an apt description for what it was like to reside in Ruth's spellbinding orbit. "You know, I saw it all happen from beginning to end. But sometimes I still can't believe what I saw: this 19-year-old kid, crude, poorly educated, only lightly brushed by the social veneer we call civilization, gradually transformed into the idol of American youth and the symbol of baseball the world over—a man loved by more people and with an intensity of feeling that has perhaps never been equaled before or since. I saw a man transformed from a human being into something pretty close to a god," Hooper said.[36]

Ruth's obituary in the *New York Times* read: "Probably nowhere in all the imaginative field of fiction could one find a career more dramatic and bizarre than that portrayed in real life by George Herman Ruth.... A creation of the times, he seemed to embody all the qualities that a sport-loving nation demanded of its outstanding hero. For it has always been debatable whether Ruth owed his fame and the vast fortune it made for him more to his ability to smash home runs in greater quantity than any other player in the history of the game or to a strange personality that at all times was intensely real and 'regular,' which was the one fixed code by which he lived."[37]

Babe is the only major league pitcher to pitch at least 10 seasons and post a winning record in all of them. Ruth's overall pitching record was 94–46 with a 2.28 ERA. He allowed 974 hits in 1,221⅓ innings and completed 107 of his 147 starts. He surrendered only 10 home runs in 163 games pitched, or 704 fewer home runs than he hit as a batter. Babe ranks in the top 20 in both career winning percentage and ERA. His lifetime ERA of 2.28 ranks 17th, while his winning percentage of .671 ranks 16th.

Ruth pitched in just five games for the Yankees, none in the postseason. He hurled single games in 1920, 1930, and 1933, and two games in 1921. Those five appearances totaled 31 innings and produced a 5.52 ERA, but he won all five games.

In 12 head-to-head games pitching versus Walter Johnson—arguably the greatest pitcher in baseball history—Ruth came out on top. He went 6–3 with a 1.68 ERA, eight complete games, three shutouts, and 6.1 hits per 9 innings. Three of Ruth's wins against Johnson were by 1–0 scores. Johnson went 4–7 pitching against Ruth with a 1.80 ERA, eight complete games, one shutout, and 7.0 hits per 9 innings. Johnson did hold Babe to a .125 average (and no home runs) in games in which both pitched. However, Ruth batted .350 with 10 home runs against The Big Train in 152 total plate appearances.

Ruth compiled unbelievable batting numbers across his career, primarily due to the fact he had no weaknesses at the plate. His batting eye was superb, and he rarely chased out of the strike zone. His 2,062 walks far outnumbered his 1,330 strikeouts, which is extremely rare for a top slugger. He led the league in on-base percentage 10 times, with 16 seasons finishing in the top 10. He led in offensive WAR 12 times, with 15 seasons in the top 10, and is the all-time leader at 154.4. He led in slugging percentage and OPS 14 times, with 16 seasons in the top 10, and is the all-time leader in both categories. Babe batted .326/.470/.744 with 15 home runs and a 1.214 OPS in 41 World Series games.

The Big Fella didn't just take advantage of Yankee Stadium's short right-field porch, which was 314 feet away. He hit 259 of his 714 home runs at Yankee Stadium—plus another 85 at the Polo Grounds, where Ruth played home games from 1920 to 1923. The Polo Grounds' dimensions were a cozy 279 feet to left and 258 feet to right but 483 feet to center. He hit more home runs in away games (367) than at home (347) during his career.

Ruth got as much of a thrill out of hitting home runs as the fans did watching them leave the yard. He explained, "If I'd just tried for them dinky singles I would've batted around six hundred."[38]

The Bambino was remarkably consistent at the plate. He batted .351 with a 1.186 OPS versus right-handed pitchers, but he was almost as good against left-handed pitchers: .319 average with 1.109 OPS. His .342 average with runners in scoring position is exactly the same as his career average. He batted .346 at home and .338 on the road. His batting average as a pitcher was .299 with 12 homers and 105 hits, which demonstrates that the dual role of pitching and batting diminished his production whether it was from fatigue or some other reason. On the other hand, he batted .483 playing 31 games as a first baseman.

When matched against baseball's best pitchers, Babe held his own. He batted .563 against Waite Hoyt with four homers in 16 at-bats, and .349 against Stan Coveleski. However, Herb Pennock held Ruth to a .250 average, while southpaw Lefty Grove struck him out 45 times and held him to a .316 average. Overall, Ruth batted .339 when facing Hall of Fame pitchers.[39]

Babe had three seasons with at least a .375 average, .500 on-base percentage, and .750 slugging percentage. In 1920, he produced .376/.532/.847; in 1921 he recorded .378/.512/.846; and in 1923 he went .393/.545/.764. No other player in baseball history recorded even one season with those benchmarks. Ruth's career slugging percentage of .690 is far ahead of second-place Ted Williams at .634. Barry Bonds, in fifth place at .607, would have to hit 247 consecutive homers to pass Ruth in slugging, or else Ruth would need to go hitless for 1,147 at-bats to fall below Bonds' slugging mark, according to baseball historian Allan Wood, who after years of studying Ruth came to the conclusion that he is underrated.[40]

CHAPTER 6

Bullet Rogan

The Negro Leagues' Greatest Triple Threat

The year 1920 marked two important moments in baseball history: Babe Ruth joined the New York Yankees and abandoned two-way playing to concentrate on batting; and Wilber "Bullet" Rogan debuted with the Kansas City Monarchs as the first star two-way player in the newly formed Negro National League.

If Rogan had debuted in the major leagues in 1920 instead of the Negro Leagues, whatever team he was on might have forced him to choose between pitching and playing the field. Setting aside how great that would have been for Rogan to be in the majors, such a scenario also would have deprived an entire generation of fans from seeing one of baseball's greatest two-way players perform his magic.

Rogan, who spent almost his entire career with the Monarchs, produced an unmatched record of achievement as a triple threat—he could beat you with his pitching arm, with his bat, and with his glove. He always batted in the middle of the lineup, because he was usually the best hitter on the team, and reportedly swung a heavier bat than Babe Ruth. When Rogan wasn't pitching, he could be found gracefully patrolling center field or some other position.

The righty threw forkballs, curveballs, spitballs, and palm balls, but it was his blazing fastball that earned Rogan the "Bullet" nickname. He didn't look intimidating on the mound at five-foot-seven and 160 pounds, but batters couldn't hit what they couldn't see.

If you include barnstorming games, Rogan played every position on the diamond. However, in league play he never played shortstop and only played a handful of games at catcher. He appeared the most at pitcher (238 games), center field (211 games) and right field (118 games), and he also had 41 pinch-hitting appearances. Author Robert Peterson notes in *Only the Ball Was White* that in one doubleheader Rogan pitched and played four other positions, demonstrating unmatched versatility.[1]

Chapter 6. Bullet Rogan

Negro League historian and author Phil Dixon conducted extensive research on Rogan's career, compiling a comprehensive record of his stats. According to Dixon, Rogan won more than 350 games and struck out more than 2,000 batters. He accumulated over 2,500 hits, 400 doubles, 200 triples, 350 home runs and 500 stolen bases, if barnstorming games are included.[2]

Imagine what his stats would look like if he had not spent nine prime years of his career in the U.S. Army, getting discharged a month before his 27th birthday. It is shocking and shameful that it took until 1998 to get Bullet Rogan inducted into the Hall of Fame in Cooperstown.

In Negro National League (NNL) history, Rogan is the all-time leader in pitching wins (116) and complete games (136), and his 900 strikeouts are 233 more than second-place Willie Foster. He ranks first in innings pitched, second in shutouts, and is fourth in ERA at 2.68, according to Seamheads. He went 8–2 with a 2.72 ERA in the postseason, winning the Negro World Series in 1924 and the NNL Championship Series in 1925.

At the plate, he batted .335/.409/.509 (155 OPS+) with 729 hits, 426 runs, 50 home runs, and 60 triples in documented Negro League play. Standing deep in the batter's box with a massive 50-ounce bat in his hands, Rogan would unleash strong wrists to explode into the ball. He feasted on curve balls and low balls.

"If you saw Ernie Banks hit in his prime, then you saw Rogan," Buck O'Neil once said of Rogan.[3] "He could hit that ball…. He was the type of guy that stood a long way from the plate. Not too close, because they'd jam you…. He was very smooth, swung that bat good," O'Neil added.[4]

Rogan got his baseball start at age 15 as a catcher with the semipro Palace Colts in Kansas City, Kansas, and he immediately stood out for his ability to throw hard. He joined the Kansas City Giants for a series against the all-white Kansas City Blues in 1911, then his next opportunity came from Uncle Sam.

Since the major leagues weren't going to let him play and Black baseball opportunities were limited by the shaky financial situation of the various clubs, Rogan enlisted in the U.S. Army in 1911. He spent his first three years stationed in the Philippines, where he quickly developed a reputation as an all-around player with unmatched ability to pitch and bat.

In 1915, he found himself with the 25th Infantry Wreckers club in Hawaii, where he would be joined by future Negro Leaguers Oscar "Heavy" Johnson, Dobie Moore, and Lemuel Hawkins. He was known as "Cap" in a sign of respect for his top-notch pitching and slugging. Rogan featured a unique pitching style with a no-windup, sidearm delivery that didn't give batters time to react to his scorching fastball. He often served as catcher when not on the mound.

With Rogan starring on the mound and at the plate, the Wreckers went virtually unbeaten for three years. On November 8, 1915, he belted three home runs and a double while catching as the Wreckers soundly defeated the St. Louis University Saints 13–1.[5] Newspaper reports the next year note a game in which Rogan struck out 18 batters but saw his 52-inning scoreless streak snapped.[6] A Chicago newspaper later reported Rogan's pitching record in the service to be 58–2, which illustrates how utterly dominant he was.[7]

While on furlough in 1917, Rogan showed off his sensational two-way abilities while playing for the Kansas City Giants and J.L. Wilkinson's All Nations club. One game he was stealing home to secure victory, while the next game he was smacking a majestic home run—Rogan had lots of ways to beat his opponent. That fall he also pitched for the Los Angeles White Sox, a Black team in the integrated California Winter League. When Rogan returned to active duty his regiment was assigned to guard the Mexican border as American troops faced heavier fighting in Europe. He had less time to devote to baseball while at Fort Huachuca, but he kept his arm in shape.

Wilkinson began recruiting players for a new all-Black team in Kansas City that would be part of the newly formed Negro National League. Rube Foster had founded the new league to provide structure, leadership, financial stability, and media coverage for the best Black players to showcase their talents. Wilkinson had found the perfect player to star on his 1920 Kansas City Monarchs team—Bullet Rogan, the extraordinary two-way player. Casey Stengel, then an outfielder with the Pittsburgh Pirates, had stumbled onto Rogan while barnstorming through Arizona, and he had told Wilkinson about the amazing pitcher with the no-windup delivery. Wilkinson, however, already knew about the famous two-way player.

To make his debut with the Monarchs, Rogan rode a series of trains for three days. He arrived in time to appear in left field and record his first professional hit on July 4, 1920. The next day, he shut out the powerful Chicago American Giants on one hit while striking out 11. For the third game, Rogan collected two hits while playing right field—a star was born.[8]

A six-game home series against the American Giants later in July served as further proof of Rogan's knack for leading his team to victory. In the second game, Rogan struck out 13 and pitched all 12 innings while knocking in the winning run with a double. For the third game, he played right field and smacked two hits including a triple. He pitched a complete game for the fifth game but took a close loss. The Monarchs ended up capturing four of six games from the eventual pennant winners, as Rogan struck out 21 in 21 innings and legged out two triples while playing three different positions.[9]

Chapter 6. Bullet Rogan

Big crowds followed the Monarchs the rest of the season so fans could witness Rogan's brilliance. He played 35 games across the outfield and made 14 pitching appearances that season for the Monarchs, who finished in third place. He went 7–5 with a 3.12 ERA and 12 complete games in 121 innings while batting .296, according to Seamheads. With some barnstorming games added in, Dixon shows him with an 11–6 record, 119 strikeouts, and five games of 10 or more strikeouts. The *Kansas City Sun* named him to its 1920 All-Negro League team as a pitcher.[10]

Dixon points out that Rogan's "Bullet" nickname was hijacked by white sportswriters, who turned him into "Bullet Joe" Rogan as a match to the Yankees' 26-game winner, Bullet Joe Bush. Rogan's given name at birth was Charles Wilbern Rogan, with Wilbern shortened to the Wilber he went by until everyone in the Army called him Cap. There was no reason to ever call him Joe or Bullet Joe, except in a disrespectful manner. Unfortunately, his Hall of Fame plaque refers to him as Wilber Joe Rogan (Bullet).

Bullet Rogan took a back seat to no one in 1921, emerging as the undisputed ace of the Monarchs and the best pitcher in the league. He went 16–8 with 22 complete games in 23 starts across 204 innings. His league-leading 1.82 ERA edged runner-up Dave Brown by two points and his adjusted ERA of 209 was 20 points higher than Dave Brown in second place. He batted .298 with eight triples and 147 OPS+. His 8.5 WAR, which led the league, included 2.8 offensive WAR, 4.6 pitching WAR, and 1.3 fielding WAR playing mainly right field.

Rube Foster's Chicago American Giants emerged again as the champions of the 1921 NNL season, but Rogan lingered as their kryptonite, beating them five times with dazzling pitching and clutch hitting. The Monarchs finished in third place but were the biggest gate attraction in the league because of Bullet Rogan's growing popularity. "Rogan easily demonstrated that he's the greatest pitcher white or black," wrote a report in the *Kansas City Sun*.[11]

In the 1922 season, Rogan again led the Monarchs' staff with a 14–8 record. He led the NNL with 20 complete games in 21 starts, and he finished second in the league in wins, strikeouts (118), innings pitched (193⅔), and ERA+ (157). Playing 47 games in the outfield, he batted a robust .369/.453/.660 (194 OPS+), finishing sixth in average, second in homers (15), OBP and OPS, and third in slugging and OPS+.

Dixon notes Rogan recorded more than 20 homers, 20 stolen bases, and 20 pitching wins with barnstorming games added.[12] No other player in baseball history has ever come close to posting 20 wins, 20 stolen bases, and 20 home runs in the same season. Rogan's two-way brilliance that season is demonstrated by his near-perfect mix of 3.6 pitching WAR and 3.8 offensive WAR.

"There are few pitchers in the game today, regardless of color, who look as good on the mound as Rogan. His stand is beautiful. His wind-up is perfect. He is a great twirler, we venture to say another Matty or Foster," exclaimed *The Chicago Whip*.[13]

To win city bragging rights in the fall of 1922, the Monarchs faced off against the Kansas City Blues, a minor league team in the American Association. The Blues featured first baseman Bunny Brief, who led the league with 40 homers that year, and 22-game winner Ray Caldwell, who had pitched the previous 12 seasons in the majors. The Monarchs easily won the series five games to one, with Rogan batting .444 and striking out nine to earn one of the wins. Newspaper coverage of the culturally significant event focused on the fact the Negro team had bucked convention by showing their superiority at every phase of the game. "Most of the quick thinking and acting was displayed by the blacks. White psychology so far as applied to Negro baseball is a dead issue," wrote Charles Starks in the *St. Louis Argus*.[14]

If anyone doubted Black players could compete at a major-league level, all they had to do was watch Bullet Rogan play. When the Monarchs came to Denver for a barnstorming series, the *Fort Morgan Evening Times* wrote: "Rogan is not only a great pitcher but can play

Bullet Rogan spent nine years of his prime in the U.S. Army but still managed to carve out a career as the greatest two-way player in Negro League history. He was a one-man wrecking crew for the Kansas City Monarchs for 15 seasons, playing center field and batting cleanup when he wasn't pitching. Historian Phil Dixon asserts that Rogan won over 350 games and hit more than 350 home runs, when a comprehensive review of his stats is conducted (National Baseball Hall of Fame and Museum, Cooperstown, N.Y.).

any position of the team and play it well. He is considered by many big-league ballplayers as one of the greatest all-around players in baseball today."[15]

He remained in top form and finally guided the Monarchs to their first NNL championship in 1923, with the team posting an overall 111–41 record. He batted a robust .362 and led the league with 16 wins, 20 complete games, four shutouts, 248⅓ innings, and 151 strikeouts while finishing second with a 2.94 ERA. Dixon credits him with 25 wins and seven shutouts that year, as the semipro and town teams that lined up to play the Monarchs had little hope of slowing him down on the mound or at the plate.

One of the highlights of the season came when Bullet teamed up with José Méndez to pitch a no-hitter for the Monarchs on August 5, 1923. Méndez, who had taken over as manager of the Monarchs that year, started the game and threw a perfect five innings. Rogan followed and allowed one base runner but no hits in his four innings. He had another no-hitter that season broken up with two outs in the ninth inning.

On May 20, 1923, Bullet pitched a three-hit shutout and belted two homers against the Detroit Stars.[16] When the team began playing games in the newly opened Muehlebach Field that July, it was a double-edged sword. Rogan and slugging teammates like Heavy Johnson found it much harder to hit homers, but the same held true when Bullet took the mound—he allowed just four home runs that year in over 248 innings. After finishing second in the league in homers the previous season, Rogan would have to adjust to hitting in a pitcher's park for the rest of his Negro League career.

The Monarchs never let up in 1924, posting a 57–22 record to win the Negro National League pennant by five games over the American Giants while posting an overall record of 83–28–1. Rogan's .396 average in the regular season was the highest in the league (although shy of at-bats to qualify) and his 16 wins in the regular season also led the league. The only other player to win a batting title and lead his league in pitching wins was Martín Dihigo in the 1938 Mexican League. If you take the Monarchs' 79 league games that year and extrapolate that into a 162-game season, Rogan would have ended up with 32 wins. His 2.8 offensive WAR that year was nearly identical to the 2.7 WAR he produced from pitching.

Winning a second straight NNL pennant was nice, but an even bigger prize was at stake for Rogan and the Monarchs in 1924. The first Negro World Series was held between the Monarchs and the Hilldale Club, champions of the Eastern Colored League, who featured Judy Johnson, Biz Mackey, and Nip Winters. Rogan pitched an eight-hitter to win the first game. "Rogan was tough. He had a good hard one and just enough meanness in him to keep you honest up there at home plate," said Hilldale shortstop Jake Stephens.[17]

Bullet Rogan helped lead the 1924 Kansas City Monarchs to the first Negro World Series championship over the Hilldale Club, batting .396 and winning 16 games that season. Shown here during the Series from left: Hurley McNair, Newt Joseph, Hal "Yellow Horse" Morris, Oscar "Heavy" Johnson, Bullet Rogan, Newt Allen, and José Méndez (Society for American Baseball Research-Rucker Archive).

Bullet came in from center field to pitch the 13th inning of game three, which ended in a tie due to darkness. He carried a 2–1 lead into the ninth inning of game five, but a series of errors and a controversial call led to a three-run, inside-the-park homer by Johnson that won it for Hilldale. The Monarchs evened the series up in the next game as Bullet recorded three hits and drove in the winning run in the bottom of the 12th inning. In game eight, Rogan pitched well but trailed 2–0 going into the ninth inning. He singled and later scored as the Monarchs rallied for three runs to stun Hilldale 3–2. The Monarchs rallied for five runs in the eighth inning to win the final game 5–0 and earn the first world championship. Rogan had played in all 10 games, pitching to a 2.89 ERA in four games, and batting .350 with 14 hits, six RBI, and three stolen bases.

In the offseason, Rogan ventured down to Cuba for the first time. He pitched a six-hitter and hit a home run to win one game for Almendares. The next game he hit a triple and shut out the powerful Habana team featuring Martín Dihigo and Cristóbal Torriente.[18] He went 9–4 in 18 pitching appearances with five complete games and tied for the league lead in wins as Almendares easily captured the 1924–25 Cuban Winter League title.[19]

Staying hot the next season, the Monarchs captured the first-half pennant with Rogan still serving as the rotation ace. He would go on to win at least 20 games for the sixth straight season, accounting for barnstorming activity. In league play, he went 15–2—both losses were by one run in May—with a league-best 1.74 ERA that was a full run lower than runner-up and teammate Nelson Dean. He also led in complete games (15), innings (155⅓), strikeouts (96), WHIP (1.01), K% (15.6%), and K/BB (3.10). He played fewer games in the field—18 games in the outfield and one at first base—but still mashed the ball at a .360 clip, slugging .592. Eight of his 45 hits were triples, illustrating that his triple-threat powers extended to his speed. Rogan's 9.0 WAR that season was almost double that of Andy Cooper in second place at 4.8.

Facing the St. Louis Stars in the playoffs, Bullet did his part by winning all three of his starts with a 2.42 ERA. He helped his cause by collecting four singles to win game four. He pitched a seven-hit shutout to win the decisive game seven and send the Monarchs back to the World Series. He batted .450 in the championship series. Then disaster struck. Rogan injured himself playing with his son and was unable to play in the World Series. Hilldale capitalized on their good fortune to win the series 4–1. Even worse for the league, attendance dropped in half without Bullet Rogan available to show off his talents.

With future Hall of Famer Cristóbal Torriente joining the Monarchs for the 1926 season, Rogan found himself surrounded by talent as he took on a new role as player-manager. Torriente paced the team with a .351 average and 65 RBI while holding down center field. Nineteen-year-old Chet Brewer went 12–1 with a 2.37 ERA that season, while William Bell led the staff with 177 innings and 15 wins. Rogan chipped in a 12–3 record with a 2.86 ERA while batting .287 as the Monarchs again won the first-half championship. He played 15 games at first base to go with 20 appearances in the outfield. Seven of his 19 pitching appearances came out of the bullpen.

A tragic shooting in May that prematurely ended the career of star shortstop Dobie Moore cast a pall over the team's season, despite a strong 60–22 record. Competing against the American Giants in the championship series, the Monarchs put all their hopes on Rogan. He pitched an eight-hitter to win one of the home games and was on the mound for game eight with the chance to clinch. Bullet pitched brilliantly but gave up a single run in the ninth to lose a 1–0 duel with Willie Foster. The two aces would face each other again in the nightcap of the doubleheader with the pennant on the line. Although Foster again came out on top, it was an incredible feat of durability by two Hall of Fame pitchers. During the series, Rogan batted .583 and won three games with a 2.84 ERA.

After a four-year run of success, the Monarchs stumbled to a third-place finish in 1927. Like many great players who turn to coaching in baseball and other sports, Rogan found it difficult to relate to players who couldn't execute in key spots like he had done his whole career. The team would not win the pennant again until 1929, although Bullet kept up his outstanding play. He went 14–7 with a 2.32 ERA in 1927 while batting .331. Adding in barnstorming games, Bullet won 20 games for the seventh consecutive year. When the game was on the line, he often called his own number as a pinch hitter or to take the mound to close out a victory.

In 1928, he batted .348 while going 10–2 with a 3.24 ERA as the Monarchs went 50–29–1 to finish second. He hit three homers in a single game for the first time that season against the Detroit Stars. The *Joplin Globe* was one of many newspapers singing his praises, writing: "In Bullet Rogan the Monarchs have who is generally termed the greatest Negro pitcher in the game. He often is ranked with Walter Johnson and Grover [Cleveland] Alexander as one of the three greatest twirlers in baseball."[20]

The Monarchs put all the pieces together in 1929 as they won the first-half and second-half pennants and ended the regular season 63–17 including a remarkable 36–4 mark at home. With teams forced to cut rosters down to 14 players due to financial constraints, it was a strategic advantage to have a versatile player like Bullet Rogan. At age 35, Rogan was needed in center field, where he played 66 games while making just one pitching appearance. His days as a premier pitcher, at least in organized Negro League play, were just about over. He produced a .359/.449/.571 batting mark while setting career highs with 93 hits, 16 homers, 65 runs, 69 RBI, nine triples, and 26 stolen bases (fourth best) in league play.

The Eastern Colored League had disbanded, so the Monarchs played an unofficial World Series against the Houston Black Buffaloes, champions of the Texas-Oklahoma-Louisiana League. It was no contest as the Monarchs swept the series in four games, highlighted by a prodigious home run blast by Rogan in the final game.

The Negro National League was hanging on by a thread as the 1930 season kicked off. The Monarchs and the St. Louis Stars were among the few teams able to field competitive clubs. The Stars easily captured the pennant while the Monarchs produced a respectable record of 40–23. Rogan batted .296 as the center fielder for the first half of the season, while Chet Brewer and William Bell were relied on to front the rotation. To keep the money coming in as the Great Depression raged on, Monarchs owner J.L. Wilkinson made barnstorming more lucrative by dragging a portable lighting system from town to town. Night games attracted larger crowds, especially when you could promise an appearance by superstar Bullet Rogan. Except Rogan got an illness that kept lingering, causing him to miss the rest of the 1930 season and all of the 1931 season.

When Rogan returned to play baseball in 1932, it was not with the Monarchs, but instead with an integrated semipro team in Jamestown, North Dakota. He unleashed his two-way skills again to great success. Rogan posted a 20-3 record for the Red Sox and played either first base or the outfield when not on the mound. At the plate, he led the team with 51 RBI and belted 11 home runs with a .315 average.[21]

One of the teams Jamestown faced was a rebooted Monarchs team, which came to town on a 20-game winning streak. Rogan undoubtedly had mixed feelings as he looked on from first base, but his competitive juices kicked in and he smashed a mammoth two-run homer in the seventh inning to prevent Jamestown from getting shut out.[22]

Rogan was no stranger to integrated play. He played five seasons in the integrated California Winter League (CWL) between 1920 and 1930, leading his team to the championship each season while routinely outclassing white major and minor league players such as Bob Meusel, Al Simmons, and Max Carey. He played all over the infield and outfield when not pitching and even managed one season. If anyone doubted how the Negro League players would fare if allowed to compete with whites in the major leagues, then Rogan and his African American teammates silenced the doubters emphatically. With the 1928–29 championship on the line, Rogan held the all-white Shell Oil lineup in check while collecting two hits and stealing a base.[23] Researcher William McNeil credits Rogan with a .362 average with 15 home runs, and a 42-14 pitching record with 52 complete games during his CWL career.[24] Dixon unearthed more CWL games for Rogan, showing him with more than 60 wins, over 300 hits, and 30 home runs.[25]

Rogan wrapped up his playing with Jamestown and rejoined the Monarchs for the rest of the 1932 season, which included a barnstorming tour in Mexico. His old pitching form had returned, and his bat remained as potent as ever. The Monarchs spent 1933 barnstorming all over the country, rarely losing no matter how stiff the competition. A spirited contest against Grover Cleveland Alexander and the stout House of David club in Carthage, Missouri, on October 1 turned into a rout for the Monarchs, as Rogan recorded three hits and drove in two runs. With Rogan working his managerial magic and showing flashes of his old brilliance on the diamond, the Monarchs sailed through the season with a 134-14 record.[26]

The Monarchs operated as an independent club that primarily barnstormed from 1934 to 1936, with Rogan contributing clutch hits with regularity but pitching less often. He stopped managing the team after 1934, finishing with a 414–280 managerial record in league play, a .678 winning percentage. The Monarchs became the first all–Black team to participate in the *Denver Post*'s prestigious tournament in 1934, which offered a $5,000 prize to the winner. In the first game, Rogan not only scored the winning run, in the sixth inning he made what the *Post* called as "spectacular a catch as anybody ever saw," with a backhanded grab of a sinking liner in right center.[27] Bullet ended up batting .261 in the tournament, with the Monarchs losing 2–0 to House of David in the title game.

A 43-year-old Rogan was voted as an outfielder for the 1936 East-West All-Star game. He went 0-for-1 in his first all-star appearance. The Monarchs joined the newly formed Negro American League for the 1937 season and ran away with the pennant. Bullet batted .333 in limited at-bats and played for the South All Stars in the North-South classic. He batted 3-for-4 with a double and two RBI as the right fielder. Although the Monarchs won the league championship that year over the Chicago American Giants, Rogan went 0-for-6 playing left field in just one game. Later that fall, the Monarchs faced Bob Feller's All-Stars and Rogan was the only player to get a hit off Feller in a 1–0 loss.

Buck O'Neil joined the Monarchs to play first base in 1938, which ended up as Rogan's last season. Bullet got the occasional key hit but was mainly a spectator as the next wave of Monarch players found their footing. He went 0-for-7 in a doubleheader on August 21, which proved to be his last home appearance in Kansas City. The remarkable playing career of Wilber "Bullet" Rogan was over after 18 seasons filled with highlights.

Although many people think of Satchel Paige as the player most representative of the Monarchs, Satchel generated 14.6 WAR playing nine years for the team. By comparison, Rogan played 18 seasons with the Monarchs and his 57.8 career WAR with the team is nearly double that of runner-up Newt Allen at 30.6.

Dizzy Dean, Casey Stengel, Babe Herman, Bob Feller, George Carr, and many others all agreed that Bullet Rogan was the best pitcher they had ever seen. Catcher Frank Duncan said if you had to choose between Paige and Rogan, you would pick Rogan because he could hit. "The pitching, you'd as soon have Satchel as Rogan, understand? But Rogan's *hitting* was so terrific. Get my point? Rogan was one of the best low-ball hitters I ever saw, and one of the best curve-ball hitters," Duncan said. Added Newt Allen: "Rogan was better than Satchel because Rogan was smarter."[28]

Chet Brewer, former pitching great for the Monarchs, who played with both Satchel and Bullet, was among many who felt Rogan was better than Paige. "[Rogan was] the best pitcher I ever saw in my life.... Rogan invented the palm ball. He was the master of the no-wind-up pitch. He wasn't as colorful as Satchel," Brewer said.[29]

Chapter 6. Bullet Rogan

Negro League historian and author John Holway touted Rogan's two-way abilities when comparing him to Paige. He wrote, "Satchel Paige was not the best Negro League pitcher. Bullet Joe Rogan was. Satch had the color and got the ink, but there were better pitchers than he was. At 5'6", Joe didn't stand as high as the letters on Babe Ruth's chest and weighed 40 pounds less than the Babe, but he ranks with Ruth as the best double-threat man, hitting and pitching, in North American history."[30]

When Cum Posey selected his All-Time All-Star Team in 1945, Rogan was one of the four pitchers he named. The *Pittsburgh Courier's* 1952 All-Time All-Star Team featured Rogan as one of the first-team pitchers. Bill James judges Rogan to be the best Negro League pitcher in three years: 1922, 1924, and 1925. He also considers him the best-hitting pitcher and among the most aggressive baserunners.[31]

Rogan was the best pitcher in baseball—Negro Leagues or major leagues—in the 1920s. His 2.62 ERA in the decade is the third-best mark behind fellow Negro Leaguers Bill Foster (2.27) and Dave Brown (2.39), who pitched half as many innings as Rogan. The major league's best pitchers in that decade trail him significantly in ERA—Grover Alexander at 3.04, Lefty Grove at 3.09, and Dazzy Vance at 3.10. Same story with ERA+, where Rogan's mark of 163 blows away Grove (137), Alexander (130), and Vance (130). Rogan's 2.36 Fielding Independent Pitching mark outshines Vance (2.84), Grove (2.96) and Alexander (3.36).

Bullet almost always finished what he started. He completed a remarkable 154 of his 177 Negro League starts. That 87 percent completion rate ranks third in Negro League history, close behind Rube Foster (87.9%) and Carlos Royer (87.3%).

The numbers also show that Bullet was the best player in the Negro Leagues in the 1920s, regardless of position. His 59.1 WAR for the decade outpaces runner-up Oscar Charleston at 44.5 WAR. Rogan's 34.5 pitching WAR in the 1920s ranks number one in the Negro Leagues, ahead of Nip Winters, who recorded 26.9 WAR; while his 24.3 offensive WAR ranks fifth behind Oscar Charleston, Cristóbal Torriente, Turkey Stearnes, and Hurley McNair. Rogan's ranking as the number one pitcher and number five position player for the 1920s demonstrates his unmatched ability as a two-way player.

Considered to be one of the best-fielding pitchers ever in the Negro Leagues, Rogan led pitchers in putouts three straight seasons and finished in the top three in assists four times. He led the Negro National League in at least one pitching category in each of his first seven seasons, and he batted over .300 in 11 of his 18 seasons with the Monarchs.

WAR figures from Seamheads demonstrate his two-way versatility. Rogan's 1921 season (8.9 WAR) is the best by a Negro League right fielder.

His 1922 season (7.8 WAR) is the third best for a center fielder. On the mound, he compiled the third-best (9.8 WAR in 1925) and seventh-best (7.7 WAR in 1923) seasons for a starting pitcher, as well as the ninth-best season for a relief pitcher (5.5 WAR in 1927) when he relieved in 14 of the 29 games he pitched.

Wilkinson, the Monarchs' owner, knew how fortunate he was to have Bullet on his team for so many years. As he said in 1926: "Yes, he's a great player, the greatest in the league. He could make any major league club and would be a star. Everywhere we go they want to see Rogan."[32]

Although he got a late start to his professional career, Bullet Rogan quickly demonstrated that he was the greatest triple-threat talent in baseball history. As the *Baltimore Afro-American* wrote in 1932: "Triple threats are not often mentioned in baseball, but there is no shorter cut to describe Rogan's ability. Bullet could pitch. Bullet could play the outfield and Bullet could hit that apple."[33]

CHAPTER 7

Martín Dihigo
Black Baseball's Versatile and Underrated Star

Watching Martín Dihigo play baseball was like watching Luciano Pavarotti sing or Eddie Van Halen play the guitar—you knew you were witnessing greatness at the highest level. It was artful grace and beauty combined with the requisite doses of speed, power, and instinct, whatever the situation required.

In Cuba he was called "El Inmortal" or "The Immortal," perhaps because his many admirers in his native country hoped they would always get to watch him perform his magic. He was known as "El Maestro" in Mexico, while in the United States everyone from John McGraw and Johnny Mize to Buck Leonard called him the greatest all-around baseball player they had ever seen.

Peter Bjarkman, a leading expert on Cuban baseball history, wrote this about Cuba's enduring national baseball hero: "In Cuba in the years before communism and the rise of amateur sports, Martín Dihigo was everywhere acknowledged as Babe Ruth, Joe DiMaggio and Walter Johnson all wrapped up in one muscular dark-skinned package."[1]

Another esteemed historian, James Riley, weighs in with this description: "The most versatile man ever to play the game of baseball was Martín Dihigo.... A natural five-point player, the graceful athlete had an exceptionally strong arm, great range in the field, very good speed on the bases, and was a superior batter with power at the plate."[2]

Bjarkman was able to flesh out Dihigo's career and compile statistics for his time in the Negro Leagues, Cuba, Mexico, the Dominican Republic, and Venezuela. He came up with an overall pitching record of 288–142 for Dihigo, or slightly more than two wins for every loss. That includes a 26–4 mark in Venezuela, 119–57 in Mexico, 107–56 in Cuba, 30–21 in the Negro Leagues and 6–4 in the Dominican Republic.[3]

What makes this pitching record even more impressive is the fact that Dihigo didn't pitch much in his 20s and basically didn't pitch more than 10 games or 75 innings in a season during his Negro League career. He didn't start pitching heavily in Cuba until the age of 30 in 1935, and he didn't spend significant time on the mound in Mexico until 1938 at the age of 33.

His career winning percentage of .670 ranks 17th in baseball history, right behind Babe Ruth's .671. However, Ruth had 140 career decisions, while Dihigo had 430 decisions. Dihigo's record in verified Black baseball games is 101–67, according to Seamheads. That .601 winning percentage ranks 31st in Black baseball history.

At the plate, Dihigo averaged .305 over 24 seasons with 1,680 hits, 252 doubles, 91 triples, and 156 home runs, according to Bjarkman. He batted .295 during 23 seasons in the Cuban League. Seamheads shows him with a .311 average in Negro League action and .313 in Latin leagues.

It seems imprecise to describe Dihigo as a two-way player—he was more like an eight-way player. He played frequently at every position except catcher (where he played infrequently), and his defense was sensational at each of these positions. It was virtually impossible to hit the ball past him at second base or over his head in center field. When his team needed him to pitch, he pitched like an ace. Powerfully built at six-foot-two and over 200 pounds, he could hit for average and power and was a fast, instinctive base runner. Blessed with a calm, friendly demeanor, Dihigo in his prime was as close as it got to the perfect baseball player.

At the Negro Leagues Baseball Museum in Kansas City is a Field of Legends that shows statues of 10 of the Negro Leagues' greatest players positioned around a baseball diamond. It is not Josh Gibson or Oscar Charleston who is shown up at bat, it is Martín Dihigo. It makes more sense when you consider how difficult it would have been to pick which position to place him at—Second base? Pitcher? Center field? He could certainly back up any of the starters while playing better defense. El Maestro was the ultimate weapon to be deployed by a manager all over the diamond, a tactic that became more interesting when Dihigo evolved into a player-manager role. It has been said that Dihigo sometimes played all nine positions in a single game to show off his versatility.[4]

Dihigo was selected by a panel of ex-players and Negro League experts as the second baseman for the All-Time All-Stars of Black Baseball, while also receiving votes as the best outfielder and the best third baseman.[5] The *Pittsburgh Courier's* 1952 All-Time All-Star Team placed Dihigo on the first team as a utility player. In 1993, he was named an outfielder on the Negro Leagues Baseball Museum's All-Time Team. In addition, he was selected as the second baseman on Cum Posey's All-Time All-Star Team.[6]

He pitched no-hitters in three countries: Puerto Rico, Mexico, and Venezuela. He was the first player to be inducted into the Baseball Halls of Fame in Cuba, Mexico, and the United States. El Inmortal ended his playing career the year Jackie Robinson broke the color barrier—1947. In 1977, he became the first Cuban-born player inducted into the Hall of Fame in Cooperstown.

Brought north by Alex Pompez to join his 1923 Cuban Stars East team in the Eastern Colored League, an 18-year-old Dihigo initially looked overmatched at the plate. In the field, his glovework and range were already spectacular as he played four positions including pitcher. He played the most games, 22, at first base while batting .208. He played six positions for the Stars in 1924, as his versatility quickly turned him into a weapon for manager Pelayo Chacón. His average climbed to .261, and he went 3–3 with a 2.39 ERA in 49 innings.

John McGraw and Buck Leonard were among the experts who called Martín Dihigo the greatest all-around baseball player they had ever seen. Dihigo batted .305 over 24 seasons and compiled a pitching record of 288–142 (National Baseball Hall of Fame and Museum, Cooperstown, N.Y.).

After getting his feet wet for a few seasons—and learning how to hit a curveball—21-year-old Dihigo emerged as a multi-faceted star in 1926 with a Cuban Stars East club that would finish third. That season he led the Eastern Colored League with 5.5 WAR, which included 3.5 offensive WAR, 1.3 fielding WAR, and 0.7 pitching WAR. He won the batting title with a .375 average, and he also led the league with 14 homers, .737 slugging, 1.212 OPS, and 245 OPS+. He went 3–1 with a 3.86 ERA on the mound that season and played every position except catcher.

He played primarily at shortstop the next season and tied Oscar

Charleston for the most home runs with 13 while batting .316. The 1928 season was spent with the Homestead Grays, with Dihigo batting .313.

Some of his slugging feats remain legendary. Buck Leonard claimed to have seen Dihigo blast a ball over the right-field fence at Pittsburgh's Greenlee Field that landed on a hospital roof more than 500 feet away.[7]

He played one verified game at catcher in 1929 with the Hilldale Club, with anecdotal information revealing that he caught in other games but infrequently. El Maestro played every position except right field that year for Hilldale, posting a .332/.448/.613 batting mark with 90 hits, 18 home runs (second best in league), 79 RBI (third best), .613 slugging (fifth best), and 56 walks (tied for first). Pitching 51⅓ innings, Dihigo posted a 2.63 ERA.

His versatility was on display during the 1935 East-West All-Star Game at Comiskey Park in Chicago. He started the game in center field and batted third in the East lineup, collecting a single and a walk with one run scored. With the game tied, Dihigo was summoned to pitch the 11th inning and surrendered a three-run, walk-off homer to Mule Suttles to take the loss. He later pitched for the East in the 1945 East-West Game, allowing one run in 3⅓ innings.

He served as player-manager for the New York Cubans in 1935 and 1936, finishing second and fourth in the Negro National League those seasons. Dihigo only pitched 69 verified games in his 12-year Negro League career, primarily because his defense was such a weapon at other positions. The most innings he psitched in the

Known as "El Maestro," Cuban native Martín Dihigo played all nine positions on the field equally well and was a feared slugger and ace pitcher in Cuba, Mexico, Puerto Rico, and Venezuela in addition to 12 seasons in the Negro Leagues. He is shown here as the batter in the Negro Leagues Baseball Museum Field of Legends (courtesy Negro Leagues Baseball Museum, used with permission).

Negro Leagues was 75⅔ for the New York Cubans in 1936, when he went 6–2 with a 3.69 ERA.

Playing 12 seasons in the Negro Leagues, Dihigo went 30–24 with a 3.45 ERA (133 ERA+) and batted .311 with 546 hits (144 OPS+), according to Seamheads. Despite playing just 492 games, he ranks 12th all-time among Negro Leaguers with 85 home runs, hitting a home run every 20.6 at-bats. Turkey Stearnes, the Negro Leagues' all-time home run leader with 200, hit a home run every 20.2 at-bats, while Oscar Charleston hit one every 26.8 at-bats.

Dihigo also ranks 14th in slugging in Negro League history at .534. He slugged over .700 two times, which has happened only 63 times in major-league history including 28 times by Negro Leaguers. He slugged .737 as a 21-year-old for the Cuban Stars East in 1926 and .739 in 1930, a season in which he didn't have enough at-bats to qualify.

In the opinion of Bill James, either Dihigo or Jelly Gardner had the best outfield arm in the Negro Leagues.[8] Script Lee said he had an arm like a cannon, while Ted Page said he had a better arm than Roberto Clemente.[9]

James also ranked Dihigo as the top right fielder in Negro League history, writing: "Fast, graceful, blessed with a powerful arm, he played every position on the field, and played them all well; this claim seems improbable but is well documented."[10]

Negro League Hall of Fame pitcher Hilton Smith remarked that Dihigo loved baseball and could do everything on the diamond. "That man could play outfield, and ooh, could he throw! You better not try to stretch a hit—he could throw. And pitching, he threw everything, overhand or sidearm. Good curve ball and a good fastball. Had he come along today, he'd lead the major leagues in winning. Would have hit .300 too. Tremendous power," Smith said.[11]

Cuban baseball historians agree that Dihigo has a strong case to be called the best player in Cuban baseball history at every position except catcher. He was named Most Valuable Player in the Cuban League a record four times: for the 1927–28, 1935–36, 1936–37, and 1941–42 seasons.

Fellow Cuban Tony Oliva, who joined him in Cooperstown in 2022, said, "Everyone in Cuba knows of him. He was a great hitter who could play every position. And when he pitched, he was out of sight."[12]

Dihigo ranks as the Cuban Winter League's all-time leader in pitching wins with 107 and complete games with 121, and he ranks fourth in games pitched (248) and winning percentage (.656). On the batting side, he is tied for fourth in triples (44), eight in runs (356), and ninth in doubles (100), according to Bjarkman's *A History of Cuban Baseball 1864–2006*.

Dihigo's home run totals in Latin league play are deceptive due to the cavernous parks where he played games. For example, Almendares Park II in Havana featured a left-field wall that was more than 500 feet from home plate and no baseball was ever hit over that wall.[13] Some of the ballparks in Cuba and Venezuela didn't even have outfield fences.

El Inmortal ranks fourth with 22 years played in Cuba and 248 games pitched, and he is second with 19 years pitching in his native country, according to Jorge Figueredo's *Cuban Baseball: A Statistical History, 1878–1961*.

Born in Matanzas, Cuba, Dihigo got his professional start as a skinny 17-year-old backup infielder playing for Habana in the 1922–23 season—he batted just .161 in 31 at-bats. Two years later, he had started to fill out his tall frame with muscle as he batted .300 and led the Cuban League with 20 pitching appearances. He would bat over .300 in 11 out of the next 12 seasons in his native land.

His versatility in the 1927–28 season for Habana played a part in him being recognized with the Cuban League's first MVP Award. That year he batted .415 with a league-best 54 hits while going 4–2 with a 3.10 ERA on the mound. On November 15, 1928, El Inmortal became the only player in Cuban League history to smack four doubles in one game. He would bat .303 that season.

After a four-year absence in Cuba, Dihigo was the player-manager for Santa Clara in 1935–1936 while leading the Cuban League in most hitting and pitching categories. He led the league in average (.358), runs (42), triples (9), victories (11), winning percentage (.846), complete games (13), and shutouts (4), while tying for first in hits (63) and RBI (38). He guided Santa Clara to the title with a 34–14 record and won his second MVP award.

The next year he switched uniforms to Marianao and won his second consecutive MVP and third overall. He went 14–10 with 22 complete games while batting .323 and tying for the league lead with five home runs. He defeated Barney Brown to win the decisive third game of the playoff series to lead Marianao to the championship.

He went 11–5 and batted .303 for Marianao the next year before returning to the Habana club for the 1938–39 season. Posting his fourth straight season with double-digit wins, he was again the top pitcher with a 14–2 record, .875 winning percentage, and 14 complete games. At the plate, his average slipped to .255 as Habana came in second place. At the age of 36, Dihigo won his fourth and final MVP Award for the 1941–42 season with Habana, when he went 8–3 with a league-best 11 complete games and four shutouts but just a .228 average.

El Inmortal was inducted into the Cuban Baseball Hall of Fame in 1951. After Fidel Castro overthrew the government during the Cuban Revolution in 1959, Dihigo returned from exile and served as Cuba's minister of sports until his death in 1971. Successive generations of Cubans tried to emulate him on the baseball diamond.

"He helped me by teaching me how to play properly," said fellow Cuban and Hall of Famer Minnie Miñoso, who idolized him growing up. "I'd have to say he was most responsible for me getting to the major leagues. He was a big man, but he was big in all ways, as a player, as a manager, as a teacher, as a man."[14]

The player known as El Maestro started his career in the Mexican League playing for Aguila in 1937 at the age of 32. In limited action, he batted .357 and went 4–0 with a 0.93 ERA and 51 strikeouts in 38⅔ innings. That year he pitched the first no-hitter in Mexican League history against Nogales on September 16.

Returning to Aguila for the 1938 Mexican League season, Dihigo won the pitcher's Triple Crown with an 18-2 record, 184 strikeouts, and 0.90 ERA (lowest in Mexican League history) in 167 innings while also winning the batting title with a .387 average. "That's amazing. That's one of the most unique double-doubles ever," said Bob Kendrick, president of the Negro Leagues Baseball Museum. "He wins the pitching title and the batting title in the same season. That is ridiculous. He had a cannon for an arm, because he was a pitcher."[15]

That 1938 season was full of highlights. On June 4, Dihigo struck out a record 22 batters in a 13-inning stint. On September 18, he became the first Mexican League batter to collect six hits in a game, not to mention it came against Satchel Paige. He also engaged in an epic duel against Satchel on September 5. The two aces were evenly matched at 1–1 heading into the ninth inning. Ramón Bragaña relieved Paige and watched as Dihigo blasted a towering walk-off home run to center field to prove he was "The Master" of two-way playing.[16]

He came back the next year and went 15–8 for Aguila with a 2.87 ERA and 20 complete games in 23 starts, while setting a Mexican League record with 202 strikeouts in 202 innings and batting .336.

In 1940, Dihigo won the first of his two Mexican League championships, guiding Veracruz to the title as player-manager. He went 8–6 with a 3.54 ERA on the mound while batting .364 (tied for second) and slugging .550 with 110 hits and 73 RBI (fourth best). When not pitching, he mainly played in the infield that season with 46 games at third base and 15 games at second base.

Dihigo almost won the pitcher's Triple Crown again pitching 35 games for Unión Laguna de Torreón in 1942. His 22 wins tied for second while he led the Mexican League with 211 strikeouts, 2.53 ERA, 26 complete games, and 181 ERA+. His 8.3 pitching WAR in 1942 is tied for the fifth-best mark in Black baseball history. That season he batted .319 while also playing 35 games at third base and 15 games at first base and leading Torreón to the championship as player-manager.

In 1943, he led the Mexican League in strikeouts for the fourth time with 134 while going 16–8 with a 3.10 ERA in 26 mound appearances. Serving as player-manager, he batted .277 playing 49 games at first base as Torreón lost the pennant by a half-game.

His last great season in Mexico was 1946, when a 41-year-old Dihigo batted .316/.427/.441 for Torreón while going 11–4 on the mound with a 2.83 ERA and a league-best .733 winning percentage.

Dihigo's .676 winning percentage as a pitcher is the best-ever in Mexican League history, while his 2.84 ERA ranks seventh. He was inducted into the Mexican Professional Baseball Hall of Fame as part of the second class in 1964.

Dihigo played in Venezuela for a brief period between 1933 and 1935. Gonzalo Gomez, the son of the country's dictator, Juan Vincente Gomez, was the owner of the Concordia Eagles, He actively recruited the best Cuban players to come to Venezuela, and Dihigo was atop his list of recruits. El Maestro posted a 6–0 record for the team in 1933 with a microscopic 0.15 ERA. He went 20–4 the next season as player-manager for Concordia, giving him a winning percentage of .867 as a pitcher in Venezuela.

That 1934 Concordia team, which went undefeated at 12–0 in league play before embarking on a barnstorming tour, is considered one of the best in Latin baseball history. Dihigo was joined in the lineup by Josh Gibson and Rap Dixon, with future major-league star Johnny Mize joining them for an exhibition series in Cuba. They won the Trujillo Cup by defeating the Dominican Republic's top two teams.

Dihigo pitched one of his no-hitters in Venezuela. Another no-hitter came in Puerto Rico while playing an exhibition game with Concordia, with Dihigo reportedly downing beers with his pals right up until game time, according to an account in his son Gilberto's biography of him.[17]

Finding the money too good to turn down, he joined Aguilas Cibaeñas for the 1937 Dominican Republic League. He tied for the league lead in home runs, hit .351 (third best) with 34 hits and 19 RBI (tied for third best) and went 6–4 on the mound (second in wins to Satchel Paige).

Dihigo's career WAR of 65.8, which includes 33.7 WAR from pitching and 28.8 offensive WAR, ranks second all-time in Black baseball history behind Oscar Charleston and places him as the number one right fielder.

The Seamheads site features an all-star team for each verified Negro and Latin league season with each position winner determined by WAR. Dihigo's first selection came as the right fielder on the All-1925 team, and he went on to earn nine more selections at five different positions to demonstrate his sensational versatility. He was the top first baseman in 1926 and 1943, the top third baseman in 1940 and 1942, the top center fielder in 1936, the top shortstop in 1929, and the top right fielder in 1925, 1931, and 1941. He was also the center fielder for the Cuban League's All-1927–28 Team.

Dihigo's 11.0 WAR season with Torreón in 1942 ranks as the top season for a third baseman in Black baseball history, while his 1940 season with Veracruz in the Mexican League ranks fourth best at third base. His 1926 and 1943 seasons are tied for the fifth-best WAR marks for a Blackball first baseman, while his 5.0 WAR as a right fielder in 1941 ranks sixth.

Hall of Fame catcher Roy Campanella, who played six seasons in the Negro Leagues before joining Jackie Robinson on the Brooklyn Dodgers, knew greatness when he saw it. "Dihigo was one of the greatest players I ever saw, in the Negro leagues and the majors," Campanella said. "There wasn't anything he could not do. He was equally good at any position he played and in three different countries. I played against him in Cuba, Mexico and the United States."[18]

Cum Posey, the Hall of Fame owner of the Homestead Grays, proclaimed that Dihigo's "gifts afield have not been approached by any one man, black or white."[19]

Negro League Hall of Famer Buck Leonard thought of Dihigo as baseball's greatest all-around player. "I say he was the best ballplayer of all time, black or white. He could play any position, except catch—and I believe he could catch. Good arm, good pitcher, good outfielder, true thrower, could hit."[20]

While Dihigo remains a legend in Cuba, many baseball fans in the United States seem unaware of what he accomplished on the baseball diamond. They don't know that he demonstrated brilliance at eight different positions on the field. Or that he played at a high level for 24 years in five countries. The unfortunate reality is that too often his name is left out of the discussion when Satchel Paige, Josh Gibson, and Oscar Charleston are mentioned as the greatest Blackball players. El Maestro was in a different class—in the conversation as the greatest two-way player in baseball history.

Chapter 8

The Negro Leagues
Teams Filled with Two-Way Players

Major League Baseball's recognition of seven Negro leagues as major leagues is a step in the right direction. Thanks to the Seamheads Negro Leagues database, we now have a more complete picture of the exceptional accomplishments of talented Negro League stars like Oscar Charleston, Hilton Smith, Smokey Joe Williams, and Ray Brown. However, there is still much work to be done to bring a more complete picture of their statistical greatness.

Black baseball's roots go back to the 19th century, but until 1920 there were no successful, organized leagues to allow Black players to easily make a living in baseball. The first all–African American professional team, the 1885 Cuban Giants, was formed to entertain white guests at the Argyle Hotel in Babylon, New York.

As Black baseball evolved, it spread around the country more fully than white organized baseball that was mainly confined to large cities in the Northeast and a few cities in the Midwest. As players like John Donaldson and Barney Brown barnstormed around the country playing in small towns, they allowed a wide cross-section of Middle America to see incredible demonstrations of baseball skill. Babe Ruth and Ty Cobb weren't rolling into town, but Satchel Paige was worth the price of admission. For many Blackball players, playing in the Latin leagues in the off-season was a good opportunity to make a little extra money while refining their two-way abilities.

A full roster for a team in the Negro Leagues was often as few as 13 or 14 players, which meant everyone had to play multiple positions. Every team was filled with two-way players, and the best pitchers were typically just as skilled at hitting. These players knew they were there to put on a show for the crowd and prove their worth to the owner, then move on to the next game. The Negro Leagues' best two-way players were always in demand.

Chapter 8. The Negro Leagues 121

As James "Cool Papa" Bell explained, "We would frequently play two and three games a day. We'd play a twilight game, ride 40 miles, and play another game, under the lights. This was in the 1940's. On Sundays, you'd play three games—a doubleheader in one town and a single night game in another.... Many a time I put on my uniform at eight o'clock in the morning and wouldn't take it off till three or four the next morning."[1]

Bell claimed he played nearly 200 games in 1933, and he likely did if you include barnstorming exhibitions against semipro and minor-league teams. Seamheads documents just 74 games for him that season, because they only include organized Negro leagues comparable in quality. Cool Papa's career counting stats should be much higher (perhaps he is baseball's all-time hit king), but there is no way of knowing if his batting average would remain as high if stats could be found for every game he played. Bell was extremely hard to throw out because of his blazing speed, so a .330 lifetime average seems reasonable.

Similar assumptions must be made for other Blackball players, making it difficult to compare their records as two-way players to that of Babe Ruth and Shohei Ohtani, who have played in documented seasons of 154 and 162 games. One is forced to rely on projections and anecdotal information, which is not always reliable. However, one must also ask: how great would Ohtani's stats be if he played 80 "official" MLB games each season but also had to play 120 exhibition games against a mishmash of competition? His stats might look very similar to Bullet Rogan's 1922 season with the Kansas City Monarchs.

In 1952, the *Pittsburgh Courier* used a panel of 31 Black baseball players, executives, and sportswriters to come up with two all-time teams of greatest players in Negro Leagues history. They did a fine job, but their work evolved in unintended directions. The paper included an honor roll of other players who received votes, supposedly in order of votes, so some decided to turn that into all-time teams three through five. Author Steven R. Greenes argues in his book *Negro Leaguers and the Hall of Fame* that it is appropriate to treat the order of ranking as having some merit.[2] We agree, and that's how players who made one of the *Pittsburgh Courier's* five all-time teams will be viewed in this chapter.

What follows in this chapter is an overview of 60 Negro League players, profiled alphabetically, who demonstrated some success as two-way players. Their stats may not be complete enough to impress, but their peers all knew who could play the game at a high level. Negro League stars Bullet Rogan, Leon Day, Martín Dihigo, and Ted "Double-Duty" Radcliffe were accomplished enough to rate their own chapters, so their feats as two-way players are covered elsewhere in this book.

Bernardo Baró

Bernardo Baró was inducted in the Cuban Baseball Hall of Fame in 1945. The native of Cárdenas, Cuba, was a five-foot-six speedy dynamo who showcased his all-around ability throughout his 17-year career in the Negro and Cuban Winter Leagues. He played from 1913 to 1930 and collected 850 total hits while batting .299 with .366 OBP, and 129 stolen bases. He batted .309 in 18 games versus major leaguers and posted a career offensive WAR of 18.5.

Baró played 334 games in center field, 306 games in right field and 32 games in left field, as well as 42 games at first base, displaying a quick temper that sometimes overshadowed his feats. He pitched in 45 games with a 13–21 record and 5.27 ERA across 283⅔ innings.

He played 11 seasons in his native country between 1915 and 1929. In the 1919–20 Cuban League, he led the league with 37 hits, 21 runs, and 105 at-bats while averaging .352. In the 1921–22 Cuban League, he was the top batter with a .424 average in an eight-game series of Cuban versus major league stars. He led the 1922–23 Cuban Winter League with a .401 average, 61 hits, and 12 doubles. Baró ranks fifth all-time in Cuban League batting average (.311).[3]

Playing for the Cuban Stars West in 1918, 22-year-old Baró saw his most extensive two-way action. That season he pitched 83⅔ innings in 14 appearances with a 4–7 record and 4.95 ERA, while batting .212 in 30 games in the outfield. He no-hit the Indianapolis ABCs on July 21, 1918.

Playing for the Cincinnati Cuban Stars in 1921, Baró set a career high with 103 hits and 64 RBI and finished sixth in the Negro National League with a .343 average, third in stolen bases with 30, and sixth in OPS+ (166) and OBP (.392).

Baró teamed up with Alejandro Oms and Pablo Mesa on the Cuban Stars East in the 1920s to form one of the most dynamic outfields in the history of the Eastern Colored League, batting .319 in 1923 and .295 in 1927. He suffered a mental collapse while playing the 1929 season and died suddenly back in Cuba in June 1930 at age 34.[4]

James "Cool Papa" Bell

Bell is often called the fastest player in baseball history. It was said that Cool Papa could score from first on a bunt (he did that in a game versus major league stars), steal two bases at a time, and beat out virtually any ball hit to the infield. Hall of Famer and teammate Judy Johnson remarked that it was impossible to throw out Cool Papa if you took your regular position in the infield.[5]

Bell started out as a skinny, left-handed pitcher, but he made his mark as a center fielder and prototypical lead-off hitter across 21 seasons in the Negro Leagues. Demonstrating breath-taking range, he could get to any ball hit in the general direction of center field. He was inducted into the Hall of Fame in 1974 as the fifth Negro League player to be enshrined.

Starting out as a righty batter, he evolved into a switch-hitter early in his career and batted leadoff in a record seven East-West All-Star games. He won Negro League championships with the Homestead Grays in 1943 and 1944, and Negro National League pennants with the St. Louis Stars in 1928 and 1930, and the Pittsburgh Crawfords in 1935. Cool Papa was listed as a second-team outfielder in the 1952 *Pittsburgh Courier's* poll of greatest Black players.

Bill James ranked Cool Papa as the best switch-hitter and fastest player in the Negro Leagues, as well as the Best Negro League Player in 1926 and 1932. James also lists the St. Louis Stars' outfield of the late 1920s with Bell, Frog Redus, and Johnny Russell as the best Negro League outfield.[6] Bell's 49 stolen bases in 1929 and 36 stolen bases in 1926 are the most documented steals in Negro League history, according to Seamheads.

He batted .366 in limited at-bats his rookie year of 1922 and finished with a .330 batting average and 1,958 hits in 1,482 games over 21 seasons. Bell likely batted over .300 in every season he played with his uncanny ability to chop the ball where the fielder couldn't retire him. He was an amazing bunter as well, who frequently bunted for hits.

Bell batted .347 in 13 documented games versus major leaguers. He also played a number of seasons in the California Winter League (CWL) against white professional players. He batted .415 in nine games during the 1931–32 CWL, then led the league in batting (.362), hits, and triples in 1933–34.

He averaged .372 in 189 games in the Latin leagues. He starred in the Mexican League from 1938 to 1941, leading the league in 1940 with a .437 average and 167 hits in 89 games. He led the 1928–29 Cuban League in home runs (five) and runs (44) while batting .325. Not known as a slugger (he had 74 career homers), on January 2, 1929, Bell became the first player to hit three home runs in a Cuban League game, with one coming off Martín Dihigo.[7] Overall, Bell hit .292 with 166 hits including 16 triples playing in Cuba between 1928 and 1941, according to Peter Bjarkman's *A History of Cuban Baseball*.

Bell is credited with 49 appearances as a pitcher—almost all with the St. Louis Stars—with a 20–15 record and 4.53 ERA. He picked up his nickname for the cool demeanor he displayed while striking out Oscar Charleston as a 19-year-old pitcher in a 1922 game in which he also homered.[8]

Relying mainly on a knuckleball, he went 11–7 in 153⅔ innings in

1923, when his 25 pitching appearances were more than the 18 games he played in the field. While hurling 40 innings for the Stars in 1924, Bell was shifted to center field to take full advantage of his speed and that was it for him pitching.

Cool Papa's speed was more intimidating to opponents than the power of any slugger, which is why he earned the honor of Mississippi's All-Time Best Player in *Baseball State by State*.[9] Seamheads credits him with 348 career steals, while Bell claims he stole 175 bases playing nearly 200 games in 1933.[10] During the 1934 East-West All-Star Game, Bell walked, stole second, and scored the only run of the game from second base on a shallow blooper.

He was one of six future Hall of Famers who played on the powerful 1936 Pittsburgh Crawfords—along with Satchel Paige, Josh Gibson, Oscar Charleston, Bill Foster, and Judy Johnson—but Bell also played on dominant championship teams with the St. Louis Stars and Homestead Grays.

Bell batted an amazing .397 in 1946 at age 43 for the Grays, then continued as a player-manager for the Detroit Senators (1947) and Kansas City Stars (1948–50). His career WAR of 44.5 (which included 5.6 WAR for pitching) ranks 13th all-time in Negro League history. The Cool Papa Bell historical marker in his hometown of Starkville, Miss., states: "Renowned as the fastest man to ever play baseball."

Cool Papa Bell started his baseball career as a pitcher before pivoting to become the greatest lead-off hitter in Negro League history (Society for American Baseball Research-Rucker Archive).

Bell said his biggest thrill was watching Jackie Robinson lead a parade of Black players to the major leagues. "They say we was born too soon, but it wasn't that. They opened the doors too late," he said.[11]

William Bell

Bell was one of the top right-handed pitchers in the Negro Leagues, relying on sharp control and pitching smarts more than overpowering stuff. Despite getting a late start at age 25, he played 15 seasons that produced a 3.20 ERA (127 ERA+) in 1,695 innings (10th in Negro League history). His 135 wins is tied with Bullet Rogan for fifth all-time and his 134 complete games rank 11th all-time.

The Center for Negro League Baseball Research credits Bell with a .723 career winning percentage that is the best in Negro League history, as well as an overall record of 207-74 against all competition. A strong case can be made that Bell belongs in the Hall of Fame, and he evidently did get close during the 2006 Negro League special election.[12]

Bell played his first eight seasons as a dependable workhorse for the Kansas City Monarchs, playing in the shadow of more famous teammates such as Bullet Rogan and Cristóbal Torriente. He won his first 10 starts for the Monarchs in 1924 and won Game Six to help them win the first Negro League World Series that season over Hilldale. In 1926, the righty won 10 of his first 11 starts on the way to a 15-6 record with a 2.46 ERA and a league-leading 16 complete games in 190 innings for the Monarchs. In 1927, Bell went 13-4 and his 2.17 ERA was just behind Willie Foster's league-leading 2.12 mark.

In the winter of 1927-28, Bell pitched for Habana Leones of the Cuban Winter League, going 6-2. He returned the next winter and led the league with nine wins and 11 complete games as Habana took a second straight title.

In his last season with the Monarchs, 1930, Bell was the ace of the staff and went 10-3 with a 2.95 ERA. Joining the Pittsburgh Crawfords late in the 1932 season, Bell reeled off nine straight wins in July and August. He also pitched and won the first night game at Greenlee Field. At the end of that season, Bell went 3-0 as the Crawfords beat Casey Stengel's All Stars five out of seven games.[13]

Known as an excellent fielder and a respectable batter, Bell got four hits in six at-bats to lead the Monarchs to the 1926 pennant over the Chicago American Giants. Overall, he batted .245 with 193 hits while making 42 appearances in the outfield and 16 as a pinch hitter. His career WAR of 35.8 (which includes 34.3 pitching WAR and 1.5 offensive WAR) ranks 23rd in Black baseball history. He was named the All-1926 starting pitcher by Seamheads after a 4.7 WAR season.

Ramón Bragaña

Bragaña started out as an infielder in Cuba but emerged as one of the most dominant Blackball pitchers of the 1940s. The Cuban-born righty played for several Negro League teams at a young age and then became a star in leagues in Mexico, Cuba, Venezuela, and the Dominican Republic in a career that spanned from 1928 until 1955. He pitched just 13 games in the Negro Leagues, because he felt he was treated better in Latin America.

Nicknamed "El Professor" for the pitching instincts he displayed on the mound, Bragaña was a power pitcher with great control who played all nine positions around the diamond including 167 games at third base.

During the 1930 American Series between big-league and Cuban stars, Bragaña held his own against Carl Hubbell, narrowly losing 2–1. Then in the 1937 American Series, he held the major-league all-stars to one run in a 6–1 win, according to Jorge Figueredo's *Cuban Baseball*.

"This Ramon Bragaña is just about as great a pitcher as I ever saw. He has speed, a wonderful assortment of curves, and control," said Hall of Famer Bill Terry, who faced him in a 1937 spring series in Cuba.[14]

Across the 1941–42 Cuban League season, Bragaña set a record with 39⅔ scoreless innings across seven games with rival Habana, which included four consecutive shutouts. He led the league with nine wins, 21 games pitched, 11 complete games, and five shutouts that season, according to Figueredo's *Cuban Baseball*.

He set a Mexican League record in 1944 with 30 wins out of 52 total victories for the pennant-winning Azules de Veracruz, pitching to a 3.29 ERA in 325⅓ innings (another Mexican League record). His 10.3 pitching WAR for Azules that season is the best pitching season in Black baseball history, according to Seamheads, while his 8.3 pitching WAR in 1940 is tied for fifth best.

A speedy player with a strong throwing arm, his best two-way season was 1942. That year he went 22–10 with a 3.74 ERA for Veracruz, a team that won just 39 games. That season he played 50 games at third, batted .299, and slugged .519 with 17 homers. He led the Venezuelan League in home runs in 1936–37.

Bragaña easily retired a 51-year-old Babe Ruth, who was in civilian clothes, during a 1946 exhibition in Mexico. However, the incident turned ugly when Bragaña didn't willingly serve up home runs to the Bambino and the revered Cuban was suspended as manager.[15]

In 1951, at the age of 42, Bragaña solved Veracruz's shortage at catcher by filling in for a few games. The next year he won his 200th game in the Mexican League. In his 18 years in Mexico, he is credited with a .243/.352/.365 mark at the plate with 544 hits and 50 home runs, as well as 218 pitching wins.[16]

According to research from the Center for Negro League Baseball Research compiled by historians Dr. Layton Revel and Luis Munoz, Bragaña was a member of 17 championship teams, compiled 310 documented pitching wins, was named to five Mexican League All-Star games, and was named MVP of the 1936 Dominican League. He is considered one of the four greatest Cuban pitchers in baseball history.[17]

Bragaña was inducted into the Cuban Baseball Hall of Fame in 1959, the Mexican League Hall of Fame in 1964 and the Latino Baseball Hall of Fame in 2012. He was named the relief pitcher on Seamheads' All-1940 Team, the third baseman on the All-1943 Team, and the starting pitcher on the All-1944 Team. His career WAR of 39.9 (which includes 37.2 WAR from pitching and 4.1 offensive WAR) ranks 18th in Blackball history and is fourth best among Cuban Baseball Hall of Fame members.

George "Chippy" Britt

Britt was a righty pitcher and catcher who could play all nine positions. He played 20 seasons between 1917 and 1942, although his activity in several years is undocumented. Britt played nine seasons with the Homestead Grays, winning 25 verified games for them with 27 complete games. However, historians have determined Britt went 21–4 for the powerhouse 1931 Homestead Grays team that went 143–29–2 against all competition.

He picked up the nickname "Chippy" because that is what he typically called everyone. It also goes with the fact he was known to be argumentative and scrappy with a temper, getting into his fair share of dustups on and off the diamond. Still, he finished second in fan voting for most popular player of the year in 1924.[18]

Britt led the Eastern Colored League with a 3.01 ERA and 163 ERA+ in 1925. Overall, he went 60–52 with a 4.10 ERA (103 ERA+) in 1,013 innings with 73 complete games. In addition to pitching 168 games, he caught 69 games, played 35 games at first base, and played at least seven games at all nine positions. For his career he batted .263 with 237 hits. His best year at the plate was 1932, when he batted .319 with a 119 OPS+.

Barney "Brinquitos" Brown

Brown, a top lefthander in the Negro National League, went 93–83 with 3.96 ERA (117 ERA+) in combined action from the Latin and Negro Leagues from 1932 to 1948. His pitching took off once he mastered the screwball.

After starting the 1932 season with Pollock's Cuban Stars, Brown jumped to the Jamestown Red Sox, an integrated semipro team in North Dakota. He was especially in demand by the Red Sox because he pitched like an ace and swung a good bat. Others Black players soon followed, and Brown started holding his own against Satchel Paige of the Bismarck Churchills while playing primarily with white teammates.

He won 16 games to lead Azules de Veracruz to the 1940 Mexican League championship, then won 16 games the next season while batting .256. He led the Puerto Rico Winter League with 16 wins and was named MVP in both the 1941–42 and 1946–47 seasons. Brown's overall record in Mexico was 84–53, a .613 winning percentage.

Overall in Black baseball, Brown batted .254 with 273 hits across 1,259 plate appearances, and his status as a strong batter was confirmed by 49 pinch-hitting appearances. He played 60 games in left field, 77 games in right field, 27 games in center field, and three games at first base.

He won seven games while batting .317 for Marianao in the 1937–38 Cuban League. He went 16–23 with 21 complete games and batted .286 playing four years in Cuba, according to Bjarkman's *A History of Cuban Baseball*.

Brown pitched in six East-West All-Star games, allowing just one run in 16⅔ innings. He also pitched the last four innings and was the winning pitcher in the final All-Star game between the Negro National League and Negro American League in 1938. Catcher Quincy Trouppe named Brown to his number one all-time Negro League team.[19]

Ray Brown

Brown was in his fourth year with the Homestead Grays in 1935 when he married the daughter of Cum Posey, who was the owner, manager, and driving force behind the team. Posey and Brown were both inducted into the Hall of Fame posthumously in 2006. A control artist who relied on a great curveball as well as a sinker and top-notch fastball, Brown pitched for the Grays in 14 of his 15 seasons and led the team to nine straight pennants. In 1937, he batted .322 and went 11–3 for the Grays.

Overall, he went 125–50 with a 3.07 ERA and 146 ERA+. He led the league in wins and complete games six times, ERA and winning percentage twice, and strikeouts and shutouts three times. Brown won the pitcher's Triple Crown in 1938 with marks of 14–0, 1.84, and 76 strikeouts.

Among his best feats on the mound: hurling a no-hitter during the 1936–37 Cuban Winter League; pitching a one-hit shutout against the Birmingham Black Barons in the 1944 Negro World Series; and throwing a seven-inning perfect game against the Chicago American Giants in 1945, his last season in the Negro Leagues.

Brown was a good hitter from both sides of the plate and typically batted in the middle of the lineup. He played a lot in center field early in his career and then less often once he demonstrated his dominance as a pitcher. He was named the center fielder on the All-1931 and All-1935 Teams by Seamheads, as well as the All-1936 right fielder and All-1938 relief pitcher.

Playing the Cincinnati Reds in Puerto Rico during spring training in 1936, Brown helped the Brooklyn Eagles win three of four contests by blasting a two-run triple on March 9.[20]

He is credited with a .268 average and 371 hits including 32 homers. As a position player, he made 85 appearances in right field, 75 in center field, 47 in left field, plus 16 more games scattered around the infield. He was used as a pinch-hitter 34 times. Brown pitched in three East-West All-Star games.

His record playing five seasons in Cuba was 46–20 with 57 complete games in 89 games, according to Bjarkman's *A History of Cuban Baseball*. His .696 winning percentage is second-best in Cuban baseball history. He produced a sensational 21-4 record for Santa Clara in the 1936–37 Cuban League, leading the league in winning percentage, wins and complete games (23) that season while batting .311. Also that season, he completed both games of a doubleheader while only allowing one run. The next year he led the Cuban League with 12 wins, 14 complete games, and .706 winning percentage. In the 1938–39 Cuban Winter League, he went 11–7 and led the league with 16 complete games.

Brown went 4-2 with a 1.32 ERA appearing in seven games in five World Series (two championships). He was listed as a fifth-team pitcher in the 1952 *Pittsburgh Courier's* poll of greatest Black players. Hall of Fame pitcher Hilton Smith ranked Brown on par with Satchel Paige and Bob Feller as a talent.[21]

His career WAR of 43.5 (which includes 37.5 WAR from pitching and 6.7 offensive WAR) ranks 14th in Negro League history, although he ranks third among pitchers. His offensive WAR total is the best all-time in Black baseball history among players identified primarily as a pitcher, according to Seamheads.

Brown continued playing in Mexico and Canada until 1953, occasionally playing the outfield and pinch hitting in addition to pitching. He won 20 games for the Thetford Miners in 1952, then closed out his career with 13 wins as player-manager for the Lachine Indians in the Laurentian League. He was just doing what he loved to do, until he ran out of teams and leagues to dazzle with his pitching brilliance.

Harry Buckner

Buckner was viewed as a top pitcher in the early days of Black baseball, becoming one of the first Americans to play in Cuba during the American Series in 1904. He played in various leagues from 1896 to 1914, when game accounts were sparse. During the turn-of-the-century period, Buckner was referred to as one of the four great Black pitching stars along with Rube Foster, Dan McClellan, and Walter Ball.[22] Nicknamed "Green River," Buckner pitched a no-hitter for the Brooklyn Royal Giants on August 31, 1907.

He is credited with a 44–35 record, 2.88 ERA (101 ERA+), .293 batting average, and 215 hits. Buckner stood out as a versatile and skilled player who could do it all, pitch, catch and play infield and outfield, according to James Riley.[23] He regularly caught when not pitching in 1909, and that year sportswriter Harry Daniels named him a pitcher on his All-American Team.[24]

Buckner played a documented 117 games in right field, often batting in the middle of the lineup. In 1914, he batted .411 in limited at-bats. Buckner compiled 9.2 pitching WAR and 7.3 offensive WAR over his career. His two seasons in Cuba produced a 1–7 pitching mark and seven complete games in 12 appearances to go with a .255 batting average, according to Bjarkman's *A History of Cuban Baseball*. He had more success in the annual American Series held between Cuban squads and Negro Leagues teams from the U.S. He won two games in 1904 and 1905, four games in 1906, and three games in the 1908 series, according to Figueredo's *Cuban Baseball*.

Bill Byrd

Byrd was a top pitcher in two decades, getting named to eight East-West All-Star teams (behind only Leon Day among pitchers). He pitched in seven East-West games representing the East, going 2–1 with a 2.12 ERA in 17 innings. He pitched six shutout innings in relief to get the win in the 1943 North-South All-Star Game, helping his cause with two hits. He posted a career mark of 102–67 with 3.39 ERA (128 ERA+) from 1933 to 1950. Playing for the Baltimore (or Washington) Elite Giants in 15 of his 17 seasons probably prevented him from gaining full recognition for his greatness.

One of his best years on the mound was 1948 with the Elite Giants. That season he went 11–4 with a 1.90 ERA (178 ERA+) and 12 complete games, then followed that up with a 12–3 mark the next season at age 42. He led the Negro National League with a 2.23 ERA in 1941, and in wins in 1942, 1945, and 1948. The Georgia native relied on a sharp curve, spitball, and occasional knuckleball to baffle batters. "He was a good pitcher and he was good for a long time," said Hall of Fame catcher Roy Campanella.[25]

He played a fair amount in the outfield (58 recorded games) and a few games around the infield. Byrd, a switch-hitter, took pride in his batting and averaged .262 with 213 hits and 17 home runs. He served as a pinch hitter 59 times including in a 1945 All-Star game. Byrd batted over .300 six times including .366 in 1937 and .339 in 1942. "They always played me [as a hitter] in Yankee Stadium, because I could drop that ball right in there [into the right field stands]. I think I hit six or seven homers in Yankee Stadium," he said.[26]

Byrd was listed as a third-team pitcher in the 1952 *Pittsburgh Courier's* poll of greatest Black players. Bill James ranks him as the best Negro League pitcher in 1944, 1948, and 1949.[27] John Holway recognized Byrd with the George Stovey Award (Cy Young) for top pitcher in the East for those same three seasons.[28]

He was named the starting pitcher for the All-1939 Team by Seamheads. He compiled 4.0 offensive WAR and his 29.7 pitching WAR is better than Negro League Hall of Famers Andy Cooper, Hilton Smith, and Leon Day. A full accounting of his lifetime stats would undoubtedly earmark his career as Hall of Fame worthy.

Tatica Campos

Campos was a right-handed Cuban pitcher and utility player. He played nine seasons in the Negro Leagues and seven seasons in Cuban leagues between 1911 and 1922. He went 21–29 with a 2.91 ERA pitching 74 games but was much more effective pitching in Cuba—2.27 ERA compared to 4.63 ERA in 21 Negro League games.

Overall, Campos batted .231 with 253 hits. He played all nine positions in the field including 66 games at first base, 50 at second base, 49 at third base, 11 at shortstop, 42 in left field, 17 in center field, 46 in right field, and four at catcher. His best season was 1918–19 with the Cuban Stars in the Cuban League, when he batted .255 and was the staff ace with an 8–7 record and 1.62 ERA (154 ERA+) in 144⅓ innings.

Walter "Rev" Cannady

Cannady was a jack-of-all-trades utility player who played 25 years with 13 teams and did everything well. Everyone knew how talented Cannady was, but his combative personality (such as when he attacked an umpire) and indifferent attitude made him unpopular with teammates and fans. He made one Negro National League All-Star team as a third baseman in 1938, although other sources have judged him as worthy of all-star status in multiple seasons.

Rev started out as an outfielder and pitcher in 1921–22, then pivoted to play primarily in the infield. He is credited with pitching in 20 games with a career mark of 8–5 and 5.52 ERA (93 ERA+). Cannady played 281 games at second base, 223 games at shortstop, 147 games at third base, 83 games at first base, and 34 games in the outfield.

In 1925, 23-year-old Cannady finished third in the Eastern Colored League in batting (.389), homers (13), OPS (1.047) and OPS+ (165), second in hits (107), and fourth in slugging (.604) for the second-place Harrisburg Giants.

In 1928, Cannady started the year batting .325 in 55 games as the Hilldale Club's first baseman, then later batted .500 in eight games as the Homestead Grays' second baseman. In 1944 at the age of 42, Cannady hit .326 playing the second half of the season as the starting second baseman for the Homestead Grays, helping them win the Negro World Series.

A strong batter who typically hit in the middle of the lineup, Cannady batted .321 lifetime in the Negro Leagues with 897 hits, 46 homers, 528 runs, and 560 RBI. He batted .533 in nine games against major leaguers.

His best year pitching was 1922, when he went 4–1 with a 2.80 ERA. Cannady was listed as a fourth-team utility player in the 1952 *Pittsburgh Courier's* poll of greatest Black players. Rev was selected as the first baseman on Cum Posey's 1924 All-Star team and the second baseman on his 1933 All-Star team.

He compiled 16.6 offensive WAR and 0.7 pitching WAR. By Similarity Score on Baseball-Reference, Cannady's production compares favorably to Hall of Famer Pop Lloyd, Sammy Hughes, and Dick Lundy—three of the best infielders in Negro League history.

Oscar Charleston

Charleston was one of the greatest, most talented players in baseball history, regardless of color. Primarily a center fielder, he was listed as a first-team outfielder in the 1952 *Pittsburgh Courier's* poll of greatest Black players. After accumulating career WAR of 78.9 (most in Negro League history), Charleston was inducted into the Hall of Fame in 1976. He won three batting titles and led the league in home runs five times, in runs scored six times, in RBI four times, and in hits three times.

Charleston, who was called "Charlie," is the Negro Leagues' all-time leader in RBI (1,317), hits (2,036), games played (1,587), doubles (378), triples (143), stolen bases (368), and walks (774). His .350 batting average ranks eighth all-time in Negro League history, while his 211 homers rank second behind Josh Gibson's 240.

Charleston had blinding speed, prodigious power, and unmatched competitiveness (often sidetracked by his temper), and he could track down every fly ball in center. He played 996 games in center field and 513 games at first base, but he only made 33 appearances on the mound—that's where his two-way status falls short of greatness. He posted a 3–7 record with a 4.54 ERA in 170⅓ innings.

He started his baseball career in 1914 as a 17-year-old southpaw in the Manila League while stationed in the Philippines with the U.S. Army. The next year he pitched 40⅔ innings with a 4.43 ERA for the Indianapolis ABCs. Charleston's bat, defense, and speed quickly proved too valuable to be wasted on the mound. Charlie's 1921 season

Oscar Charleston won three batting titles and ranks second in Negro League history with 211 home runs. "Charlie" made just 33 appearances on the mound, so he made minimal impact as a two-way player (Society for American Baseball Research-Rucker Archive).

with the St. Louis Giants illustrates his awe-inspiring talent. That year he batted .423 and slugged .743 with 17 home runs, 14 triples, 32 steals, 101 RBI, and 108 runs—all in 82 games. That is basically half an MLB season.

Playing in Cuba between 1920 and 1931, Charleston produced a .361 average with 19 home runs and 360 hits in 996 at-bats, according to Bjarkman's *A History of Cuban Baseball*. He led the Cuban League with a .371 average in 1930–31, with 59 runs in 1923–24, and with five home runs and 11 stolen bases in 1927–28.

John Holway recognized Charleston with the Fleet Walker Award (MVP) in the West for the 1918, 1919, and 1921 seasons plus 1933 (just one league).[29] Seamheads ranks him as the best center fielder in 1919, 1920, 1921, and 1925, and the best first baseman in 1925 and 1933. Charleston was the easy choice as Indiana's All-Time Best Player in *Baseball State by State*.[30]

Buck O'Neil was quoted saying: "The greatest MLB player I ever saw was Willie Mays. But, the greatest baseball player I ever saw was Oscar Charleston."[31]

Phil Cockrell

Cockrell was listed as a third-team pitcher in the 1952 *Pittsburgh Courier's* poll of greatest Black players. Nicknamed "Fish" and "Georgia Rose," Cockrell posted an overall record of 97–71 in Negro League action with a 3.98 ERA (100 ERA+). He rose to the occasion in six outings against major leaguers, going 5–1 with a sparkling 0.89 ERA.

The crafty spitballer pitched no-hitters for Hilldale in 1921 and 1922. Cockrell pitched two games in each of the 1924 and 1925 World Series for Hilldale, winning the decisive Game Six in 1925. He ranks seventh in Negro League history with 135 complete games and ranks 13th in wins.

"If you were to ask me who is the smartest hurler in our league, there could be but one answer, and that is 'Cockrell,'" said W. Rollo Wilson, a sportswriter and commissioner of the Negro National League.[32]

Cockrell did not make much of an impact at the plate, batting .246 with 189 hits playing 49 games in the outfield, eight games in the infield, and 18 games as a pinch hitter. His 11.8 pitching WAR outshines his 2.1 offensive WAR.

Homer "Goose" Curry

Curry started his career as a righty pitcher and ended up going 26–39 with 5.51 ERA in 101 pitching appearances. He did pitch a seven-inning no-hitter for the Memphis Red Sox on September 5, 1931, against inferior competition. He fared better at the plate with a .301 career average, .404 OBP, and 124 OPS+. Batting lefty, he totaled 561 hits while hitting more for contact than power. The Texas native appeared in 223 games in right field, 182 games in left field, 75 games in center field, and 46 games as a pinch hitter.

Curry is documented playing 10-plus games as a pitcher and position player in 1928, 1929, and 1932. He saw the most two-way action in 1932 with the Memphis Red Sox and Monroe Monarchs, pitching in 12 games and playing 33 games in the outfield. He went 5–8 with a 4.06 ERA and batted .291. A shrewd strategist, Curry served as player-manager in eight seasons.

Johnny Davis

Davis led the Newark Eagles to the 1946 Negro League championship, averaging .292 and getting the clinching hit in the series. Nicknamed "Cherokee," he appeared in East-West All-Star games in 1944, 1945, and 1949 as an outfielder. The righty slugger posted a career average of .301 with 318 hits, 31 home runs, and 135 OPS+. He appeared in 284 games in the outfield, plus eight games at first base.

Although he started out as a pitcher with the semipro Mohawk Giants, Davis pitched in just 13 Negro League games with a 5.35 ERA across 69 innings. However, he was primarily a pitcher in the Puerto Rican winter leagues, pitching a no-hitter and leading the league in strikeouts in 1944.[33] He was named MVP of the 1947–48 winter season after going 12–7 with a 3.22 ERA, belting 11 homers, and setting a record with eight consecutive hits. Davis batted .279 playing in the Cuban League between 1946 and 1948.

In 1953 at age 36, he hit .321 with a league-record 35 homers and 136 RBI for the Class B Fort Lauderdale Lions. Davis narrowly missed making it to the majors after the color barrier was shattered but had an untimely broken ankle.

Walter "Steel Arm" Davis

Davis was a lefty ace hurler and outfielder for minor-league teams in the Texas Negro League in 1919, 1921, and 1922, sandwiched between three games in the Negro National League in 1920. Other than pitching 12 games for the Detroit Stars in 1923, Steel Arm went on to make his mark as a slugging outfielder.

In a career that lasted until 1935, Davis accumulated 567 hits with a .324 lifetime average and 147 OPS+. He batted .268 playing in the Cuban League in 1927–28.

In 1927, Davis batted .393 with 149 hits for the Chicago American Giants. He helped them win the Negro World Series that year by averaging .361 in the series with a homer. He led the Negro Southern League with four home runs in 1932 after batting .331 in 1930. Overall, Steel Arm pitched in 21 games with a 5.47 ERA (82 ERA+). He appeared in 307 games in the outfield and 184 games at first base.

Davis made one All-Star team in 1933 with the Chicago American Giants, and he was named the right fielder on the All-1930 Team by Seamheads.

John Donaldson

Donaldson was legendary, one of the greatest pitchers in Blackball history, yet his official career stats from a 33-year career from 1908 to 1940 are unimpressive. A visit to The John Donaldson Network site reveals the incredible accomplishments: 30 consecutive no-hit innings in 1915, 424 verified wins, 5,221 verified strikeouts including two games with at least 30 strikeouts, 14 no-hitters including two perfect games, complete games pitched in 92 percent of his pitching appearances, and he played in over 763 cities.[34] He gave people in small, out-of-the-way towns a chance to see what a generational talent could do with a baseball.

Most of the games he played were barnstorming exhibitions—he was a fixture on J.L. Wilkinson's All Nations multi-racial squad, along with José Méndez—so his stats did not come against reliable competition. Donaldson was continually billed in the press as the world's greatest pitcher as he traveled from town to town, and he didn't disappoint the fans who came out to see the pitching sensation dominate. He pitched seven of his 14 no-hitters for All Nations, turning fans into true believers everywhere from Beach, North Dakota, to Lismore, Minnesota. He helped his cause by bringing thunder from the middle of the lineup.

Pitching for Brown's Tennessee Rats in Humboldt, Iowa, on September 14, 1911, Donaldson pitched all 18 innings and struck out 31 batters. He did not allow a hit from the seventh inning to the 18th inning.[35] In 1915, he hurled 30 consecutive no-hit innings, leaving local sportswriters baffled as they tried to come up with new superlatives to describe his performances.

Relying on a sharp curve that was faster than most pitchers' fastballs, a fastball that was a notch beyond blazing and impeccable control, the southpaw hurler kept demonstrating that he was Black baseball's best pitcher. His stout legs, sturdy frame and smooth, repeatable delivery were a scout's dream. Facing tougher competition in 1916, he led All Nations to series victories over C.I. Taylor's Indianapolis ABCs and Rube Foster's Chicago American Giants.[36] Pitching in his first game against white major leaguers in the 1917 California Winter League, Donaldson emerged victorious while striking out 16.[37]

John McGraw famously said, "If Donaldson were a white man.... I would give $50,000 for him."[38] McGraw was not the only luminary in the white baseball world to gaze at Donaldson's other-worldly skills and envision what-if scenarios, as Branch Rickey, Charles Comiskey, Frank Chance and many others had similar thoughts—and Hall of Fame pitcher Grover Cleveland Alexander said he would have given $100,000 to sign Donaldson.[39]

He was known to be fast on the bases and smooth in the field playing the outfield and shortstop. While resting his sore pitching arm, Donaldson batted .294 with 89 hits as the leadoff hitter and center fielder for the 1920 Kansas City Monarchs. His five home runs that season tied Oscar Charleston for third most in the league. He batted .281 with 115 hits the next season, finishing seventh in runs with 67. He continued playing extra games with All Nations to make side money. The money became so good, Donaldson mainly played with semipro teams in Minnesota from 1924 to 1930.

He is credited with 224 games in center field but only 63 verified pitching appearances with a 23–29 record and 2.98 ERA (114 ERA+). The 1918 season is his only Negro League season with more than 100 innings pitched. Overall, he batted .280 with 335 hits across 12 documented Negro League seasons.

He was named the right fielder on Seamheads' All-1917 Team and the starting pitcher for the All-1918 Team. Donaldson was listed as a first-team pitcher in the 1952 *Pittsburgh Courier's* poll of greatest Black players—he is the only one of their five all-time-greatest pitchers to not make the Hall of Fame. In 1949, the Chicago White Sox hired Donaldson as the American League's first African American scout.

One newspaper report summarized his appeal: "One player always stands out in our memory—that of graceful polished and classy John Donaldson. He was the poetry and rhythm of baseball."[40]

Charles Earle

Earle was the ace pitcher for the 1909 Brooklyn Royal Giants, who were recognized as Black champions after a best-of-five series against the Cuban Stars. Earle outpitched Luis Padrón to win the first game, outdueled

José Méndez 2–1 in the second game and then closed out the series by defeating Padron again in the fourth game.

The next season he alternated between the mound and left field, going 2–2 with 3.75 ERA and batting .370. He is credited with 223 games in the outfield to go with 40 appearances on the mound. Overall at the plate, the speedy Florida native batted .294 with 291 hits. He batted .333 in limited action in Cuba.

Earle, who was sometimes called "Frank," was named the left fielder on Seamheads' All-1910 Team. Sportswriter Harry Daniels named Earle the left fielder on his 1909 All-American team, writing: "Earl (sic) of the Royals, is the best hitter in base ball; a sure fielder, going back or coming forward after a ball, and as fast as they come as far as speed is concerned, both in the field and on the bases."[41]

Isidro Fabré

Fabré was a five-foot-six righty pitcher who spent 11 seasons with the Cuban Stars East. He ranks third all-time with 18 seasons pitching in the Cuban League. He went 55–63 with a 4.03 ERA across 198 appearances while batting .244 with 337 hits. The Havana native played 252 games in the outfield during a career that lasted from 1918 to 1939. His best year on the mound was 1918–19 with Almendares in the Cuban League, when he went 9–9 with a 2.63 ERA and 17 complete games in 177⅔ innings. He led the Cuban League with 20 games pitched in 1923–24.

Playing for Almendares in the 1927–28 winter season, Fabré tied for third in the league in home runs, batted .250, and went 4–2 on the mound. He was named the left fielder on Seamheads' All-1918 Team. Fabré was inducted into the Cuban Baseball Hall of Fame in 1956.

Luther Farrell

Farrell showed flashes at the plate and on the mound during a 13-year career. He ended up batting .299 with 239 hits across 13 seasons. He appeared in 122 games in the outfield and made 11 pinch-hit appearances. He posted a career record of 52–62 with a 4.71 ERA from 157 pitching appearances in 966⅔ innings.

Farrell's best season was 1927 for the Atlantic City Bacharach Giants. His 18 wins, 22 complete games, 160 strikeouts (Phil Cockrell was second with 78) and 257⅔ innings all led the league. At the plate that year, Farrell posted a .309/.383/.511 mark with 55 hits and 36 RBI playing 21 games in the outfield to lead the team to the Eastern Colored League pennant. He pitched a seven-inning no-hitter in the fifth game of the Negro World Series and won another game, but the Giants lost the series to the Chicago American Giants.

The Giants also won the Eastern Colored League pennant in 1926, and Farrell hit a home run in Game One of the Negro World Series but again in a losing effort to the Chicago American Giants. Farrell was the ace of the 1928 Giants, going 9–7 with a 3.63 ERA in 124 innings while leading the team with a .395 average. He also batted .405 in 1928, and baseball historian John Holway credits him as the 1926 ECL batting champion with a .359 average.[42]

Farrell's offensive WAR total of 5.8 ranks second in Black baseball history among players identified primarily as a pitcher, according to Seamheads.

Wilmer "Red" Fields

Fields was an ace pitcher for the Homestead Grays' 1948 team, which won the last Negro World Series. That season he went 6–1 with a 3.21 ERA while also batting .260 from 19 games at third base. Named to the 1948 East All Stars, he pitched three scoreless relief innings in one of the East-West Games. His career record was 21–6 in 218 innings and his .778 winning percentage is second best in Negro League history. Overall, he batted .247 in Negro League action with 58 hits playing 43 games in the field.

Fields, who was a sturdy six-foot-two, started out his career with the Grays in 1940 and 1941 while also playing for the football and basketball teams at Virginia State College for Negroes. After serving in the U.S. Army for four years during World War II, he returned to the Grays in 1946. That was Fields' best year on the mound, when he went 8–1 with 2.63 ERA while batting .267.

Fields also played all over Latin America and Canada, winning seven MVP awards in various leagues. Playing four seasons for the Brantford Red Sox in Canada, Fields posted a 38–7 record with a .392 batting average, winning three MVP awards.[43] He played four seasons in the Puerto Rico Baseball League, winning MVP honors in 1948–49 after going 10–4 on the mound and batting .330 with 11 home runs.

Playing mainly in right field, Fields garnered MVP honors in the 1951–52 Venezuelan Professional Baseball League after leading the league in average (.357), hits (74), and RBI (48) and helping Cerveceria win the pennant. Fields, who rejected multiple overtures from major-league teams between 1948 and 1952 because he was content with his life in Black baseball, kept playing until 1958. He was inducted into the Caribbean Baseball Hall of Fame in 2001.

Andrew "Rube" Foster

Foster went into the Hall of Fame for his visionary leadership as the founder of the Negro National League, as he wore multiple hats as owner, manager, and league commissioner in addition to organizing activities that solidified Black baseball's future.

He was also a star pitcher in Black baseball's Deadball Era, posting a 69–32 record in a career that spanned 1902–17. His .683 winning percentage ranks 14th in Negro League history while his 2.32 ERA ranks 10th. Foster is credited with six no-hitters in games where one or both teams were minor league or semipro.

In 1903, Foster won four of the five games as the Cuban X-Giants won the Colored World Championship over the Philadelphia Giants. The next year, he joined Philadelphia and helped them win the rematch by striking out 18 to win the first game and tossing a two-hitter to win the decisive third game while batting .445 in the Colored World Championship series. Philadelphia swept the 1905 championship as Foster won the second game, then he went 3–0 as the Giants swept again in 1906—Foster's fourth straight title.

"Andrew Foster deserves every word of praise ever said of him. He is undoubtedly among the very best pitchers that America affords," proclaimed the *Indianapolis Freeman*.[44]

He was a trailblazer in another way by becoming one of the first Negro League players to compete in Cuba in 1903. He led the Cuban Winter League in 1905–06 with 15 complete games. In 1907, he led the Cuban League with 10 wins. Overall, Foster went 17–12 with 24 complete games pitching four seasons in Cuba.

Sol White, his manager on the Philadelphia Giants, listed Foster among the many colored players he believed to be of major-league caliber. In an essay in Sol White's 1907 book, *History of Colored Base Ball*, Foster wrote: "The three great principles of pitching are good control, when to pitch certain balls, and where to pitch them."[45]

Foster's teams were disciplined and fundamentally sound, and all his players followed his dictates to act like gentlemen on and off the field. He first became a player-manager for the 1907 Chicago Leland Giants. Foster's 1910 Leland Giants team is considered one of the greatest in baseball history, finishing with a record of 123–6 and unable to find a team to challenge them for the unofficial colored championship. Foster went

18-2-1 that season. His 1912 Chicago American Giants team went 112–20, then won the California Winter League championship for an encore. He managed and pitched the Chicago American Giants to a 126–16 record in 1914 and a sweep of the Brooklyn Royal Giants for the Colored World Championship.

Foster batted a respectable .277 with 170 hits while playing 29 games at first base, 26 games in the outfield, and making five pinch-hit appearances. The 1906 season with the Philadelphia Giants is the only documented year he played 10-plus games in the field and on the mound. He batted .319 playing eight games in right field and five games at first base, and he led the Giants with 72 innings pitched and 10 appearances while recording a 2.00 ERA.

Honus Wagner judged Foster to be "one of the greatest pitchers of all time. He was the smartest pitcher I have ever seen in all my years of baseball."[46]

Foster's trailblazing achievements as a founder, organizer, and manager in the Negro Leagues overshadow his Hall of Fame worthy achievements as a pitcher, which in turn vastly outshine what he accomplished as a two-way player. The larger-than-life figure who many called "The Father of Black Baseball," spent the last years of his life in an insane asylum, unable to unleash his baseball tactical skills on another unlucky opponent.

Manuel "Cocaína" Garcia

Garcia was a good-hitting pitcher who dominated batters in the Latin leagues with a lightning-fast fastball and a sharp-dropping curve. His nickname derived from his ability to lull batters to sleep as if he drugged them.[47] He posted a record of 73–52 and 3.93 ERA with a .282 average and 250 hits in the Cuban and Mexican leagues, according to Seamheads. He led the 1942–43 Cuban League in wins (10) and winning percentage (.769) while batting .340 that season. He also went 10–3 in 1946–47.

Garcia is credited with 182 games in the outfield plus 13 games as a pinch hitter in addition to 210 pitching appearances. With 5.6 WAR, he was named the center fielder on Seamheads' All-1945 Team.

As a 21-year-old rookie in 1927, the Cuban-born Garcia went 3–6 with a 4.96 ERA for the Cuban Stars West. Playing 25 games in the outfield that season, he led the team with a .342 average. The short and stocky Cocaína went 96–68 with a 3.83 ERA playing eight seasons in the Mexican League and chipped in a .281/.339/.374 mark at the plate.[48]

Playing for Habana during the 1943–44 Cuban Winter League, Garcia batted .431 and won 12 games in a row including a no-hitter on

December 11, 1943. He ended up pitching 17 seasons in Cuba, winning 85 games in 222 appearances with 93 complete games.[49] Garcia was elected to the Cuban Baseball Hall of Fame (in exile in Miami) in 1969.

Bill Gatewood

Gatewood bounced around to 14 teams over an 18-year pitching career between 1906 and 1927. Nicknamed "Big Bill" because he was six-foot-seven, Gatewood went 61–60 with a 3.64 ERA in Negro League action. He relied on a spitball, an emery ball, and knowing when to brush back the batter, and he is credited with teaching Satchel Paige his famous hesitation pitch.[50]

At the plate, he averaged .266 with 149 hits while appearing occasionally at first base and right field. He was used to pinch-hit nine times. His best seasons were 1920, when he batted .273 and went 15–6 with a 2.66 ERA in 172⅔ combined innings for the Detroit Stars and St. Louis Giants; and 1916, when he went 6–2 with a 1.75 ERA (179 ERA+) in 77 innings and batted .300 for the St. Louis Giants.

Pitching for the Detroit Stars in Mack Park, Gatewood threw the first no-hitter in the Negro National League against the Cincinnati Cuban Stars on June 6, 1921. He had previously tossed a no-hitter for the St. Louis Giants on May 13, 1916, against the Cuban Stars.

Willie "Three Finger" Gisentaner

Gisentaner had an index finger that was cut off below the joint on his left pitching hand, which meant he could only throw his wicked curveball with three fingers—just like Hall of Famer Mordecai "Three Finger" Brown. Gisentaner went 44–55 with a 5.00 ERA (95 ERA+), while batting .255 with 178 hits playing 91 games in the outfield. The lefty swinger was used as a pinch hitter 20 times.

Playing for the New York Lincoln Giants in 1926, Gisentaner had his only season with 10-plus documented games as a pitcher and position player—he played 10 games in the outfield and made 13 pitching appearances. That year he batted .296 and went 5–4 with a 2.87 ERA in 84⅔ innings. His best year at the plate was 1922, when he averaged .347 for the Kansas City Monarchs. On June 7, 1925, Gisentaner completed and won both games of a doubleheader for the Harrisburg Giants.[51]

The well-traveled Alabama native played for 16 Negro League teams in 16 seasons. His manager on the Homestead Grays, Cum Posey, praised Gisentaner as the smartest pitcher in the Negro National League.[52]

Carl "Butch" Glass

Glass was a curveball pitcher who went 46–52 with a 3.65 ERA and 56 complete games in a career that spanned 1923–30. He batted .238 with 140 hits. In addition to 143 games as a pitcher, Glass played 55 games in the outfield and 21 games in the infield. The lefty was used as a pinch hitter 21 times.

His best season was 1928, when he went 12–10 as player-manager for the last-place Memphis Red Sox with a 2.96 ERA (6th in NNL) and 15 complete games (2nd in NNL) in a league-leading 200⅔ innings. His only seasons with 10-plus games as both a pitcher and position player were 1924 and 1925. In 1924, Glass went 3–6 with a 2.61 ERA in 17 pitching appearances while batting .216. The next year he batted .238 while going 8–7 with a 4.31 ERA in 20 mound appearances.

Bob "Schoolboy" Griffith

Griffith was a spitball pitcher who pitched in the East-West All-Star game in 1935, 1948, and 1949, representing three different teams. He finished with a career record of 33–39 in Negro League action with a 4.62 ERA. He batted .260 with 75 hits playing 17 games in the outfield. In his last season, 1949, Griffith posted a 9–3 mark for the Philadelphia Stars and batted .340. He started and won that year's East-West All-Star Game. He also pitched six innings as the winning pitcher in the North-South All-Star Game in 1938.

Griffith was selected to be part of an elite team of Negro National League stars who competed in the 1936 *Denver Post* tournament. He pitched a three-hitter and a five-hitter to win two of the games, striking out 16 batters in one game as the NNL coasted to the championship.

Schoolboy shone in the California Winter League, where he went 20–2 and recorded 228 strikeouts in 214 innings. He ranks second all-time in CWL winning percentage and fifth in strikeouts.[53] Playing for Nuevo Laredo in the Mexican League in 1940, he won seven games and batted .321. He went 16–11 with 18 complete games pitching two seasons in Cuba. Overall, his record in Latin leagues was 42–30.

Lewis Hampton

Hampton was primarily a pitcher during his seven seasons with six teams, but he demonstrated power at the plate. He posted a 51–43 record and 3.95 ERA in 127 mound appearances. His best year and most two-way action came in 1922, when he went 12–6 with a league-leading 2.49 ERA (181 ERA+) for the third-place Indianapolis ABCs. That year he batted .348 and slugged .596 while playing 20 games in the outfield. He played 49 career games in the field and 10 as a pinch hitter. In 557 plate appearances, Hampton batted .303 with 154 hits, 23 home runs, and 105 RBI.

Hampton was named the All-1922 Team starting pitcher by Seamheads. His 4.0 offensive WAR for his career is tied with Bill Byrd for fourth best in Black baseball history for a player identified primarily as a pitcher. He added 7.2 WAR from pitching.

Dave Hoskins

Hoskins made it to the major leagues at age 35, pitching in 40 games for the Cleveland Indians in 1953–54. He went 9–3 with a 3.99 ERA in 112⅔ innings in 1953, making seven starts and 19 relief appearances. The next year he posted a 3.04 ERA for the Indians in 14 mound appearances. Hoskins batted .227 and collected 15 hits including one home run for the Indians. Hoskins had suffered through a rough 1952 season, facing racial hatred after becoming the first Black player in the Double-A Texas League. He persevered and made the All-Star team after batting .328 and going 22–10 with a 2.12 ERA in 280 innings.

Nicknamed "Wahoo," the Mississippi native began his career with five seasons in the Negro Leagues, batting .290 with 161 hits (101 OPS+). With the Homestead Grays in 1944, he posted a 5–2 record with 3.75 ERA, but they couldn't keep his lefty bat out of the lineup and he played 47 games in the outfield. He batted .324 that season with 67 hits in 207 at-bats, driving in 46 runs.

Hoskins batted .286 to help the Grays win the 1944 Negro World Series over the Birmingham Black Barons. The Grays lost to the Cleveland Buckeyes in the 1945 Negro World Series, as Hoskins contributed a .267 mark in a losing effort.

His career mark in 21 Negro League appearances on the mound was 7–7 with a 4.88 ERA (86 ERA+). Overall, Hoskins played 116 games in right field, 21 games in left field, and five games in other positions.

Jesse "Mountain" Hubbard

Hubbard bounced back and forth between pitching and batting throughout his 16-year career. His 10–3 record with 2.87 ERA helped lead the Atlantic City Bacharach Giants to the 1927 Eastern Colored League pennant, although he was ineffective in the Negro World Series (7.80 ERA in three starts). That season he also batted .261 with 72 hits and eight homers in 318 plate appearances. His only major two-way action came in 1927, when he pitched in 17 games and played 56 games in the outfield. With 3.9 WAR that season, Seamheads ranks him as the right fielder on the All-1927 Team.

Hubbard was also part of the 1919 rotation of the Brooklyn Royal Giants that included Dick Redding and Smokey Joe Williams. He pitched a no-hitter that season on July 6 against the semipro Logan Squares. He finished with a 37–50 record and 4.68 ERA while batting .283 with 262 hits. Overall, he played 181 games in the field and pitched in 114 contests.

Hubbard saw more success playing three seasons in the California Winter League (CWL). In the 1927–28 season, he led the league with a .442 average and slugged .558. His .390 average is fourth best in CWL history.[54]

Wade Johnston

Johnston, an Ohio native, played 13 seasons as a left-handed outfielder. The diminutive Johnston—listed at five-foot-seven and 142 pounds—appeared in 19 games on the mound, with a 5–10 record and 4.67 ERA (105 ERA+). He played 701 games in the outfield. His only real two-way season was 1922, when he played 47 games in the outfield and batted .246 with a weak 64 OPS+. On the mound for the Cleveland Tate Stars that year, Johnston posted a 3–6 record in 71⅓ innings across 12 appearances with a 4.16 ERA.

Johnston batted an even .300 for his career with 844 hits and .369 OBP. He had three terrific years at the plate: 1923, when he batted .336 with 91 hits and 63 runs; 1927, when he batted .329 with a career-high 110 hits and 57 RBI; and 1929, when he batted a career-high .357 with 89 hits, 16 homers, and 64 RBI. Johnston posted six seasons with an average over .300. He led the Negro National League with 10 triples in 1930. For his career he hit 44 home runs and scored 519 runs.

Harry Kenyon

Kenyon joins Bullet Rogan as the only Negro League players with multiple seasons with at least 10 games pitched and more than 200 plate appearances—Kenyon did it in 1921 and 1925. In 1921 playing for C.I. Taylor's Indianapolis ABCs, Kenyon went 7–11 (23 games pitched) with a 4.02

ERA in 168 innings and 13 complete games. That year he typically hit third in the lineup and batted .286 with .361 OBP and career-high 85 hits in 342 plate appearances, playing 62 games in the outfield. Then in 1925, he averaged .283 with 60 hits in 224 plate appearances while going 8-6 in 22 pitching appearances with a high 6.41 ERA across 112⅓ innings for the Detroit Stars.

Kenyon's 1926 season with the Detroit Stars was another two-way showcase. That year saw him bat .308 playing 38 games in the field and go 5-6 with a 5.85 ERA in 14 pitching appearances. He won 31 total games across 11 seasons with a 4.95 ERA and batted .276 with 361 hits playing the most games in left field—125. Kenyon was an above-average fielder and a good contact hitter but lacked a put-away pitch.

Holsey "Script" Lee

Lee was a submarine pitcher who also excelled at bunting. He finished with a 42-42 record and 4.57 ERA in 127 games pitched across 12 Negro League seasons. His best year pitching was 1926, when he joined Nip Winters, Phil Cockrell, and Red Ryan to form a fearsome rotation for the first-place Hilldale Club. That year Lee went 8-4 with a 3.56 ERA in 126⅓ innings and batted .276.

Lee played a pivotal role for Hilldale in the 1924 Negro World Series against the Kansas City Monarchs. He pitched 10 relief innings in the third game that ended in a tie. He came out of the bullpen in the first inning of Game Six and pitched well but ultimately surrendered the decisive run in the eighth inning. Getting the start in the Game 10 finale, Lee matched José Méndez with seven shutout innings before oddly deciding to switch to an overhand delivery in the eighth inning—he quickly gave up five runs and the Monarchs took the title. Lee pitched to a 3.09 ERA in 23⅓ innings in the series.

Script was the ace of the 1931 Baltimore Black Sox team, going 6-7 with a 3.28 ERA (118 ERA+). Overall, Lee batted .216 with 86 hits and 23 sacrifice hits. He played 30 games in the outfield and eight games in the infield. After retiring, Lee became an umpire and even worked the 1942 Negro World Series.

Bill Lindsay

Lindsay was a promising right-handed spitball pitcher and outfielder with a blazing fastball who died on September 1, 1914, while the Chicago

American Giants were getting ready to start a championship series against the Brooklyn Royal Giants—he was just 23 years old. His teammates went on to win the World Series in a sweep. Lindsay had spent nine days in the hospital with urinary tract problems and ultimately succumbed to uremia that contributed to uremic coma and sepsis, according to his death certificate filed by Cook County in Illinois.

"I have lost a great ball player, a fine gentleman and a noble friend," commented Rube Foster, his manager on the Giants.[55]

Nicknamed "The Kansas Cyclone," Lindsay posted a 4–0 record that 1914 season with 1.09 ERA and batted .476 in limited at-bats. He finished his short six-year career with a 30–11 record and 2.28 ERA (130 ERA+). In 1913, he played 23 games in the outfield, batting .262 with 32 hits, and went 10–6 pitching in 18 games with a 3.24 ERA in 133⅓ innings. He was named the center fielder on the All-1913 Team by Seamheads.

Verdell "Lefty" Mathis

Mathis was a very good center fielder, a skill that was overshadowed by his stellar pitching. A four-time All-Star selection, Mathis started the 1944 All-Star game for the West on the mound and contributed a single. He started the 1945 East-West Game and pitched three shutout innings and helped his cause with two hits.

He went 30–28 for his career with a 3.73 ERA, leading the Negro American League with seven wins in 1944 and six complete games in 1942. He batted a solid .269 with 104 hits playing across the outfield and 11 games at first base. Mathis was considered one of the best southpaw hurlers in the Negro Leagues in the 1940s, relying on an excellent curveball to go with a deceptive fastball, changeup, and screwball. Although he played for other teams, Lefty played for the Memphis Red Sox in each of his nine seasons. Known for his great pickoff move, he managed to nab Jackie Robinson multiple times.

His only season with 10-plus games on the mound and in the field was 1943, when he pitched 10 times and played nine games in the outfield and three games at first base. That year Mathis went 6–4 with a 3.46 ERA but batted just .208. Mathis generated 1.3 career WAR from fielding, according to Seamheads—that's the highest total for a player identified as a pitcher in Black baseball history.

Mathis pitched 13 games for Tampico in the Mexican League in 1941, recording a 3.98 ERA in 74⅔ innings. He joined other Negro League stars that barnstormed in Venezuela in the 1945 offseason. In addition to Mathis, Satchel Paige, Roy Campanella, and Buck Leonard, Jackie

Robinson was included so these veterans could help prepare Jackie for his eventual move into the major leagues.[56]

Dan McClellan

McClellan was a standout left-handed pitcher in Black baseball before the Negro National League formed. He joined the rotation for powerful Cuban X-Giants teams from 1900 to 1904 and played the outfield when he was not pitching. McClellan was praised in the press as "the best colored pitcher in the country."[57]

McClellan, who was often called Danny, relied on a masterful curveball, deceptive speed, and wily pitching instincts. He is credited with pitching the first perfect game in Black baseball on June 17, 1903, although it happened against a semipro team. He also pitched both ends of a doubleheader during the 1903 Colored World Championship—pitching a two-hitter to win the opener—to help the Cuban X-Giants defeat the Philadelphia Giants.[58]

Seamheads documents his pitching record as 34–27 with a 2.91 ERA in 71 appearances, with many other games not counted because they were against inferior competition. SABR historian Phil Williams estimates McClellan's win total to be around 300,[59] which would normally ensure induction into the Hall of Fame.

McClellan's overall record in 1905 was verified by Negro Leagues historian Phil Dixon to be 32–7 in 345 innings pitched (with just one home run allowed) as the Philadelphia Giants rolled to a 128–23–3 record against all competition and repeated as Eastern champs.[60] McClellan would help lead the team to the Eastern championship in 1906, 1907, and 1909 and his verified record for 1907 was 10–1. In 1906, he played 24 games in the outfield and batted .282 for the first-place Philadelphia Giants, while going 6–1 with a 1.78 ERA (175 ERA+) in 65⅔ innings pitched, according to Seamheads. A more complete accounting shows him with a 15–7 mark that year.

For his career, he batted .266 with 195 hits playing 117 games in the outfield and 20 games at first base. "At bat, McClellan was known to be the best left-handed hitting pitcher in baseball," Dixon writes.[61] He batted .348 while often batting cleanup for the Giants in 1909. He played outfield and pitched for Habana in the 1906–07 Cuban Winter League. He was also part of the first American all–Black team to play baseball in Cuba when his Cuban X-Giants team went 2–9 against Cuba's best players in 1903.

McClellan was listed as a first-team coach and a fourth-team pitcher in the 1952 *Pittsburgh Courier's* poll of greatest Black players, and he was named to sportswriter Harry Daniels 1909 All-American Team.[62]

Terris McDuffie

McDuffie was a three-time Negro League All-Star as a righty pitcher who went on to success in five Latin leagues and the California Winter League. His overall pitching record in all leagues is believed to be 172–143 with 45 wins coming in the Negro Leagues. Seamheads shows him with a 55–54 record and 3.94 ERA across 153 games. Pitching eight seasons in the Cuban League, he went 37–43 with 38 complete games in 135 appearances.

McDuffie batted .246 with 132 hits playing in the outfield. He combined with two other pitchers to throw a no-hitter for the Homestead Grays in 1941.

McDuffie pitched six innings with no earned runs to outduel Satchel Paige in the 1944 North-South All-Star Game. He also started and won two games in the 1937 All-Star series between the Negro National League and Negro American Leagues, then pitched a complete game win in the 1938 series. His 15.7 pitching WAR was supplemented by 1.5 offensive WAR. McDuffie was named the starting pitcher on Seamheads' All-1937 Team.

Henry McHenry

McHenry was a two-time All-Star pitcher who starred as a two-way player in the Mexican League. He led the Negro National League in wins in 1939 and 1946, in strikeouts in 1940, in complete games in 1939 and 1941, in shutouts in 1930, and in games pitched in 1939, 1941 and 1946. He started the 1940 East-West All-Star game and pitched three shutout innings to get the win. McHenry appeared in the 1941 East-West All-Star game in relief, pitching two scoreless innings.

McHenry posted 27.3 career WAR with a 125–103 record and 4.20 ERA (105 ERA+). His Negro League record was 73–58 with a 4.02 ERA, winning 54 games with the Philadelphia Stars. Overall, McHenry batted .254 with 317 hits. In 1942, his combined marks in the Negro and Mexican Leagues were .355 with 92 hits including 16 home runs. He went 8–7 pitching three seasons in the Cuban League.

He won 17 games pitching in the Mexican League in 1943. Overall, he made 341 mound appearances and played 101 games in the outfield, 22 at first base, one at catcher and 41 as a pinch hitter. He was nicknamed "Cream" due to his light skin complexion. McHenry compiled 24.2 pitching WAR and 3.8 offensive WAR. He was named Seamheads' starting pitcher for the All-1938 Team and top right fielder for the All-1942 Team.

Hurley McNair

McNair was an underrated outfielder and southpaw pitcher who had a distinguished 27-year career. He once got five hits in a game while playing for the Kansas City Monarchs. When McNair was in his prime in his 20s, much of his playing took place with independent teams so those stats are not included in career totals. Still, Black baseball historian Phil Dixon believed McNair deserved to be in the Hall of Fame and Bill James ranked him as the 10th-best left fielder in the Negro Leagues.[63]

His batting was clutch, especially with two strikes. "Mac could have taken two strikes against Jesus Christ and base hit the next pitch," gushed teammate George Giles.[64]

Joining the Kansas City Monarchs in 1920 at age 31, McNair proceeded to bat .320, .345, .376, .324, .317, and .327 for the Monarchs over the next six seasons. He led the Negro National League with a .466 OBP and 50 walks in 1922, a year in which he had a .376/.464/.554 slash line and 1.018 OPS. He posted a career average of .321 (15th all-time in Negro League history) with 1,038 hits, 77 triples, 49 homers, and 134 stolen bases in 858 Negro League games. Another good season came in 1921, when he batted .345 with 144 hits, 11 triples, 12 homers, and 84 RBI.

McNair played great defense in the outfield and was fast on the bases, but he didn't pitch enough to be considered a true two-way player. In 23 appearances on the mound, his record was 7–4 with a 3.80 ERA (104 ERA+) in 120⅔ innings. He did defeat Rube Foster in a 10-inning duel in 1911.[65]

He won a Negro World Series title with the Kansas City Monarchs in 1924 but batted just .143 in the series. He saved Game Three by throwing out Judy Johnson at home in extra innings. McNair batted .322 in 79 games in the California Winter League, winning the championship all four seasons. McNair, who continued playing until the age of 48, compiled 29.3 offensive WAR and 0.9 pitching WAR. He was named the left fielder on the All-1920, All-1922, and All-1923 Teams, and the right fielder on the All-1924 Team by Seamheads.

José Méndez

Méndez stood out from his peers with a sharp-breaking curve and deceptive fastball. He received votes as a pitcher in the *Pittsburgh Courier's* 1952 poll of greatest Black players. Inducted into the Hall of Fame in 2006, Méndez's career WAR of 47.9 (including 2.1 offensive WAR) ranks 11th all-time in Negro League history and is third best among members of the Cuban Baseball Hall of Fame.

Chapter 8. The Negro Leagues

Known as "El Diamante Negro (The Black Diamond)" and described as Cuba's "Black Mathewson," Méndez had a legendary career in his native country and was inducted into the Cuban Baseball Hall of Fame in the initial class of 1939. He led the Cuban League in winning percentage four times, and in wins, complete games, and games pitched twice. He was named the Cuban pitching champion five times: 1908, 1909, 1910, 1911, and 1914.

Méndez pitched a 10-inning no-hitter for the Cuban Stars on July 24, 1909, against an inferior opponent, Rogers Park. He also teamed up with Bullet Rogan to pitch a no-hitter for the Kansas City Monarchs on August 5, 1923. Méndez started the game and threw a perfect five innings, while Rogan followed and allowed one base runner in his four innings.

The five-foot-ten Méndez battled arm injuries that curtailed his pitching production off and on throughout the 1910s, so he played more in the field. He played shortstop and outfield while joining Sam Crawford and John Donaldson in the 1919 rotation for the Detroit Stars—he had previously joined Donaldson in the rotation for J.L. Wilkinson's traveling All Nations team. Then in 1920, he pitched 47 innings with a 2.87 ERA as player-manager for the Monarchs, while also playing 58 games in the field.

His best year at the plate was 1921, when he batted .275 with a career-high 55 hits for the Monarchs. That season he played 41 games in the infield and 15 games in the outfield but pitched just 24⅓ innings. Méndez was dominant on the mound in 1923 for the pennant-winning Monarchs, going 12–4 with 3.18 ERA—joining an all-time-great rotation that included Bullet Rogan, Bill Drake, Rube Curry, and William Bell—while batting .239 and playing 16 games in the field.

In 1924, Méndez went 2–0 with a 1.42 ERA to lead the Monarchs to the title in the inaugural Colored World Series against Hilldale. He tossed a three-hit shutout to win the decisive 10th game against Script Lee, despite a doctor's warning he risked permanent injury if he kept pitching.

He went 9–0 in his first Cuban League season to lead Almendares to the 1908 pennant. Later that year he faced off against the Cincinnati Reds, who were in Cuba to tour, and pitched 25 consecutive scoreless innings against them with 24 strikeouts in three games. He then extended his scoreless streak to 45 innings.[66]

In the 1908–09 season, Méndez led the Cuban League in wins (15), winning percentage (.714), games (28), shutouts (five), and complete games (18). For the shortened 1910 Cuban season, he posted another undefeated mark at 7–0. For the 1910–1911 season, he accounted for half of Almendares' victories and led the Cuban League in wins (11), winning percentage (.846), games (18), complete games (12), and shutouts (four). When the Philadelphia A's championship club came to Cuba in November 1910, Méndez twice defeated future Hall of Famer Eddie Plank.[67]

Pitching for Almendares, Méndez went 9–0 in his 1907–08 debut and later went 10–0 in 1913–14. His 7.6 pitching WAR in the 1908–09 and 1910–11 seasons is tied for the seventh best in Black baseball by a pitcher.

Philadelphia Athletics catcher Ira Thomas, who faced Méndez during a 1911 tour, told *Baseball Magazine*, "More than one big leaguer from the states has faced him and left the plate with a wholesome respect for the great Cuban star. It is not alone my opinion but the opinion of many others who have seen Méndez pitch that he ranks with the best in the game."[68]

Overall, he went 76–28 in 14 seasons in Cuba and is the all-time leader with a .731 winning percentage.[69] He played on the 1923–24 Santa Clara team that is considered by some experts as the best in Cuban League history. The championship team was so stacked with pitchers like Dave Brown, Bill Holland, and Rube Curry that Méndez pitched out of the bullpen, with a 4–1 record and 3.64 ERA in 47 innings.

Pitching 204 innings in 24 games against major leaguers, Méndez proved he could rise up to the challenge—he recorded a 1.85 ERA. MLB.com credits Méndez with a lifetime average of .232 with 270 hits and a 59–20 record with a 2.82 ERA. Méndez is ranked as the starting pitcher on Seamheads' All-1911 Team with 4.2 WAR, as well as the right fielder on the All-1912 Team with 2.5 WAR that season.

Eddie Miller

Miller won a Negro World Series championship in 1927 with a Chicago American Giants team that featured Steel Arm Davis, Hall of Famer Bill Foster, and Dave Malarcher as player-manager.

Miller went 29–28 with a 3.97 ERA (95 ERA+) as a righty hurler playing six of his eight seasons for the Chicago American Giants. He batted just .220 with 138 hits playing 139 games in the infield and 11 games in the outfield, along with 91 pitching appearances. His best season pitching was 1924, when he went 10–2 with a 2.92 ERA in 114 innings for the Giants. Nicknamed "Buck," Miller got 250 plate appearances with the Giants in his last season, 1930, batting .226 with 48 hits.

George Mitchell

Mitchell was primarily a right-handed pitcher during a 13-year career from 1924 to 1941. He batted .252 with 137 hits playing 45 games at first and 22 games in the outfield, plus appearing 40 times as a pinch hitter. His best year at the plate was 1931, when he averaged .303 in 130 plate appearances. Mitchell, who was nicknamed "Mountain Drop" and "Toad," was a player-manager in his last three seasons. He was named the starting first baseman on the All-1931 Team by Seamheads, with 2.8 WAR that season.

Mitchell went 48–45 with a 4.26 ERA in 134 games pitched. His best season on the mound was 1928, when he went 13–8 with a 3.57 ERA in 153⅔ innings as ace for a Detroit Stars team featuring Cristobal Torriente, Ted Radcliffe, and Turkey Stearnes. His batterymate on the 1924 St. Louis Stars was his twin brother Robert, who batted .290 that season.

José Muñoz

Muñoz was considered one of the best pitchers in Cuba during his career and was elected to the Cuban Baseball Hall of Fame in 1940. He ranks third in complete games (117) and sixth in wins (82) in Cuban Winter League (CWL) history. He went 8–1 in 1906 and led the Cuban League with 10 wins in 1905, and with 13 wins and five shutouts in 1908.

Muñoz played 13 seasons for Almendares in the Cuban League and his time in the Negro Leagues was spent with Cuban-focused teams in the Western Independent and International League like the All Cubans, Cuban Stars, Cuban X-Giants, and the Stars of Cuba. He went 9–5 with a 1.62 ERA for Almendares in 1901, leading the CWL with 15 complete games and 82 strikeouts that year. In the 1906 CWL, he completed all nine games he pitched and went 8–1 with a 0.67 ERA.

Seamheads shows him with an overall 108–89 record and his 1.89 career ERA is second best in Black baseball history, while he ranks sixth in complete games (172), 11th in shutouts (17), and eighth in innings pitched (1,838⅔).

When not pitching, he played the outfield and often batted in the top half of the lineup. He batted just .183 overall with 184 hits in 1,154 plate appearances, but he did average .259 in Negro League action. He batted .310 for the 1909 Cuban Stars, when he played 12 games in the field and pitched to a 6–3 record and 2.30 ERA in 12 mound appearances across 94 innings.

Luis Padrón

Padrón is another member of the Cuban Baseball Hall of Fame (class of 1943) who played just four seasons in the Negro Leagues but spent 17 seasons in Latin leagues and seven seasons in the minors. He is frequently confused with another Cuban Hall of Famer, Juan Padrón, who was a more accomplished pitcher but less of a two-way player.

Luis Padrón primarily played right field and third base but also pitched 154 games. His overall pitching record is 80–47 in all leagues including 41–23 with a 2.08 ERA in Latin leagues. He batted .270 with 850 hits and 189 stolen bases in his Blackball career. His .463 batting average for Habana in 1902 is the highest-ever in the Cuban Leagues—he also led the league in homers and triples that season.[70]

Padrón batted a league-best .320 for Habana in 1900, while becoming the first player to lead the Cuban League in both pitching victories (13) and hits (31). Including his 1–2 mark in the Cuban League playoffs, he went 13–6 that season with a 1.36 ERA and 20 complete games. He also led the Cuban League in home runs in 1908.

"El Mulo" led the 1909 Cubans Stars of Havana with a .344 average while playing 21 games in the field; on the mound that year he posted a 3.21 ERA in 42 innings. Padrón batted .333 playing 19 games in the field for the Long Branch Cubans in 1915, while recording a 3.00 ERA in 33 innings.

Hank Aaron and his teammates Horace Garner and Felix Mantilla, along with Al Israel and Buddy Reedy of Savannah, are credited with integrating the South Atlantic League in 1953.[71] Actually, they merely succeeded in re-integrating the Sally League, a notorious white league in the Deep South. It was Padrón who first integrated the South Atlantic League playing for the Jacksonville Jays in 1906. He batted .286 with 40 hits that season playing 36 games in the outfield. He later got a tryout with the Chicago White Sox in 1909, but he did not get signed.

Tom Parker

Parker was an outfielder and right-handed pitcher who played 11 seasons between 1929 and 1949. He spent 1935–39 with the Homestead Grays and then returned to win the Negro World Series with the team in 1948. Overall, Parker went 34–33 with a 5.45 ERA and batted .284 with 213 hits while playing frequently in the outfield.

Nicknamed "Big Train" and "Country," Parker continued playing into his 40s in minor and independent leagues. He batted .405 for the Grays in 1937 while going 7–1 on the mound despite a 5.55 ERA—the Grays team that year won almost as many games as the bottom-three teams combined. Parker started and won the ninth game of the 1937 series between the Negro National League and Negro American League.

Roy "Red" Parnell

Parnell was a left fielder and two-time All-Star from Austin, Texas, who battled a drinking problem during a 13-year career that lasted from 1927 to 1943. As a 23-year-old rookie with the Birmingham Black Barons, he won the Negro National League batting title in 1927 with a .422 average. That year he also led the league in hits (141), OBP (.464), and OPS+ (208), and he slugged .653 with 1.117 OPS. Parnell batted over .300 eight times and collected 742 hits with 43 homers.

He pitched in just 12 verified games since all but one of the years he played in the Negro Southern League are not considered major league. As a result, his record as a two-way player is incomplete. In 1932, he went 5–1 with a league-leading 0.83 ERA (421 ERA+) in 54 innings for the Monroe Monarchs. At the plate that year, he batted .350 and led the Negro Southern League in doubles (12), triples (11), RBI (50), and slugging (.556). He posted 5.3 WAR that season and was named the center fielder for Seamheads' All-1932 Team.

Roy Partlow

Partlow was a southpaw hurler who had five good years with the Homestead Grays, 1938–43, then four largely successful seasons with the Philadelphia Stars. Partlow is credited with a verified record of 38–24 with 3.13 ERA (134 ERA+) while batting .254. Pitching for the Grays in 1939, he led the league with a 1.74 ERA and was the losing pitcher in the first East-West All-Star Game that year.

"Silent Roy" went 6–2 with a league-leading 1.69 ERA for the Grays in 1942, pitching a seven-inning no-hitter against the Chicago American Giants on August 30. He pitched in two games in the 1942 Colored World Series in a losing effort for the Grays. Partlow engaged in a pitchers' duel with Johnny Markham of the Birmingham Black Barons in the seventh game of the 1943 Negro World Series. The two pitchers matched zeroes until Partlow surrendered a run with two outs in the bottom of the 11th inning—the Grays clinched the title two days later.

Pitching as the Philadelphia Stars' 1945 ace, Partlow went 8–4 with 2.47 ERA in 113 innings. It was his best two-way season, as he played 12 games in the field and batted .279.

Known for his speed on the bases, Partlow had spotty success pitching in Cuba, Mexico, and Puerto Rico. He went 7–4 with 10 complete games in 13 appearances in the 1939–40 Cuban League.

The Brooklyn Dodgers selected Partlow to be Jackie Robinson's roommate with the Montreal Royals in 1946, a curious choice considering Partlow was known to be temperamental and had battled a problem with alcohol throughout his career. It was not a pairing that lasted long, and Partlow finished out his career playing with the Stars through 1948.

Eustaquio Pedroso

Pedroso was a two-way Cuban star who played mainly in the Deadball Era from 1907 to 1927. Nicknamed "Bombin," he played all nine positions around the diamond but stood out the most with his pitching. One of the highlights of his career was pitching an 11-inning no-hitter for Almendares against Bill Lelivelt and the Detroit Tigers in the 1909 Cuban-American Series.

His career record was 123–122 with 192 complete games and a 3.42 ERA, but he was 66–49 with a 2.79 ERA in Latin leagues. He was 7–10 with a 2.51 ERA in 143⅓ innings versus major leaguers, generally matching up favorably with his above-average fastball and sharp control. Pedroso was a strong batter, averaging .264 with 646 hits and 355 RBI. He played 247 games at first base, 219 games in the outfield, 130 games at other infield spots, and even six games at catcher.

Some seasons Pedroso had mixed success with his two-way play. In 1915 with the Cuban Stars of Havana, he batted just .218 while playing 40 outfield games and even catching a game. However, he starred on the mound that year with a 9–7 record, 3.31 ERA and 13 complete games in 138⅔ innings. Playing on the 1922 Cuban Stars West, Pedroso pitched to a 6.75 ERA in 113⅔ innings, but he batted .315 with 67 hits while playing 42 games at first base and six games in left field.

Playing for Almendares in the 1913–14 Cuban Winter League, he batted .345 and went 11–6 with a 1.74 ERA and 13 complete games in 17 starts. In 1915–16, he batted a league-best .413 for Almendares playing 15 games in the outfield, while 16 pitching appearances produced a 9–2 record with a 2.50 ERA. He led the Cuban League in complete games and games pitched three times, and in pitching wins twice. His 79 complete games rank seventh in Cuban Winter League history.

Pedroso's career WAR of 42.5 (which includes 34.6 WAR from pitching and 14.6 offensive WAR) ranks 16th in Black baseball history and is the highest total for a Negro Leaguer who is not in the Hall of Fame. He was named the right fielder on the All-1914 and All-1915 Teams, as well as the left fielder on the All-1916 Team by Seamheads. He was inducted into the Cuban Baseball Hall of Fame (in exile in Miami) in 1962.

Alonzo Perry

Perry was too good a hitter to stay as a pitcher. He played for the Birmingham Black Barons in the final years of the Negro Leagues, then emerged as a star in the Mexican League through 1963. He went by several nicknames including "His Majesty," "Speedy," and "Tapya"—in Mexico they called him "The King." Perry won 10 games for the Black Barons' 1948 Negro American League champion squad while batting .325, then went 12–4 with a 3.45 ERA the next season. He started at first base and collected one hit in the 1950 East-West All-Star game.

A reputation as a troublemaker might have prevented him from making it to the majors, because he was one of the biggest stars in the history of the Latin leagues. Perry recorded a 32-game hitting streak in the Dominican Republic winter league in 1951 and he won batting titles there in 1954 and 1957. In 1956, he batted .392 and led the Mexican League with 28 homers, 118 RBI, 103 runs, and 177 hits.[72]

Willie Powell

Powell was a top-notch pitcher from 1925 to 1934, starring initially for the Chicago American Giants from 1925 to 1929. "Wee" Willie led the league with a 2.00 ERA in 1928, then in the offseason had the misfortune to be shot accidentally in the face by his father-in-law.[73]

His overall record was 62–49 with a 3.57 ERA in 148 pitching appearances. Powell took pride in his batting, but the results were not always there. Overall, he batted .180 with 62 hits in documented Negro League and Cuban League action. He pitched in 12 postseason games across four seasons, going 6–1 with a 2.52 ERA and winning Negro World Series titles with the Chicago American Giants in 1926 and 1927.

Powell was reported to be a fast runner and good fielder who batted as high as .412 in the Cuban Winter League. He threw a no-hitter on August 14, 1927, for the Chicago American Giants against the Memphis Red Sox, and he also pitched an 18-inning complete game in 1931 that ended in a tie.

Connie Rector

Rector had a few bright moments as a pitcher, but nothing like his 1929 season when he led the Negro American League in pitching wins, shutouts, and winning percentage, and generated 4.9 pitching WAR. He went 18–1 for the New York Lincoln Giants that year, recording a 4.21 ERA in 188 innings. With Chino Smith batting .451, George Scales .380, and Pop Lloyd .365, but only Rector shining on the mound, the team slugged its way to a second-place finish.

Rector was fond of the New York nightlife, picking up the nickname "Broadway," so most of his 22-year career was spent with New-York based teams like the New York Black Yankees, New York Lincoln Giants, and New York Cubans. He even pitched four games in 1944 at age 52.

Rector's most significant two-way seasons were 1923 and 1924. In 1923, he pitched 43⅔ innings over eight appearances while batting .214 playing 10 games in the outfield. In 1924, he batted .255 from 11 outfield stints and pitched 47 innings across seven appearances.

Ed Rile

Rile started out as a pitcher but then transitioned into four seasons where he alternated pitching with batting and playing first base. Then he finished his last seven seasons primarily at first and is now acknowledged as one of the greatest first basemen in Negro League history. Numerous sources including Seamheads and Baseball-Reference list him as six-foot-two, while several other sources list him as six-foot-six. We can say for sure that the lefty batter and righty pitcher was tall.

Nicknamed "Huck," Rile posted a career average of .311 with 494 hits and 38 homers in Negro League action. As a pitcher, he went 55–43 with a 3.72 ERA (110 ERA+) and led the NNL with 2.53 ERA in 1923 with the Chicago American Giants while going 15–7 in 184⅔ innings.

Rile's greatest two-way season came in 1927 with the Detroit Stars. He went 11–6 with a 2.43 ERA and 14 complete games in 140⅔ innings, generating 3.4 pitching WAR. At the plate that year, he finished third in the NNL with a .389 average while collecting 103 hits as a first baseman, generating 3.7 offensive WAR. He was named the All-1927 first baseman by Seamheads after his 6.9 WAR season—the 12th-highest season total in Negro League history and the fourth-highest season total by a position player.

Huck came back strong for the Stars the next year, leading the NNL with .425 OBP and finishing third in doubles (22) and fifth with a .348 average and 63 RBI. He pitched only 13 innings with a 2.77 ERA. Rile's versatility as a two-way player was demonstrated by his career WAR totals: 10.3 for batting and 9.8 for pitching.

Lázaro Salazar

Salazar often played in the outfield or first base when the underrated Cuban lefty wasn't pitching. A star batting and pitching in his native Cuba, Salazar was called the "Cuban Peach." His career WAR of 33.6 shows how well-rounded Salazar was as a two-way player—16.7 WAR came from pitching and 16.5 WAR came from offensive contributions. He spent 14 seasons playing in the Mexican League and was inducted into Baseball Hall of Fames in Mexico, Cuba, and Venezuela. He is credited with a .342 average with 459 hits in Latin leagues and a .309 average with 188 hits in six Negro League seasons.

In 1934–35, he became the first player to lead the Cuban Winter League (CWL) in batting average and pitching wins—he batted .407 and won six games for the champion Almendares as he was named league MVP. That marked the last time a player batted over .400 in Cuban League play. He led the Cuban League with 47 runs scored in 1936–37 and won another batting title with a 316 average in 1940–41. Salazar was again named MVP for the 1937–38 CWL season, when he batted .318 and led Santa Clara to the title as player-manager. Salazar batted .333 for the New York Cubans in 1935 and .363 for Monterrey in the Mexican League in 1942.

Seamheads has documented Salazar having an outstanding two-way season with Monterrey in 1944, batting .379/.495/.498 and playing 48 games at first base when he wasn't pitching to a 14–8 record with 2.87 ERA. Salazar's career record is 60–50 with a 3.59 ERA in 154 games, according to Seamheads. Other sources show him with 112 wins in Mexico and 35 wins in Cuba.[74]

He played 208 games at first base and 148 games in center field. Seamheads lists him as the starting center fielder on the All-1942 Team with 8.1 WAR that season, the starting first baseman on the All-1944 Team with 8.8 WAR, and the starting first baseman on the All-1945 Team with 6.2 WAR. He is credited with a lifetime .342 average in Latin leagues and .309 in Negro League action by Seamheads—his combined average of .331 ranks 35th all-time in Black baseball history.

Salazar also managed teams to seven straight pennants in Mexico and 14 championships in leagues in four countries—winning 1,153 games overall with a .562 winning percentage—making him a frontrunner for greatest manager in Latin American baseball history.[75]

Hilton Smith

Smith was inducted into the Hall of Fame in 2001 on the strength of his pitching, as he was described as having the best curveball in Black baseball history. A true ace, he pitched primarily with the Kansas City Monarchs (1936–48) in a career that started in 1932. Smith, who was five years older than he let on during his career,[76] was frequently overshadowed by his more famous teammate, Satchel Paige. Smith was sometimes referred to as "Satchel's caddy," because Paige would often pitch the first three innings and then Smith would come in and finish the game. He resented doing more of the heavy lifting without the glory.[77] He pitched 68 games in relief for the Monarchs.

Smith, who threw an assortment of six pitches with impeccable control, went 77–40 with a 2.94 ERA and 134 ERA+ in 15 Negro League seasons. His record pitching two seasons in Cuba was 10–5. He won two games against major leaguers in six appearances, posting a 1.85 ERA in 34 innings. He was no slouch at the plate, batting .291 overall across 602 plate appearances with 166 hits and 93 RBI. He appeared in 212 games on the mound, 53 games as a pinch hitter, and 28 games in the outfield.

He found himself frequently in the outfield for the 1935 Bismarck Churchills—an integrated semipro team based in North Dakota—as he watched Paige get the pitching assignments. "I didn't lose a ball game with Bismarck the whole year, but I didn't pitch much. I played right field on that club most of the time and batted third or fourth," Smith said in an interview with baseball historian John Holway.[78]

"Hilton, besides being a great pitcher, could have played outfield with any team in the league—with anybody. Hilton could have played outfield with the great teams—the Grays, Black Barons, Monarchs. He didn't just come in to hit the long ball—he could hit," said teammate Sherwood Brewer.[79]

Smith's most significant two-way seasons were 1938 and 1943 with the Monarchs. In 1938, he led the Negro American League in wins (10), ERA (1.92), innings (112⅔), and strikeouts (88), while batting .371 with three home runs playing six games in the outfield. In 1943, he posted a 2.70 ERA in 50 innings across nine pitching appearances, while batting .208 playing 11 games in left field.

Smith was the losing pitcher in the 1937 East-West All-Star Game but was the winning pitcher for the 1938 game, going on to pitch in seven consecutive All-Star games representing the West. He pitched the first no-hitter in the Negro American League on May 15, 1937, against the Chicago American Giants.

He spent most of his time pitching, but Smith was proud of his two-way abilities. "In '37, '38, and '39 I had tremendous years. I could pitch and hit, both. Andy Cooper'd pinch-hit me for his fourth-place hitters as quick. Several years I hit over .400 pinch-hitting, outfield, first base and pitching," Smith said.[80]

In another interview, Smith stated, "I could have probably made it into the majors as an outfielder; my hitting was so good. I was one player they didn't have a pinch hitter for.... I had a fastball estimated at 95 miles per hour and one of the best curveballs that has ever been in baseball."[81]

Those who watched Smith play every day verified his supreme talent. Buck O'Neil, Smith's roommate for most of his time with the Monarchs, stated, "He was an outstanding hitter, could wear the ball out. For a span of maybe five or six years, Hilton Smith may have been the best pitcher in the world."[82]

Theolic Smith

Smith had the honor of being the starting pitcher for the first East-West All-Star Game at Chicago's Comiskey Park in 1939. He would get the starting nod 12 years later for the 1951 East-West Game. In between, he pitched in the 1943 East-West All-Star Game. That year he led the Negro American League with a 2.22 ERA, eight complete games, and two shutouts pitching for the Cleveland Buckeyes. Smith was named the right fielder on the All-1940 Team and the left fielder on the All-1944 Team by Seamheads.

Nicknamed "Fireball" for his fastball, Smith also threw a curve and occasional knuckleball but battled control problems. He batted .299 with 478 hits mainly coming in the Mexican League. He went 79–59 while averaging 223 innings for his five seasons in the Mexican League. He won 19 games for Rojos del Mexico in 1940 while batting .364 (tied for second in league) in 50 outfield appearances. In 1944, Smith played 46 games in the outfield and batted .299 for Rojos while winning 16 of the team's 28 games.

Joe Strong

Strong played 16 seasons from 1922 to 1937, ending his career with six seasons with the Homestead Grays. He batted .370 for the Cleveland Tate Stars in 1922 and won consecutive pennants with the St. Louis Stars in 1930–31. Overall, he batted .259 with 186 hits and went 77–75 with a 4.08 ERA.

Strong played 68 games in the outfield, pitched in 238 games, and appeared 18 times as a pinch hitter. His most plate appearances (106) came in 1932, when he posted a .400/.495/.576 slash line. His best years on the mound were 1925, when he went 11–10 with a 3.94 ERA and a league-best two shutouts in 146⅓ innings; and 1929, when he went 9–3 with a league-leading 3.03 ERA in 110 innings.

Strong made the history books on July 31, 1927, with an 11-inning no-hitter against the Hilldale Club—it's the longest no-hitter in major-league history. He also led the league with a 2.07 ERA and 212 ERA+ in 1932.

Ben Taylor

Taylor was inducted into the Baseball Hall of Fame in 2006 as a slick-fielding, sweet-swinging first baseman who lived up to his nickname, "Old Reliable." He was listed as a second-team first baseman in the 1952 *Pittsburgh Courier's* poll of greatest Black players, while Bill James describes him as an "exceptional fielder and also a fine pitcher" while ranking him as the third-best first baseman in the Negro Leagues.[83]

Taylor batted .330 with 1,261 hits (ninth all-time in Black baseball), 737 RBI (11th best) and 16 seasons over .300. His 21-year career in the Negro Leagues included eight seasons with the Indianapolis ABCs managed by his brother C.I. Taylor and often joined by brothers Candy Jim and Steel Arm Johnny Taylor.

Overall, Ben Taylor went 16–8 from 60 mound appearances with a 3.26 ERA in 282 innings. Historian James Riley reports that his pitching record for the 1911 St. Louis Giants was 30–1 if exhibitions are included.[84]

In 1920, he pitched to a 2.70 ERA in 10 appearances and had 343 at-bats with a .321 average and league-best 64 RBI to establish his credentials as a two-way player. Taylor batted .366 (fourth best in league) for the ABCs in 1914, his 27 stolen bases ranked second and his 50 runs led the league. On the mound that year, Taylor went 4–0 with a 1.53 ERA (264 ERA+) in 59 innings.

Taylor went 7–0 with a 4.03 ERA in 51⅓ innings for the 1911 St. Louis Giants while batting .353 in limited at-bats. His best year at the plate was 1921, when the lefty-swinging South Carolina native batted .392/.448/.520 with 89 RBI and a league-leading 160 hits for the ABCs. Pitching in four games that year, he posted an ERA of 0.87.

Newspaper reports touted his greatness, with the *Kansas City Times* writing: "Ben Taylor, the big left hand first sacker, is considered one of the hardest hitters in baseball."[85]

Taylor also won 211 games as a manager, although he had a losing record. His career WAR of 36.0 (22nd all-time) includes 31.5 offensive WAR, 5.4 defensive WAR and 2.8 pitching WAR. Using WAR figures, Seamheads ranks him as the top first baseman in 1914, 1920, 1921, and 1922.

Cristóbal Torriente

Torriente was a powerful left-handed slugger who made it into the Hall of Fame's Class of 2006 as an outfielder. The Cuban native was listed as a first-team outfielder in the 1952 *Pittsburgh Courier's* poll of greatest Black players, while Bill James ranks him as the second-best center fielder in the Negro Leagues after Oscar Charleston.[86]

Torriente produced a slash line of .342/.426/.516 across 17 Negro League seasons. Add in his eight seasons of Latin league action and he ranks third in Black baseball history with 256 stolen bases and 116 triples, fourth in walks (618), fifth in hits (1,513), sixth in runs (888), seventh in doubles (249), eighth in OPS+ (174), and 13th in home runs (83).

He was a standout defensive center fielder with a strong throwing arm, playing 677 games there plus 307 games in right field and 189 games in left field. While playing on Rube Foster's Chicago American Giants from 1921 to 1923, Torriente joined with Jimmie Lyons and Jelly Gardner to form one of the best defensive outfields in baseball history. The team won the first three Negro National League titles in 1920, 1921, and 1922. Torriente pitched 55 innings in 10 games in those years, while averaging .411, .352, and .289. He played 489 games for Chicago across seven seasons, but otherwise jumped around a lot.

Fellow Cuban star Martín Dihigo felt Torriente didn't get the credit he deserved, saying: "He did everything well, he fielded like a natural, threw in perfect form, he covered as much field as could be covered; as for batting, he left being good to being something extraordinary."[87]

Torriente went 23–17 on the mound with a 3.80 ERA in 64 appearances, recording 27 complete games and four shutouts. The 1928 season with the Detroit Stars was his most action as a two-way player. That season he batted .324 playing 20 games in the outfield and went 6–2 pitching 74 innings across 14 appearances—he surrendered 101 hits and had a high 6.45 ERA. Torriente was simply too good a center fielder and slugger to be used as a pitcher, so his two-way abilities were largely untapped.

He tore the cover off the ball playing in his native country, averaging .352 in a dozen seasons, which is third best in Cuban Winter League history.[88] He led the Cuban League in runs scored four times, in hits and average twice, and in home runs once. He led the Cuban League with a .387 average, 48 hits, 33 runs, and five triples in 1914–15. When Babe Ruth came to Cuba for an exhibition game with John McGraw's Giants on November 5, 1920, Torriente stole the spotlight by slugging three homers and a double (while Ruth went hitless) as Almendares won 11–4.[89]

His career WAR of 63.3 (including 3.1 WAR from pitching) ranks third all-time in Negro League history. Using WAR season totals, Torriente was named the All-1914, All-1918, and All-1923 center fielder; the All-1919 and All-1924 left fielder; and the All-1913 right fielder by Seamheads. He was inducted into the Cuban Baseball Hall of Fame in the initial class of 1939.

Smokey Joe Williams

Williams earned the nicknames "Cyclone Joe" and "Smokey Joe" from his blazing fastball. He threw fast most of his career and had impeccable control. The right-handed Hall of Fame hurler produced a lifetime mark of 160–96 with 2.47 ERA (144 ERA+), according to Seamheads. Pitching three years in Cuba, Williams went 22–15 with 26 complete games in 48 appearances, leading the league with 21 games pitched in 1912.

Williams posted a 1.14 ERA for the New York Lincoln Giants in 1918 across 134⅔ innings. He is credited with playing 27 games at first base, 12 in right field, one in center, and nine as a pinch hitter. His career average was .275 with 284 hits and 159 RBI.

Smokey Joe pitched for the New York Lincoln Giants from 1911 to 1923 and the Homestead Grays from 1925 to 1932. He pitched a no-hitter for the Lincoln Giants on May 9, 1919, against the Brooklyn Royal Giants. Baseball historian James Riley says Williams went 41–3 in 1914 against all forms of competition and 20–7 in exhibitions against major leaguers.[90]

On August 7, 1930, Williams, at the age of 44, struck out 27 batters and allowed just one hit in a 12-inning night game played under portable lights. He was matched up against Chet Brewer of the Kansas City Monarchs, who struck out 19 himself. Smokey Joe prevailed in the 1–0 game.

John McGraw called Smokey "one of Blackball's four top talents."[91] Bill James declared him the best Negro League pitcher from 1914 to 1916 and ranked him as the 52nd-best player in baseball history.[92]

Baseball author Joe Posnanski slots Smokey Joe into the number 62 spot in his book, *The Baseball 100*, sharing Ty Cobb's belief that Williams would have been a "sure 30-game winner in the major leagues."[93]

Posnanski also quotes Williams on his two-way abilities: "When I wasn't pitching, I had to play the outfield. In those days, there was no two-platoon system. You had to pitch to everyone, lefties as well as righties. And you had to finish every game you started unless there was an emergency. We had no pinch-hitters. Couldn't afford them."[94]

Williams' 50.0 career WAR from pitching trails only Satchel Paige in Black baseball history, and he finishes ahead when his 4.9 offensive WAR is added. Williams' offensive WAR trails only Ray Brown and Luther Farrell in Black baseball history (per Seamheads) among players identified primarily as a pitcher. Williams finished ahead of Paige in voting for all-time best pitcher in the 1952 *Pittsburgh Courier* poll.

Nip Winters

Winters is acknowledged as one of the greatest left-handed pitchers in Negro League history, although his period of dominance was short. He was listed as a second-team pitcher in the 1952 *Pittsburgh Courier's* poll of greatest Black players. He led the Eastern Colored League in wins each season from 1923 to 1926 and Seamheads shows his career record to be 105–56 with a 3.65 ERA (123 ERA+) across 11 seasons.

Baseball historian James Riley declared Winters the "best pitcher in the Eastern Colored League's history" and credits him with a 32–6 record in 1923 against all competition.[95] The tall lefty (six-foot-five) went 3–0 with a 3.13 ERA in five verified games against major leaguers.

Known for his blazing fastball on the mound, Hall of Famer Smokey Joe Williams recorded a lifetime mark of 160–96 with a 2.47 ERA. He batted .275 for his career but was too valuable as an ace pitcher to spend much time as a position player (Society for American Baseball Research-Rucker Archive).

Winters led the ECL in winning percentage in 1926 and in ERA in 1923, relying heavily on his fastball, sharp curveball, and occasional spitball. In 1924, he led in eight categories including wins (23), games started (28), complete games (24), shutouts (3), innings pitched (246⅔), and strikeouts (135).

In the 1924 Negro World Series, Winters hurled four complete games including a shutout and pitched to a 1.63 ERA with three wins, but Hilldale lost 5–4 to the Kansas City Monarchs. He got a complete-game victory as

Hilldale rebounded to win the 1925 Negro World Series rematch with the Monarchs.

Winters, who battled alcoholism throughout his career and control problems on the mound, pitched a no-hitter for the Atlantic City Bacharach Giants on July 26, 1922, at the age of 23. He came back the next day and got the last five outs for an unofficial save in the finale of a six-game series. He pitched another no-hitter for Hilldale against the Harrisburg Giants on September 3, 1924, narrowly missing a perfect game—it was the first no-hitter in the history of the Eastern Colored League.

An accomplished batter who was used to pinch-hit 13 times, Winters batted .286 with 228 career hits with a high of .391 in 1928. In 1929, he played 28 games at first base and batted .277 while going 5–6 in 19 pitching appearances. His other significant two-way season was 1927, when he went 13–8 with a 4.04 ERA in 176 innings for the Hilldale Club while batting .295 from nine games at first base and six pinch-hitting chances.

His 105 wins rank 10th in Negro League history, his .652 winning percentage and 708 strikeouts rank 15th, and his 117 complete games place 12th. He compiled 3.9 offensive WAR (sixth-most by a pitcher in Blackball history) and 28.3 pitching WAR. His 8.0 WAR in 1924 is the fourth-highest single-season total in Negro League history and third-highest mark by a pitcher. Bill James lists him as the best Negro League pitcher in 1924 (with Bullet Rogan) and 1926.[96]

CHAPTER 9

Ted "Double Duty" Radcliffe
Baseball's Greatest Catcher-Pitcher Combo

Ted "Double Duty" Radcliffe lived to be 103 years old, which gave him plenty of time to tell stories about his fascinating career. He claimed to be the only player to strike out Josh Gibson and hit a home run off Satchel Paige.[1] According to Double Duty and his biographer Kyle McNary, he recorded 500 wins and 4,000 strikeouts as a pitcher, and 4,000 hits, 400 home runs, and a .303 average as a batter in 3,800 games.[2]

"'Double Duty' Radcliffe—he was a good one. Pitched and catch. He was a legend," said Negro League first baseman Red Moore.[3]

Radcliffe had a long, distinguished career in the Negro Leagues, supplemented by games all over North America and Latin America. What made Double Duty's career noteworthy was that he alternated between catching and pitching, the two most physically demanding positions on the field. On top of that, he served many years as player-manager and frequently drove the team bus.

The number of times he pitched and caught in the same game or in the same doubleheader remains a mystery. He played both positions at a high level, although his production in verified Negro League action shows he was below the caliber of a Hall of Fame player. His lifetime on-base percentage of .304 in Negro League play shows he swung for the fences and often fell short.

The righty was a six-time All-Star who pitched in three East-West All-Star games and caught in three East-West All-Star games—no other player has ever appeared in All-Star games as a pitcher and a catcher. Radcliffe played on three of the greatest Negro League teams in consecutive seasons: the 1930 St. Louis Stars, 1931 Homestead Grays, and 1932 Pittsburgh Crawfords.

Double Duty reportedly got his nickname from famous sportswriter Damon Runyon after a 1932 doubleheader in which he caught Satchel Paige pitching a shutout in Yankee Stadium in the first game and then pitched his own shutout in the nightcap. None of these details have been verified to date, but there is evidence of him being referred to as "Double Duty" for the first time in the May 19, 1932, *Philadelphia Tribune*.[4] Everyone called him Double Duty or Duty after that, and a legend was born.

His pitching produced 7.1 WAR for his career, although 3.9 of that came from the 1930 season. He added 2.2 offensive WAR and 1.9 WAR from fielding. Bill James ranked Radcliffe as the fourth-best catcher in the Negro Leagues and commented: "He was both a fine pitcher and a fine catcher."[5]

Growing up in Mobile, Alabama, he lived a few blocks from Satchel Paige. The two joined another future Negro League player, Bobby Robinson, in playing "top ball," using sticks for bats and bottle caps as baseballs. "We'd make cotton balls and soak them in oil and play night ball. We'd light them and run like hell," Radcliffe said.[6]

It was in Mobile where a 15-year-old Radcliffe got his first taste of catching. He had the unfortunate task of catching the lightning-fast but wild Paige, who was actually two years older than his pal and not four years younger like he had people believe his whole career. "That's right—I was Satchel's first catcher and I caught him more than any catcher who ever lived," Radcliffe proudly noted.[7]

Thirty-six years of catching eventually took a toll on Radcliffe's body. The worst of it was the mangled and deformed hand he got from catching Satchel for hundreds of games, which didn't overshadow the fact he caught seven of his no-hitters. "Catching Satchel is like trying to catch a freight train barreling at you with the brakes gone bad," he said.[8]

After starting his career playing a few games with the Mobile Black Bears as a teenager, Radcliffe and his younger brother Alex hitchhiked to Chicago in 1919 to join another brother. He signed with the semipro Illinois Giants for about $100 a month, a team he would play with from 1920 into 1927.

1920 was the year Rube Foster founded the Negro National League to establish a national footprint for Black players. While the Live Ball Era was replacing the Deadball Era in the segregated major leagues, Black baseball had not gone all in on the long ball yet. Teams still needed catchers who could control the running game and Radcliffe took that responsibility seriously. Catching in an exhibition game, Radcliffe once wore a chest protector that said, "Thou shalt not steal."[9]

Radcliffe traveled all over with the Giants, from Wisconsin to Montana and up into Canada, enduring exhausting travel and persistent racial discrimination. While on the Giants he learned to throw what he called a scratch ball or emery ball. "They called me the emery champ. I was the best at throwing it. I could make my emery ball break any kind of way I want. Got that piece of emery cloth in the chewing gum and slice the ball like that. Then I'd take my finger and open up the seam a little and make it break four feet down," he said.[10]

After spending a month with the Detroit Stars in 1926, he hooked up with another traveling team, Gilkerson's Union Giants, and played off and on with them from 1927 through 1929. While on that team he got extensive tutoring on the finer points of catching from wily veteran Clarence "Pops" Coleman, who forged a 40-year career as a catcher in Black baseball.

With his apprenticeship over, Radcliffe officially joined the Negro Leagues when he signed with the Detroit Stars for the 1928 season, playing for manager Bingo DeMoss. The Stars had future Hall of Famers Turkey Stearnes and Cristóbal Torriente in the lineup, but the pitching staff was not capable of holding down the opposition. Radcliffe was needed behind the plate, and he contributed a .278 average with 75 hits and eight home runs as the Stars limped to a third-place finish. Base runners were starting to learn it was not advisable to run on the young catcher from Mobile.

Radcliffe was batting .310 for the Stars midway through the 1929 season when he jumped at the chance to make more money with Gilkerson's Union Giants, an elite traveling team that would finish the year with a 115–15 record.

He finally got a chance to demonstrate what he could do on the mound, and he delivered with a 9–0 record in 61 innings. He combined an above-average fastball with a sharp curve, mixing in the emery ball when necessary. He batted .310 for the Stars and .355 overall for the year. They won a big tournament in Nebraska with Radcliffe catching the first eight innings of the final game and then striking out two to close out the ninth on the mound.

Enlisted to join a post-season all-star team that was loosely comprised of the Chicago American Giants team, Radcliffe pitched a four-hit shutout as the American Giants demolished the Homestead Grays to establish the West's superiority over the East.

Double Duty's season had one more chapter to write. The American Giants faced off against a big-league all-star team that featured future Hall of Famers Charlie Gehringer, Heinie Manush, and Harry Heilmann. Radcliffe won the third game in relief and contributed a double as the American Giants handily won three out of four. "Hell, they couldn't hit me in our league. How the big-leaguers gonna do any better? You can't hit that," he said.[11]

Radcliffe found himself traded to the St. Louis Stars for the 1930 season. He had the good fortune to join a strong team that would go on to win 69 games while the second-place Monarchs won 40 games. The Stars' lineup featured Cool Papa Bell, Willie Wells, and Mule Suttles, while

Radcliffe joined Logan Hensley, Ted Trent, Roosevelt Davis, and Leroy Matlock in a strong rotation.

Double Duty led the Negro National League that year in ERA (2.58), ERA+ (195), and winning percentage (.833) while going 10–2 with nine complete games in 115⅓ innings. He pitched a three-hitter to knock off the Homestead Grays and outpitched Willie Foster twice as the Stars defeated the Chicago American Giants.

When he wasn't pitching, he was catching 55 games and batting .284. It was his first extensive action as a two-way player in the Negro Leagues. Stout at five-foot-11 and 210 pounds, he was known for talking a big game to distract the opposition, whether he was on the mound or behind the plate. Radcliffe's 4.4 WAR that year tied for third best in Black baseball. He was listed as the All-1930 Team catcher by Seamheads. "We didn't lose often that year. We beat the Grays five out of seven and we beat the Monarchs 12 out of 14," he said.[12]

After winning the first-half pennant, St. Louis' Stars matched up against Detroit's Stars for the Negro National League championship. Double Duty prevailed in the first game, although Detroit's slugger Turkey Stearnes took him deep in the first inning. He ended up pitching in three of the games and batting .333 as St. Louis won the series. "Double Duty was a good ball player. [He could] catch and pitch. He used to think he could strike me out. Broke his arm trying it," commented Stearnes.[13]

Double Duty's unique two-way abilities were always in demand. He signed with the Homestead Grays for the 1931 season, because owner Cum Posey made him the best offer. The Grays were not part of an official league, but they became a hot ticket on the regional barnstorming circuit. That was no small feat in an era of financial instability due to the Great Depression.

A number of baseball historians regard the 1931 Homestead Grays as the greatest baseball team ever, regardless of color. Radcliffe backed up 19-year-old phenom Josh Gibson at catcher, with Oscar Charleston, Jud Wilson, Ted Page, and George "Tubby" Scales rounding out the formidable lineup. Future Hall of Famers Willie Foster and Smokey Joe Williams led the pitching staff, with Lefty Williams, George Britt, and Radcliffe rounding out the rotation. Like Double Duty, Britt was a unique player who caught and played all over the diamond when he wasn't pitching.

Baseball historian Phil Dixon documented the '31 Grays' record against all competition to be 143–29–2, with a 42–19–1 mark against rival African American clubs. They compiled two win streaks of 17 games. The team featured four 20-game winners, and Radcliffe contributed a 16–4 record while batting .307 for the year. "At utility, few men could rival the offensive and defensive efforts of Ted 'Double Duty' Radcliffe, who joined

Posey's Grays from St. Louis' Stars," Dixon wrote.¹⁴

Shortstop Bill "Happy" Evans said, "The Homestead Grays of 1931 are in the baseball books as being the greatest team of all-time. I agree that it was. We beat the Kansas City Monarchs 13 out of 17 times. There wasn't a team that beat us in a series."¹⁵

The team played 48 doubleheaders and one triple-header as it traveled to nearly 100 cities. Double Duty recalled playing a tournament that started at eight in the morning and they played the last game at eight at night. "I pitched one game and didn't give up but three or four hits, so I started the next one and threw a shutout and then I relieved in the last game," he said.¹⁶

The Grays declared themselves the unofficial champions of the Negro Leagues that year, because no team was willing to face them in a playoff series. They

Ted Radcliffe excelled at two demanding positions—catcher and pitcher—which is how he acquired the "Double Duty" nickname. It is estimated that he hit 500 home runs and won 400 games over a four-decade career (Society for American Baseball Research-Rucker Archive).

destroyed a major-league all-star team led by Lefty Grove by scores of 10–7 and 18–0. Posey named Double Duty to his 1931 All-Star Team as one of the pitchers.

Gus Greenlee, owner of the Pittsburgh Crawfords, opened a new ballpark, Greenlee Field, for the team to play in for the 1932 season. Greenlee spared no expense to wrest the mantle of dominance from Posey and the Grays. He raided the team and signed Double Duty, Gibson, Charleston, Wilson, Page, and shortstop Jake Stephens to join Satchel Paige and Judy Johnson on the Crawfords and form the Negro League's next powerhouse team.

Radcliffe was excited to join his boyhood friend Paige, and the two engaged in a friendly rivalry to see who was the better pitcher that year. McNary documents Paige with a 14–8 record and Double Duty with a 13–5 record against other Negro League teams that year.[17] The *Pittsburgh Courier* credited Radcliffe with winning 19 games in 27 contests while effectively serving as a pitcher and catcher.[18] He batted .284 that year in league action, according to Seamheads.

Paige pitched a no-hitter against the New York Black Yankees on July 8, 1932, with Double Duty catching him. Radcliffe came close to matching him later in the season, but he had his no-hitter broken up in the ninth inning by his brother Alex.

The Crawfords defeated the top team in the Negro Southern League, the Monroe Monarchs, to earn the unofficial title of world champions for 1932. Radcliffe outpitched Hilton Smith in the second game and then drove in the winning run in the decisive sixth game to help his team win a third straight championship.

For the years 1933–37, Double Duty turned into a baseball nomad, often playing for three or four teams in a season. In 1933, he suited up with the Detroit Stars in spring training but had moved to the Homestead Grays by the time the season started. He also played with the Columbus Blue Birds and New York Black Yankees that year, batting a combined .269.

The 1934 season saw Double Duty pitch to a 17–3 record and bat .355 playing mainly for one of the appealing semipro clubs in North Dakota: the Jamestown Red Sox. He got his managerial start with Jamestown, an integrated team that was in a heated rivalry with the Bismarck club. The competition he faced while playing in North Dakota was not that inferior to what he had been competing against in the Negro Leagues—he might pitch against Pete Alexander in one game and duel with Satchel Paige in the next.

Whatever the level of competition, Radcliffe found himself on a hot steak. He pitched a shutout to win his first game for Jamestown, then soon after collected five hits in a game, followed by winning both games of a doubleheader. He struck out 18 while beating the respected House of David traveling team. In another game against the House of David, Radcliffe was a one-man wrecking crew after smacking three hits, throwing out two runners from behind the plate, making a diving catch in right field, and striking out two in one inning of pitching.[19]

At the end of the 1934 season, the top players from the Jamestown and Bismarck clubs teamed up to sweep the Chicago American Giants in a five-game series. Double Duty played a major role in the wins, hitting a home run to win one game and winning both games of a doubleheader, one by shutout. Later that fall he joined the American Giants' travel squad and shut down the Homestead Grays from the mound.[20]

The next season he started out with the Brooklyn Eagles before jumping to the Bismarck Churchills, where he joined Satchel, Barney Morris, Hilton Smith, and Chet Brewer in a fearsome rotation. Double Duty pitched a one-hitter to win his first game for Neil Churchill's integrated club. When Satchel came down with a sore arm for a month, Radcliffe would catch him for the first four innings and then replace him on the mound for the final five innings—Double Duty to the rescue!

Bismarck's 1935 team, which went 7–0 to win the National Baseball Conference tournament in Wichita, is considered one of the greatest semipro teams in baseball history. Double Duty's combined stats for the year were .299 average and 11–4 record in 108 innings pitched, according to McNary.

Back in the Negro American League with the Cincinnati Tigers in 1937, Double Duty batted .279 in the first half of the season and won the fan vote as the West's All-Star catcher. Dr. W.S. Martin, co-owner of the Memphis Red Sox, recruited him at that year's East-West All-Star game and convinced him to take over as player-manager of the Red Sox for the rest of the season. Despite taking on this new role in addition to catching and pitching, no one called him "Triple Duty."

He shined in his new role in 1938, leading the Red Sox to the first-half pennant. Double Duty caught fewer games, but he went 7–2 pitching 71 innings that season. The Red Sox easily defeated the Atlanta Black Crackers for the Negro American League championship as Double Duty won the first game of the series 6–1.

Named to the 1938 East-West All-Star team as a pitcher, Double Duty contributed a single and hurled four scoreless innings to close out the West's win in front of a crowd of 30,000 people. Lloyd Lewis, a white sportswriter for the Chicago *Daily News*, was on hand to witness the quality of Negro League baseball and he came away impressed, writing: "It has pitchers who could fill places in half the leading teams of the top white leagues.... 'Schoolboy' Taylor, the 23-year-old pitcher from the Pittsburgh Crawfords, showed class that was only rivaled by the crafty old 'Double Duty' Radcliffe, who slow-balled four shutout innings to protect the West's one-run lead."[21]

Double Duty played in Cuba from 1938 to 1940 and enjoyed the level of competition and the pay. He went 7–3 and tied for the Cuban League lead with three shutouts for first-place Almendares in 1939–40. Overall, he went 12–11 with 12 complete games in 35 appearances, according to Jorge Figueredo's *Cuban Baseball*.

Representing the West again in the 1939 East-West All-Star game,

Double Duty singled and scored the go-ahead run in the eighth inning and pitched the last three innings to get the win. Overall, he went 1–0 with a 2.35 ERA in All-Star games while batting .308.

Double Duty would primarily play and manage for the Red Sox into 1942, apart from the 1940 season he spent playing in Mexico and pitching to a 6.64 ERA. He also played sporadically in Mexico in 1936 and 1942–46. He went 6–1 with a 3.13 ERA for the Red Sox in 1939, and he was the hero of the East-West All-Star game that year. Entering the game in the eighth inning, he singled and scored the tying run on a home run that gave the West the lead. Then he went out and pitched a one-two-three ninth to secure the win.

He stayed with the Red Sox long enough for a sip of coffee in 1942 before jumping to the Birmingham Black Barons, where he was able to play with his brother Alex not far from their hometown of Mobile. He batted .333 for the season while bouncing back and forth between the Black Barons, the Chicago American Giants, and the St. Paul Gophers. "People said I jumped to so many teams to get the most money, but in the Negro Leagues the owners got together and asked me to go to different teams because I was a drawing card," Radcliffe said.[22]

For the 1943 season, Double Duty was player-manager for the Chicago American Giants, who were the second-half champions. His brother Alex led the team with a .369 average as the starting third baseman, while 39-year-old Double Duty batted .275 as the primary catcher. Both brothers were voted as starters for the East-West All-Star game.

Traded to the Birmingham Black Barons for the 1944 season, Double Duty started at catcher in the East-West All-Star game. Even with a broken finger he ended up the star of the show before a crowd of 46,247 fans at Chicago's Comiskey Park. He unleashed a long, two-run homer in the fifth to break a tie and added a single and double—all this despite getting knocked out briefly by a foul tip behind the plate. His brother Alex chipped in with a triple and two RBI as the West prevailed 7–4. Double Duty would later call that All-Star game home run his most outstanding achievement in baseball, according to his player file at the Baseball Hall of Fame.

The Black Barons were solid all year, winning the pennant for the first half and the second half. They met the Homestead Grays in the World Series. Five Birmingham players were injured from a car accident before game three, which ended up a 9–0 loss as Double Duty's single was their only hit off Ray Brown. Radcliffe's hitting was one of the few bright spots as the Grays won the series 4–1.

Jackie Robinson batted .375 and led the Negro American League in doubles, home runs, and WAR in 1945 playing shortstop for the Kansas City

Monarchs. His roommate was Double Duty Radcliffe. Double Duty batted .278 that year in limited at-bats and witnessed Robinson's recruitment and signing by the Dodgers. While he was happy to see Jackie break the color barrier, Double Duty knew he was too old at 44 to get a shot at the majors. He also knew it signaled the beginning of the end for the Negro Leagues. "It broke up the league 'cause nobody was going to see us play when Jackie was on TV and the radio. But it helped in the long run," he said.[23]

As for Double Duty, he pivoted to manage the Harlem Globetrotters baseball team owned by his friend, Abe Saperstein, even serving as secretary of the basketball team and handling their bookings. "Saperstein was my man.... He was the greatest friend to the colored athlete of anybody I know today," Radcliffe said.[24]

Whether it was batting against Bob Feller and smacking a double or striking out Ted Williams, Double Duty proved numerous times over the course of his career that he could hold his own against the major league's best players. He batted .376 against major leaguers, according to John Holway's *Blackball Stars*. When asked once why he wasn't in the big leagues, Radcliffe responded, "You have to ask the two Grand Dragons of the Ku Klux—J. Edgar Hoover and Judge Landis."[25]

Double Duty knew there wasn't a team in the Negro Leagues that couldn't use his services, whether it was for his catching, pitching, managing, or all of the above. Cum Posey, the owner of the Homestead Grays, told Double Duty that he needed him to mentor a young pitching staff. So, the player often called "the smartest catcher in baseball" joined other aging stars such as Buck Leonard, Cool Papa Bell, and Josh Gibson on the 1946 Grays. Double Duty shared his pitching secrets with youngsters Alonzo Perry, Wilmer Fields, and Harold Hairston while occasionally showing them how it was done from the mound.

In 1948, Radcliffe wound down his official Negro League career with a short stint as player-manager for the Chicago American Giants. With other Black players such as Larry Doby, Willard Brown, and Dan Bankhead following Jackie Robinson to the majors, the Negro Leagues were nearing the end of their viability. That year Double Duty became the first Black player in the Southern Minnesota League when he joined the Rochester Aces, and he became the first Black player in the Michigan-Indiana League when he joined the semipro South Bend Studebakers.[26]

He showed he still had some baseball life left in his bat, as he belted a grand slam and a two-run homer off Sam Jethroe of the Cleveland Buckeyes to lead the Studebakers to a win on July 2, 1948. On August 20, Double Duty hit a home run as part of four-hit game while catching a no-hitter from Ed Hanyzewski to become the only player to catch and pitch two no-hitters, not that anyone else had ever done that once.[27]

He averaged .312 for the Studebakers in 1948 with seven home runs at age 46, including a home run that he called ahead of time on August 24. As the *South Bend Tribune* reported it: "The thrill came in the second when, after biting at a low pitch, the Norfolk bench began to razz Ted Radcliffe, Studebaker catcher. Radcliffe turned to the bench and said in an audible voice, 'If you puts one in around my neck, I'll put it out of the park.' This challenge was accepted by Norfolk pitcher Johnny Banks. The next pitch came in around Radcliffe's neck and Ted smashed it over the left-field wall, a drive of some 339 feet."[28]

Double Duty was back managing and playing occasionally for the Chicago American Giants in 1949 and 1950, in a league that was no longer considered to be major. The team won the 1949 pennant, and his old friend Satchel returned from the majors to pitch a few times to him in 1950. History was made again in 1950 when the American Giants signed Lou Chirban and Louis Clarizio as the first white players in Negro League history, followed shortly after by two more: Frank Dyll and Stanley Miarka. As skipper, Double Duty had no problem integrating races on the team, but it was a short-lived experiment that didn't produce the desired boost in attendance.

He continued playing as manager for the Elmwood Giants of the Man-Dak league in 1951–52, playing only when he didn't have better options. It's not like anyone was playing better than him in a league filled with many ex–Negro Leaguers. Double Duty batted .459 in 1951 and .364 in 1952 at age 50, going 4–0 on the mound in nine appearances. He played the occasional tournament game in Canada over the next two years before finally hanging up his cleats in 1954.

In 498 verified Negro League games, he produced a 52–42 record and 4.23 ERA (101 ERA+), along with a .269 batting average, 402 hits, and 20 home runs, according to Seamheads. It's not Double Duty's fault that he played the majority of his career games against white semipro, town, and outlaw teams, which don't count in official stats.

When the *Pittsburgh Courier* released its 1952 All-Time All-Star Team, Double Duty was listed as a third-team catcher and a fourth-team pitcher. Even the great two-way player Bullet Joe Rogan was only listed as a pitcher, which speaks to the level of respect Double Duty engendered from the public and his peers for his two-way ability. Lots of Negro League players excelled at two-way playing, but most ended up spending significantly more time at either pitching or playing the field. Only Double Duty excelled at the demanding positions of catcher and pitcher for four decades.

Radcliffe always took good care of his body, which he credits as the reason he was able to play for 36 years. "I never had a sore arm in my life. I never was prone to injuries.... You see, by me being big and rugged, I never was out much with injuries."[29]

Double Duty did finally make it to the major leagues—as a scout with the Cleveland Indians in 1962. He helped discover players such as Tommy Agee and Mudcat Grant before quitting in disgust at the low pay.

Joe Black, who pitched six years in the Negro Leagues and in the major leagues, believed Double Duty belonged in the Hall of Fame. "He was a great defensive catcher, one of the best ever, always talking to the hitters, distracting them, always encouraging his pitchers, never negative. He was a good pitcher with a nice little breaking ball, and he could always hit."[30]

Buck O'Neil agreed, saying in a 2005 interview with Chicago sportswriter Dave Hoekstra: "He should be in the Hall. 'Double Duty' was good enough. He was a good hitter, and he had hard stuff as a pitcher."[31]

What did Double Duty think? He pretended not to care about recognition as a Hall of Famer, calling it a politicized process, but he clearly felt he belonged. "My record stands out. I played against the best and I held my own. Nobody ever played like I did 'cause I'm Double Duty."[32]

Baseball historian James Riley summed up Double Duty this way: "There may have been better pitchers, better catchers, and better hitters, and there may have been a more colorful player, but there has never been another single player embued with the diverse talents he manifested during his baseball career. 'Double Duty' was unique in baseball annals."[33]

CHAPTER 10

Leon Day

More Than Just an Ace Pitcher

The Negro Leagues Baseball Museum in Kansas City has a Field of Legends, which shows statues of 10 all-time greats positioned around a baseball diamond. Leon Day is the right fielder, but he could just as easily have been positioned as the pitcher, the second baseman, or the center fielder. Day was a versatile, five-tool star wherever he was deployed.

Hall of Famer Monte Irvin called Day the finest all-around player he had ever seen. "He was a good pitcher, had the heart of a lion, and a real good fastball. He threw as hard as Bob Gibson. And he had a small but good curve, and had control of it. He could field his position, he was a good hitter, he could outrun me, he played second base, and played a great outfield," Irvin said.[1]

Another Hall of Famer, Larry Doby, viewed Day as an incomparable pitcher. "I didn't see anybody in the major leagues that was better than Leon Day. If you want to compare him with Bob Gibson, stuff-wise, Day had just as good stuff. Tremendous curve ball, and a fastball at least 90–95 miles an hour. You talk about Satchel; I didn't see any better than Day," Doby said.[2]

Doby was not just spouting hyperbole—Day beat Paige in three out of four head-to-head matchups over the course of his career. Perhaps if Day matched Satchel's charisma and flair for self-promotion he would have been more widely recognized as the Negro Leagues' best pitcher. The *Pittsburgh Courier* ranked Day ahead of Paige as the best pitcher in the Negro Leagues in 1942 and 1943.

Day was as sturdy as a five-foot-nine, 170-pound man could be, and he played every position on the field except catcher. He always pitched from the stretch, because he said that was the only way he could throw without hurting his shoulder. By cocking the ball beside his ear and flinging it to the plate without a wind-up, batters didn't have a chance to pick up his delivery. He also believed in regularly pitching high and tight to

Chapter 10. Leon Day

keep batters honest, part of a competitive streak that belied his low-key personality.

The righty pitched in a record nine East-West All-Star games in six seasons: 1935, 1937, 1939, 1942, 1943, and 1946. In All-Star competition, he holds records for most strikeouts (22) and innings pitched (21⅓ innings) with a sparkling 1.27 ERA. He won the Negro World Series with the Newark Eagles in 1946.

Day, who was born in Alexandria, Virginia, in 1916, was already pitching in the Negro Leagues at age 17 in 1934. He had been discovered by Rap Dixon, player-manager for the Baltimore Black Sox. It was an inauspicious debut with the Black Sox, who played 15 games that season before folding. Day did not impress in his short stint, surrendering 11 hits and 11 earned runs in three innings pitched. He impressed plenty over the next 21 years.

Leon Day combined a powerful fastball, a knee-buckling curveball, and a no-windup delivery to dominate in the Negro Leagues from 1934 to 1949. A lifetime .307 batter, Day was equally adept playing the infield or the outfield (National Baseball Hall of Fame and Museum, Cooperstown, N.Y.).

He rebounded to emerge as the ace pitcher for the Brooklyn Eagles the next season, making a salary of $50 a month. Day went 7–4 with a 4.34 ERA in 103⅔ innings (fourth in the Negro National League) while completing eight of his 13 starts. One of those wins was a one-hitter, which served notice of more dominance to come. His bat remained a work in progress with a .209 average. Representing the East, Day pitched four innings in the 1935 East-West All-Star game and retired future Hall of Famers Turkey Stearnes, Buck Leonard, and Mule Suttles in key spots. Making the first of many trips to Puerto Rico for winter ball, Day batted .307.

The Eagles moved to Newark for the 1936 season, and Day—still just

19 years old—focused on pitching. On the mound that year, he teamed up with Terris McDuffie and William Bell, who at 38 was twice the age of Day. Relying on sharp control and a deceptive fastball, Day led Newark in every pitching category, posting a 3.30 ERA (third in the NNL) in 76⅓ innings, good for an adjusted ERA of 151. He batted .361 in limited at-bats as the Eagles limped to a fourth-place finish.

According to Day's recollection, he batted .320 and went 13–0 with a 3.02 ERA in league play with the Eagles in 1937, calling it his best season.[3] Seamheads credits him with a 3–0 mark, 3.99 ERA, and .429 average but only documents 31 of the Eagles' 59 league games. Despite having the "million-dollar infield" of Mule Suttles, Dick Seay, Ray Dandridge, and Willie Wells behind him, Day was only able to pitch the team to a second-place finish behind the powerful Homestead Grays. Bill James ranks Day as the best pitcher in the Negro Leagues in 1937.[4] Pitching to a 7–3 record in Cuba that winter, Day slipped in the shower and hurt his arm, causing him to miss most of the 1938 season.

Day was back with the Eagles for the 1939 season. He batted .333 while filling in at second base, shortstop, or center field when not pitching. However, he was needed on the mound to prop up a thin rotation. Day led the team with 87 innings pitched on the way to a 7–3 record, 3.41 ERA (142 ERA+) and a league-leading 11 starts. His 87 innings ranked second in the league. Playing in two East-West All-Star games that year, Day threw six hitless, scoreless innings.

On January 9, 1940, Day set a record for the Puerto Rican league by striking out 19 in an 18-inning duel with spitballer Bill Byrd. The game ended in a 1–1 tie due to darkness. He showed off his two-way skills by batting .330 for Aguadilla. Next, he moved on to Venezuela, where he posted a 12–1 record for Vargas.

Delighted to be making $350 a month to play in Mexico for the 1940 season—double his salary with the Eagles—Day had the good fortune to be on a stacked Azules de Veracruz team with Josh Gibson, player-manager Martín Dihigo, Willie Wells, Ted Radcliffe, Barney Brown, and Ramón Bragaña. Day batted .298 and went 6–0 on the mound with a 3.22 ERA in 67 innings. The team raced to a 61–30 record and captured the championship.

Some of his peers questioned why the Eagles didn't make him a full-time position player to take better advantage of his speed, defense, and batting. "Day was the best athlete I've ever seen in my life. When the second baseman got hurt, he'd go in and play second," said teammate Clarence "Half a Pint" Israel. "He was the most complete ball player I've ever seen."[5]

When Day returned to the U.S. for the 1941 season, he battled his way through a sore arm as the Eagles tried once again to overcome the Homestead Grays' hold on first place. He ended up playing 22 games at second base and 20 games in center field while only pitching in five games. Day batted .310 but didn't contribute much from the mound as the Eagles fell to third place. Back in Puerto Rico for the 1941–42 winter season, Day batted .351 and recorded a 2.93 ERA with a league-record 168 strikeouts for Aguadilla.

"He had plenty of speed and a pretty fair curve. The best thing he had going for him was he could get it over the plate," said Hall of Famer Buck Leonard.[6]

Day set a Negro League record on July 31, 1942, by striking out 18 Baltimore Elite Giants while surrendering only one hit—Paige's career high was 17 strikeouts. The Elite Giants' lineup featured Roy Campanella, Sammy Hughes, and Wild Bill Wright, but they were helpless against Day's fastball-curve combination. He struck out Campanella three times and helped his own cause by rapping out a hit at the plate.

The Eagles had defeated the Grays three times in two days in early July, with Day winning the opener 6–2 while batting sixth in the lineup. The next day he collected three hits including a double that led to the winning run in the 14th inning. The Grays had their way with the rest of the Negro National League that year, but they were no match for Day's all-around play.

Day and Satchel matched up again in the 1942 East-West All-Star game before a crowd of 45,000 at Comiskey Park, with each entering a 2–2 game in the seventh inning. Day was asked to put out a rally with two outs and the tying and go-ahead runs on base. He got the final out of the seventh on a ground ball and then shut out the West the rest of the way to earn the win. He struck out the last four batters and five of the last six to close the door with a thud, while Paige gave up three runs to take the loss.

The Homestead Grays brought in Day as a ringer as they faced Satchel and the Kansas City Monarchs in the first World Series between the Negro American League and Negro National League in 1942. Day pitched a complete game five-hitter while striking out 12 to beat Paige 4–1 in Game Four. However, the Monarchs swept the rest of the games and later got Day's win overturned under protest. With 4.9 WAR that season, Day emerged as the center fielder for Seamheads' All-1942 Team.

Watching Day's splendid pitching throughout that season caused Cum Posey, the owner of the Grays, to proclaim in the *Pittsburgh Courier*: "Leon Day was the best pitcher in Negro baseball—despite the fact he is used daily either as a pitcher, outfielder, or infielder."[7]

Shortly after pitching two shutout innings in the 1943 East-West All-Star game, 26-year-old Day got drafted into the U.S. Army. Nine months later and a few days after D-Day, he was driving a "duck" amphibious landing vehicle onto the shores of Utah Beach with the 818th Amphibian Battalion. "When we landed, we were pretty close to the action, because we could hear the small arms fire," Day recalled.[8]

Day survived several months of combat action unscathed and then had the experience of a lifetime. He competed in the G.I. World Series as part of the OISE (Overseas Invasion Service Exposition) All-Stars representing Com-Z units in liberated territories. He and fellow Negro League slugger Willard Brown—the only Blacks on the team—were joined by Pirates pitcher Russ Bauers on an otherwise ragtag group of semipro journeymen. It was a form of baseball integration two years before Jackie Robinson broke the color barrier.

In the best-of-five World Series, OISE was matched up against the 71st Division Red Circlers featuring All-Star Harry Walker, Ewell Blackwell, and seven other major leaguers. A crowd of roughly 50,000 GIs watched as Day took the mound for Game Two. Despite a long layoff during the war, Day proved up to the challenge by striking out 10 to win a close game. He didn't fare as well taking the loss in Game Four in Reims, France, but OISE pulled off the upset in the decisive fifth game back in Nuremberg Stadium. Both Day and Brown got to eat with their white teammates at the victory banquet, a right they did not enjoy back in the States.[9]

Day and OISE traveled to Italy to play the Mediterranean Theatre of Operations champion, with many of the major leaguers begging their way onto the team. Day got the honor of pitching the first game and struck out nine as OISE won 19–6. A third series took place, with Day switching sides to shut out his former team while striking out 10. He had successfully demonstrated his pitching abilities against major-league talent on a big stage.

Walker, who would go on to win the NL batting title in 1947, was impressed by Day. "Good control, he didn't overpower you. Nothing flim-flam about him. Would have been a real good pitcher in the major leagues probably. And wasn't too bad a hitter," Walker said.[10]

With Day (and many of his teammates) returning from the war for the 1946 season, no one knew how rusty he would be after missing two-and-a-half years of his prime. As he prepared to face the Philadelphia Stars on Opening Day on May 5, Day admitted, "I was a little nervous, like I always was at the beginning of a game, but after I got started, everything was all right."[11]

He ended up pitching a no-hitter. Bob Feller, in 1940, is the only other major leaguer to throw a no-hitter on Opening Day. No player from the Stars reached second base and Day faced 29 batters, with one walk and two errors marring an otherwise perfect performance. The Stars' side argued vehemently that one of the errors should have been ruled a hit. Stars catcher Bill Cash was ejected after he forcefully shoved the umpire after a close call at the plate in the sixth inning, which caused a mini riot on the field. Goose Curry, player-manager for the Stars, was also ejected after he kicked the umpire while he was down. All the excitement did not phase Day at all. Despite tweaking his arm while fielding a bunt, Day had enough left to strike out pinch hitter Henry McHenry with three fastballs to end the game. His teammates carried him off the Ruppert Stadium field on their shoulders. He had made a loud statement in his return to Negro League action—Leon Day was still the litmus test other Negro League pitchers needed to measure themselves against.

As teammate Monte Irvin said, "If we had one game to win, we wanted Leon to pitch."[12]

In the first game of a doubleheader on August 11, 1946, Day struck out 10 batters while pitching all 15 innings against the Homestead Grays, the Eagles' longtime rival. Day came out on top 8–7 when he smacked a long home run to left in the bottom of the 15th inning.

It proved to be a charmed season for Day and the Eagles. Irvin batted .369, Larry Doby batted .363, and Day batted .362 to anchor the lineup. On the mound, Day went 13–2 and led the league in wins, complete games (14), innings (132), strikeouts (109) and shutouts (three), while finishing second with a 2.45 ERA (178 ERA+). Newark won the Negro National League by 12½ games over the New York Cubans.

They faced off against the Kansas City Monarchs in an epic seven-game World Series. The Monarchs had Satchel Paige, Hilton Smith, and Connie Johnson in the rotation, and Willard Brown, Buck O'Neil, and Ted Strong in the lineup. With big-league scouts in the stands, Day squared off against Smith in Game One, allowing one run in five innings as the Monarchs prevailed 2–1.

Down 3–2 in the Series, a sore-armed Day was tabbed as the Eagles' Game Six starter. Rocked for four runs in the first inning, Day left the mound without recording an out and moved to center field. He made a spectacular over-the-shoulder catch off a drive from O'Neil to save the game 9–7 for the Eagles. Newark hung on for a 3–2 win in Game Seven to win their first championship.

Day had reached the pinnacle of his league just as his arm ran out of juice. He played two more years in Puerto Rico and Mexico, then signed with the 1949 Baltimore Elite Giants as the Negro Leagues tried to carry on at a lesser level after Jackie Robinson opened the door to the majors. The Elite Giants won the pennant that year, but without much contribution from Day. He moved on to Canada in 1950, then found himself with Toronto in the International League the next season, a minor league team for the St. Louis Browns. Pitching 40 innings out of the bullpen, Day recorded a 1.58 ERA at age 34.

Day went 13–9 with a 3.41 ERA and batted .314 with Scranton in the AA Eastern League in 1952, followed by a 5–5 record with Edmonton in 1953. No major-league team reached out with interest. He finished his career in Canada in 1955. Day would later say his arm never felt the same after he returned from the war, despite pockets of success in the years immediately following. That unfortunate reality prevented him from joining his younger teammates Doby, Irvin, and Don Newcombe, who had made it to the integrated major leagues.

Tucked into Day's file at the Hall of Fame in Cooperstown is Buck O'Neil's scouting report for the Kansas City Royals. Here is what O'Neil had to say about Day: "Front line starter. Short arm type. Everything quick. Strikeout pitcher. Very durable. Worked with 3 days rest. Played 2B or CF between starts. Top athlete. Very desirable." O'Neil graded him at the highest level—excellent—and recommended him as someone worth acquiring.

Seamheads documents Day with a 57–24 record and 3.50 ERA in 114 games, along with a .307 batting average. Day estimated that he won about 300 games against all competition. He generated 19.3 WAR from pitching and 3.8 WAR from offense. In 1993, Day was inducted into the Puerto Rican Baseball Hall of Fame.

"And Leon Day—it's a shame he was born when he was. He played every position on the field except catch, and played them all magnificently," said Effa Manley, co-owner of the Newark Eagles during Day's tenure.[13]

Day settled in Baltimore for the last 15 years of his life, and there was an organized effort to see him recognized for his baseball achievements. January 31, 1992, was Leon Day's Day in Baltimore, and May 18, 1992, was Leon Day Day in Maryland. A street near Camden Yards is named Leon Day Way, and he has a park named after him in Baltimore.

After throwing out the first pitch at a 1992 Orioles game, Day chose not to reflect on the fact that he had been forced to leave the segregated city to chase his baseball dreams. Instead, he expressed a hopeful but realistic approach to his chances of getting into Cooperstown. "It would mean a lot to me to get into the Hall of Fame, to be grouped with some of the greatest players in history," Day said.[14] He fell one vote short when the Veterans Committee met in 1993.

Fast forward to March 1995. Day is stuck in a hospital bed battling diabetes and heart-related ailments. He had tried not to get his hopes up about making the Hall, but it had to be weighing on his mind. Then, with his family and former teammates by his side, he got the call that changed everything—he had been elected to the Baseball Hall of Fame, Class of 1995.

"I'm so happy. I don't know what to do. I never thought it would come," Day said.[15] He died five days later on March 13, 1995, at the age of 78. With Mike Schmidt and Richie Ashburn being inducted into the Hall that year, the induction ceremony on July 30 attracted a then-record 40,000 baseball fans to Cooperstown. One of the Negro League's greatest pitchers never got to hear the applause and recognition for his splendid career, but a great Day was honored on a great day in Cooperstown. Leon Day died knowing he would forever be a member of baseball's most prestigious club.

Chapter 11

Live Ball Era 1920–Present
Two-Way Play That Bucked the System

Coming off a catastrophic end to the Deadball Era, Major League Baseball was not in trouble for long. The Black Sox Scandal of 1919 was the unfortunate culmination of a decade of declining attendance as fans were turned off by the lack of offense. Most of the best players of the Deadball Era were not larger than life, other than the fact everyone hated Ty Cobb.

Then Babe Ruth stopped trying to be a two-way player and, more importantly, found himself in New York City on the Yankees. His 54 homers in 1920 nearly doubled his major-league record of 29 set the year before in Boston. The game of baseball would never be the same—the Live Ball Era had arrived with a bang.

Home runs started flying out of the park, batting averages rose sharply, and the spitball and emery ball were banned. Another long-overdue change—as a result of Ray Chapman's tragic death in 1920 when hit in the head by a dirty ball—was that batters no longer had to hit the same slimy and dark baseball throughout each game.

These changes happened just in the nick of time, because MLB had new competition for attention as the Roaring '20s evolved into the Golden Age of Sports. The formation of the Negro National League in 1920 heralded the dawn of a new age of Black baseball. Negro League players finally had financial backing, stable and organized league structure, visionary leadership, and an increasing number of African American newspapers devoted to covering their games and star players.

Ruth's transformation from a pitcher to a two-way player and finally to an outfielder reflected the value of an everyday star player in the Live Ball Era, especially one who was a gate attraction. In the 19th century, the best everyday players were pitchers and the teams with the most durable pitchers (who could hopefully hit) came out on top. Two-way players were less common in the Deadball Era, but it was still a thing. The Negro Leagues could not have survived without players able to pitch and play the field.

Chapter 11. Live Ball Era 1920–Present

After a half-century of constant, ground-breaking changes to the game, baseball settled down in the 1930s. The ball was undoubtedly tinkered with a little as offensive production got out of hand. The first night baseball game in 1935 marked a gradual transformation from a sport played during the day to one played almost always at night. The player-manager became an infrequently used solution as franchises started viewing the manager as a role with more singular importance. Front offices took firm control of player acquisition and development, although Branch Rickey still seemed to be the first to discover every great player.

Teams were no longer stocked solely with farm boys from the Midwest, Southern rednecks, and the sons of immigrants from the Northeast. California was turning into a hotbed of talent with the likes of Joe DiMaggio, Ted Williams, and Duke Snider about to flash their skills.

When a large number of players went off to serve their country during World War II, teams had to fill rosters with anyone who seemed remotely qualified. Benches were not as deep or experienced, and managers had nothing to lose trying a position player out on the mound and vice versa. In many cases, a sore pitching arm led a player to see if he could extend his career as a position player. A two-way career typically meant pitching and playing the field in separate seasons, not together. Once the war was over and players returned from military service, two-way playing became a rarity. Shohei Ohtani's emergence will undoubtedly inspire a new generation of two-way players, if their teams allow them to try.

What follows in this chapter is a snapshot of 26 Live Ball Era players since 1920 who had experience as two-way players. They are featured in the order in which their careers started.

Clarence Mitchell

Mitchell debuted in the majors in 1911 during the Deadball Era, but the bulk of his two-way playing came between 1920 and 1922 and his career lasted until 1932. He was one of 17 spitball pitchers allowed to continue throwing the pitch after the 1920 ban and the last remaining lefty spitballer. "You never heard of a spitballer with a sore arm," he remarked.[1]

Mitchell's other claim to fame came when he hit into the only triple play in World Series or postseason history in Game 5 of the 1920 Series. It was executed in the fifth inning by Indians second baseman Bill Wambsganss unassisted, making it one of 15 unassisted triple plays in baseball history. With the hit-and-run sign on, Mitchell's hard shot up the middle was snagged in a leaping grab by Wambsganss, who dashed to second to double off the runner and then tagged the runner coming from first.

"He stopped running and stood there, so I just tagged him. That was all there was to it," Wambsganss explained.[2] As for Mitchell, he rapped into a double play in his next at-bat to round out a forgettable day.

Mitchell's career was marked by promising fits and starts. After an unsuccessful five-game stint with Detroit in 1911, Mitchell spent the next four years pitching and playing outfield in the minors. He batted .333 in 1913 for the Providence Grays in the International League. His 22–11 record with a 2.77 ERA for Denver in the Western League in 1915 attracted the attention of Cincinnati. He went 11–10 across 194⅔ innings for the seventh-place Reds in 1916 with a 3.14 ERA and 17 complete games—seven of the losses were in one-run games.

Brooklyn gave some thought to converting Mitchell to first base for the 1919 season, but the team acquired Ed Konetchy instead.[3] Mitchell batted .367 that year in limited at-bats and went 7–5 with a 3.06 ERA in 19 appearances on the mound. He went 6-for-18 as a pinch hitter in 1920.

Spitball pitcher Clarence Mitchell finished sixth in the National League in ERA in 1921 and won 125 games during an 18-season career. At the plate, he was just a .252 batter (Library of Congress, Prints & Photographs Division, LC-DIG-ggbain-340094).

His best year pitching was 1921 with the Brooklyn Robins. He went 11–9 with a 2.89 ERA (sixth best in NL; 136 ERA+) in 190 innings and tied for the league lead with three shutouts. Mitchell was able to baffle batters as a southpaw spitballer at a time when Dutch Leonard was the only other lefty spitball pitcher in the majors.

Mitchell's best year at the plate came in 1922, when he batted .290 with 45 hits. That season he played 42 games at first base while pitching just five games. Traded to Philadelphia in advance of the 1923 season, he was mainly used as a starting pitcher by the Phillies over the next five seasons but pitched to a 4.98 ERA. He wasn't over the hill yet, but he was slowing down, as evidenced by the nickname he acquired: "Old Bullet Ball."

After getting released by the Phillies in 1928, Mitchell was signed by the Cardinals, who were on their way to win the NL pennant. Mitchell did his part to contribute. On August 5, he started and pitched into the 15th and final inning as the Cardinals defeated the second-place Giants 6–4. He would start 18 games and post eight victories for the Cards that year. He was traded to the New York Giants early in the 1930 season and produced a 10–3 record in 129 innings.

Mitchell's career-high in wins (13) came in his next-to-last season, 1931, at age 40. The Nebraska lefty won 125 games pitching 18 seasons for six teams. He would continue pitching in the minors, and throwing the spitball, until the age of 46 in 1937. His career record in the minors was 91–70. His career marks at the plate were .252 with 324 hits and 133 RBI. He appeared 144 times as a pinch hitter, collecting 31 hits for a .225 average. Across his 18 seasons, he played 80 games at first base, 18 games in the outfield, and made 390 pitching appearances. In 1953, Mitchell—the pride of Franklin, Nebraska—was named to the Nebraska Sports Hall of Fame.[4]

Jack Bentley

Bentley was a slugging and pitching sensation in the minor leagues, who was unfairly held back from the majors. The southpaw toiled for 13 years in the minors, playing 1,300 games, while seeing action in just 287 major-league games over nine seasons. He gained notoriety as the losing pitcher in the famed "pebble" game of the 1924 World Series.

Bentley debuted with the Washington Senators at age 18 in 1913, pitching in three games that year and then 30 the next season. His 2.37 ERA in 1914 was strong, but he walked too many batters. Sent to the minors for more seasoning in 1915, he wouldn't return to the majors for extended action until 1923. He emerged as a star first baseman with the 1917 Baltimore Orioles in the International League, batting .343 that season while letting a sore pitching arm heal. He served in the U.S. Army and was deployed to France during World War I, which caused him to miss all of 1918. He returned to the Orioles to help them win the first of seven straight International League pennants in 1919, batting .324 and playing 92 games at first.

He broke out as a two-way star the next season, batting .371 with 20 homers, 161 RBI, and 231 hits playing 125 games at first base for the Orioles. On the mound, he went 16–3 with a 2.10 ERA in 167 innings. He did not get called up to the majors, because Orioles Owner Jack Dunn had learned his lesson. Back in July 1914, he had sold Babe Ruth (and two other players) to the Boston Red Sox for $25,000 out of financial desperation. After watching Ruth turn into the game's biggest attraction with 54 home runs that season with the Yankees, Dunn had no intention of repeating his mistake.

"Baltimore's Jack Bentley typifies the minor-league superstar, ruthlessly penalized because he was a local draw. The versatile Bentley was often called the Babe Ruth of the International League.... When he was not pulverizing baseballs, Bentley was mystifying batters, as he went 16 and 3 for a winning percentage of .842," wrote William Curran in *Big Sticks: The Batting Revolution of the Twenties*.[5]

Bentley performed even better for the Orioles in 1921. He won the league Triple Crown by batting .412 with 24 homers and 120 RBI, pounding out a league-record 246 hits while playing 129 games at first base. On the mound he went 12-1 with a 2.34 ERA. More of the same in 1922: .351 average, 217 hits, 13-2 record with a league-best 1.73 ERA. Bentley was frustrated to be stuck in the minors, saying, "An ambitious ballplayer can't be satisfied with anything he may do below the highest rank."[6]

Lots of major-league teams were interested in Bentley's services, and Dunn finally got an offer he couldn't refuse—the New York Giants ended up paying $72,500 to acquire his rights for the 1923 season.

Bentley, at age 28, won 13 games for the Giants but with a high 4.48 ERA. He mashed the ball at a .427 clip—a National League record for a pitcher—while slugging .573 and generating 1.6 offensive WAR in 94 plate appearances but not playing any in the field. He batted .421 (8-for-19) and slugged .790 as a pinch hitter that season. He was rocked making two appearances in the World Series that year, recording a 9.45 ERA but collecting three hits in five at-bats. His pitching improved in 1924, compiling an eight-game winning streak on the way to a 16-5 record with a 3.78 ERA in 188 innings.

He won the fifth game in the 1924 World Series while hitting a homer off Walter Johnson, but he will be remembered more as the losing pitcher of Game 7. With the score tied in the bottom of the 12th inning, Earl McNeely stepped to the plate with runners on first and second and grounded a ball that struck a pebble and bounced high over the head of Giants' third baseman Freddie Lindstrom, allowing the winning run to score.

"When we lost, I felt lower than a snake's belly in a rut. But as I walked off the field and heard all those people hollering, I was a little bit pleased that I had brought so much happiness to so many people," Bentley recalled years later.[7] Bentley's .417 lifetime batting average in World Series action is among the best-ever by a pitcher.

He went on to play four games in the field in 1925, making 34 pinch-hitting appearances on the way to a .303 average while posting a 5.04 ERA

Chapter 11. Live Ball Era 1920–Present

Jack Bentley set a National League record by batting .427 as a pitcher in 1923. He was stuck playing 1,300 games in the minors despite a .354 average and 114 home runs. His 80–30 pitching record in the minors eventually led to 138 pitching appearances in the big leagues (Library of Congress, Prints & Photographs Division, LG-DIG-ggbain-17097).

on the mound. The highlight of his season was belting a walk-off home run on August 29, 1925—he pitched the last two innings to get the win. In the offseason, Bentley was traded to the Phillies, who let him play 56 games at first base in 1926. He batted .258 with 63 hits but was so horrible on the mound (8.17 ERA in 25⅓ innings), that he was shifted permanently to first base. His career would end the next year with the Giants.

Bentley finished his career with a .291 batting average and 170 hits in the majors, including a .250 average from 21 pinch-hits. He recorded a .354 average with 114 home runs and 1,551 hits in the minors. On the mound he went 46–33 with a 4.01 ERA in 138 major-league pitching appearances and a record of 80–30 with a 3.08 ERA in in the minors.

Rube Bressler

Bressler pitched from 1914 to 1917, then did a little bit of two-way playing from 1918 to 1920, before settling into an outfield role until 1932. He

Rube Bressler played 48 games in the outfield with the Cincinnati Red in 1919 while also pitching in 13 games. He ended up winning 26 games in 107 pitching appearances but spent the last 12 years of his career as an outfielder and first baseman, recording a .301 average with 1,170 hits (Library of Congress, Prints & Photographs Division, LG-DIG-ggbain-17265).

played 840 games in the outfield, 147 games at first base, and 107 games as a pitcher, mainly for the Cincinnati Reds (11 seasons).

His best year on the mound came as a 19-year-old rookie with the Philadelphia Athletics in 1914, when he went 10–4 with a 1.77 ERA (148 ERA+) in 10 starts and 19 relief appearances. *Sporting Life* noted that Bressler "looks like the sure successor of Eddie Plank as the Athletic Club's star southpaw."[8]

His arm started failing him the next season and his production dropped sharply to 4–17 with a 5.20 ERA. He managed to produce an 8–5 mark with a 2.46 ERA in 1918 with Cincinnati but had already started shifting to be an outfielder. Playing with the Class A Atlanta Crackers in 1917, Bressler smashed the longest home run ever hit at Ponce de Leon Park.[9]

He played 48 games in the outfield in 1919 and 13 games as a pitcher, batting a weak .206 for a Reds team that would win the infamous World Series against the Black Sox. Bressler found his batting stroke in 1921, averaging .307 with 99 hits. On April 21, he posted a four-hit day while batting fifth in the lineup. He rapped four hits again on June 16 while batting third. In 1922, he was mainly utilized as a weapon off the bench, leading the league with 13 pinch-hits and 43 pinch-hit appearances.

Bressler credited Edd Roush with teaching him how to play the outfield and Jake Daubert with how to play first base. "And I made myself into a hitter. I changed my whole style of batting. Went into a deep crouch," he explained in Lawrence Ritter's *The Glory of Their Times*.[10]

Bressler was a force at the plate from 1924 to 1930, with averages as high as .347 (6th in NL), .348, and .357. He recorded a 25-game hitting streak in 1927. He ended his 19-year career with 1,170 hits and a .301 average (110 OPS+), .378 OBP, 87 triples, and 586 RBI. His pitching mark was 26–32 with a 3.40 ERA. In 1963, Bressler was inducted into the Cincinnati Reds Hall of Fame.

George Sisler

Sisler started out as a pitcher in high school, college, and the majors, but it wouldn't take long for the sweet-swinging lefty to establish himself as one of the best batters in baseball history.

Sisler excelled as a southpaw hurler at the University of Michigan, where he attracted the attention of Branch Rickey, the school's head baseball coach. He posted 16 strikeouts in a seven-inning game—causing *Sporting Life* to proclaim him the "greatest college pitcher"[11]—but recurring arm trouble allowed Sisler to shine more with the bat. He gained recognition as a two-time All-American and led the Wolverines to the unofficial 1914 college baseball championship.[12] Rickey, who had moved on to become an executive and manager of the St. Louis Browns, won a contract battle with the Pirates to sign Sisler.

Playing 36 games at first base, 29 games in the outfield, and 15 games on the mound, Sisler debuted with the Browns in 1915 with a .285 average and 78 hits. His pitching record was 4–4 with a 2.83 ERA (101 ERA+) and six complete games in 70 innings. On August 29, 1915, he outpitched the great Walter Johnson to win 2–1 with a complete-game six-hitter.

"Sisler can be counted a baseball freak," gushed a report in the *Washington Post*. "[Rickey] plays him in the outfield and he makes sensational catches … he plays him on first base and actually he looks like Chase when Hal was king of the first sackers, and then on the hill he goes out and beats Johnson."[13]

Sisler was able to make only three pitching appearances in 1916, and his only win of the season came on September 17, when he again outpitched Johnson with a six-hit shutout. He ended the year with a 1.00 ERA in 27 innings but emerged as a solid, all-around player as the Browns' first baseman. He batted .305 that season with 177 hits, 76 RBI, and 34 stolen bases. His days as a pitcher were over.

Sisler went on to establish himself as one of the best first basemen of the 20th century, relying on a flat-footed batting style that allowed him to spray the ball all over the field. Hitting 10 homers in 1919 and 19 long balls the next season, Sisler trailed only Babe Ruth in that newly important category. His 257 hits in 1920 set a major-league record that held until Ichiro Suzuki collected 262 hits in 2004. His 41-game hitting streak in 1922 is the fifth best in baseball history, while his 35-game hitting streak in 1924–25 is tied for 11th best.

Nicknamed "Gorgeous George" for his good looks, Sisler was named the American League's Most Valuable Player over Ruth in 1922, a year in which he batted .420 and also led the league in runs (134), hits (246), triples (18) and stolen bases (51). That year, future Hall of Fame pitcher Christy Mathewson commented that Sisler was "every bit as valuable as Ruth, some people think more valuable."[14]

George Sisler was an outstanding two-way player at the University of Michigan who once recorded 16 strikeouts during a seven-inning game. Recurring arm trouble turned the southpaw into a Hall of Fame first baseman who batted over .400 twice and finished with a .340 career average (Library of Congress, Prints & Photographs Division, LG-DIG-ggbain-12855).

Sisler also batted over .400 in 1920 and finished his career with a .340 average, which ranks 19th in baseball history. He recorded six seasons with 200 or more hits, led the league in stolen bases four times, and batted over .300 13 times.

Sisler finished his 15-year career with 2,812 hits, 164 triples (30th all-time), 375 stolen bases, 1,284 runs scored, and an OPS+ of 125. In 1999, Sisler was ranked number 33 on *The Sporting News*' list of "Baseball's 100 Greatest Players."[15] He ranks 19th all-time among first basemen, according to JAWS—the Jaffe WAR Score System developed by Jay Jaffe.

Sisler was part of the first induction class of the National Baseball Hall of Fame in 1939. "I think it's the greatest honor the game can offer a retired player and it's a satisfaction to know that your career is still remembered, years after you have hung up your glove," he said.[16]

Lefty O'Doul

O'Doul is like many two-way players who turned into position players after experiencing arm trouble from pitching. He debuted with the New York Yankees in 1919 as a lefty pitcher and pinch hitter, making just 11 appearances on the mound with a 3.65 ERA over the next four years. Returning to the minors for the 1921 season, O'Doul went 25–9 with a 2.39 ERA in 312 innings for the San Francisco Seals while batting .338. A 23-game stint pitching for the Red Sox in 1923 produced disappointing results. That would be the end of his pitching experiment.

As O'Doul explains in *The Glory of Their Times*: "I was a pitcher at first. Spent seven years at it, but never got very far. Was up with the Yankees and the Red Sox, but hurt my arm and never did much. So I said to the manager, 'I am now an outfielder.' 'You don't know how to play the outfield,' he says. 'Well,' I said, 'I'll learn.'"[17]

O'Doul found his batting stroke playing outfield in the Pacific Coast League—he even caught 32 games for Salt Lake City in 1925. He batted .392 for Salt Lake City in 1924 and followed up with a .375 average and an astounding 309 hits playing 198 games the next season. Moving to Hollywood in the same league, he averaged .338 with 223 hits in 1926, followed by .378 with 278 hits for San Francisco in 1927.

Picked up by the New York Giants for the 1928 season, the 31-year-old O'Doul showed promise with a .319 average playing left field despite missing time with a broken ankle. Traded to the Phillies, he just missed hitting .400 in 1929 but still led the league at .398 and with a .465 on-base percentage while finishing second in runs (152) and eighth in RBI (122). His 254 hits that season set a National League record that was matched by Bill Terry the next year but has never been surpassed. He finished second in the MVP voting to Rogers Hornsby.

O'Doul batted .383 (4th in NL) with 202 hits in his last season with the Phillies. Next, he was traded to Brooklyn, where he averaged .336 in 1931 and then won his second batting title with a .368 average in 1932. He was able to squeeze in six seasons as a regular outfielder before his career ended in 1934. His .349 lifetime average trails only Ty Cobb, Rogers

Hornsby, Joe Jackson, and Negro Leaguers Oscar Charleston and Jud Wilson. His .413 lifetime on-base percentage ranks 32nd all-time.

The pedestrian bridge that takes fans to Oracle Park in San Francisco is named after O'Doul, a San Francisco native who managed the San Francisco Seals for 17 years after his playing career ended. One of the players he managed and mentored: 20-year-old Joe DiMaggio, who batted .398 for him in 1935.

O'Doul made many trips to Japan to spark friendly interest in the game there before and after World War II, and he helped found the Nippon Professional Baseball League. For his efforts as a baseball ambassador, O'Doul was inducted into the Japanese Baseball Hall of Fame in 2002.[18]

Johnny Cooney

Cooney came from a family of major leaguers. His father, Jimmy, and brother, Jimmy, Jr., both played in the majors. Cooney started out as a pitcher with modest success, dabbling a little bit in the outfield and first base, before being forced to return to the minors for four years. He returned to the majors as an outfielder at the age of 34 and was an effective starter into his 40s.

He debuted as a southpaw with the Boston Braves at age 20 in 1921, appearing in 12 games in two years. He refined his pitching in the minors, going 19–3 with a 1.94 ERA for New Haven in 1922.

Returning to the Braves for 1923, Cooney pitched to a 3.31 ERA in 98 innings but broke out with a .379 average. He appeared in 11 games as an outfielder and six games as a pinch runner. He started 16 games in the outfield early in the 1924 season before settling into a role as a spot starter and reliever. He went 8–9 with a 3.18 ERA and 12 complete games in 181 innings. He batted .254 with 33 hits.

Cooney, who was a righty batter, saw his average climb to .320 the next season while making 29 starts on the mound with his patented "hesitation" pitch to throw off the batter's timing. He posted a 14–14 record with a 3.48 ERA and 20 complete games in 245⅔ innings. Ongoing arm trouble, which later required surgery, forced Cooney to contribute as a position player. He played 31 games at first base in 1926, which resulted in a .302 average.

Playing for former teammate Casey Stengel at Toledo in Double A ball, Cooney batted .291 while playing 64 games in the outfield and recording a 2.49 ERA in 25 pitching appearances. He pitched 174 innings the next season in Indianapolis while batting .291, then spent three more years in Indianapolis as an outfielder with averages of .330, .308, and .372 (with 224 hits).

The Brooklyn Dodgers finally signed Cooney for the 1936 season on the recommendation of their manager, Stengel. He offered no power, but Cooney could hit and play above-average defense in center field.

"I think Cooney is the best outfielder I ever saw in my life or ever heard of. He's not fast, but he doesn't have to be. He's just always there when a ball has to be caught," commented teammate Van Lingle Mungo.[19]

After batting .282 with 143 hits in 1936 and .293 in 1937, the popular Cooney was traded back to the Cardinals, who wanted to send him down to the minors. He refused and was released, signing with the Boston Bees to rejoin Stengel, his favorite manager. He started in the outfield and batted .271 and .274 the next two seasons. He hit the only two home runs of his major-league career on back-to-back days at the Polo Grounds, September 24 and 25, 1939.[20]

At the age of 39, Cooney saw his productivity jump to a .318 average (3rd best in NL) in 1940 and then set career highs the next season with 141 hits and 25 doubles with a .319 average (2nd best) as a 40-year-old starting center fielder. *The Sporting News* named him "Veteran Player of the Year."[21] It would be his last hurrah, and he played his last game in 1943 with the Yankees at age 43. He finished with 965 hits and a .286 average (87 OPS+) playing 794 games in the outfield and 93 games at first base.

On the mound, Cooney threw 795⅓ innings with a 34–44 record and 3.72 ERA (106 ERA+). He generated 9.2 pitching WAR to go with 8.5 WAR as a position player but never played in the postseason during his 20-year career.

Bob Smith

Smith debuted in the majors as a 28-year-old shortstop in 1923. He finished his career as a 42-year-old relief pitcher in 1937. He started his professional baseball career in the minors with Beaumont in 1921, which is when he first lied about his age and said he was 23 instead of 26. He waited 56 years before fessing up to this deception. "If they had known I was really 38 when I was telling them I was 35, they never would have kept me," he explained.[22]

The Boston Braves gave Smith a two-year trial as the starting shortstop. He batted .251 with 35 errors in 1923 and .228 with 20 errors playing 80 games at short in 1924. The first-place Giants had Travis Jackson batting .302 as their shortstop, while the last-place Braves had Smith posting the lowest average of anyone on the team.

Smith possessed a strong arm, so the Braves gave him a shot at pitching in 1925. He went 5–3 with a 4.47 ERA in 92⅔ innings, while also appearing in 21 games at short and 15 games at second base and batting .282. His first win came on July 18, 1925, when he pitched an 11-inning complete game to win 2–1.

The next year he worked strictly as a pitcher. His 3.75 ERA in 1926 came in 201⅓ innings and included 14 complete games. The Tennessee native would post double-digit win totals every season from 1926 to 1931, with a career-high 15 wins and 3.22 ERA for the third-place Cubs in 1931. He played five games at shortstop in 1929, but otherwise focused on pitching. He pitched at least 200 innings seven times but operated as a swingman over the last half of his career.

He started and lost both games of a doubleheader on September 14, 1928. After he surrendered four straight hits at the start of the opener, he was taken out and suffered the loss. Back on the mound for the nightcap, he pitched into the seventh inning but again took the loss.

One of the highlights of Smith's career came in a loss he suffered on May 17, 1927. He pitched all 22 innings as the Braves fell 4–3 to the Cubs. After falling behind 3–0 through five innings, Smith shut out the Cubs for the next 16 innings. He even chipped in a single and scored a run in the sixth inning. Manager Dave Bancroft asked several times if he needed relief, but Smith waved him off. He finally gave up a run in the 22nd inning that proved decisive. He scattered 20 hits and nine walks while facing 89 batters, and he was helped out by four double plays behind him.

Smith got to pitch in Game One of the 1932 World Series for the Cubs, retiring both Babe Ruth and Lou Gehrig in a series the Cubs lost.

He was released by the Reds in the middle of the 1933 season despite pitching to a 2.20 ERA in 16 games. He resigned with the Braves. Smith was the best pitcher on the 1935 Boston Braves team that lost 115 games. Despite an 8–18 record, his 3.94 ERA and 96 ERA+ demonstrated he could still get batters out at age 40.

Pitching mostly for bad teams during his 15-year career, Smith posted a record of 106–139 with a 3.94 ERA that was exactly average (100 ERA+). He recorded 128 complete games and finished 157 games as the last man out of the bullpen. His career pitching WAR was 23.7.

Playing 208 games at shortstop and 48 games at second and third, Smith averaged .242 with 409 hits. His career OPS+ of 54 demonstrates he was of greater service on the mound.

Red Lucas

Lucas was a righty pitcher and lefty batter who played just 18 games in the field but was a valuable weapon off the bench. He appeared 479 times as a pinch hitter during a 15-year career, batting .272 with 68 RBI. His 117 career pinch-hits are tied with Steve Braun for 11th-most all-time, according to Baseball-Reference. Lucas held the major-league record for career pinch-hits until Smoky Burgess broke it in 1965.

Nicknamed "The Nashville Narcissus," Lucas was known for his impeccable control on the mound, pitching in 396 games with 204 complete games and 2,542 innings. He went 157–135 with a 3.72 ERA, but the only time his team won the pennant was his 1923 rookie year in which he pitched in three games.

He went 18–11 with a 3.38 ERA and 19 complete games in 1927, finishing 11th in MVP voting. In 1929 he led the NL in complete games (28), WHIP (1.204) and hits/9 innings (8.9) while winning a career-high 19 games and finishing sixth in MVP voting. He also led the league in shutouts with four in 1928 and in complete games in 1931 and 1932. Despite a 13–17 record in 1932, Lucas produced his only sub-3.00 ERA that year with a 2.94 mark. His 1.61 BB/9 ranks 31st all-time.

At the plate, Lucas batted over .300 six times and averaged .281 for his career with 404 hits, 190 RBI, and .340 on-base percentage. He had at least one hit in each of the nine batting positions. The most he played in the field was nine games at second base, shortstop, and left field in 1927. His managers tried to make him an outfielder and a second baseman at various times, but it never stuck for long. In 1931, he appeared in 68 games as a pinch hitter and collected 15 pinch-hits.

Lucas narrowly missed a no-hitter on July 22, 1927. The only base runner reached on a questionable call that probably should have been ruled an error, and then was wiped away by a double play. Perhaps more impressive was his 17-inning complete game to beat the Cardinals on April 25, 1928, or in 1932, when he went 250 consecutive innings without being relieved.[23]

Lucas surrendered Babe Ruth's 712th home run on May 25, 1935. Famed sportswriter Grantland Rice paid tribute to him with a poem titled "Red Lucas, Ball Player." He was inducted into the Cincinnati Reds Hall of Fame in 1965.

Ben Chapman

Chapman is best known as the person who symbolized the racial hatred directed at Jackie Robinson when he broke baseball's color barrier. Chapman, who was the manager of the Phillies in 1947, believed it was his obligation to heckle and direct slurs at the opposition to gain an edge. He started the abusive comments and encouraged three of his players to join in. Chapman clearly crossed the line into unacceptable, racist behavior with Robinson and has been rightfully condemned since then.

As Branch Rickey, Dodgers general manager, pointed out, "Chapman did more than anybody to unite the Dodgers. When he poured out that string of unconscionable abuse, he solidified and unified thirty men.... Chapman made Jackie a real member of the Dodgers."[24]

"Robinson is just another ballplayer to us.... We'll ride anybody if it'll help us win," explained Chapman in a 1947 interview.[25]

In fairness to Chapman, he was an equal opportunity irritant who had feuded with Babe Ruth when they were teammates, fought with umpires and opponents, taunted Jewish fans with Nazi salutes, and berated players he was managing.[26] It was representative of the competitive streak that carried him to success in his playing career.

Known for his speed, the "Alabama Flash" was one of the premier base stealers of the 1930s. He led the American League in stolen bases four times and finished with 287 career steals during a 15-year career. He won a World Series title with the New York Yankees in 1932 as a teammate of Ruth and Lou Gehrig. A four-time All-Star, his career slash line of .302/.383/.440 produced a 114 OPS+.

He batted .316 as a rookie with the Yankees in 1930, playing 91 games at third base and 45 games at second base. Switching to the outfield after that, he ended up in the outfield for 1,495 games before switching to pitcher in 1942. He led the AL in triples in 1934 and finished fourth in runs scored three times.

Chapman served as player-manager for the Richmond Colts in 1942. In addition to playing 62 games at third base and batting .324, he went 6–3 with a 1.71 ERA in 16 mound appearances. However, he slugged an umpire near the end of the season and that caused him to be suspended for the 1943 season.[27]

Returning to Richmond for 1944, Chapman pitched in 21 games with a 13–6 mark and 2.21 ERA. He played 23 games at third base and batted .303. That led to a late-season appearance for the Dodgers, where he pitched in 11 games (5–3, 3.40) and batted .368.

Chapman took the mound for 25 games in the majors over his last three seasons while also playing 18 games in the field. He went 8–6 with a 4.39 ERA (84 ERA+) in 141⅓ innings.

Bobby Reis

Reis showed flashes of promise playing all nine positions around the diamond, but ultimately his major-league career consisted of 142 games played between 1931 and 1938. He debuted with the Brooklyn Robins in 1931, playing six games at third base and batting .294.

Reis played 21 games in the outfield in 1935 but batted just .247. That year he went 3–2 in 14 pitching appearances with a 2.83 ERA. The next season he pitched 138⅔ innings and led the NL in games finished with 24 but his 74 walks led to a 4.48 ERA. Four years of pitching led to a 10–13 career record and 4.56 ERA.

At the plate, he averaged .233 with 70 hits playing 51 games in the outfield, 21 games in the infield, and one game at catcher. Reis batted .297 with 864 hits in nine minor-league seasons but pitched just six times in the minors.

Bucky Walters

Walters made it to the major leagues as a third baseman before pivoting to become one of the top right-handed pitchers of the late 1930s and 1940s. Depending on your perspective, he was either a below-average hitter for a third baseman or an above-average hitter for a pitcher.

Walters won 20 games in three seasons and led the league in wins, complete games, and innings pitched three times; in ERA, ERA+ and WHIP twice; and in shutouts and strikeouts once. The six-time All-Star recorded a lifetime 116 ERA+ and 46.5 pitching WAR. His 42 shutouts rank 38th all-time.

From 1939 to 1946, Walters led the majors with 141 wins. Bill James once ranked Walters as the 69th-best pitcher in baseball history,[28] while he ranks 85th all-time among starting pitchers, according to JAWS (the Jaffe WAR Score System).

Tommy Lasorda called Walters "a great player, a great pitcher, and certainly deserving of being inducted into the Hall of Fame."[29] He was inducted into the Cincinnati Reds Hall of Fame in 1958.

Walters debuted with the Boston Braves in 1931 and batted .191 in 31 games over the next two seasons. Traded to the Red Sox for the 1933 season, he batted 250 with 50 hits in 52 games. He played third base in 1934 and batted .256 with 97 hits, but he also pitched in two games for the Phillies at the end of the season as they recognized his strong throwing arm at third.

The Phillies preferred Johnny Vergez at third, so they mainly had Walters pitch in 1935. He pitched in 24 games with a 4.17 ERA in 151 innings and played eight games in the field. He would play 11 games in the field over the remaining 13 years of his career as his pitching took off.

Some of his pitching numbers were poor in 1936—league-leading

21 losses, 4.26 ERA, 284 hits in 258 innings—but Walters led the league with four shutouts. He was a groundball pitcher who relied on a sinker and sharp slider to get batters out.

Walters was nonplussed about making the switch from position player to pitcher, although he greatly preferred playing every day. "Hell, if the game was half as complicated as some of these writers make out it is, a lot of us boys from the farm would never have been able to make a living at it," Walters said.[30]

Walters was traded to the Reds on June 13, 1938, right in between Johnny Vander Meer's back-to-back no-hitters for the team. Walters was booed as he warmed up in the bullpen in the late innings of Vander Meer's second no-hitter, but luckily, he wasn't needed.

The righty hurler was named the National League MVP in 1939 with the Reds, when he won the pitcher's Triple Crown with 27 wins, 2.29 ERA, and 137 strikeouts in 319 innings. He helped his cause by batting .325 with 16 RBI. On September 8, 1939, he slugged a home run while scattering five hits for the complete-game win. On August 26, 1939, Walters pitched a complete-game two-hitter for the Reds as they beat the Dodgers in the first ballgame ever televised.[31]

He followed up his MVP season with another strong year in 1940. He led the league in wins (22), ERA (2.48), complete games (29), innings (305), ERA+ (154), WHIP (1.092) and hits/9 (7.1) as the Reds won the pennant. They beat the Tigers in the World Series as Walters pitched a complete-game two-hitter to win Game Two and pitched a five-hit shutout to win Game Six. In that elimination game he belted a home run in the eighth inning and drove in two of the four runs in a 4–0 victory.

Nineteen wins and a league-leading 27 complete games and 302 innings followed in 1941, then Walters again led the league with 23 wins in 1944 while finishing second with a 2.40 ERA. Two more strong years followed—2.68 and 2.56 ERA—before he threw his last pitch in 1950 at age 41.

On April 20, 1946, Walters was locked up in a pitchers' duel with Rip Sewell of Pittsburgh. He bunted his way on in the sixth inning and then stole home to score the only run of the game for the Reds as Walters lost the 2–1 decision.[32] Walters stole nine bases as a pitcher.

His infield background undoubtedly helped him with his fielding from the mound, which was exceptional. He led NL pitchers in double plays four times, fielding percentage once, and finished in the top five in putouts five times. He also had his moments with the bat, although he batted .183 in 67 pinch-hitting appearances. Walters batted .247 with 10 home runs and 59 doubles as a pitcher.

It seems fitting that Walters' 198th and final win came on September

9, 1947. It was Bucky Walters Appreciation Night and he rose to the occasion and pitched a two-hit shutout.

Lovill "Chubby" Dean

Dean pitched in 162 games and played 157 games at first base during a career that lasted from 1936 to 1943. He also batted .241 with 46 hits in 220 appearances as a pinch hitter. Dean batted .287 with 98 hits as a 20-year-old rookie first baseman for Connie Mack's Philadelphia Athletics in 1936, but he was unpolished in the field. The next season he batted .262 with 81 hits, then transitioned to focus on pitching. "Chubby seems to have an idea with pitching. He thinks about every pitch he makes," Mack commented.[33]

One of the highlights of Dean's major-league career came on April 16, 1940. Mack gave him the opening day start against the defending champion Yankees. He outpitched future Hall of Famer Red Ruffing to win 2-1, pitching all 10 innings and driving in the winning run in the bottom of the 10th inning.

Dean's best year pitching was 1942 with Cleveland, when he started out 6-2 before faltering and finishing with an 8-11 record and 3.81 ERA in 172⅔ innings. He batted .351 in 1939 with 42 of his plate appearances coming as a pinch hitter—he would often stay in the game as a reliever. He missed the 1944-45 seasons serving overseas in the military and was unable to make the Indians when he returned in 1946.

Overall, the lefty won 30 games pitching seven seasons with an ERA+ of 80. He averaged .270 at the plate with 287 career hits.

René Monteagudo

Monteagudo pitched and played the outfield in four seasons between 1938 and 1945. His career record of 3-7 is the same as his son, Aurelio, who pitched in seven major-league seasons. The Cuban-born Monteagudo debuted with five pitching appearances with the Washington Senators in 1938, posting a 5.73 ERA while battling a sore arm.

He appeared in 27 games on the mound in 1940 but recorded a 6.08 ERA in 100⅔ innings. A 14-game stint in 1945 was even worse, so he pitched in the Mexican League from 1946 to 1949.

Monteagudo also played 35 games in the outfield for the Phillies in 1945, batting .301 with 58 hits. That season he became the first player since Babe Ruth in 1919 to pitch at least 10 games in the majors while making at least 200 plate appearances. For his career he batted .372 with 16 pinch-hits.

Max Macon

Macon started out as a promising pitcher with the St. Louis Cardinals and Brooklyn Dodgers before transitioning to first base with the Boston Braves. The tall and skinny lefthander pitched more than 200 innings in the minors each year from 1934 to 1937 and won 21 games for the Cardinals' Double A team in Columbus in 1937.

His debut with the Cardinals in 1938 was spotty, with a 4–11 record and 4.11 ERA in 129⅓ innings, but he was pitching with a damaged arm. He got good results pitching 84 innings for Brooklyn in 1942—5–3 with a 1.93 ERA and a 19-inning scoreless streak. Branch Rickey described him as a "pitcher who has nothing and uses every bit of it."[34]

A 5.96 ERA followed in 1943 and that was it for Macon's once-promising pitching career. In 1944, he played 72 games at first base and 22 games in the outfield. He had a five-hit game on May 14 to raise his average to .373, and he would finish the year with a .273 average and 100 hits. He batted .256 from 46 pinch-hitting appearances during his career.

Macon continued his career as a player-manager in the minors, recording a 34-game hitting streak for Modesto in 1949—while pitching 11 games—and posting averages of .383, .392, and .409. Overall, he won 98 games in the minors and 17 games in the majors; and he collected 916 hits in the minors and 133 hits in the majors. He won 1,100 games managing 14 seasons in the minors.

Johnny Lindell

Lindell won his second and last game pitching for the New York Yankees on July 18, 1942. His next major-league win came 11 years later on May 3, 1953. In between, he showed what he could do as an outfielder.

Advancing in the minors as a pitcher, Lindell's track record was strong. He went 23–4 with a league-best 2.05 ERA pitching for Newark in Double A ball in 1941. That production led *The Sporting News* to name him Minor League Player of the Year.[35] He would win 117 games across eight seasons in the minors with 110 complete games, while collecting 296 hits playing 84 games in the outfield and first base.

He pitched 52⅔ innings for the Yankees in nine games his rookie season, 1942, recording a 3.76 ERA. Manager Joe McCarthy was not impressed with his repertoire—which consisted of a slider, curve, and weak fastball—so he converted him to be an outfielder. All he had to do was replace Joe DiMaggio in center field in 1943—Joltin' Joe was off to serve in the Air Force.

Lindell, who was a solid six-foot-four and 217 pounds, made the AL All-Star team in 1943. That year he led the league with 12 triples, although he batted just .245 that season. His best year was 1944, when he led the AL in triples (16) and total bases (297) while batting .300 with 18 homers, 178 hits, 91 runs, and 103 RBI. That was followed by his own stint in the U.S. Army, which sidelined him for much of the 1945 season.

In 1947, he averaged .275 and accumulated 131 hits for the pennant-winning Yankees. Lindell was a fan favorite who starred in the World Series that year, as he batted .500 and drove in seven runs as the Bronx Bombers won the title. He also got World Series rings with the Yankees in 1943 and 1949 and did not play in the 1942 Series they lost.

Lindell set career highs in 1948 in average (.317) and slugging (.511). On the side, he had started fooling around with a knuckleball. He came up clutch in the next-to-last game of the 1949 season against the Red Sox, who led the Yanks by one game. His third hit of the game was an eighth-inning home run that proved to be the decisive run in a 5–4 win. The next day he chipped in a single and two walks as the Yankees clinched the pennant. He spent eight seasons as an outfielder for the Yankees, batting .273 with 762 hits, and OPS+ of 114.

Traded first to the Cardinals and then to the Dodgers in 1950, Lindell found himself in the minors. He served as a two-way player for the Hollywood Stars in 1951, appearing in 14 games in the outfield, 13 at first base and 26 on the mound. His 24-9 record with 2.52 ERA for the Stars in 1952—largely on the strength of his new knuckleball—attracted the attention of the Pirates, who called him back up to the majors.

He went 5-16 for Pittsburgh in 1953, as he had trouble controlling his knuckleball. "About all I possess is a knuckleball," Lindell noted in an interview with the Associated Press. "I have a dinky slider and a straight ball. No curve whatsoever. I throw the knuckleball about 85 percent of the time. It's a pretty difficult pitch to hit except that half the time I can't get it over the plate."[36]

He did manage to hit two pinch-hit home runs for the Pirates that season before they traded him to the Phillies in August 1953, Lindell made five more appearances on the mound before getting released. He ended up leading the NL in walks and wild pitches that year but also batting average (.320) and home runs (four) by a pitcher. His career record ended up 8–18 with a 4.47 ERA.

Erv Dusak

Dusak played nine seasons between 1941 and 1952, missing three years for military service. Nicknamed "Four Sack" as a tribute to his homer-hitting ability in the minors,[37] he hit only 14 homers in the majors. He played 271 games in the outfield and 64 in the infield but made only 23 pitching appearances.

Dusak pitched in 14 games in 1950 for St. Louis, posting a 3.72 ERA. He had more than 300 plate appearances each year from 1946 to 1948, batting .240, .284, and .209.

He made key contributions to the Cardinals' 1946 championship team. On July 16, he pinch-hit a three-run, walk-off home run in the bottom of the ninth inning as the Cards beat the Dodgers. He batted .250 in 61 appearances as a pinch hitter.

Clint Hartung

Hartung was supposed to be the next Babe Ruth, the successor to his throne as the greatest two-way player in history. It didn't work out that way, but he did enjoy one moment of glory.

The six-foot-four, 215-pound "Honda Hurricane" looked the part hitting .359 while pitching to a 3.60 ERA in a 1942 minor-league season. Then he got drafted into the Army Air Corps in 1943. "When Clint went into the army he was smacking the ball 450 feet or further," noted Garry Schumacher, the Giants' publicity man.[38]

Hartung was able to keep playing while in the service. It's reported that he batted .567 and went 25–0 on the mound playing for a team based in Pearl Harbor.[39] "In all my time in sports, I had never seen a ballplayer so heralded before he had played game one in the major leagues. Not DiMaggio ... not Mantle ... not Williams nor A-Rod or any of them," commented Bill Gallo, columnist for the *New York Daily News*.[40]

Signing with the Giants for $35,000 in advance of the 1947 season, Hartung's pitching demonstrated he needed more seasoning. He threw fast but had no deception. His ERA went up four straight years from 4.57 to 6.61 while his walk-rate stayed high. His career mark was 29–29 with a 5.02 ERA (80 ERA+).

He played seven games in the outfield in 1947 and batted .309 with four home runs. He batted .302 in 1950 but he never reached 100 plate appearances in his six-year career despite shifting to the outfield for his last two seasons. The next Babe Ruth finished with 14 career home runs and slugged a weak .407.

Hartung did play a minor role in one of baseball's most famous plays. He had been a forgotten player all year in 1951, with just 87 plate appearances and no innings pitched. The Giants and Dodgers tied at the end of the regular season, which necessitated a three-game playoff series. In the decisive third game, the Giants trailed by two runs in the bottom of the ninth when Don Mueller broke his ankle sliding into third. His roommate on the road, Hartung, was inserted as a pinch runner.

What came next has been played on rewind millions of times. Bobby Thomson hit "The Shot Heard 'Round the World" for a three-run, walk-off home run off Ralph Branca to win the pennant for the Giants. The video clip shows an exuberant Hartung crossing the plate while waving both arms frantically like a windmill. He later described winning the 1951 pennant "was like knocking out Joe Louis."[41]

Hal Jeffcoat

Jeffcoat tried pitching in five games in the low minors in 1946, but it didn't go well (7.36 ERA). Instead, he concentrated on playing the outfield. In 1947, he batted .346 with 218 hits (including 13 triples) and 118 RBI for the Nashville Sounds in Double A ball, breaking out a 35-game hitting streak to show his promise.

Jeffcoat batted .279 with 132 hits his rookie year with the Cubs in 1948, leading NL center fielders with 11 assists. He was named to *The Sporting News'* all-rookie team.[42]

"Hal Jeffcoat ... is proving it was no mistake to make him over from a pitcher to an outfielder," commented Jack Hand of the Associated Press.[43]

Unable to bat consistently, Jeffcoat would spend the next five seasons largely as a fourth outfielder. He took advantage of his speed to finish third in the league with 12 steals in 1949. He also continued to impress with his strong arm, collecting 16 outfield assists in 1952 in just 95 games but batting a weak .219.

"Hal Jeffcoat has unlimited potential.... To me, he's the greatest center fielder in the league and a tremendous asset regardless of what he hits," gushed Wid Matthews, general manager of the Cubs.[44]

In 1953, Manager Phil Cavarretta mainly used Jeffcoat as a defensive replacement late in games. He averaged an uninspiring .235 with a 66 OPS+. Overall, he batted .248 for his career with 487 hits.

Players and coaches on the Cubs had admired Jeffcoat's pitching ability for several years as he threw during batting practice. When Stan Hack was brought in as Cubs manager for 1954, he quickly saw the upside of converting Jeffcoat back to pitching.

He pitched mainly out of the bullpen for the Cubs in 1954, recording a 5.19 ERA while mixing in a screwball to go with a fastball and curve. He fared much better the next season as his 50 appearances and 2.95 ERA both led the team. He started 16 games for the Redlegs in 1956 to go with 22 relief appearances, posting an 8–2 record and 3.84 ERA in 171 innings. "Adding a sidearm curve helped me fool the hitters, and I improved ... by getting better control," Jeffcoat said after the season.[45]

Working as a starter in 1957, Jeffcoat went 12–13 with an unimpressive 4.52 ERA in 207 innings. There were high moments such as his six-hit shutout of the Dodgers in June, but he seemed to tire as the season wore on. Working exclusively out of the bullpen in 1958, he worked to a 3.72 ERA in 49 appearances—a 113 OPS+. Baseball-Reference retroactively gives him nine saves for the year, although that stat did not become official until 1969.

Jeffcoat had a 3.32 ERA in 17 relief appearances for the Reds when he got traded to the Cardinals in June 1959. He was released after producing a bloated ERA of 9.17 in 11 outings. His major-league career on the mound was 39–37 with a 4.22 ERA in 245 appearances—not bad for a converted outfielder.

Jeffcoat had a brother, George—11 years older—who helped raise him for a period after their mother died.[46] George pitched four seasons in the majors, winning seven games. Two other brothers pitched in the minors.

Dick Hall

Hall excelled as a two-way player at Swarthmore College in Pennsylvania, but Branch Rickey signed him for the Pirates for his batting ability. Working his way up in the minors, Hall bounced around the diamond playing shortstop, outfield, and second base, but he struggled to hit consistently. He saw action in 102 games in the outfield for the Pirates in 1954 and batted .239.

The only time Hall saw extensive action as two-way player was in the Mexican Winter League in 1954 and with the Lincoln Chiefs in Class A ball in 1955. He pitched 19 games for Lincoln and played 73 games in the outfield, batting .302 and going 12–5 with a league-best 2.24 ERA in 153 innings. It was enough to get called back up to Pittsburgh, where he recorded an encouraging 3.91 ERA in 15 appearances (13 starts). He struck out 11 batters in his first start on July 24, 1955.

Hall batted .345 in limited at-bats with the Pirates in 1956, but his pitching took a step back with an 0–7 record and 4.76 ERA and then injuries slowed his progress. He won eight games in 28 starts for Kansas City in 1960. He had good success starting and relieving for Baltimore in 1961 (3.09 ERA in 122⅓ innings) and then settled into a 10-year stretch as a valuable reliever. He went 9–1 with a career-best 1.85 ERA for the Orioles in 1964 and posted a 1.92 ERA for the 1969 Orioles team that lost to the Miracle Mets in the World Series.

As he refined his pitching style, Hall developed an awkward delivery. "The best description I've heard of what I look like on the mound is a drunken giraffe on roller skates," he said.[47]

Still pitching in 1971 as the oldest player in the American League at 41, Hall wound down his career with 27 appearances with a 4.98 ERA. He threw his last pitch to save Game Two of the 1971 World Series, which the Orioles won over his former team the Pirates.

Overall, Hall made 74 starts and 421 relief appearances with a 3.32 ERA (111 ERA+) and a 93–75 record. His lifetime batting average was .210 playing 127 games in the field.

Willie Smith

Smith played for five teams in the majors from 1963 to 1971, but 1964 was his only real season as a two-way player. He remains the only African American player (outside the Negro Leagues) to play at least 15 games as a pitcher and 15 games as a position player in the same major-league season.[48] He is the only player to accomplish this in the Negro Leagues and the major leagues. Smith was the last player to hit these two-way thresholds until Shohei Ohtani did it in 2021.

Smith got his start pitching and playing outfield and first base for the Birmingham Black Barons in the waning years of the Negro Leagues, 1957–59. Statistics available from the Howe News Bureau show he went 6–2 with a 2.67 ERA pitching in 10 games in 1958 while batting .458 with 11 hits. He was a starting pitcher in the East-West Negro American League All-Star games in both 1958 and 1959, singling in the winning run in 1958 and hitting a home run in the 1959 game.

He rose through the minors mainly pitching but also playing some in the outfield. His .304 batting mark left as big an impression as his 2.93 ERA, leading to the nickname "Wonderful Willie." Smith only pitched in 11 games after being called up in June 1963 by the Tigers. After the Los Angeles Angels acquired him a few weeks into the 1964 season, they saw his two-way potential.

Smith, who batted and threw left-handed, was fast on the bases but not fast with his pitches. Instead, he relied on a curveball. He averaged .301

with 108 hits and 11 home runs in 1964 while playing 87 games in the outfield for the Angels. On the mound he made one start and 14 relief appearances, posting a 1–4 record with a 2.84 ERA in 31⅔ innings.

"If I got a chance to pitch regularly in the big leagues, I'd be a pretty good pitcher. If I keep getting the chance, I'll be a pretty good hitter here, too," Smith said in an interview with *Baseball Digest*.[49]

Serving as the Angels' starting left fielder in 1965, Smith set career highs in hits (120), runs (52), triples (nine), stolen bases (nine), and plate appearances (459). "Smith reminds me of Willie McCovey. He has the same quick wrists," said Bill Rigney, his manager on the Angels.[50]

He was used frequently as a pinch hitter but hit just .228 in 266 career pinch-hitting chances. One of the highlights of Smith's career was hitting a pinch-hit, walk-off two-run homer for the Cubs on Opening Day 1969.

Smith pitched in only 29 games covering 61 innings over three seasons with a 3.10 ERA (114 ERA+). He appeared in 339 games in the outfield and 93 games at first base. He batted .248 with 410 hits, 46 home runs, and 94 OPS+. After his major-league career ended in 1971, Smith played two seasons in Japan, batting .259 and pitching in two games.

Mel Queen

Queen gained insights into what it took to be a big leaguer by watching his father, Mel, pitch eight years in the majors. The son made it to seven years. Starting as a third baseman in the minors, Queen switched to outfield and made his debut with the Cincinnati Reds in 1964. Playing 20 games in right field and showing off a strong right-handed arm, he batted .200 that year swinging from the left side.

Blocked by Frank Robinson, Vada Pinson, and Tommy Harper in the Reds' outfield, Queen had a revelation while throwing batting practice. "My fastball would really move and the guys would talk about it. I can make it take off or sink depending on how I hold it," he said.[51]

Without taking time to refine his craft in the minors, Queen made his first pitching appearance for the Reds on July 15, 1966. The next season he started 24 games and impressed with a 14–8 record, 2.76 ERA (10th in the NL), and 154 strikeouts in 195⅔ innings. He pitched a six-hit shutout on April 16 while striking out eight.

Unfortunately, a torn rotator cuff suffered that season would prevent Queen from building on that promise. Queen finished his career with a 20–17 record and a 3.14 ERA (114 ERA+). He played 53 games in the outfield and batted .179.

Ron Mahay

Mahay started out as an outfielder in the minors from 1991 to 1995, getting called up to play five games in center field for the Red Sox in 1995. He resurfaced in 1997 as a valuable contributor in the bullpen. He made 28 relief appearances that season pitching to a 2.52 ERA. He would go on to pitch in 514 games for eight teams across 14 seasons.

Mahay pitched in 60 games for the Rangers in 2004 with a 2.55 ERA. He made 58 relief appearances for Texas and Atlanta in 2007, recording a 2.55 ERA. With a lifetime record of 27–12 and a 3.83 ERA (120 ERA+), Mahay made the right move converting to the mound. He batted .250 with 316 hits playing 348 games in the outfield during 19 minor-league seasons.

Brooks Kieschnick

Kieschnick lived up to his nickname, "Toolshed," by adding relief pitcher to his resume after starting his big-league career as an outfielder.

Playing for Milwaukee in 2003, Kieschnick became the first player in major-league history to hit a home run as a pitcher, pinch hitter, and designated hitter in the same season. He was called on to pinch-hit 24 times that season and also appeared in four games as a designated hitter, three as an outfielder, and 42 as a relief pitcher. He batted .300 with seven homers while pitching to a 5.26 ERA in 53 innings.

Before Kieschnick became a three-time All-American and two-time college baseball "Player of the Year" at the University of Texas, he showcased his two-way abilities at the 1990 World Junior Championships, where he batted .414 with two homers and pitched two shutout innings. During his time at Texas, he batted .360 with 43 homers and went 34–8 on the mound.

Drafted by the Cubs in the first round of the 1993 MLB draft, they saw his future as a middle-of-the-lineup force. "Oh, I'd love to hit and to pitch, that would be awesome. But, I'm in the hands of the Cubs," he said.[52]

Instead, Kieschnick played outfield, first base, and third base during four seasons in the minors. He batted .295 with 23 homers for Iowa at the Triple A level in 1995, but mainly saw action as a pinch hitter for the Cubs in 1996 as he batted .345.

Kieschnick hit well in the minors but didn't get extended opportunities to show what he could do in the majors. He bounced from the Cubs to the Devil Rays, followed by the Reds, Rockies, Indians, and White Sox organizations.

Finally, at the age of 30 in 2002, he got a chance to show what he could do pitching for the White Sox's Triple A team in Charlotte. He struck out 30 in 31⅓ innings with a 2.59 ERA. "I had to do something. I had to make myself more valuable. I pitched in college, and my arm was rested for 10 years, so that's what I wanted to do," he said.[53]

The White Sox couldn't find a spot for him, but the Brewers signed him because they saw his versatility as a strength. "If a player like Brooks can be your 12th pitcher and a bat off the bench, he is performing two roles," explained Brewers General Manager Doug Melvin. "He can hit for the pitcher in the fifth inning and stay out there. If he comes up and you don't want to make a change, he allows a manager to manage an American League game. We love the idea."[54]

With the Brewers in 2003, Kieschnick pitched in 42 games out of the bullpen, played three games in left field, four games as designated hitter, and made 24 pinch-hitting appearances. He batted .300 and slugged .614 with seven home runs, but he pitched to a 5.26 ERA.

"I don't think people realize how hard it is to be a major-league player in the first place, and he did both (pitching and playing the outfield) and he did them well. It was awesome to see and awesome to be a part of," commented teammate Glendon Rusch.[55]

The Brewers used him in a similar manner in 2004. He appeared 48 times as a pinch hitter and batted a decent .270. On the mound, he recorded a 3.77 ERA in 32 outings as a reliever (117 ERA+). Released by the Brewers, Kieschnick spent one more season pitching in the minors with the Astros before deciding to retire at 33. He had proved to himself how far he could go as a hitter, pitcher, and two-way player.

"Now when I turn 40, I won't be lying awake wondering what I should have done. This has brought peace to the rest of my life," he told Peter Gammons in an interview.[56]

Kieschnick batted .248 with 76 hits in the majors, along with a .279 average, 164 homers, and 932 hits in 13 minor-league seasons. He went 2–2 with a 4.59 ERA in 74 major-league appearances, to go with a 3–5 record and 5.79 ERA in 87 appearances in the minors.

Rick Ankiel

Ankiel debuted with the St. Louis Cardinals as a 20 year old, flame-throwing southpaw in 1999. He won 11 games the next year, striking out 194 in 175 innings and finishing second in Rookie-of-the-Year voting. The Cards were counting on him as a key starter in the playoffs. That's when the wheels fell off.

Starting the first game of the 2000 National League Division Series against the Braves' Greg Maddux, Ankiel lasted just 2⅔ innings as he lost control of the strike zone. He threw five wild pitches (the most in a single inning since 1890) and walked six batters before he was taken out.

Starting the second game of the 2000 NL Championship Series against the Mets, Ankiel faced just six batters before getting pulled—he had walked three and thrown two more wild pitches. Given one final chance in Game Five, Ankiel walked two of the four batters he faced and threw his eighth and ninth wild pitches of the series before being removed. His rising star had crashed.

"'The Thing,' 'The Yips,' 'The Monster,' whatever you want to name it," Ankiel said. "You lose your ability to do something that you've done your whole life without the explanation of why."[57]

It was asking a lot of the 21-year-old phenom to start pressure-packed playoff games, especially since Ankiel's father had been sentenced to prison on drug charges and his parents had gone through a divorce that year. Cardinals Manager Tony LaRussa has long regretted putting his young star pitcher in position to fail.[58]

Ankiel had risen quickly through the minors after being drafted in the second round of the 1997 MLB draft. He struck out 162 batters in 74 innings to be named the *USA Today* High School Player of the Year. He struck out 222 in 161 innings in 1998, followed by 194 strikeouts in 137⅔ innings in 1999, when he was named Minor League Player of the Year by *Baseball America*.[59] He didn't always exhibit sharp control, but there were no harbingers of his upcoming inability to throw strikes.

Coming back for the 2001 season, Ankiel walked 25 batters in 24 innings and that was largely it for his major-league pitching career. After his control problems persisted in the minors, he shifted to the outfield in 2005 and made it back to the majors in 2007. He hit a home run in his first game back on August 9, 2007. He finished the season batting .285 with 11 homers in 49 games, showing off his strong arm in right and center field. At the end of the year, Ankiel was one of numerous players mentioned in the Mitchell Report for alleged involvement in performance-enhancing drugs.[60]

Ankiel belted 25 homers and slugged .506 in 2008—an OPS+ of 120. He played five more seasons for five different teams but never had the same success at the plate. He finished his career with 462 hits including 76 homers, a .240 average, and OPS+ of 92. His pitching record was 13–10 with a 3.90 ERA in 242 major-league innings.

He is the first player since Babe Ruth to hit 70 career homers and win at least 10 career games as a pitcher—Shohei Ohtani joined the club in 2021. Ankiel and the Babe are the only players to hit a home run as a position player in the postseason and start a game as a pitcher in the postseason. Ankiel is also the last player since Clint Hartung in 1947 (and before him, Babe Ruth) to hit his first homer as a pitcher and then hit a homer as a position player.

Michael Lorenzen

Lorenzen showed off his two-way ability while serving as both a starting outfielder and the team's closer while at Cal State Fullerton. That led to him being named a finalist for the John Olerud Two-Way Player of the Year Award. He batted .322 with 11 home runs in college while recording a 1.61 ERA and 35 saves on the mound. The Cincinnati Reds drafted him as a pitcher in the first round of the 2013 MLB draft.

He debuted in the majors early in the 2015 season and posted a 4–9 record with 5.40 ERA in 27 appearances (21 starts). He lowered his ERA to 2.88 the next season while pitching 35 games out of the bullpen. Lorenzen had some bright moments pitching seven seasons mainly in relief for the Reds, with a 4.07 ERA in 295 appearances. On August 19, 2016, he homered while in the game as a relief pitcher. On April 6, 2017, he homered as a pinch hitter.

He made his first outfield appearance in 2018—along with 13 pinch-hitting chances—and batted .290 with four homers. He continued to make more headlines with his bat than his pitching arm. He hit home runs in three consecutive at-bats: a pinch-hit homer on June 24, while in the game to pitch on June 29, and then a pinch-hit grand slam on June 30.

Seeing the success the Angels had with Shohei Ohtani in 2018, Reds Manager David Bell decided to deploy Lorenzen as a multi-faceted weapon in 2019. He played 29 games in the outfield, mainly as a late-inning defensive replacement, and appeared 13 times as a pinch runner and seven times as a pinch hitter while pitching in 73 games out of the bullpen. His average dropped to .208 but his ERA was a sparkling 2.92.

On September 4, 2019, Lorenzen accomplished something last done by Babe Ruth in 1921—he was the winning pitcher, played in center field, and hit a home run, all in a game he entered in the seventh inning.[61]

Lorenzen moved on to the Angels for the 2022 season and began working exclusively as a starting pitcher. He won eight games in 18 starts with an adjusted ERA of 95. He split 2023 with Detroit and Philadelphia—making the All-Star team with the Tigers—starting 25 games with a 4.18 ERA in 153 innings. In his first home start with the Phillies, he pitched a no-hitter on August 9, 2022.

Through the 2023 season, Lorenzen batted .192 in 29 pinch-hitting chances and .233 overall and recorded a 4.11 ERA in 342 pitching appearances.

Matt Bush

Bush is both a cautionary tale and a tale of redemption. Selected number one in the 2004 MLB draft as a high school shortstop, Bush was thrilled to be picked by his hometown San Diego Padres. He signed for $3.15 million and set about silencing critics who questioned his batting ability. He batted .191 in brief action his first year and hit just .221 in 2005. Then his life snowballed out of control.

Bush developed a problem with alcohol, got into a bar fight, and broke his ankle in 2006. His strong defense at short didn't make up for his weak bat. After watching him play shortstop for 205 games, the Padres decided to convert Bush into a pitcher. He pitched well in seven appearances before needing Tommy John surgery in 2007. He got in another fight while drunk in 2009, which led the Padres to release him and then trade him to the Blue Jays. The Blue Jays released him less than two months later after he allegedly assaulted a woman at a party. In June 2009, Bush was arrested for DUI. Tampa Bay gave him another shot, but he was involved in a hit-and-run crash with a motorcyclist in which he was charged with his third DUI—that led to a 34-month prison stint until October 2015.[62]

"I don't want to be the guy that always screwed everything up and threw everything away," Bush said in 2016 interview, shortly after he began his last-chance comeback.[63] Still able to throw a fastball at 98, Bush was signed to a minor league deal by the Rangers as a relief pitcher.

After 12 games in the minors to knock off the rust, he made his major-league debut at the age of 30 on May 13, 2016, and he pitched a one-two-three inning. Two days later, he won his first game but the feat was overshadowed by José Bautista's hard slide into second that started a fight with Rougned Odor—it had been precipitated by Bush drilling Bautista with a purpose pitch. He was officially a big leaguer after that, accepted by his teammates. Bush would go on to pitch in 58 games out of the bullpen for the Rangers that season, with a 7–2 record, 2.48 ERA, and 184 ERA+.

"A lot of his success is self-taught. I don't think he has any pressure at all on the mound. His pressures are off the field," commented Rangers pitching coach Doug Brocail, who had been Bush's teammate in the minors.[64]

Bush worked as the Rangers' closer for part of 2017, ending up with 10 saves in 57 appearances with a 3.78 ERA. A second Tommy John surgery was required in 2018 and then another surgery the next year, as Bush ended up missing most of three seasons.

In six seasons through 2023, Bush had pitched in 217 games and struck out 227 in 211 innings. His .219 batting average as a shortstop in the minors was a distant memory. He was with the Rangers during the 2023 World Series but not on the playoff roster. His career ERA+ of 120 through the 2023 season shows he has been 20 percent better than average, but Bush has learned through experience that expectations are hard to live up to and it's better to focus on one day at a time.

CHAPTER 12

Shohei Ohtani
On the Path to Baseball Immortality

One eventually runs out of superlatives to describe Shohei Ohtani. It seems like at least once a week, the Japanese two-way sensation sets a record or does something no one else has ever done. While baseball fans, peers, teammates, and historians marvel at his feats and rush to anoint him the greatest two-way player ever, Ohtani has a more ambitious goal—become known as the greatest baseball player of all-time. He hates to lose and views his multi-threat ability to hit home runs, steal bases, and strike out batters as the best way to lead his team to wins.

If the rest of his career goes like his first six seasons have gone, there is a good chance he will reach his goal. He is the only player in MLB history to win the MVP Award three times unanimously, which he did while turning in the greatest all-around seasons in baseball history in 2021, 2023 and 2024. It took a 62-homer season by Aaron Judge in 2022 to keep Ohtani from winning four straight MVP awards.

"He kind of reminds you of Nolan Ryan, and then he reminds you of freaking Barry Bonds. He's both of those guys," said Hall of Fame pitcher Greg Maddux. "I mean, he's got great stuff and he can hit a home run with the best of anybody. Nobody else has done it before; I mean, the last guy was who, maybe Babe Ruth? Nobody's been able to do that."[1]

Ohtani has already accumulated 34.7 WAR through his first six seasons, one of them the pandemic-shortened 2020 season. He has batted .274/.366/.556 with 171 homers, 437 RBI, 681 hits, 86 stolen bases, and 148 OPS+. In 86 mound appearances he has recorded a 3.01 ERA, 608 strikeouts, and 142 ERA+. Babe Ruth's first six seasons—which included three as a pitcher, two as a two-way player, and one as a batter—produced 103 home runs, or 68 fewer than Ohtani. Ruth struck out 231 batters in his first 86 games on the mound, or 377 fewer than Ohtani.

The Japanese star has played 627 games as a designated hitter (DH) to go with the 86 pitching appearances through the 2023 season. He has lost significant pitching time due to two Tommy John surgeries, and he struggled at the plate in 2020. Other than that, he has been a transformational, transcendent talent unlike anything seen before on the diamond.

Dave Winfield, who was a successful two-way player in college, has been impressed with how well Ohtani has handled the pressures and workload of his dual roles. "You have to train different parts of your body. That's a pretty big deal; it's hard enough to stay healthy doing one or the other. And you have to study twice as much. Plus, expectations are so hard," Winfield said, in an interview with baseball writer Joe Posnanski.[2]

Baseball observers throw out two scenarios for debate: could Ohtani become the greatest slugger of all-time if he concentrated just on hitting? Also, what is his ceiling if he performed exclusively as a pitcher? In other words, by going all in as a two-way player is Ohtani sacrificing some of his potential hitting and pitching production? Hall of Famer John Smoltz has expressed the opinion that Ohtani could be as good as Jacob deGrom if he focused solely on pitching.[3]

The general consensus seems to be that Ohtani is at his best when he is able to perform full time as a two-way player, and the stats back that up. He batted just .259 with 25 home runs from 2019 to 2020 when he was unable to pitch. Angels' hitting coach Jeremy Reed offers this theory: "When Shohei thinks about two things, he doesn't think about one thing. He's so detail-oriented that detail can turn into a single-minded, 'want-to-be-great' thing. When he dedicates his time throughout the day to 'I've got to do this, this and this' to be ready to play, I think there is less focus on one thing to be great and he's great at both."[4]

Ohtani grew up in Ōshū in the Iwate Prefecture, which is not known as a hotbed for Japanese baseball talent. His father, Toru, played baseball for a company-sponsored semipro team. Toru regretted not being able to help his oldest son, Ryuta, more with his baseball, so he vowed to be more involved with his youngest son's training. He began coaching Shohei early on and served as his manager in junior high. The importance of playing hard and showing respect for the game took priority over techniques and fundamentals. Toru advised a diligent Shohei to adopt a clean form and place his fingers firmly on the seam of the ball when pitching. For his batting, he taught him the best way to strike with the meat of the bat.[5]

His father also coached him through the pivotal decision on whether to bat lefty or righty. When Ohtani settled on batting left-handed to go with his right-handed pitching, that inadvertently worked to counterbalance the strain of doing both skills with regularity. It also affords him the platoon advantage with the majority of his at-bats at the plate and on the mound, and it's a trait he shares with Ted Williams, Ty Cobb, Yogi Berra, and Japan's greatest baseball player—Ichiro Suzuki, who Ohtani idolized growing up.

Chapter 12. Shohei Ohtani

When Ohtani began playing in high school at Hanamaki Higashi, his power hitting developed faster than his pitching. As a high school freshman, he filled out a goal matrix grid containing 81 areas to focus on to reach his highest potential as a baseball player. It revolved around his overarching goal—be picked at the top of the Nippon Professional Baseball draft list—surrounded by focused goals in specific areas such as pitching speed (99 mph), building body, ball control, and the mental aspect. The grid identified specific actions he could take to reach his goals including lead with lower body, maintain a consistent release point, even a need to show respect to others and be someone people want to support.[6]

When sportswriter Tom Verducci asked Ohtani what gives him the most joy in baseball, his answer had nothing to do with winning games, striking out batters, or launching home runs, but instead harkened back to his formative years. "It's about setting goals," Ohtani replied. "My first goal was to play in the national tournament. And I was actually able to play there. It was a joy that led from the result of my practice. I don't think it had to be baseball, but for me, it just happened to be baseball. I love setting goals and achieving them."[7]

As he developed and filled out his large frame in high school, Ohtani captured the attention of scouts across Japan and the United States. He launched mammoth home runs and touched 99 mph with his fastball, providing a mesmerizing blend of power, speed, and athleticism. At age 18, Ohtani announced his intentions to go to the United States and start his professional career with a major-league team, which would break the established protocol between the two countries' baseball leagues.

While he hoped his announcement would deter a Japanese team from drafting him, that strategy didn't work—the Hokkaido Nippon-Ham Fighters in the Pacific League of Nippon Professional Baseball drafted him as their top pick. The Fighters convinced him to sign by pointing out that a major-league team would make him work his way up through the minors and would force him to choose between batting or pitching, while they would support and encourage his desire to be a two-way player. It proved to be a pivotal moment to help launch him to two-way stardom.

Ohtani played with the Fighters for five years, living the entire time in the team dormitories so he could concentrate on baseball. He played 64 games in the outfield for the Fighters while making 92 pitching appearances, growing a reputation as the "Babe Ruth of Japan." Most of those outfield appearances came in his first season with the Fighters—after that he balanced pitching with being a designated hitter. He hit .231, .274, and .202 his first three seasons before breaking out with a .322 average with 22 homers in 2016 and .332 his last season. He only hit 48 home runs in 1,045 at-bats in the 414 games he played in his native country. That is

Shohei Ohtani has already won two unanimous MVP Awards for his sensational two-way play in 2021 and 2023, and he continues to do things that have never been done before. No player in the modern era has ever attempted Ohtani's ambitious regimen of two-way play, which paid off for him when he signed the largest free-agent contract in baseball history before the 2024 season—$700 million from the Los Angeles Dodgers (Conor P. Fitzgerald / Shutterstock, 2190501331).

despite the fact Japanese pitchers did not throw inside to Ohtani as a sign of respect—a much different code than the one followed by pitchers in the major leagues.

On the mound, he started to dominate in his second season when he went 11–4 with a 2.61 ERA and 179 strikeouts in 155⅓ innings, leading the league with 10.4 K/9. Ohtani typically pitched every Sunday, which was always followed by a day off on Monday—a good opportunity for him to rest. During the 2014 Mazda All-Star Game he set a Japanese record by throwing a 101-mph pitch.

The next year, 2015, he went 15–5 with a league-leading 2.21 ERA with 199 strikeouts and three shutouts in 162⅔ innings. Instead of playing the outfield, he started seeing some action at designated hitter. Ohtani was nearly unhittable in 2016, going 10–4 with a 1.86 ERA and allowing only 89 hits in 140 innings while striking out 174. That season he set a Nippon Professional Baseball record by throwing a pitch at 102.5 mph—pretty good for someone who had a 1.004 OPS as a batter that season.

The most games he played was 104 of the 140 the Fighters played in

2016. He was named league MVP that season with 253 of the 254 first-place votes and led his team to the Japan Series championship. He was named to the All-Star team all five seasons in Japan, and in 2016, he was named to the Best Nine at pitcher and designated hitter. An ankle injury curtailed his playing in 2017, and he only pitched 26⅓ innings but still averaged 96.6 mph on his fastball and topped out at 101.6 mph.

While the world marveled at Ohtani's ability to master two difficult skills, to him it was just maximizing his ability to play the sport he loves. "Hitting and pitching, it's the only baseball I know. Doing only one and not the other doesn't feel natural to me. I suppose it's an accomplishment—I'm doing what others are not. But, to me, this is just normal," Ohtani said in an interview with a Canadian sportswriter.[8]

With 543 innings on the mound in Japan, Ohtani had a good foundation to tackle the challenge of facing major-league batters. Combining raw power and speed with durability at six-foot-five and 220 pounds, he possessed the perfect sculpted body to approach two-way playing as a long-term pursuit.

The sky was the limit for Ohtani, according to multiple executives from big-league clubs who had been scouting him for several years. A major league international scouting director told ESPN sportswriter Tim Keown in 2017 that "Ohtani could be the best pitcher in the history of baseball, and I don't say that lightly. He has equal if not better stuff than all of them."[9]

The major leagues awaited as his proving ground, and Ohtani looked forward to the challenge. "This may sound like a cliche, but I do not feel pressure at all when it comes to playing baseball, and this is being 100 percent honest," he said. "Playing baseball is genuinely fun for me, and I enjoy every moment of my time on the field, whether it's practice or game time."[10]

Although some in the baseball community were surprised to see Ohtani sign with the Los Angeles Angels, the decision came down to where he felt most comfortable and a team that would best support his goal to be a two-way player. The team also needed to be in the American League so he could serve as the designated hitter. "I never thought a professional team in Japan would let me do both hitting and pitching before I was drafted, so I can only imagine that it would be a tougher decision for an MLB team to let me do both," Ohtani said.[11]

When future Hall of Famer Albert Pujols observed his new teammate on the Angels taking swings in the cage for the first time, he called his former teammate Mark McGwire to rave about what he was witnessing. "Mac, you aren't going to believe this," Pujols recounted to *USA Today* sportswriter Bob Nightengale. "This new guy from Japan that we have, he's got more power than I've ever seen in my life. I've never seen a guy hit the ball this far."[12]

The new guy from Japan got off to a slow start in his first major-league spring training, but once the season began he showed off his tantalizing talent. He won his pitching debut on April 1, 2018, striking out six in six innings. He hit a three-run homer in his first home at-bat on April 3. Then in his home pitching debut on April 8 against the A's, he retired the first 19 batters before allowing a single with one out in the seventh inning. He struck out the final batter he faced to end the seventh inning, giving him 12 strikeouts on the way to the win. Ohtani had just done something last accomplished by "Grunting Jim" Shaw of the Washington Senators 99 years earlier in 1919—win two games and hit three home runs in the first 10 games of the season.[13]

Shaw, who was once compared to a young Walter Johnson as his career got underway, picked up the odd nickname for his habit of grunting every time he exerted himself to throw a pitch. Shaw also accidentally shot himself in the jaw and throat with a shotgun in a 1915 hunting accident, so perhaps the shotgun pellets that remained stuck in his neck for the rest of his life caused odd sounds to escape on occasion.[14]

As MLB batters quickly learned, when Ohtani is in rhythm and throwing strikes, they are at a distinct disadvantage. If it's not a blazing fastball that reaches 100 mph or a filthy splitter that ranges from 86 to 91 mph, then Ohtani might baffle them with a wipeout slider, or a drop curve that he throws to lefty and right batters. Rather than tiring at the end of his pitching outings, he often threw harder and with more precision.

The Angels came up with a plan to ease his workload. He did not bat on the days he pitched, and he typically did not bat the day after or the day before he pitched. In essence, he was a part-time two-way player, restrictions that were never adopted by Negro League two-way stars like Bullet Rogan and Martín Dihigo. Despite having to make lots of adjustments to a new league in a foreign country, Ohtani was named American League Rookie of the Month for April. His teammates were impressed with how polite and humble he was in the face of relentless media attention, as well as what a good teammate he was. Then they wondered if their eyes were deceiving them as they watched him launch a home run during batting practice at Angel Stadium on May 18, 2018, that struck the scoreboard past the outfield seats. It was later measured to be 513 feet.

The first hiccup came when he was placed on the disabled list in early June with an elbow strain. He returned with a splash, belting a pinch-hit home run on July 8, 2018, that proved to be the winning run. Returning to the mound on September 2, he was pulled from the game in the third inning after losing velocity. A few days later it was announced he would require Tommy John surgery—he still clubbed two home runs that day.

For the 2018 season, Ohtani batted .285/.361/.564 with 22 homers and a 151 OPS+ while serving as designated hitter in 82 games. He batted .316 with two home runs in 22 pinch-hitting appearances. He made just 10 starts with 63 strikeouts in 51⅔ innings for a 127 ERA+. Ohtani's major-league debut was impressive—he was 51 percent better than the average batter and 27 percent better than the average pitcher—but it still seemed like he fell short of the ultra-high expectations for him. He was named Rookie of the Year with 25 of the 30 first-place votes.

Despite all the precautions the Angels had taken to reduce the strain on Ohtani's body, his arm had not held up. They were aware when they signed him that he had a strain of the ulnar collateral ligament in his pitching arm. This new injury would keep him from pitching during the 2019 season, and it would cause some people to speculate that Ohtani would have to abandon his dream of being a two-way player.

Hall of Famer Reggie Jackson was among those who were skeptical that Ohtani could keep performing at a high level as a two-way player. "I just don't know how this pitching and hitting is going to work out for him. I don't know, what's harder? Just throwing 15 minutes of batting practice, I was sore and tired. And he's throwing 98 mph…. How much longer can he do this?" Jackson said.[15]

Although he was not able to pitch in 2019, Ohtani still managed to hit. After playing his first 162 games in the major leagues midway through the 2019 season, Ohtani had produced a .290/.358/.556 batting mark. His best baseball was still to come.

Facing the Rays on June 13, 2019, Ohtani became the first Japanese player to hit for the cycle in the major leagues. He blasted a 414-foot homer in the first, followed by a double in the third. In the fifth, he smacked a sharp drive into the right-field corner and hustled his way to third for a triple. Although he was trying for another homer in his fourth at-bat, he settled for a perfectly placed single to right-center. Only 74 players have hit for the cycle in the Japanese professional leagues, compared to 330 in the U.S. major leagues.[16]

After the game, Ohtani said, "Simply very happy to accomplish this. There's been so many great Japanese players that have come before me. Being the first one to accomplish it [makes me] really happy and makes for a lot of confidence down the road."[17]

Ohtani's 2019 season ended early when a congenital knee problem flared up that required minor surgery. He finished the year with a pedestrian (for him) .286/.343/.505 batting mark with 18 homers, 62 RBI, and just 2.5 WAR in 106 games. The Angels, featuring the game's two best players in Ohtani and Mike Trout, finished out of the playoffs in fourth place.

Major League Baseball adopted several new rules that only benefited Ohtani. In 2020, MLB allowed Ohtani to remain on the Angels' roster as a batter and then leave periodically to pitch in rehab games in the minors while he got his pitching arm in shape. The pandemic-shortened 2020 season was a challenge for all teams and players, but it was especially challenging for Ohtani. His pitching was cut short after two starts due to a forearm strain. He walked eight batters and allowed seven runs in less than two innings. At the plate, he struggled to a .190 average with seven home runs and a 79 OPS+.

In the 2023 Disney documentary *Shohei Ohtani: Beyond the Dream*, Ohtani admitted taking two years off from pitching due to injury made him seriously considering scrapping his plans for two-way domination. "After the Tommy John surgery in 2019, the following year was also a struggle. I didn't feel that I was recovering how I should. I started to doubt. I thought it might be better to focus on one position to obtain results. That was the time when I honestly considered dropping the two-way path," he said.[18]

Baseball in the 21st century has devolved into a game of risk avoidance. Starters are pulled before they face a lineup for a third time and before they exceed 100 pitches. A right-handed batter is brought in to face the southpaw reliever. Approaching the 2021 season, Angels Manager Joe Maddon and General Manager Perry Minasian decided they had nothing to lose and removed the restrictions on how Ohtani would be used. Treating Ohtani with kid gloves had resulted in him pitching just 53 innings across his first three seasons. There would be no more days off batting before and after games he pitched. It was time to see what he could produce when his talents were fully unleashed. Ohtani was excited about the possibilities and began skipping pre-game batting practice to save his energy for games.

During a spring training game on March 21, 2021, Ohtani batted leadoff as the pitcher. That was unheard of for an American League game since the adoption of the DH rule in 1973 and was an exceedingly rare occurrence before then. He singled in his first at-bat, then took the mound. In the third inning he threw a fastball to Fernando Tatis, Jr., that hit 102. "He definitely has another gear when the other team is threatening," said Maddon.[19]

Once the 2021 season started, the Angels forfeited their use of the DH for the first time on April 4, as Ohtani pitched and batted on the same day for the first time. All he did was slug a 451-foot homer with 115.2 exit velocity in his first at-bat and throw a 100-mph pitch in the first inning. With refined mechanics and a heavier workload, his sensational two-way feats would continue throughout the season. "It' s like you're adding two stars.

You're adding an ace and you're adding a guy to the middle of the lineup who can bang," said Trout.[20]

Ohtani hit his seventh home run on April 25, 2021, to take over the lead in the American League. The next day he made history when he started the game on the mound. For the first time in nearly 100 years, a player who was starting the game as a pitcher was leading his league in home runs. The last time that had happened was June 13, 1921, when Babe Ruth made his only pitching start of the season for the Yankees while leading the AL with 19 homers.[21]

The Japanese sensation blasted a 470-foot home run off the Royals' Kris Bubic at Angel Stadium on June 8, 2021. It was the longest home run of his career to date. "That's the farthest ball I've ever seen hit here. I've never seen one hit there before," said Maddon.[22]

A month later on July 9, he smashed a 463-foot homer into the Upper Deck in Seattle's T-Mobile Park, becoming just the sixth player to reach that area in the park's 21-year history. Then on July 27, he matched it with a 463-foot shot at home off the Rockies' Austin Gomber on July 27. The day before, Ohtani had become the first American League pitcher since Luis Tiant in 1970 to throw a scoreless half-inning and record a hit, an RBI, a stolen base, and a run scored in the same inning.[23]

Ohtani again made history in 2021 by becoming the first player to be elected to the All-Star Game as both a position player and a pitcher—the first two-way All-Star. Going into the game, he was slugging .698 and leading MLB with 33 homers while recording 87 strikeouts with a 3.49 ERA on the mound.

On July 12, 2021, he became the first pitcher and the first Japanese player to participate in the All-Star Game Home Run Derby. Despite hitting several gargantuan shots more than 500 feet, he was eliminated in the first round by Juan Soto as a huge global audience watched in fascination.

MLB adjusted the rule to allow the American League to keep the designated hitter for the All-Star Game once Ohtani had left the game as a pitcher—the rule would be extended to the whole league the next season. Ohtani opened the All-Star Game batting first as the designated hitter and also serving as the starting pitcher, which was another first. Ohtani ended up the winning pitcher after pitching a one-two-three bottom of the first, while he went 0-for-2 at the plate as the American League All-Stars won 5–2.

"As a fan of baseball, being able to see what he's accomplishing and doing day in and day out, you've just got to take a step back and watch, and realize the greatness that Shohei Ohtani is," said Freddie Freeman, then of the Braves, who is now his teammate on the Dodgers. "What he's doing, I don't think is going to come around ever again."[24]

No one has ever produced a year like Ohtani did in 2021. Literally no one. He is the only player in baseball history to record more than 100 innings and 100 strikeouts as a pitcher with at least 100 RBI, 100 runs scored, and 100 hits in the same season. You can even find that stat in the Guinness World Records. The best Babe Ruth could do was 100+ runs, hits, RBI, and innings pitched in 1919, but only 30 strikeouts. Bob Caruthers hit the mark in four out of five categories in 1887, but he never came close to 100 RBI in a season. Major League Baseball recognized Ohtani's groundbreaking season by awarding him the Commissioner's Historic Achievement Award.

Also in 2021, Ohtani led all players in barrel rate (22.3%) and ranked third with a maximum exit velocity of 119 mph. He played in 155 of the 162 games. Overall, he produced a .304 average (4th in AL), 46 homers (3rd), 100 RBI, 26 stolen bases (5th), league-leading 20 intentional walks, 103 runs (8th), and .592 slugging, .965 OPS, 80 extra-base hits, and 157 OPS+ (2nd). His 8.9 WAR led the AL. As a pitcher he went 9–2 with a 3.18 ERA in 130⅓ innings with a 141 ERA+, ranking ninth in opponent batting average (.209). He played seven games in the outfield that season covering eight innings, with the Angels pulling double switches to keep his bat in the lineup after he was replaced on the mound. No balls were hit to him in the outfield.

By collecting three triples in his last eight games to finish with a league-high eight triples in 2021, Ohtani

In 2023, Shohei Ohtani led the American League in home runs (44), slugging (.654), and on-base percentage (.412), while also making 23 pitching starts with a 3.14 ERA and 167 strikeouts in 132 innings (Conor P. Fitzgerald / Shutterstock, 2190493173).

matched another impressive feat. He became the first player since Bullet Rogan with the Kansas City Monarchs in 1925 to record at least eight triples and 20 pitching appearances in the same season. Rogan and Harry Kenyon of the Indianapolis ABCs also accomplished that feat in 1921.[25]

Rick Ankiel, who wanted to be a two-way player with the Cardinals but settled for tackling pitching and hitting separately, has been amazed at what Ohtani has accomplished, calling him a role model for kids. "Watching what he can do, it blows me away. I think that you're looking at someone that could win the batting title and the home run title and the Cy Young. In the same year. That's what's so incredible," Ankiel said.[26]

Ben Lindbergh, writing for *The Ringer*, shared more fascinating stats to summarize Ohtani's historic 2021 season. His 46 homers matched the 46 earned runs he allowed on the mound. He easily led the majors in batting OPS in high-leverage situations (1.276). On the mound he allowed a .380 OPS with runners in scoring position compared to .724 OPS with bases empty. Ohtani's 1,172 combined plate appearances as a hitter and batters faced as a pitcher is the highest mark of this century. He was the only American League pitcher to get hit by a pitch—he got hit four times. He had the highest standard deviation for pitch usage from start to start, throwing his fastball as low as 19 percent and as high as 76 percent, his splitter between seven and 52 percent, and his slider between two and 49 percent. In the first half of the season, Ohtani walked twice as many batters as he took walks at the plate—he reversed those numbers in the second half. His 4.09 average home-to-first time was the fastest in baseball (among those with 100 or more "competitive" runs). Finally, his 9.0 WAR represented 40 percent of the Angels' total team WAR.[27]

"He's definitely a 'unicorn,' and I think that's the best way to describe it," said teammate Jared Walsh, during one of the many times he was asked to describe Ohtani to the Japanese press that followed his every move.[28] Walsh knows how difficult it is to be good at both elements of the game. He had been a two-way player throughout college and did it in 2019 as a rookie in the majors, playing 24 games at first base while pitching in five games.

More historic milestones and awe-inspiring feats occurred in 2022. Ohtani became the first pitcher to bat lead-off on Opening Day in major league history. On May 9, he slugged the first grand slam of his professional career—it was his second home run of the game. He belted his 100th career homer on May 14 against the A's, becoming the third Japanese player to reach that figure.

Facing the Royals at Angel Stadium on June 21, 2022, Ohtani smacked two homers and a single to drive in eight runs. He returned the next day and struck out 13 Royals while hurling eight shutout innings, allowing two hits. At the plate, he singled and walked twice. He had just become the first major leaguer to both drive in eight runs and strike out 13 batters, and he had accomplished this amazing feat on consecutive days.

While beating the Marlins on July 6, 2022, Ohtani became the first player to strike out at least 10 batters without allowing an earned run in three consecutive starts. On September 29, he lost a no-hitter with two outs in the eighth inning but managed to extend his hitting streak to 14 games with a two-hit game. Appearing in the 2022 All-Star Game solely as a designated hitter, Ohtani collected a single and a walk in two plate appearances. From September 14 to October 3, he compiled an 18-game hitting streak, batting .348 over the stretch.

When the 2022 season ended—with the Angels again eliminated from the postseason—Ohtani had become the first player with 30 homers and 200 strikeouts in a season, the first with 30 homers and 10 wins, as well as the first with 300 total bases and 150 innings pitched. He also became the first player to qualify for the batting title and the ERA crown in the same season since Dave Foutz in 1888. He ended up batting .273/.356/.519 with 34 home runs (4th in AL) and 95 RBI to go with 15 wins with a 2.33 ERA (both fourth best) and 219 strikeouts (third best) in 166 innings. His 9.6 WAR trailed only Judge of the Yankees, his 6.2 pitching WAR trailed only Dylan Cease of the White Sox, and he finished fourth in voting for the Cy Young Award.

The highlight of Ohtani's 2023 season came during the World Baseball Classic (WBC). He had been disappointed to miss the 2017 WBC with an ankle injury, so this time around he was determined to lead his country to victory. He won Japan's first pool play game with four shutout innings while adding a single, double, and two RBI. In the final game of pool play he smashed a three-run homer on the way to four RBI.

With the final rounds held at LoanDepot Park in Miami, Ohtani stepped up his game. In the quarterfinals against Italy, Ohtani started and struck out five in 4⅔ innings while adding a hit. Japan won a close 6–5 game in the semifinals against Mexico, as Ohtani contributed a single, double, and two runs scored. In the final game on March 21, Japan would have to defeat a stacked U.S. lineup featuring Mookie Betts, Mike Trout, Paul Goldschmidt, Nolan Arenado, Trea Turner, and Kyle Schwarber. Batting third, Ohtani had a single and a walk as Japan took a 3–2 lead into the ninth inning. Ohtani went from the dugout to the bullpen several times in the later innings to complete warmups in case he was needed to pitch.

Of course his country needed him to pitch. Ohtani was brought in to replace Yu Darvish and preserve the win. After walking Jeff McNeil, he got Betts to hit into a double play. Hollywood couldn't have written a better script as the U.S., down to its final out, sent Trout up to the plate to face his famous teammate and friend. As Trout said of the matchup after the game,

"Did you think that it was going to end any other way?"²⁹ Trout, the three-time MVP about to start his 13th MLB season, had only competed in one postseason series back in 2014. The Angels had been swept by the Royals while he batted .083. The dream matchup of Trout versus Ohtani with the WBC championship on the line was the most pressure-packed moment either player had faced so far in their illustrious careers.

Ohtani started him off with a slider that missed outside for ball one. Trout then swung through a 100-mph fastball for strike one. The third pitch was a 99.8-mph fastball that was outside for ball two. Pitch four was a 99.8-mph fastball that Trout swung at and missed for strike two. A 101.6-mph fastball was way off the plate for ball three. Of course there would be a full count, with a capacity crowd of 36,098 and a record TV audience of 5.2 million in the U.S. watching on the edge of their seats. Trout, undoubtedly expecting Ohtani to challenge him again with a fastball, swung and missed at a sweeping slider for strike three. In terms of spin rate and velocity, it was the best breaking pitch Ohtani had thrown since leaving Japan for the major leagues in 2018. Another surprising stat: in 6,174 career plate appearances in the majors, Trout had only had three swinging strikes 24 times. In a bit of an understatement after the game, Ohtani said, "I believe this is the best moment in my life."³⁰

That thrilling at-bat seemed like an official changing of the guard, with the mantle of baseball's best player shifting from Trout to Ohtani, if it hadn't already. Asked his thoughts on facing and failing against his teammate in that key moment, Trout said, "He's a competitor, man. That's why he's the best."³¹

Ohtani got at least one hit in all seven games of the tournament, batting .435/.606/.739 with four doubles, a home run, and 10 walks. On the mound, he struck out 11 batters in 9⅔ innings with a 1.86 ERA. He had hit the longest home run—448 feet against Australia. And he had thrown the fastest pitch—102 mph against Italy. In addition to being named World Baseball Classic MVP, Ohtani was named the DH and pitcher on the 2023 All-World Baseball Classic team.

The 2023 regular season started with extra pressure on the Angels and Ohtani. He was in the final season of his contract with the team and had been awarded a record $30 million salary in arbitration. Would he finally lead the team to the playoffs, and would the Angels consider trading him if they fell out of contention?

Ohtani went out and continued dominating the competition on the mound and at the plate, finding new ways to wow fans, teammates, and peers. He demolished a 493-foot home run with an exit velocity of 115.1 mph on June 30, 2023. It was his 30th home run of the season and it came off lefty Tommy Henry of the Diamondbacks. The four longest home runs of his career have all come against left-handed pitchers, either destroying the myth that lefties cannot consistently hit lefties, or perhaps it's another illustration that comparing Ohtani to mere mortals is unfair.

"I hear about all those 500-foot shots from guys in the past, but I don't think I'm ever going to see one. Because I [don't think it's possible] to see one hit farther than the one I saw," said Angels manager Phil Nevin.[32]

Ohtani led all American League players in votes for the All-Star Game, making his third team as the DH. On June 27, 2023, he had his first multi-homer game as a pitcher, striking out 10 in a 4–2 win over the White Sox. "MVP with ease. He should win it every year. What he's doing is insane. All of us at the highest level can't believe our eyes. Truly remarkable. Be thankful you get to witness a real GOAT!" Cubs pitcher Marcus Stroman posted on Twitter after that game.

A month later on July 27, Ohtani found a way to top his performance. In the first game of a doubleheader against the Tigers, he pitched a one-hit shutout with eight strikeouts—he also batted five times without a hit. Then in the nightcap, he hit a two-run homer in the second inning and followed with a solo shot deep to right-center field in the fourth inning.

The Angels, still clinging to a faint hope to make the playoffs, decided not to trade their iconic player, and then proceeded to fall apart down the stretch. On August 23, the team announced Ohtani had again torn the ulnar collateral ligament in his arm and would need Tommy John surgery for the second time that would prevent him from pitching in 2024. It was a cruel blow to the team and the player.

Babe Ruth led the American League in home runs, slugging, and on-base percentage in 1920, his first season as a batter only. In 2023, Ohtani led the American League in home runs (44), slugging (.654) and on-base percentage (.412), while also making 23 pitching starts with a 3.14 ERA and 167 strikeouts in 132 innings. He led the league with a 184 OPS+. In his 23 games as a starting pitcher, he batted .372 with seven home runs. He ranked fifth in WAR for pitchers with 3.9 and his 10.0 total WAR led the league. At the end of the year, Ohtani was selected as the Male Athlete of the Year by the Associated Press for the second time in three years to go with his second unanimous AL MVP trophy.

"We should make a new award for him. He's just a different breed. This is something MLB hasn't seen since Babe Ruth…. He's not the best hitter, he's not the best pitcher, but if you combine everything, he's the best player," said Red Sox manager Alex Cora.[33]

Ohtani had also done something for the fourth time in 2023 that had never been done before in baseball history—hit at least 10 home runs as a batter while striking out at least 50 batters as a pitcher. He had barely hit the threshold in his rookie campaign with 22 homers and 63 strikeouts in 2018, then he had shattered those marks in 2021, 2022, and 2023.

As he rehabbed his arm in the winter of 2023, Ohtani commanded attention as the highest-profile free agent in baseball history. How high would a team be willing to go to sign the sport's best two-way player? As it turned out, as high as $700 million. Signing that record contract with the Dodgers—with $680 million deferred—did not change how Ohtani approached his craft. By taking slightly above the minimum salary for the 10-year length of the contract, he demonstrated that he wanted to win and experience the thrill of a postseason more than anything.

The gambling scandal involving Ohtani's interpreter and best friend Ippei Mizuhara, which broke in late March 2024 during MLB's highly anticipated World Tour Seoul Series in South Korea, did little to disrupt the focus of baseball's biggest star. The two had been inseparable since Ohtani burst onto the major-league scene in 2018, with Mizuhara working as his trainer, workout partner, and the person who shielded the intensely private star from much scrutiny. "To summarize how I'm feeling right now, I'm just beyond shock," Ohtani said during a statement to the media after the scandal broke.[34]

From what has been reported of Ohtani's character and aversion to gambling, it seemed inconceivable that he personally bet on baseball or any other sport. Major League Baseball officials undoubtedly breathed a sigh of relief once Mizuhara admitted to the theft of more than $16 million from his friend's account and was charged with felony bank fraud. "Mr. Ohtani is considered a victim in this case. There is no evidence that Mr. Ohtani authorized the transfers to the bookmakers," said United States attorney Martin Estrada.[35] Most people would be aware if someone was stealing that much money from their bank account, but it further demonstrates Ohtani's single-minded focus on baseball.

His teammates and coaches, who are kept at arm's length from Ohtani's detailed and rigorous daily routines, are amazed to see that he goes through his full pre-pitch routine before every swing he takes in the batting cage. There are no half-measures and no wasted effort in practices. Early in the 2024 season, he began practicing with a customized cricket bat to help him keep his bat in the hitting zone longer. "Everything he does is intentional, which is pretty amazing but not surprising," said Dodgers manager Dave Roberts.[36]

For his part, Ohtani looked forward to the challenge of taking his batting to another level in 2024. "I feel like there's not just one level but several levels ahead offense-wise. It's just going to depend on what kind of lineup I'm in and everything. But at the end, my focus is going to be the same—keep the focus on my hitting and trying to get better," Ohtani said.[37]

He began a throwing program near the end of 2024 spring training, and the Dodgers said they had not ruled out using him in the field later on in the season if the need came up. No one doubts that he could be an excellent outfielder or first baseman, and that might be a new path for him to follow if it ever gets to the point where his pitching contributions are curtailed.

On April 21, 2024, Ohtani again made history when he clubbed his 176th career home run to pass Hideki Matsui for the most home runs in MLB history by a Japanese-born player.

Ohtani ended up having a history-making season in 2024, setting numerous franchise records in his first season with the Dodgers while becoming the first player in baseball history to have a 50–50 season—50 home runs and 50 stolen bases. He finished with a league-leading 54 home runs, while his 59 steals were second behind Elly De La Cruz of the Reds. He narrowly missed the Triple Crown by falling four points shy of the batting title. While he previously had seasons with 20 and 26 stolen bases, no one saw him putting such a unique twist on another type of two-way excellence. Only Ronald Acuña, Jr., of the Braves, who produced the first 40–70 season in 2023 with 41 home runs and 73 stolen bases, has produced such lofty heights as a dual threat on the bases and as a slugger.

On September 19, 2024, Ohtani had what some were calling "the greatest day in baseball history" to join the 50–50 club. He clubbed three home runs in his last three at bats, went six-for-six with 10 RBIs, two doubles, two runs scored, and two stolen bases while helping the Dodgers clinch a playoff spot with a 20–4 win over the Marlins at Dodger Stadium. He just missed hitting for the cycle when he was thrown out trying to stretch a double into a triple. Ohtani became the first player to hit three home runs and steal two bases in a game and he tied a major-league record with five extra-base hits. "It's unexplainable witnessing history like that. What we see is expected," gushed teammate Mookie Betts.

In the press conference after his historic game, Ohtani said: "I'm happy, I'm relieved, and very respectful to peers and everybody who came before me to play the sport of baseball. I've had perhaps the most memorable moments here in my career and this stadium has become one of my favorite stadiums. Ideally, aiming for a home run for me is not the best way of hitting a home run, so what I focus on is having quality at bats. In terms of the stolen base, my attitude was just be aggressive and when the opportunity arises be aggressive at all times."

It is a short list of players who are faster and better baserunners than Ohtani. It is an even shorter list of pitchers who are currently as good or better than Ohtani. A case can be made for Aaron Judge as a better slugger and Juan Soto as a better overall hitter, but that's about it. No one alive has witnessed a singular baseball player who combines all those skills in one package like Shohei Ohtani. It seems fitting to describe him as a unicorn, since unicorns symbolize power, innocence, and purity. With unmatched purpose and drive, Ohtani will undoubtedly continue to produce historic achievements at MLB ballparks all over North America, building a legacy that future generations will find hard to believe. Back in Japan, an entire nation will continue to anxiously await the result of every at-bat and every pitch he throws, hearkening back to the days when Mantle and Maris were fighting for the home run crown in 1961 and folks stayed glued to their TVs and radios.

"I've never seen anyone like Shohei, especially his popularity in Japan," said Lon Rosen, Dodgers executive vice president and chief marketing officer. "He is revered not just because he is a sports figure. Like M.J. and Magic, he has that special something that people see he is authentic."[38] In his hometown of Ōshū back in Japan, the seventeenth of every month is "Ohtani Day" in homage to his jersey number, with many in the city wearing his jersey that day as an outpouring of pride.[39]

Ohtani is not striving to be better than Babe Ruth or Bullet Rogan or even Aaron Judge. He is striving in pursuit of something unique, something that has not been done before. Becoming the best baseball player ever is just part of the journey. While he hopes to return baseball to its former status as the most popular sport in America and says he is comfortable being seen as the face of baseball, those are not the things that drive him to seek perfection. For a player who was named after a Japanese warrior who died in the 12th century, the game of baseball is a chance to test the limits of his performance as a two-way player. His toughest competition may prove to be the standards he sets for himself.

A generation of boys grew up wanting to play center field like Mickey Mantle. Then another generation grew up wanting to play shortstop like Derek Jeter. Now a new generation of budding baseball stars will grow up wanting to be a great two-way player just like their idol Shohei Ohtani.

Chapter 13

Pitchers at the Plate

Profiling the Best-Hitting Pitchers

For the first 100 or so years of professional baseball, the pitcher was just another batter in the lineup who was expected to contribute. The pitchers who were strong batters gave their manager one less reason to pull them from the game. In the 19th century and especially in the Negro Leagues, if a pitcher was one of the best batters on the team he often batted in the middle of the lineup.

Hall of Famer Red Ruffing batted in all nine positions during his career. He batted in the one through five spots in 37 games and averaged .429 batting third. Red Lucas also batted in all nine spots, a total of 351 times outside the ninth spot. Wes Ferrell batted 97 times in a lineup position other than ninth.

When relief pitchers came more into vogue in the 1950s and 1960s, managers didn't trust them batting in key spots and would instead rely on pinch hitters. Pitchers who could swing the bat were frequently deployed as pinch hitters, which enabled managers to expand their late-game options. Bullet Rogan is credited with 41 pinch-hitting chances with the Kansas City Monarchs.

The adoption of the designated hitter in the American League in 1973 changed the role of the pitcher to specialist, but for only half of baseball. When the National League finally adopted the designated hitter in 2022, the evolution was complete.

Pitchers now have one main job (apart from fielding), and fans no longer have to see poor-hitting pitchers like Ron Herbel (career average .029) flail helplessly at pitches. However, apart from Shohei Ohtani and any unicorn players who follow in his footsteps, we will no longer see good-hitting pitchers come to the plate and make history. Historic baseball moments like the following will become a thing of the past:

- Madison Bumgarner becoming the only pitcher to belt two home runs on Opening Day, which he accomplished while pitching for the San Francisco Giants on April 2, 2017.

Chapter 13. Pitchers at the Plate

- Dave McNally hitting the first (and probably only) grand slam by a pitcher in the World Series on October 13, 1970.
- Nixey Callahan getting five hits in a game three times—in 1897, 1902, and 1903.
- Guy Hecker getting six hits (including three home runs) and scoring seven runs for Louisville on August 15, 1886.
- Jouett Meekin hitting three triples on July 4, 1894.
- Ken Brett homering in four consecutive starts as a pitcher in June 1973.
- Harry Staley driving in a record nine runs with two homers, a single, and two sacrifice flies on June 1, 1893.
- Tony Cloninger hitting two grand slams and knocking in a record-tying nine runs on July 3, 1966.
- Rick Wise hitting two home runs for the Phillies on June 23, 1971, while also pitching a no-hitter.
- Dixie Howell entering the game in the fifth inning for the White Sox on June 16, 1957, and slugging two home runs and getting the win while pitching only 3⅔ innings.

The statistical analysis that follows comes from Sports-Reference's Statfinder tool. Looking at players who pitched, didn't play any other positions, and had a minimum of 200 plate appearances, we find:

- Erv Brame has the highest lifetime batting average at .306.
- George Uhle has the most RBI (190) and most hits (393).
- Wes Ferrell has the most home runs with 36.
- Micah Owings has the highest slugging percentage at .502, followed by Chad Kimsey at .432, and Erv Brame at .429.

The pitchers who were the best batters of the 19th century—Bob Caruthers, Dave Foutz, Guy Hecker, Win Mercer, Scott Stratton, and Jack Stivetts—were all covered extensively in Chapter 3. Top-hitting Negro League pitchers were covered extensively in Chapter 8 and their stats are too incomplete or not able to be defined in this section. For example, we are not able to break down Bullet Rogan's at-bats for when he was a pitcher. However, if one looks at career slugging percentages for players who pitched (with no restriction on games played elsewhere) and had at least 200 plate appearances, five of the top seven spots go to Negro League players: Lewis Hampton #2 at .527, Bullet Rogan #3 at .521, Ed Rile #5 at .492, Luther Farrell #6 at .462, and Nip Winters #7 at .456.

Looking just at Negro League players who played at least 75 percent of their games at pitcher, Edsall Walker has the highest career slugging percentage at .405, followed by Charles Corbett at .392. Using the same criteria, William Ross has the highest batting average at .286, followed by Sam Streeter at .285. By comparison, Bullet Rogan had a career slugging percentage of .510 and he batted .335 while pitching in about one-third of the games he played.

Here are the top Negro League players for offensive WAR:

Most Offensive WAR for Negro League Pitchers

(at least 60 percent games as pitcher, minimum 250 at-bats)

1. Lewis Hampton   5.3
2. Bill Byrd   4.9
3. Hilton Smith   4.3
4. Nip Winters   4.3
5. Joe Strong   4.1
6. William Bell   2.5
7. Henry McHenry   2.5
8. Sam Streeter   2.4
9. Edsall Walker   2.3
10. William Ross   2.1
11. Willie Cornelius 2.1

Source: Statfinder, Sports-Reference

Most Offensive WAR for Negro League Pitchers

(minimum 250 at-bats)

1. Bullet Rogan   22.5
2. Homer Curry   12.9
3. Ed Rile   11.1
4. Ray Brown   6.3
5. Luther Farrell   5.7
6. Lewis Hampton   5.3
7. Bill Byrd   4.9
8. Hilton Smith   4.3
9. Nip Winters   4.3
10. Joe Strong   4.1

Source: Statfinder, Sports-Reference

The highest batting average by a pitcher in the designated hitter era is Dan Haren, who batted .364 in 2010, followed by Orel Hershiser at .356

Chapter 13. Pitchers at the Plate

in 1993, and Mike Hampton at .344 in 2002. The highest slugging percentage in the DH era is Micah Owings' .683 in 2007, while Jim Rooker of the Pirates collected the most single-season hits with 29 in 1974.

Looking at the top single-season slugging percentages by a player who got a minimum of 60 percent of their games at pitcher with at least 100 at-bats, we find Don Newcombe atop the list at .632 in 1955, followed by Wes Ferrell at .621 in 1931, Red Ruffing at .582 in 1930, and Scott Stratton at .559 in 1884.

Looking at the top career batting averages by a player who got at least 75 percent of their games at pitcher with a minimum of 250 at-bats, Al Spalding ranks first at .313, followed by Erv Brame at .306, Bert Inks at .300, and George Uhle at .289.

Babe Ruth, Bucky Walters, and Jack Stivetts are covered elsewhere in this book for their feats as two-way players and are not featured in the list that follows, which focuses on players who pitched almost exclusively. It should be pointed out that Ruth compiled 5.4 offensive WAR (oWAR) for the 1914–17 seasons when he only pitched, and he batted .344 with 21 hits as a pitcher in 1918. As a pitcher, the Bambino batted .304 and hit 15 of his 714 home runs.[1] Walters produced 8.3 oWAR from 1935 to 1950, when he was almost exclusively a pitcher. Stivetts hit 20 of his 35 home runs as a pitcher.[2]

What follows are the top 25 best-hitting pitchers in major league history as ranked by career offensive WAR from Statfinder (minimum 250 at-bats, played at least 90 percent of games at pitcher).

1. Red Ruffing, 13.3 career oWAR—Ruffing's best year at the plate was 1930, when he batted .364 with four home runs, 40 hits, and 1.7 oWAR. He batted .273 in six games for the Red Sox that season before getting traded to the Yankees, batting an impressive .374 (157 OPS+) for them—15 points higher in batting average than Babe Ruth. Ruffing's .596 slugging in 1930 trailed only Ruth and Gehrig on the team, and his .415 on-base percentage topped that of future Hall of Famers Bill Dickey, Tony Lazzeri, and Earle Combs. His .582 combined slugging percentage that season is tied for the third-best mark in baseball history by a pitcher.

Ruffing had three three-hit games that year for the Bronx Bombers. On September 18, 1930, he belted two home runs and drove in three runs in a 7–6 win over the St. Louis Browns. Yankees Manager Bob Shawkey knew to ride the hot hand, calling on Ruffing 20 times to pinch hit that season—he got six pinch hits. His .364 average in 1930 is tied for the seventh-best mark by a pitcher.

Ruffing had a salary dispute with the Yankees in 1937, because he expected to be paid an extra $1,000 for his exceptional hitting.[3] He had hit .291 with five home runs the previous season. He batted .269 in seven seasons with the Red Sox and .270 in 15 seasons with the Yankees. His 13 doubles in 1928 tied Smoky Joe Wood for the most by a pitcher in the modern era (since 1900).

He batted over .300 eight times and led AL pitchers in batting average four times including 1930–32. Ruffing's 34 career home runs rank fourth among pitchers in major league history. He batted .262 with 56 hits in 233 appearances as a pinch hitter—second-most pinch hits by a pitcher. Red was called on to pinch hit for Hall of Famer Bill Dickey (a lifetime .313 batter) four times. Overall, Ruffing batted .270 lifetime with 437 hits, 87 doubles, 12 triples, and 215 RBI as a pitcher. He hit two home runs in a game as a pitcher twice.

2. **George Mullin**, 12.9 oWAR—"Wabash George" was one of the best-hitting pitchers of the Deadball Era in addition to winning 228 games with a 2.82 ERA. He batted .262 lifetime with 401 hits and 139 RBI, and he led pitchers in his league in batting average three times.

Walter Johnson is shown taking batting practice for the Washington Nationals in 1925, the year he batted .433, which is the highest batting average ever recorded by a pitcher (Library of Congress, Prints & Photographs Division, LG-DIG-npcc-14700).

His best years at the plate were 1904, when he batted .290 with 45 hits and produced 1.8 oWAR; and his rookie season, 1902, when he collected 39 hits with a .325/.367/.408 slash line. He hit three doubles during his pitching debut on May 4, 1902. The righty batter proved his consistency by batting .262 against right-handed pitchers and .262 against left-handed pitchers.

Mullin was sent up to pinch hit in Games 3, 5 and 7 of the 1909 World Series for Detroit. Pitching in Game 6, he got two hits including a double while pitching a complete game for the win. Pitching on his 32nd birthday in 1912, Mullin hurled a no-hitter against the St. Louis Browns and helped his cause by rapping three hits and knocking in two runs.[4] He would bat .278 that season with an on-base percentage of .393.

3. Walter Johnson, 12.8 oWAR—One of the greatest pitchers of all time, Johnson's .433 batting average in 1925 is the highest ever by a pitcher. It was his 19th season in the majors and his previous career high for average had been .283 the year before. Johnson posted a .433/.455/.577 slash line in 1925 with 42 hits and 1.8 oWAR. His 1.033 OPS that season is the best-ever mark by a pitcher.

Also in 1925, the 37-year-old Johnson blasted a game-winning two-run homer as a pinch hitter on May 19. Playing in the 1907–08 California Winter League after his rookie season, Johnson hit .372 and slugged .628. His six triples in 1913 remain tied for the second most by a pitcher in the modern era, and he holds the record for career triples by a pitcher with 41.

4. Red Lucas, 12.0 oWAR—Lucas posted a .287/.342/.348 slash line while batting as a pitcher with 256 hits in 893 at-bats. He batted over .300 six times, and his best year at the plate was 1927, when he batted .313 with a career-high 47 hits and 28 RBI. In 1926, Lucas hit .303 to join a trio of Reds pitchers to bat over .300—Dolf Luque batted .346 and Pete Donohue batted .311 and the trio combined for 10 triples that season. Lucas threw right-handed but batted as a lefty. Lucas led the National League in pinch hits four times and still remains Cincinnati's all-time leader with 80 pinch-hits.[5]

5. Wes Ferrell, 11.3 oWAR—Bill James views Ferrell as the best hitter among the top 100 pitchers, estimating that he created four times the number of runs as an average pitcher would from hitting.[6] In 1935, Ferrell's 2.5 oWAR is tied with Guy Hecker (1884) for the highest single-season total by a pitcher. He added 8.2 pitching WAR while leading the AL with 25 wins, and his 10.6 total WAR led the league as he finished second in the MVP voting. That year he batted .347 with seven home runs, 32 RBI, and 52 hits.

On July 21, 1935, Ferrell hit a walk-off three-run homer as a pinch hitter to lift the Red Sox to a dramatic 7–6 win over the Tigers. The next day he hit another walk-off homer while pitching a complete game to get his 15th win of the season. "What he did while on the mound and at bat made everybody forget the other players," read the game report in the *Boston Globe*.[7]

His 1931 season at the plate—.319 average with nine homers, 30 RBI, and 37 hits—produced 1.8 oWAR and set a single-season record for home runs by a pitcher that still stands. He batted .216 in 157 career pinch-hitting chances.

Ferrell's 36 career home runs are the most all-time by a pitcher and his career OPS+ of 100 is very respectable for a hurler. Ferrell produced two seasons with OPS over .900: .994 in 1931 and .960 in 1935—those seasons he produced the two-highest RBI totals for a pitcher in the modern era with 32 RBI in 1935 and 30 RBI in 1931. His .621 slugging percentage in 1931 is the second highest by a pitcher in baseball history. He hit two home runs in a game five times. His strong batting ability sometimes overshadowed what he accomplished as a pitcher, but Ferrell was a two-time All-Star who won 20 games six times. He pitched a no-hitter in 1931 while driving in four runs with a homer and double.

Wes generated twice as much career WAR as his older brother Rick (60.1 to 30.8), yet it was his brother the catcher who was elected to the Hall of Fame. Rick had a huge advantage in at-bats (7,076 to 1,176), yet Wes out-homered his brother 38–28 and outslugged him .446 to .363. At least Wes was able to win a World Series ring with the Yankees in 1938, although he didn't play in the Series.

> **6. Bob Lemon**, 10.6 oWAR—Lemon started out as a third baseman and batted .286 in the minors before getting called up to the Indians in 1946. The team was not convinced he would hit enough (he couldn't hit changeups) and noticed the natural sinking motion on his throws from third, so he became a pitcher. His best year at the plate was 1950, when he batted .272 with six homers, 26 RBI, and 37 hits, producing 1.8 oWAR. On July 24, 1949, Lemon hit two home runs in the first game of a doubleheader as the Indians beat the Senators.

Lemon batted .288 with 32 hits (two home runs) in 117 pinch-hitting appearances. His 35 career home runs are tied for second most by a pitcher in major league history, and his seven home runs in 1949 are tied for second most in a season by a pitcher. Lemon led AL hurlers in home runs four straight seasons (1948–51). His .394 slugging percentage as a pitcher is fourth best since 1900.[8]

7. **George Uhle**, 10.5 oWAR—The Ohio righty recorded a lifetime average of .289 with 393 hits and 190 RBI. He batted over .300 nine times with a high of .381 in his last season, 1936. His best year at the plate was 1923, when he batted .361 with 22 RBI and 52 hits (a modern-era record for pitchers), which generated 1.9 oWAR. Overall, Uhle recorded 43 pinch-hits (third most by a pitcher) in 190 pinch-hitting opportunities for a .261 average.

On April 28, 1921, Uhle collected three hits including a grand slam to drive in six runs as he pitched a complete game to beat Detroit. On May 24, 1929, an undefeated Uhle got his eighth win of the season after pitching the first 20 innings of a 21-inning marathon against the White Sox—he went 4-for-9 at the plate to raise his season average to .412.

8. **Early Wynn**, 9.5 oWAR—The Hall of Famer was a decent hitter, but his oWAR is largely a function of compiling for 23 seasons. The switch-hitter's best year with the bat was 1953, when he batted .275 with three home runs and 1.2 oWAR. He hit a grand slam as a pinch hitter on September 15, 1946, and his career marks were .214 average, 14 home runs, and 321 hits. On May 1, 1959, Wynn pitched a one-hitter and beat the Red Sox 1–0, helping his cause by hitting a home run in the eighth inning for the only run.

9. **Don Newcombe**, 8.9 oWAR—Newcombe impressed with the bat at an early age, as he batted .311 in his first year in the minors, 1946. His 2.3 oWAR in 1955 is the third best by a pitcher in baseball history. That season Newcombe batted .359 and slugged .632 for the Brooklyn Dodgers with seven homers (setting an NL record that has not been surpassed), 17 extra-base hits, 23 RBI, and 42 hits, with an incredible 1.028 OPS. Newcombe belted two home runs and drove in three runs in his first start of the season on April 14, 1955. The next month on May 30, he hit two more homers and added a single with three RBI while pitching a complete game for the win.

Newcombe's total of 2.3 oWAR on the 1955 Dodgers outpaced the team's starting third baseman, Jackie Robinson, who produced 2.2 oWAR. His .632 slugging in 1955 outpaced the team's center fielder, Duke Snider, who finished second in the NL with a .628 slugging percentage that season (among qualifiers)—only Willie Mays topped Newcombe in slugging that year. It remains the highest single-season slugging percentage by a pitcher in baseball history.

Newk went 20-for-88 as a pinch hitter and averaged .276 with 218 hits and 15 home runs batting as a pitcher. His .361 average in 1958 is the 10th best in major-league history by a pitcher, and his .359 mark in 1955 is 13th best. He hit two home runs in a game three times and led NL pitchers in batting average three times.

   10. **Schoolboy Rowe**, 8.3 oWAR—The three-time All-Star batted .266 for his career with 15 home runs. His best year at the plate was 1943, with a .300 average (tops for NL pitchers), four homers, 36 hits, and 1.9 oWAR. Rowe batted .283 as a pinch hitter with two home runs and 26 pinch-hits. He started drawing comparisons to Babe Ruth in his second season, 1934, when he hit .303 with 33 hits and 22 RBI and smacked two walk-off home runs. He hit a double off Lon Warneke in Game 1 of the 1935 World Series. In 1943, Rowe led the NL with 15 pinch-hits while leading the Phillies with a .300 average.

   11. **Warren Spahn,** 7.9 oWAR—His 35 career home runs as a pitcher are tied for second most in major league history. Spahn's best year at the plate was 1958, when he batted .333 with 36 hits and 1.9 oWAR. His next-highest batting mark was .231 the next season. Spahn accumulated 363 wins and 363 hits. He clubbed four home runs in both 1955 and 1961 (at the age of 40).

   12. **Carl Mays**, 7.7 oWAR—In a season in which he won a league-best 27 games, 1921, Mays batted .343 for the New York Yankees. Babe Ruth was the only starter on the '21 Yankees to post a higher average. Mays had 49 hits and 1.4 oWAR that year. He would collect 291 hits over his 15-year career but had zero pinch-hits in six at-bats. Appearing in six World Series with the Red Sox and Yankees, Mays batted just .118 in 18 postseason plate appearances.

Carl Mays batted .343 while winning 27 games for the New York Yankees in 1921 (Library of Congress, Prints & Photographs Division, LG-DIG-ggbain-29157).

His .277 average in 1914 while winning 24 games for the Providence Grays in the minors was just behind the team's other pitching and hitting sensation, Ruth, who batted .300 in a 12-game stint with the Grays.

13. Earl Wilson, 7.6 oWAR—Wilson's 33 career homers as a pitcher rank fifth all-time. He belted a home run on June 26, 1962, while pitching a no-hitter, becoming the third MLB pitcher to accomplish that feat. His best season was 1966, when he batted a combined .240 with seven home runs, 22 RBI, and 1.3 oWAR for the Red Sox and Tigers. He also hit seven homers in 1968 and slugged six homers in 1965. Wilson led AL pitchers in home runs five straight seasons from 1964 to 1968.

Wilson started out as an outfielder but actually began his professional career as a catcher in 1953. He batted a strong .268 with 10 home runs during seven seasons in the minors, but he was quickly switched to pitching due to his strong arm. When Wilson won his first major league game pitching in relief on August 20, 1959—becoming just the second Black player in Red Sox history—he drove in three runs with a single and double.

14. Mike Hampton, 7.6 oWAR—A five-time Silver Slugger winner, Hampton was considered one of the best-hitting pitchers of his era. He hit seven home runs in 2001, which are the most by a pitcher in the designated hitter era and tied the National League record. That season the two-time All-Star batted .291 with 23 hits, slugged .582, and generated 1.0 oWAR. That .582 mark is tied for the third-highest slugging percentage ever by a pitcher. In 2002, Hampton put up a .344/.354/.516 mark and he also batted over .300 in 1999, 2005, and 2009.

For his career, he averaged .246 with 16 home runs and 178 hits. On June 5, 2001, Hampton slugged two homers and drove in three runs for the Rockies while pitching into the eighth inning to get the win.

15. Bob Gibson, 7.3 oWAR—Gibson's tremendous athleticism carried over to his fielding (nine Gold Gloves) and his batting. He batted .206 lifetime with 274 hits including 24 home runs, leading NL hurlers in batting average in 1970 with a .303 mark. Gibson's best year at the plate was 1965, when he batted .240 with five home runs and 25 hits for 1.3 oWAR. In his last start of the 1965 season on September 29, Gibson hit a grand slam off Gaylord Perry to go with two singles as he won his 19th game of the year. His last career home run was a grand slam on July 26, 1973, against the Mets.

He hit home runs in the 1967 and 1968 World Series. On June 21, 1972, Gibson belted a three-run homer in the seventh inning to help his cause as he won his 211th career game to become the Cardinals' all-time leader in wins. He had injured his hamstring after singling and scoring in the second inning but stayed in to pitch seven innings.

16. Tom Glavine, 6.8 oWAR—The Hall of Fame pitcher won four Silver Slugger Awards and finished with 216 sacrifice bunts for his career (tied for 69th all-time)—it's the most by a pitcher. Since pitchers don't bat anymore, he should hold that record forever. He batted over .200 in just nine of 22 seasons and only hit one home run. His best year at the plate was 1996, with a .289 average and 1.0 oWAR.

Overall, Glavine batted .186 with 244 hits and 90 RBI as a pitcher. He smashed a bases-clearing triple in the first inning of Game Seven of the 1996 National League Championship Series, as the Braves rolled to a 15–0 win over the Cardinals.

17. Jim Tobin, 6.7 oWAR—In a year in which he would lead the National League with 21 losses, Tobin set a modern-era record for pitchers by blasting three home runs for the Boston Braves on May 13, 1942. Tobin, who had smashed a pinch-hit homer the day before, homered in three consecutive at-bats, driving in four runs. The first home run he hit that day went completely out of the ballpark. "It was a mighty swat, clearing both the billboard fence and the park's outer boundaries and landing in the freight yards that fringe the Charles River," wrote the *Boston Post*.[9]

Tobin's third homer of the game was a two-run blast in the eighth inning that provided the final margin as he pitched a complete game to defeat the Cubs 6–5. He narrowly missed a fourth homer in the game, as he hit a long drive in his first at-bat that was caught at the right field fence. The *Boston Daily Globe* wrote that Tobin "went absolutely berserk with the bat and with piledriving power."[10]

Howell Stevens of the *Boston Post* went so far as to call Tobin's hitting that day "one of the most astounding feats of baseball history."[11] The only other pitcher to hit three home runs in a single game was Guy Hecker, whose three homers in an 1886 game were all inside-the-park hits. So, Tobin is indeed the only pitcher in baseball history to hit three balls over the fence for home runs in a single game.

Tobin's best year at the plate was 1942, when he batted .246 with six home runs, 28 hits, and 1.8 oWAR—the six homers tied the NL record. He also batted .441 in 34 at-bats his rookie season in 1937, and .280 with a career-high 30 hits in 1943. In 1945, he led NL pitchers with three home runs and tied for the lead among AL pitchers with two home runs. The one-time All-Star hit .258 with 148 hits and 13 home runs as a pitcher. He batted just .079 (6-for-76) as a pinch hitter.

18. Gary Peters, 6.7 oWAR—The two-time All-Star and 1963 Rookie of the Year hit at least one home run in nine straight years—no pitcher has matched that feat since—and hit 19 home runs total over his 14-year career. The lefty swinger's best year at the plate was 1963, when he batted .259 (tops among AL hurlers) with three homers, 21 hits, and 1.1 oWAR. On July 19, 1964, he hit a walk-off, pinch-hit two-run homer for the White Sox. After that dramatic feat, he emerged as one of the team's primary left-handed pinch hitters the rest of the season with 16 pinch-hitting chances.

Peters batted .221 with 163 hits as a pitcher, and he batted .235 as a pinch hitter. His four pinch-hit home runs are the most ever by a pitcher.

19. Christy Mathewson, 6.5 oWAR—One of the greatest pitchers of the Deadball Era was also one of the best-hitting pitchers. "Big Six" recorded 12 straight seasons with at least 20 hits, averaging .215 lifetime with 362 hits. His best year at the plate was 1906, when he batted .264 with 24 hits for a 103 OPS+. He legged out three triples in 1904.

Mathewson batted .600 with three hits in a losing effort in the 1913 World Series. Overall, he batted .281 with nine hits in four World Series.

20. Vern Law, 6.4 oWAR—His best year at the plate was 1964, when he batted .311 with 116 OPS+ and 1.0 oWAR. He also batted .311 in 1962 and a career-high .344 in 1951. During his 16-year career, he batted .216 with 191 hits and 11 home runs. Law appeared in three games for the Pirates in the 1960 World Series, collecting a single and a run-scoring double in Game Four and ending the Series with a .333 average to go with two pitching wins.

Branch Rickey, while he was the Pirates' general manager, considered converting Law to an everyday role in the outfield due to his athleticism, base-running, and hitting ability.[12]

21. Burleigh Grimes, 6.3 oWAR—The Hall of Fame hurler recorded four seasons with at least 30 hits, topped by 42 in 1928, when he led NL hurlers with a .321 average. Another strong year at the plate was 1920, when he batted .306/.358/.432 (124 OPS+) with 34 hits for Brooklyn, generating 1.4 oWAR. He averaged .248 with 380 hits over his 19-year career. Grimes batted .321 in 1928 and .306 in 1920.

Grimes started out his professional baseball career as a two-way player before quickly pivoting to full-time pitching. Appearing in four World Series with three different teams, he hit a stout .316 with six hits.

22. Claude Hendrix, 6.1 oWAR—Hendrix was an all-around athlete who excelled at fielding (leading the league twice in assists as

Christy Mathewson, shown here taking batting practice during the 1911 World Series, batted .600 during the 1913 World Series. One of baseball's greatest pitchers, he recorded 12 straight seasons with at least 20 hits (Library of Congress, Prints & Photographs Division, LG-DIG-ggbain-09868).

pitcher) and running the bases (stealing nine bases). That athleticism translated into his batting abilities. For his career he batted .241 with 222 hits, 97 RBI, 14 home runs, and 17 triples.

His six triples in 1912 are tied for the second-most by a pitcher in the modern era and his 17 extra-base hits that year was a pitcher record for the 20th century. His three home runs in 1918 led all NL hurlers—Babe Ruth had one fewer that year to lead AL pitchers. He batted .322 that season and slugged .529 (135 OPS+) with 39 hits for the Pirates, which registered 1.4 oWAR. Hendrix made 29 appearances as a pinch hitter. He got a pinch-hit single in his only at-bat in the 1918 World Series for the Cubs.

23. Don Larsen, 5.9 oWAR—Larsen was named MVP of the 1956 World Series mainly for pitching a perfect game in Game Five against the Dodgers, but he also batted .333 with one RBI in the series. He batted .284 with three homers in his rookie year, 1953, and he averaged .251 lifetime with 132 hits and 12 home runs as a pitcher. In 1958, Larsen batted .306 with four homers and a .935 OPS, producing 1.0 oWAR.

Larsen showed enough with the bat in the minors—.242 with 10 homers between 1947 and 1950—that the St. Louis Browns considered making him an outfielder. In 1953, Larsen set a major league batting record for pitchers with seven consecutive hits across three games for the Browns.[13]

24. Don Drysdale, 5.8 oWAR—Drysdale twice hit seven home runs in a season, in 1958 and 1965, to tie Don Newcombe for the National League single-season record for a pitcher. In the '65 season, he batted .300 with 19 RBI, 39 hits, and 2.1 oWAR. He hit a two-run homer on Opening Day that season on the way to a complete-game win.

The only other time he batted over .200 during his 14-year career was a .227 mark in 1958. During that 1958 season, Drysdale hit five of his seven home runs in the month of August including two in a game against the Milwaukee Braves on August 23. Drysdale batted just .186 with 218 hits for his career, but his 29 homers rank sixth all-time for pitchers.

25. Bullet Joe Bush, 5.8 oWAR—His best year batting was 1924, when he posted a .339/.374/.484 mark (120 OPS+) for the Yankees with 42 hits and 1.4 oWAR. Babe Ruth at .378 was the only regular to have a higher average on the team that season. Bush had other strong years at the plate, batting .325 with 39 hits in 1921, .326 with 31 hits in 1922, and .274 with a career-high 21 RBI in 1923. Bush collected three hits including a double and batted .429 in the 1923 World Series for the champion Yankees. His 12 doubles in 1925 are tied for third best by a pitcher in the modern era. Overall, he batted .253 with 313 hits and seven home runs and went 17-for-61 (.279) as a pinch hitter.

Chapter Notes

Introduction

1. Jeff Fletcher, *SHO-TIME: The Inside Story of Shohei Ohtani and the Greatest Baseball Season Ever Played* (New York: Diversion Books, 2022), 145–146.
2. Bill James, *The New Bill James Historical Baseball Abstract* (New York: Free Press, 2003), 32.
3. Anthony Castrovince, "Negro Leagues had their own two-way stars," www.mlb.com/news/negro-leagues-two-way-stars, February 5, 2022.

Chapter 2

1. Bryan Di Salvatore, *A Clever Base-Ballist: The Life and Times of John Montgomery Ward* (New York: Pantheon Books, 1999), 3.
2. Bill Lamb, "John Montgomery Ward," Society for American Baseball Research (SABR) Biography Profile, https://sabr.org/bioproj/person/john-montgomery-ward/.
3. Di Salvatore, *A Clever Base-Ballist*, 3.
4. David Stevens, *Baseball's Radical for All Seasons: A Biography of John Montgomery Ward* (Lanham, MD: Scarecrow Press, 1998), 5.
5. Di Salvatore, *A Clever Base-Ballist*, 102.
6. Lamb, Ward SABR Biography.
7. Di Salvatore, *A Clever Base-Ballist*, 118.
8. L. Robert Davids, ed., and Mike Cook, *Great Hitting Pitchers* (Phoenix: Society for American Baseball Research, 2012), 83.
9. "Troublesome for the opponents," *New York Clipper*, February 12, 1880.
10. *Providence Journal*, August 18, 1882.
11. Lamb, Ward SABR Biography.
12. Di Salvatore, *A Clever Base-Ballist*, 140–141.
13. *Sporting Life*, April 30, 1884.
14. Fred Stein, *And the Skipper Bats Cleanup: A History of the Baseball Player-Manager, with 42 Biographies of Men Who Filled the Dual Role* (Jefferson, NC: McFarland, 2002) 36.
15. Lamb, Ward SABR Biography.
16. Stevens, *Baseball's Radical for All Seasons*, 29.
17. Gary Ashwill, "Switch Pitchers in the Negro Leagues," https://agatetype.typepad.com/agate_type/2015/06/switch-pitchers-in-the-negro-leagues.html, June 8, 2015.
18. David Nemec, *Major League Baseball Profiles, 1871–1900, Volume 2* (Lincoln: University of Nebraska Press, 2011), 71.
19. *Sporting Life*, June 3, 1885.
20. Di Salvatore, *A Clever Base-Ballist*, 190.
21. John M. Ward, "Is the Base-Ball Player a Chattel?" *Lippincott's*, August 1887, 310–319.
22. Joe Posnanski, "Walk, Don't Run: The Surprising History of the Free Pass in Baseball," *Esquire*, August 3, 2023.
23. John Thorn, "The Dauvray Cup," https://ourgame.mlbblogs.com/the-dauvray-cup-d2ce9bb8fba4, April 2, 2018.
24. John Montgomery Ward, *Base-Ball: How to Become a Player* (Philadelphia: The Athletic Publishing Company, 1888), 46.
25. Ward, *Base-Ball*, 126.
26. John Thorn, "A Pictorial Chronology of Baseball in the 19th Century, Part 15: 1888–1889," https://ourgame.mlblogs.com/a-pictorial-chronology-of-baseball-

in-the-19th-century-part-15-1888-1889-ecab278682b9, August 13, 2019.
27. Mike Attiyeh, "Who Was Baseball's Most Interesting Character? Monte Ward," BaseballLibrary.com, posted July 19, 2001.
28. Di Salvatore, *A Clever Base-Ballist*, 275–277.
29. Charles Alexander, *Turbulent Seasons: Baseball in 1890–91* (Dallas: Southern Methodist University Press, 2011).
30. *New York Clipper*, November 3, 1894.
31. Benjamin Hoffman, "First He Was Perfect, and Then Things Got Interesting," *The New York Times*, June 30, 2023.
32. Natalie A. Naylor, "Long Island's Gentleman Athlete: John Montgomery Ward," *The Nassau County Historical Society Journal*, 2001, 21.
33. Bill James, *The New Bill James Historical Baseball Abstract* (New York: Free Press, 2003), 135.

Chapter 3

1. Jules Tygiel, *Past Time: Baseball as History* (New York: Oxford University Press, 2001).
2. John Snell, "The Invention of the Baseball Glove: The Case for the Forgotten 1901 Web-Pocketed Glove," *Baseball Research Journal*, Spring 2023.
3. Frank Vaccaro, "Origin of the Modern Pitching Win," *Baseball Research Journal*, Spring 2013.
4. *The Sporting News*, April 23, 1892.
5. Brian Angelhardt, "George Bradley," Society for American Baseball Research (SABR) Biography Profile, https://sabr.org/bioproj/person/george-bradley/.
6. Neil W. McDonald, *The League That Lasted: 1876 and the Founding of the National League of Professional Base Ball Clubs* (Jefferson, NC: McFarland, 2004), 149.
7. *The Sporting News*, as cited in Baseball-Reference BR Bullpen.
8. "One Good Fellow: General Tribute to the Memory of 'Charley' Buffinton, Old Ball Player," reprinted in Philip T. Silvia, Jr., ed., *Victorian Vistas: Fall River, 1901–1911* (Fall River, MA: R.E. Smith Print Co., 1992), 527.
9. Joseph M. Overfield, "Charles G. Buffinton," *Nineteenth Century Stars* (Phoenix: Society for American Baseball Research, 2012), 41.

10. "Buffinton Released," *Baltimore Sun*, July 1, 1892.
11. "One Good Fellow: General Tribute to Memory of 'Charley' Buffinton, Old Ball Player," *Fall River Herald*, September 24, 1907.
12. Gary Belleville, "Cleveland's Pete Dowling tosses the American League's first no-hitter—or does he?" SABR Games Project, https://sabr.org/gamesproj/game/june-30-1901-cleveland-pete-dowling-tosses-the-american-leagues-first-no-hitter-or-does-he/.
13. James Elfers, "Nixey Callahan," SABR Biography Profile, https://sabr.org/bioproj/person/nixey-callahan/.
14. Elfers, "Nixey Callahan" SABR Bio.
15. James E. Elfers, "Jimmy Callahan," *Deadball Stars of the American League* (Dulles, VA: Potomac Books, 2006), 472.
16. "SABR 47: Bob Caruthers selected as Overlooked 19th Century Baseball Legend for 2017," Society for American Baseball Research, https://sabr.org/latest/sabr-47-bob-caruthers-selected-overlooked-19th-century-baseball-legend-2017/.
17. Charles F. Faber, "Bob Caruthers," SABR Biography Profile, https://sabr.org/bioproj/person/bob-caruthers/.
18. Bob Bailey, "Guy Hecker: Hitting Pitcher," *Inventing Baseball: The 100 Greatest Games of the Nineteenth Century* (Phoenix: Society for American Baseball Research, 2013), 180–181.
19. Charles F. Faber, Caruthers SABR Biography.
20. Bill Lamb, "Dave Foutz," SABR Biography Profile, https://sabr.org/bioproj/person/dave-foutz/.
21. Lamb, Foutz SABR Biography.
22. Bill James, *The New Bill James Historical Baseball Abstract* (New York: Free Press, 2003), 135.
23. "Death of 'Dave' Foutz," *The New York Times*, March 7, 1897.
24. *Sporting Life*, March 13, 1897.
25. James, *Historical Baseball Abstract*, 524–525.
26. David Adler, "These MLB careers spanned 4 decades," mlb.com, January 7, 2022.
27. Garrett J. Kelleher, "More Than a Kid: The Story of Kid Gleason," *Baseball Research Journal*, No. 17, 1988.
28. Kelleher, "More Than a Kid," *Baseball Research Journal*.

29. Bob Bailey, "September 19, 1882: Guy Hecker throws Louisville's second no-hitter of season," SABR Games Project, https://sabr.org/gamesproj/game/september-19-1882-guy-hecker-throws-louisvilles-second-no-hitter-of-season/.
30. Bob Bailey, "Guy Hecker: Hitting Pitcher," *Inventing Baseball*, 180–181.
31. L. Robert Davids, ed., and Mike Cook, *Great Hitting Pitchers* (Phoenix: Society for American Baseball Research, 2012), 10–11.
32. Darlene Langley, "The Ladies Day Riot That Didn't Happen," District on Deck, January 9, 2015.
33. "Winnie Mercer a Suicide," *The New York Times*, January 14, 1903.
34. David Nemec, *Major League Baseball Profiles, 1871-1900, Volume 2* (Lincoln: University of Nebraska Press, 2011), 404.
35. *Baltimore Sun*, July 19, 1882.
36. *Boston Herald*, April 8, 1884.
37. Jerry Grillo, "Mullane Goes Both Ways," *Inventing Baseball*, 138–140.
38. James, *Historical Baseball Abstract*, 903–904.
39. "Old Providence Manager Tells Inside History of Old Hoss Radbourn Winning 26 out of 27 Games," *New Castle Herald*, July 7, 1908.
40. Alex Bonilla, "Old Hoss Radbourn: 59 or 60 Wins?" https://www.sports-reference.com/blog/2019/04/old-hoss-radbourn-59-or-60-wins/, April 10, 2019.
41. Nemec, *Major League Baseball Profiles*, 58–59.
42. Bill James and Rob Neyer, *The Neyer/James Guide to Pitchers: An Historical Compendium of Pitching, Pitchers, and Pitches* (New York: Simon & Schuster, 2004), 349–350.
43. Edward Achorn, "Radbourn the Slugger," *Inventing Baseball: The 100 Greatest Games of the Nineteenth Century*, 141–143.
44. *Sporting Life*, June 14, 1890.
45. *Sporting Life*, July 21, 1894.
46. Bill Nowlin, "August 6, 1892: Boston's Jack Stivetts no-hits the Bridegrooms," SABR Games Project, https://sabr.org/gamesproj/game/august-6-1892-boston-jack-stivetts-no-hits-the-bridegrooms/.
47. *Sporting Life*, October 22, 1892.

48. L. Robert Davids, ed., and Mike Cook, *Great Hitting Pitchers* (Phoenix: Society for American Baseball Research, 2012), 57.
49. "Two Players in Collision," *New York Tribune*, September 11, 1887.
50. Larry DeFillipo, "Adonis Terry," SABR Biography Profile, https://sabr.org/bioproj/person/adonis-terry/.
51. *Sporting Life*, November 1, 1890.
52. DeFillipo, Terry SABR Biography.
53. James, *Historical Baseball Abstract*, 135.
54. "But Few Old-Timers Left," *Fall River Globe*, June 5, 1891.
55. *Sporting Life*, December 4, 1915.
56. Mark Pestana, "Grasshopper Snatches the Pennant," *Inventing Baseball*, 152–154.
57. Bill Lamb, "Jim Whitney," SABR Biography Profile, https://sabr.org/bioproj/person/bill-lamb/.
58. Davids and Cook, *Great Hitting Pitchers*, 12.

Chapter 4

1. Bill James, *The New Bill James Historical Baseball Abstract* (New York: Free Press, 2003), 204.
2. David Jones, ed., *Deadball Stars of the American League* (Dulles, VA: Potomac Books, 2006).
3. Steve Steinberg, "Ray Caldwell," SABR Biography Profile, https://sabr.org/bioproj/person/ray-caldwell/.
4. Fred Lieb, *The Sun* (New York), December 19, 1918.
5. Steve Steinberg, "Ray Caldwell," *Deadball Stars of the American League*, 721.
6. Ryan Hockensmith, "The incredible story of Ray Caldwell, the MLB pitcher who survived a lightning strike to finish a game," ESPN.com, August 24, 2021.
7. Steinberg, "Caldwell," *Deadball Stars of American League*, 721.
8. Hockensmith, "The incredible story of Ray Caldwell," ESPN.com.
9. Hockensmith, "The incredible story of Ray Caldwell," ESPN.com.
10. R.J. Lesch, "J.O. 'Doc' Crandall," *Deadball Stars of the National League* (Dulles, VA: Brassey's, 2004), 67.
11. R.J. Lesch, "Doc Crandall," SABR

Biography Profile, https://sabr.org/bioproj/person/doc-crandall/.

12. Lesch, "Crandall," *Deadball Stars of National League*, 68.

13. Eric Sallee and David Jones, "Harry Howell," *Deadball Stars of the American League*, 780.

14. Glen Sparks, "Harry Howell's Best Pitch was Wetter than a Rainstorm," dazzyvancechronicles.wordpress.com, November 14, 2014.

15. Sallee and Jones, "Howell," *Deadball Stars of American League*, 780.

16. Sallee and Jones, "Howell," 781.

17. Eric Gouldsberry, "1910: A Carload of Trouble," thisgreatgame.com.

18. Rick Huhn, *The Chalmers Race: Ty Cobb, Napoleon Lajoie, and the Controversial 1910 Batting Title That Became a National Obsession* (Lincoln: University of Nebraska Press, 2014).

19. Andrew Simon, "MLB rookies to throw no-hitters," mlb.com, May 9, 2023.

20. Chris Hauser, "Albert Lewis Orth," *Deadball Stars of the American League*, 710.

21. Hauser, "Al Orth," *Deadball Stars*, 711.

22. Marty Appel, *Pinstripe Empire: The New York Yankees from Before the Babe to After the Boss* (New York: Bloomsbury, 2012).

23. Hauser, "Orth," *Deadball Stars of American League*, 711.

24. Richard Smiley, "Reb Russell," *Deadball Stars of the American League*, 514.

25. *Washington Post*, July 8, 1913.

26. Richard Smiley, "Reb Russell," SABR Biography Profile, https://sabr.org/bioproj/person/reb-russell/.

27. Smiley, "Russell," *Deadball Stars of American League*, 516.

28. Nathaniel Staley, "Jess Tannehill," *Deadball Stars of the American League*, 430.

29. Appel, *Pinstripe Empire*, 25.

30. L. Robert Davids, ed., and Mike Cook, *Great Hitting Pitchers* (Phoenix: Society for American Baseball Research, 2012), 17.

31. John Bennett, "Guy Harris 'Doc' White," *Deadball Stars of the American League*, 488.

32. John Bennett, "Doc White," SABR Biography Profile, https://sabr.org/bioproj/person/doc-white/.

33. Bennett, "'Doc' White," *Deadball Stars of American League*, 489.

34. Bennett, Doc White SABR Biography.

35. Bill Nowlin, Len Levin, Dan Descrochers, and Maurice Bouchard, eds., *Opening Fenway Park with Style: The 1912 Champion Red Sox* (Phoenix: Society for American Baseball Research, 2012), 175.

36. Paul Dickson, *Baseball's Greatest Quotations* (New York: HarperCollins, 2008), 274.

37. James T. Farrell, *My Baseball Diary* (Carbondale: Southern Illinois University Press, 1998).

38. Dickson, *Baseball's Greatest Quotations*, 604.

39. Lawrence S. Ritter, "Joe Wood," *The Glory of Their Times* (New York: Harper Perennial Modern Classics, 2010), 166–167.

40. Michael Foster, "Joe Wood," *Deadball Stars of the American League*, 443.

41. Ritter, *Glory of Their Times*, 169.

42. Michael Foster, "Smoky Joe Wood," SABR Biography Profile, https://sabr.org/bioproj/person/Smoky-Joe-Wood/.

43. C. Paul Rogers III, "John Coombs," *Deadball Stars of the American League*, 614.

44. Rogers, "John Coombs," *Deadball Stars*, 615.

45. *Sporting Life*, January 12, 1907.

46. Dan Ginsburg, "John Taylor," *Deadball Stars of the National League*, 93.

47. Gregory H. Wolf, "June 11, 1904: Chicago's Bob Wicker begins game with 9⅓ hitless innings—or does he?" Society for American Baseball Research Games Project, https://sabr.org/gamesproj/game/june-11-1904-chicagos-bob-wicker-begins-game-with-9⅓-hitless-innings-or-does-he/.

Chapter 5

1. Lawrence S. Ritter, "Rube Bressler," *The Glory of Their Times* (New York: Harper Perennial Modern Classics, 2010), 205–206.

2. Brother Gilbert, C.F.X., *Young Babe Ruth*, ed. Harry Rothberger (Jefferson, NC: McFarland, 1999), 10, 11, 14.

3. Bill Gutman, *Giants of Baseball* (New York: Tempo Books, 1975).

4. Gilbert, *Young Babe*, 12.

5. George Herman Ruth, *Babe Ruth's Own Book of Baseball* (Lincoln: University of Nebraska Press, Bison Books, 1992), 5–6.
6. Gilbert, *Young Babe*, 49.
7. Gilbert, *Young Babe*, 63.
8. Jesse Linthicum, "Homer by Ruth Feature of Game," *Baltimore Sun*, March 8, 1914.
9. Gilbert, *Young Babe*, 115.
10. Babe Ruth, "Why a Pitcher Should Hit," World Series Program, 1916.
11. Gilbert, *Young Babe*, 127.
12. "Ruth Combines Confidence and Natural Power," *Los Angeles Examiner*, July 28, 1918.
13. Bill Jenkinson, "Baseball's First Five-Hundred Foot Home Run," https://firstfivehundredfoothomerun.jimdofree.com/history-of-the-first-500-home-run/.
14. Paul Shannon, "Ruth Smashes Up Hopes of Dodgers," *Boston Post*, March 25, 1918.
15. Edward Martin, "Babe's Crash Good for Four Sox Runs," *Boston Globe*, March 25, 1918.
16. Jenkinson, "Baseball's First Five-Hundred Foot Home Run."
17. Robert W. Creamer, *Babe: The Legend Comes to Life* (New York: Simon & Schuster, 1974), 152.
18. "Baseball Gossip," *Wichita Daily Eagle*, May 7, 1918.
19. F.C. Lane, "The Season's Sensation," *Baseball Magazine*, October 1918, 472.
20. Allan Wood, "Babe Ruth's Lost 715th Home Run," sabr.org/journal/article/babe-ruths-lost-715th-home-run/.
21. Creamer, *Babe: The Legend*, 187.
22. Lawrence S. Ritter, "Harry Hooper," *The Glory of Their Times* (New York: HarperCollins, 2010), 145.
23. Jane Leavy, *The Big Fella* (New York: HarperCollins, 2018), 490.
24. "Babe Ruth Accepts Terms of Yankees," *New York Times*, January 7, 1920, 22.
25. Gilbert, *Young Babe*, 32.
26. Gilbert, *Young Babe*, 153.
27. Mike Huber, "July 18, 1921: Babe Ruth's 560-foot blast against Tigers sets career home run record," sabr.org/gamesproj/game/July-18–1921-babe-ruths-560-foot-blast-against-tigers-sets-career-home-run-record/.
28. Ritter, "Sam Jones, *The Glory of Their Times*, 246.
29. Hugh Fullerton, "Why Babe Ruth is Greatest Home-Run Hitter," *Popular Science Monthly*, October 1921, 19.
30. Robert Weintraub, *The House That Ruth Built* (New York: Little, Brown, 2011), 30.
31. Ken Schlager, "Babe Ruth Called His Shot, From the Mound," *New York Times*, August 16, 2008.
32. Joe Lawler, "Today's Battery: Ruth and Glenn," *SABR Baseball Research Journal*, 1983, 8–11.
33. "'Pitcher Babe' Would Rather Stay in Field," *Brooklyn Daily Eagle*, October 2, 1933.
34. Leigh Montville, *Big Bam* (New York: Broadway, 2006), 41.
35. Marty Appel, *Pinstripe Empire* (New York: Bloomsbury, 2012), 270.
36. Ritter, "Harry Hooper," *The Glory of Their Times*, 145.
37. Murray Schumach, "Babe Ruth, Baseball's Great Star and Idol of Children, Had a Career Both Dramatic and Bizarre," *New York Times*, August 17, 1948.
38. William Curran, *Big Sticks: The Batting Revolution of the Twenties* (New York: William Morrow, 1990).
39. Ed Gruver, "Even Against Hall of Fame Hurlers, Babe Ruth Was King of Swing," sabr.org/journal/article/even-against-hall-of-fame-hurlers-babe-ruth-was-king-of-swing/.
40. Allan Wood, "Cool Babe Ruth Facts," *The Babe* (Phoenix: Society for American Baseball Research, 2019), 30.

Chapter 6

1. Robert Peterson, *Only the Ball Was White* (New York: Gramercy Books, 1970), 214.
2. Phil S. Dixon, *Wilber "Bullet" Rogan and the Kansas City Monarchs* (Jefferson, NC: McFarland, 2010), 180.
3. Larry Lester, *Baseball's First Colored World Series: The 1924 Meeting of the Hilldale Giants and Kansas City Monarchs* (Jefferson, NC: McFarland), 90.
4. John B. Holway, *Blackball Stars* (New York: Carroll & Graf, 1988), 184.
5. "Twenty-fifth hands up mark for hitting," *Hawaiian Gazette*, November 9, 1915, 8.
6. "Rogan strikes out eighteen men and twenty-fifth wins from All-Stars," *Chicago Defender*, November 25, 1916.

7. "Bullet Rogan," *Chicago Whip*, July 1, 1922, 7.
8. Dixon, *Wilber "Bullet" Rogan*, 31–33.
9. Dixon, *Bullet Rogan*, 33–34.
10. Dixon, *Bullet Rogan*, 34.
11. *Kansas City Sun*, October 15, 1921.
12. Dixon, *Bullet Rogan*, 41.
13. *The Chicago Whip*, July 1, 1922.
14. Charles A. Starks, "Negro Baseball breaking down the race prejudice," *St. Louis Argus*, November 3, 1922.
15. "K.C. team plays Denver Bears in Morgan Thurs.," *Fort Morgan Evening Times*, September 23, 1922.
16. "Monarchs blank Detroit Stars 6–0," *Detroit Free Press*, May 21, 1923.
17. Holway, *Blackball Stars*, 176.
18. Dixon, *Bullet Rogan*, 128.
19. Jorge Figueredo, *Cuban Baseball: A Statistical History, 1878–1961* (Jefferson, NC: McFarland, 2003), 158–159.
20. *Joplin Globe*, April 13, 1928.
21. "Jamestown baseball season one of greatest in history; Hancock leads bat average," *Jamestown Sun*, August 23, 1932, 6.
22. Dixon, *Bullet Rogan*, 109, 111.
23. "Cleveland Gts. Champions of Coast League," *Kansas City Call*, March 8, 1929, 13.
24. William F. McNeil, *The California Winter League: America's First Integrated Professional Baseball League* (Jefferson, NC: McFarland, 2002), 260, 269.
25. Dixon, *Bullet Rogan*, 137, 138.
26. Dixon, *Bullet Rogan*, 117, 121.
27. "Defeat Denver A.C., 4 to 3," *Denver Post*, August 5, 1934.
28. Holway, *Blackball Stars*, 167, 169.
29. Dixon, *Bullet Rogan*, 185.
30. John Holway, "Hats off to Bill James' Negro Leagues 100-Best List," https://baseballguru.com/jholway/analysisjholway05.html.
31. Bill James, *The New Bill James Historical Baseball Abstract* (New York: Free Press, 2003), 176, 178.
32. Dixon, *Bullet Rogan*, 139.
33. *Baltimore Afro-American*, 1932, as cited in Dixon, *Bullet Rogan*, 181.

Chapter 7

1. Peter C. Bjarkman, *A History of Cuban Baseball 1864–2006* (Jefferson, NC: McFarland, 2007), 28.
2. James A. Riley, *The Biographical Encyclopedia of the Negro Baseball Leagues* (New York: Carroll & Graf, 1994), 234.
3. Bjarkman, *Cuban Baseball*, 29.
4. Bjarkman, *Cuban Baseball*, 29.
5. James A. Riley, *All-Time All-Stars of Black Baseball* (Cocoa, FL: TK Publishers, 1983), viii.
6. John B. Holway, *Blackball Stars* (New York: Carroll & Graf, 1992), 386.
7. Holway, *Blackball Stars*, 237.
8. Bill James, *The New Bill James Historical Baseball Abstract* (New York: Free Press, 2003), 177.
9. Holway, *Blackball Stars*, 236.
10. James, *Historical Baseball Abstract*, 191.
11. Holway, *Blackball Stars*, 236.
12. Bob Fowler, "Twins' Cubbage Earns Raves with Bat, Glove," *The Sporting News*, August 27, 1977, 14.
13. Bjarkman, *Cuban Baseball*, 91.
14. Peter C. Bjarkman, "Martín Dihigo," SABR Biography Profile, https://sabr.org/bioproj/person/martin-dihigo/.
15. Bill Ladson, "2-way player Dihigo a HOFer in 5 countries," mlb.com/news/martin-dihigo-career-profile, October 15, 2020.
16. Bjarkman, Dihigo SABR Bio.
17. Gilberto Dihigo, *My Father Martin Dihigo "The Immortal"* (independently published, 2021).
18. Jack Lang, "Dihigo and Lloyd Voted Into Shrine," *The Sporting News*, February 19, 1977, 42.
19. Robert Peterson, *Only the Ball Was White* (New York: Gramercy Books, 1970), 243.
20. Buck Leonard and John Holway, "Grays Brought Night Baseball to Washington," *The Sporting News*, March 11, 1972, 27.

Chapter 8

1. Donald Honig, *Baseball When the Grass Was Real: Baseball from the Twenties to the Forties Told by the Men Who Played It* (Lincoln: University of Nebraska Press, 1993).
2. Steven R. Greenes, *Negro Leaguers and the Hall of Fame* (Jefferson, NC: McFarland, 2020), 48–50.
3. Jorge Figueredo, *Cuban Baseball: A Statistical History, 1878–1961* (Jefferson, NC: McFarland, 2003), 502.

4. James A. Riley, *The Biographical Encyclopedia of the Negro Baseball Leagues* (New York: Carroll & Graf, 1994), 64.
5. Robert Peterson, *Only the Ball Was White* (New York: Gramercy Books, 1970), 239.
6. Bill James, *The New Bill James Historical Baseball Abstract* (New York: Free Press, 2003), 175–177.
7. William Rogers, "Cool Papa," Mississippi History Now, mshistorynow.mdah.ms.gov/issue/cool-papa-bell, August 2008.
8. Rogers, "Cool Papa."
9. Chris Jensen, *Baseball State by State* (Jefferson, NC: McFarland, 2012), 164–165.
10. Riley, *Biographical Encyclopedia*, 72.
11. *Pittsburgh Journal*, September 14, 1988, as cited by Leslie Heaphy, *The Negro Leagues 1869–1960* (Jefferson, NC: McFarland, 2003), 198.
12. Greenes, *Negro Leaguers and the Hall of Fame*, 153.
13. Dr. Layton Revel and Luis Munoz, "Forgotten Heroes: William Bell," Center for Negro League Baseball Research, 2014.
14. Peter Williams, *When the Giants Were the Giants: Bill Terry and the Golden Age of New York Baseball* (Chapel Hill: Algonquin Books of Chapel Hill, 1994), 225.
15. Dr. Layton Revel and Luis Munoz, "Forgotten Heroes: Ramon 'El Professor' Bragana," Center for Negro League Baseball Research, 2011.
16. Pedro Treto Cisneros, *The Mexican League: Comprehensive Player Statistics* (Jefferson, NC: McFarland, 2022).
17. Revel and Munoz, "Forgotten Heroes: Ramon 'El Professor' Bragana."
18. *New York Amsterdam News*, January 28, 1925, as cited by Leslie Heaphy, *The Negro Leagues*, 66.
19. Greenes, *Negro Leaguers and the Hall of Fame*, 163.
20. Tom Van Hyning, "Ray Brown: Underrated Cooperstown Hall of Famer and Caribbean Legend," Beisbol101.com, September 19, 2020.
21. Chris Rainey, "Raymond Brown," SABR Biography Profile, https://sabr.org/bioproj/person/Raymond-Brown/.
22. Riley, *Biographical Encyclopedia*, 131.
23. Riley, *Biographical Encyclopedia*, 131.
24. Harry Daniels, "The Base Ball Spirit in the East," *Indianapolis Freeman*, December 25, 1909, 7.
25. James A. Riley, *Of Monarchs and Black Barons* (Jefferson, NC: McFarland, 2012), 168.
26. John B. Holway, *Black Giants* (Bloomington, IN: Xlibris, 2009), 164.
27. James, *Historical Baseball Abstract*, 176.
28. John Holway, *The Complete Book of Baseball's Negro Leagues: The Other Half of Baseball History* (Roxbury, CT: Hastings House, 2001).
29. Holway, *Complete Book of Negro Leagues*.
30. Jensen, *Baseball State by State*, 89.
31. Sarah Langs, "The Negro Leagues: Oscar Charleston," www.mlb.com/history/negro-leagues/players/oscar-charleston.
32. "Detroit Stars Fail to Twinkle Once," *Philadelphia Inquirer*, September 6, 1921.
33. Riley, *Biographical Encyclopedia*, 216.
34. The John Donaldson Network, https://johndonaldson.bravehost.com.
35. *Humboldt Republican*, September 15, 1911, 1.
36. Riley, *Biographical Encyclopedia*, 242.
37. *Atlanta Daily World*, March 31, 1935.
38. Frank G. Menke, "Color Line Loses 3 Great Pitchers to Major Leagues," *Colorado Springs Gazette Telegraph*, June 9, 1915.
39. Todd Peterson, ed., *The Negro Leagues Were Major Leagues* (Jefferson, NC: McFarland, 2020), 167.
40. *Lake Wilson* [Minnesota] *Pilot*, June 4, 1942.
41. Harry Daniels, "The Base Ball Spirit in the East," *Indianapolis Freeman*, December 25, 1909, 7.
42. John B. Holway, *Blackball Stars* (New York: Carroll & Graf, 1992), 224.
43. Brent Kelley, *Voices from the Negro Leagues: Conversations with 52 Baseball Standouts of the Period, 1924–1960* (Jefferson, NC: McFarland, 2005).
44. Peterson, *Negro Leagues Were Major Leagues*, 149.
45. Sol White, *History of Colored Base Ball* (Lincoln: University of Nebraska Press, 1995), 100.
46. Robert Peterson, *Only the Ball Was White* (New York: Gramercy Books, 1970), 115.
47. Riley, *Biographical Encyclopedia*, 303.

48. Cisneros, *The Mexican League*.
49. Figueredo, *Cuban Baseball*.
50. Larry Tye, *Satchel: The Life and Times of an American Legend* (New York: Random House, 2009).
51. "Gisentauer [sic] in Iron Man Role," *Harrisburg Evening News*, June 8, 1925.
52. Stephen V. Rice, "Willie Gisentaner," SABR Biography Profile, https://sabr.org/bioproj/person/williegisentaner/.
53. William F. McNeil, *The California Winter League: America's First Integrated Professional Baseball League* (Jefferson, NC: McFarland, 2002).
54. McNeil, *California Winter League*, 245, 246.
55. "Bill Lindsay's Record," *Indianapolis Freeman*, September 12, 1914.
56. Leslie A. Heaphy, *The Negro Leagues 1869-1960* (Jefferson, NC: McFarland, 2003), 175, 176.
57. "Cuban X Giants Win a Good Game," *Poughkeepsie Eagle*, July 29, 1902.
58. Greenes, *Negro Leaguers and the Hall of Fame*, 164.
59. Phil Williams, "Dan McClellan," SABR Biography Profile, https://sabr.org/bioproj/person/dan-mcclellan/.
60. Phil Dixon, *Phil Dixon's American Baseball Chronicles, Great Teams: The 1905 Philadelphia Giants, Volume Three* (Charleston, SC: BookSurge, 2006), 22-26, 260-261, 268-276.
61. Dixon, *American Baseball Chronicles*, 261.
62. Harry Daniels, "The Base Ball Spirit in the East," *Indianapolis Freeman*, December 25, 1909, 7.
63. James, *Historical Baseball Abstract*, 189.
64. Dr. Layton Revel and Luis Munoz, "Forgotten Heroes: Hurley McNair," Center for Negro League Baseball Research, 2016.
65. Level and Munoz, "Forgotten Heroes: Hurley McNair."
66. Gary Ashwill, "José Méndez vs. Major League Teams, 1908-1913," https://agattype.typepad.com/agate_type/2006/05/jos_mndez_vs_ma.html, May 2, 2006.
67. Peter C. Bjarkman, *A History of Cuban Baseball 1864-2006* (Jefferson, NC: McFarland, 2007), 424.
68. Lawrence D. Hogan, *Shades of Glory: The Negro Leagues and the Story of African-American Baseball* (Washington, D.C.: National Geographic, 2006), 169.
69. Figueredo, *Cuban Baseball*.
70. Bjarkman, *A History of Cuban Baseball*, 110.
71. Anthony Castrovince, "Aaron broke barriers during rise to Majors," mlb.com, February 5, 2023.
72. Riley, *Biographical Encyclopedia*, 620.
73. Riley, *Biographical Encyclopedia*, 640.
74. Cisneros, *The Mexican League*.
75. Joseph Gerard, "Lazaro Salazar," SABR Biography Profile, https://sabr.org/bioproj/person/Lazaro-Salazar/.
76. Stew Thornley, *Baseball in Minnesota: The Definitive History* (St. Paul: Minnesota Historical Society, 2006), 136.
77. Hogan, *Shades of Glory*, 309.
78. John Holway, *Voices from the Great Black Baseball Leagues* (New York: Da Capo Press, 1992) 286-287.
79. Kyle P. McNary, *Ted "Double Duty" Radcliffe: 36 Years of Pitching & Catching in Baseball's Negro Leagues* (St. Louis Park, MN: McNary Publishing, 1994), 106.
80. Thomas Kern, "Hilton Smith," SABR Biography Profile, https://sabr.org/bioproj/person/Hilton-Smith/.
81. "Kansas City Monarchs, fielding prejudice," *Vibrations*, Sunday magazine of the *Columbia Missourian*, August 2, 1981, 3.
82. Phil S. Dixon, *Wilber "Bullet" Rogan and the Kansas City Monarchs* (Jefferson, NC: McFarland, 2010), 172, 173.
83. James, *Historical Baseball Abstract*, 182.
84. Riley, *Biographical Encyclopedia*, 761.
85. "Indianapolis A.B.C. to Meet Local Negro Club," *Kansas City Times*, May 27, 1921, 14.
86. James, *Historical Baseball Abstract*, 189.
87. Hogan, *Shades of Glory*, 147.
88. Peter J. Bjarkman, "Cristóbal Torriente," SABR Biography Profile, https://sabr.org/bioproj/person/Cristobal-Torriente/.
89. Bjarkman, *A History of Cuban Baseball*, 425.
90. Riley, *Biographical Encyclopedia*, 855.
91. Greenes, *Negro Leaguers and the Hall of Fame*, 241.

92. James, *Historical Baseball Abstract*, 176, 365.
93. Joe Posnanski, *The Baseball 100* (New York: Avid Reader Press, 2021), 253.
94. Posnanski, *Baseball 100*, 253.
95. Riley, *Biographical Encyclopedia*, 877.
96. James, *Historical Baseball Abstract*, 176.

Chapter 9

1. John B. Holway, *Josh and Satch* (New York: Carroll & Graf, 1992), 1.
2. Kyle P. McNary, *Ted "Double Duty" Radcliffe: 36 Years of Pitching & Catching in Baseball's Negro Leagues* (St. Louis Park, MN: McNary Publishing, 1994), 5.
3. Brent Kelley, *Voices from the Negro Leagues: Conversations with 52 Baseball Standouts* (Jefferson, NC: McFarland, 1998), 53.
4. Thomas Kern, "Ted 'Double Duty' Radcliffe," SABR Biography Profile, https://sabr.org/bioproj/person/ted-double-duty-radcliffe/.
5. Bill James, *The New Historical Baseball Abstract* (New York: Free Press, 2003), 180-181.
6. Larry Tye, *Satchel: The Life and Times of an American Legend* (New York: Random House, 2009), 12.
7. McNary, *Ted "Double Duty" Radcliffe*, 12.
8. Tye, *Satchel*, 248.
9. Fred Mitchell, "Ted 'Double Duty' Radcliffe, 103; Star Catcher in Negro League Also Pitched," *Los Angeles Times*, August 12, 2005.
10. Kern, Radcliffe SABR Biography Profile.
11. McNary, *Ted "Double Duty" Radcliffe*, 44.
12. McNary, *Radcliffe*, 50.
13. John B. Holway, *Blackball Stars* (New York: Carroll & Graf, 1992), 257.
14. Phil S. Dixon, *Phil Dixon's American Baseball Chronicles Great Teams: The 1931 Homestead Grays Volume I* (Bloomington, IN: Xlibris Corporation, 2009).
15. McNary, *Ted "Double Duty" Radcliffe*, 53.
16. McNary, *Radcliffe*, 55.
17. McNary, *Radcliffe*, 68.
18. Chester Washington, "Sez Ches, And Now—The Craws' Pitchers' Records," *Pittsburgh Courier*, January 28, 1933.
19. McNary, *Radcliffe*, 92.
20. McNary, *Radcliffe*, 93, 97.
21. Lloyd Lewis, "How Good is Negro Baseball? It's Faster, For One Thing," *Chicago Daily News*, August 26, 1938.
22. McNary, *Radcliffe*, 161.
23. McNary, *Radcliffe*, 183.
24. John B. Holway, *Voices from the Great Black Baseball Leagues* (Boston: Da Capo Press, 1992), 182.
25. Kern, Ted "Double Duty" Radclifee SABR Biography.
26. McNary, *Radcliffe*, 204, 208.
27. McNary, *Radcliffe*, 214.
28. McNary, *Radcliffe*, 215.
29. Holway, *Voices*, 185.
30. Michael Bamberger, "Man of a Century Double Duty Radcliffe Nemesis of Ty Cobb, Close Friend of Satchel Paige, A Negro Leagues Legend Remains the Life of the Party as He Celebrates His 100th Birthday," *Sports Illustrated*, July 15, 2002.
31. Dave Hoekstra, "Ted 'Double Duty' Radcliffe—1902–2005," davehoekstra.com.
32. McNary, *Radcliffe*, 245.
33. James A. Riley, *The Biographical Encyclopedia of the Negro Baseball Leagues* (New York: Carroll & Graf, 1994), 650.

Chapter 10

1. James A. Riley, *Dandy, Day and the Devil* (Cocoa, FL: TK Publishers, 1987), 58.
2. John B. Holway, *Blackball Stars* (New York: Carroll & Graf, 1992), 344.
3. Riley, *Dandy, Day and the Devil*, 68.
4. Bill James, *The New Bill James Historical Baseball Abstract* (New York: Free Press, 2003), 176.
5. Holway, *Blackball Stars*, 349.
6. Holway, *Blackball Stars*, 349.
7. Riley, *Dandy, Day and the Devil*, 66-67.
8. Riley, *Dandy, Day and the Devil*, 72.
9. Gary Cieradkowski, "Leon Day: The 1945 G.I. World Series," posted August 12, 2018, https://studiogaryc.com/2018/08/12/leon-day-gi-world-series/.
10. Holway, *Blackball Stars*, 350.
11. James A. Riley, *Of Monarchs and Black Barons: Essays on Baseball's Negro Leagues* (Jefferson, NC: McFarland, 2012), 154–155.

12. Thomas Kern, "Leon Day," Society for American Baseball Research (SABR) Biography Profile, https://sabr.org/bioproj/person/Leon-Day/.
13. John B. Holway, *Voices from the Great Black Baseball Leagues* (Boston: Da Capo Press, 1992).
14. "Baltimore's Day had Hall of Fame numbers," *Daily Mail*, September 25, 1992.
15. Brad Snyder, "'You made it, man': Day named to Hall of Fame," *Baltimore Sun*, March 8, 1995.

Chapter 11

1. "Clarence Mitchell, Former Spitball Pitcher, Dies at 72," *The Baltimore Sun*, November 7, 1963.
2. *The Sporting News*, January 22, 1966.
3. Charles F. Faber, "Clarence Mitchell," SABR Biography Profile, https://sabr.org/bioproj/person/clarence-mitchell/.
4. Faber, Mitchell SABR Bio.
5. William Curran, *Big Sticks: The Batting Revolution of the Twenties* (New York: William Morrow, 1990).
6. *Baseball Magazine*, February 1924.
7. "Jack Bentley Saw Dramatic Baseball Days," *Montgomery County Sentinel*, October 27, 1955.
8. *Sporting Life*, September 12, 1914.
9. *Atlanta Constitution*, July 25, 1917.
10. Lawrence S. Ritter, "Rube Bressler," *The Glory of Their Times* (New York: Harper Perennial Modern Classics, 2010), 203–204.
11. Rick Huhn, *The Sizzler: George Sisler, Baseball's Forgotten Great* (Columbia: University of Missouri Press), 30.
12. Huhn, *The Sizzler*, 39.
13. Bill Lamberty, "George Sisler," *Deadball Stars of the American League* (Dulles, VA: Potomac Books, 2006), 796.
14. Huhn, *The Sizzler*, 135.
15. "Baseball's 100 Greatest Players," baseballalmanac.com/legendary/lisn100.shtml.
16. Huhn, *The Sizzler*, 252.
17. Ritter, "Lefty O'Doul," *The Glory of Their Times*, 273.
18. Brian McKenna, "Lefty O'Doul," SABR Biography Profile, https://sabr.org/bioproj/person/brian-mckenna/.
19. Roscoe McGowen, "Mungo Nominates Randy Moore as Preferred Dodger Catcher," *New York Times*, April 7, 1937.
20. Ray Birch, "Johnny Cooney," SABR Biography Profile, https://sabr.org/bioproj/person/johnny-cooney/.
21. Birch, Cooney SABR Bio.
22. Eugene Murdock, *Baseball Players and Their Times* (Westport, CT: Meckler, 1991), 45.
23. Al Quimby, "Red Lucas," SABR Biography Profile, https://sabr.org/bioproj/person/Red-Lucas/.
24. Jackie Robinson, *I Never Had It Made* (New York: Fawcett, 1974), 74.
25. *Washington Post*, May 4, 1947.
26. Bill Nowlin, "Ben Chapman," SABR Biography Profile, https://sabr.org/bioproj/person/ben-chapman/.
27. Nowlin, Chapman SABR Bio.
28. Bill James, *The New Bill James Historical Baseball Abstract* (New York: Free Press, 2003), 204.
29. Sheldon Appleton, "Bucky Walters," SABR Biography Profile, https://sabr.org/bioproj/person/bucky-walters/.
30. Wayne Stewart, ed., *The Little Red Book of Baseball Wisdom* (New York: Skyhorse Publishing, 2012), 49; also Paul Dickson, *Baseball's Greatest Quotations* (New York: HarperCollins, 2008), 584.
31. Appleton, Walters SABR Bio.
32. Leonard Gettelson, "Pitchers Stealing Home," *Baseball Research Journal*, 1976.
33. Cy Peterman, "The Science of Pitching Also Aided by Thought," *Philadelphia Inquirer*, June 27, 1940.
34. Harold Parrott, "Both Sides," *Brooklyn Eagle*, August 16, 1942.
35. Edgar G. Brands, "Barrow, Southworth, Williams Ranked as Outstanding in '41," *The Sporting News*, January 1, 1942.
36. Associated Press, February 20, 1953.
37. Eric Vickrey, "Erv Dusak," SABR Biography Profile, https://sabr.org/bioproj/person/erv-dusak/.
38. Peter M. Gordon, "Clint Hartung," SABR Biography Profile, https://sabr.org/bioproj/person/clint-hartung/.
39. *New York Times*, December 12, 1967.
40. *New York Daily News*, July 23, 2010.
41. *Texas Monthly*, July 1983, 80–84.
42. Andrew Sharp, "Hal Jeffcoat," SABR Biography Profile, https://sabr.org/bioproj/person/hal-jeffcoat/.
43. Sharp, Jeffcoat SABR Bio.
44. Sharp, Jeffcoat SABR Bio.
45. Tom Swope, "Three-Year Mound

Rise Under Tebbetts Buoys Reds' Hopes," *The Sporting News*, December 5, 1956.
46. Swope, *Sporting News*.
47. "Cincinnati Joins Mexico in Hall's Legend," *Newsday*, October 12, 1970.
48. Andrew Sharp, "Willie Smith," SABR Biography Profile, https://sabr.org/bioproj/person/willie-smith-2/.
49. Bill Libby, "The Amazing Transformation of Wonderful Willie Smith," *Baseball Digest*, September 1964.
50. Bill Becker, "Willie Smith moves to the outfield; Angels move up," *The New York Times*, June 28, 1964.
51. Dick Peebles, *Houston Chronicle*, April 24, 1967.
52. Bill Jauss, "Cubs get versatile No. 1 draft pick; Sox stick with pitching," *Chicago Tribune*, June 4, 1993.
53. Doug Miller, "Before Ohtani, Kieschnick did it all for Brewers," mlb.com, December 16, 2017, mlb.com/news/brooks-kieschnick-played-both-ways-for-brewers/c-263664078.
54. Peter Gammons, "Kieschnick impresses Brewers," ESPN.com, February 21, 2003, espn.com/gammons/s/2003/0221/1512192.html.
55. Miller, "Before Ohtani."
56. Gammons, "Kieschnick impresses."
57. Brian Plaspholer, "August 9, 2007: Cardinals' Rick Ankiel homers in return to major leagues as outfielder," https://sabr.org/gamesproj/game/august-9-2007-cardinals-rick-ankiel-homers-in-return-to-major-leagues-as-outfielder/.
58. Buzz Bissinger, *Three Nights in August: Strategy, Heartbreak and Joy Inside the Mind of a Manager* (New York: Houghton Mifflin, 2006).
59. Gary Weilek, "Former MLB Hurler Remembers 5 Pitches That Detailed His Career," https://www.wbur.org/onlygame/2017/05/19/rick-ankiel-baseball.
60. George J. Mitchell, "Report to the Commissioner of Baseball of an Independent Investigation into the Illegal Use of Steroids and Other Performance Enhancing Substances by Players in Major League Baseball," December 13, 2007, 242–244.
61. Michael Lorenzen BR Bullpen biography, Baseball-Reference.
62. Rick Gosselin, "How Matt Bush's journey to big-league redemption began with a friend at a Golden Corral," *Dallas News*, May 13, 2016.
63. Bryce Miller, "Matt Bush out of prison, back on the mound," *The San Diego Union-Tribune*, March 4, 2016.
64. Bob Nightengale, "Matt Bush aims for sobriety while filling crucial role for Texas Rangers," *USA Today*, June 20, 2016.

Chapter 12

1. Nick Friedell, "Greg Maddux gives Angels' Shohei Ohtani legendary MLB praise," espn.com, April 13, 2023.
2. Joe Posnanski, *Why We Love Baseball: A History in 50 Moments* (New York: Dutton, 2023) 119.
3. Ken Rosenthal, "Shohei Ohtani keeps pushing MLB's boundaries. Whatever his future holds, let's enjoy his remarkable present," *The Athletic*, July 8, 2021.
4. Rosenthal, "Ohtani keeps pushing," *The Athletic*.
5. "Father of baseball star Ohtani coached son with life tips in 'very ordinary' upbringing," *The Mainichi*, December 11, 2017.
6. Jared Diamond, "How Shohei Ohtani Visualized His Baseball Success," *The Wall Street Journal*, September 11, 2018.
7. Tom Verducci, "The Icon Among Us," *Sports Illustrated*, April 2024, 35.
8. Andrew Zwelling, "The Next Babe Ruth: How Shohei Ohtani became MLB's most dominant two-way player in a century," www.sportsnet.ca/baseball/mlb/big-read-meet-shohei-ohtani-next-babe-ruth/.
9. Tim Keown, "The one baseball's been waiting for," *ESPN The Magazine*, April 23, 2018.
10. Scott Miller, "Shohei Ohtani: The 'Best Baseball Player in the World Isn't in MLB … Yet," Bleacher Report, March 6, 2017.
11. Miller, "Ohtani," Bleacher Report.
12. Bob Nightengale, "Hall of Famers in awe of Shohei Ohtani," *USA Today*, July 13, 2021.
13. Laura H. Peebles, "April 8, 2018: Shohei Ohtani's home pitching debut is almost perfect," SABR Games Project, https://sabr.org/gamesproj/game/april-8-2018-shohei-ohtanis-home-pitching-debut-is-almost-perfect/.
14. Bill Lamb, "Jim Shaw," SABR

Biography Profile, https://sabr.org/bio proj/person/jim-shaw/.
15. Nightengale, "Hall of Famers," *USA Today*.
16. J. Scott Shaffer, "June 13, 2019: Shohei Ohtani becomes first Japanese player to hit for the cycle," SABR Games Project, https://sabr.org/gamesproj/game/june-13-2019-shohei-ohtani-becomes-first-japanese-player-to-hit-for-the-cycle/.
17. Jeff Fletcher, "Shohei Ohtani Hits for the Cycle in Angels' Victory over Rays," *Orange County Register,* June 13, 2019.
18. *Shohei Ohtani: Beyond the Dream* documentary, 2023.
19. Jeff Fletcher, *SHO-TIME: The Inside Story of Shohei Ohtani and the Greatest Baseball Season Ever Played* (New York: Diversion Books, 2022), 136.
20. Fletcher, *SHO-TIME*, 137.
21. Fletcher, *SHO-TIME*, 145.
22. Rhett Bollinger, "Ohtani's longest career HR a sight to behold," mlb.com, June 9, 2021.
23. Daniel Guerrero, "Ohtani Pitches, Hits and Runs Through Rox," www.mlb.com/news/shohei-ohtani-does-it-all-against-rockies?utm_source=ground.news&utm_medium=referral, July 27, 2021.
24. Ryan Fagan, "'Beyond incredible': Shohei Ohtani constantly left MLB peers in awe during historic 2021 season," *The Sporting News*, October 28, 2021.
25. Bill James, *The Bill James Handbook 2022* (Chicago: ACTA Sports, 2022), 12–14.
26. Fletcher, *SHO-TIME*, 198.
27. Ben Lindbergh, "Ten Stats That Sum Up Shohei Ohtani's Historic 2021 Season," *The Ringer*, October 5, 2021.
28. Yukitsugu Sasada, "How did his teammates describe Shohei Ohtani's 'extraordinary talent'?" *Number*, April 19, 2021.
29. Steve Gardner, "A classic final boss battle: Breaking down Shohei Ohtani's strikeout of Mike Trout to conclude WBC," *USA Today*, March 22, 2023.
30. Stephen Cannella, "Ohtani vs. Trout at the 2023 WBC Was an Instant Classic Moment for Baseball," *Sports Illustrated*, December 28, 2023.
31. Tyler Kepner, "Transcendent Athlete Transforms an Event," *The New York Times*, March 23, 2023.

32. Rhett Bollinger, "Ohtani obliterates the longest HR in MLB this season for No. 30," mlb.com, July 1, 2023.
33. Steve Hewitt, "Alex Cora 'in awe' of Angels two-way sensation Shohei Ohtani," *Boston Herald*, July 5, 2021.
34. Tim Keown, "Shohei Ohtani stands alone in spotlight amid gambling scandal," espn.com/mlb/story/_/id/39816463/Shohei-ohtani-dodgers-interpreter-gambling-betting-scandal-ippei-mizuhara, March 27, 2024.
35. Andy McCullough, "Ippei Mizuhara, Shohei Ohtani's former interpreter, charged with bank fraud and stealing more than $16M," theathletic.com, April 11, 2024.
36. Fabian Ardaya, "Dodgers learning quickly that Shohei Ohtani loves the details," *The Athletic*, February 27, 2024.
37. Alden Gonzalez, "Shohei Ohtani says he feels like a rookie again with Dodgers," ESPN.com, February 9, 2024.
38. Tom Verducci, "The Icon Among Us," *Sports Illustrated*, April 2024, 28.
39. Fletcher, *SHO-TIME*, 162.

Chapter 13

1. L. Robert Davids, ed., and Mike Cook, *Great Hitting Pitchers* (Phoenix: Society for American Baseball Research, 2012), 19.
2. Davids and Cook, *Great Hitting Pitchers*, 13.
3. Marty Appel, *Pinstripe Empire* (New York: Bloomsbury, 2012), 170–171.
4. David Jones, ed., *Deadball Stars of the American League* (Dulles, VA: Potomac Books, 2006), 534.
5. Al Quimby, "Red Lucas," SABR Biography Profile, https://sabr.org/bioproj/person/Red-Lucas/.
6. Bill James, *The New Bill James Historical Baseball Abstract* (New York: Free Press, 2003), 871–872.
7. James C. O'Leary, "Wes Ferrell's Home Run Wins Another in the Ninth," *Boston Globe*, July 23, 1935.
8. Davids and Cook, *Great Hitting Pitchers*, 56.
9. Gerry Hern, "Tobin Content to Remain Pitcher," *Boston Post*, May 14, 1942.
10. Jerry Nason, "Tobin Hits 3 Homers,

New Pitchers' Mark," *Boston Daily Globe*, May 14, 1942.

11. Howell Stevens, "Jim Tobin Slams Three Home Runs," *Boston Post*, May 14, 1942.

12. C. Paul Rogers III, "Vern Law," SABR Biography Profile, https://sabr.org/bioproj/person/Vern-Law/.

13. Pete Cava, *Indiana-Born Major League Baseball Players* (Jefferson, NC: McFarland, 2015), 113.

Bibliography

Appel, Marty. *Pinstripe Empire.* New York: Bloomsbury USA, 2012.

Bissinger, Buzz. *Three Nights in August: Strategy, Heartbreak and Joy Inside the Mind of a Manager.* New York: Houghton Mifflin, 2006.

Bjarkman, Peter C. *A History of Cuban Baseball, 1864-2006.* Jefferson, NC: McFarland, 2007.

Bruce, Janet. *The Kansas City Monarchs: Champions of Black Baseball.* Lawrence: University Press of Kansas, 1985.

Cava, Pete. *Indiana-Born Major League Baseball Players.* Jefferson, NC: McFarland, 2015.

Chiarello, Mark, and Jack Morelli. *Heroes of the Negro Leagues.* New York: Abrams, 2007.

Cisneros, Pedro Treto. *The Mexican League: Comprehensive Player Statistics.* Jefferson, NC: McFarland, 2022.

Creamer, Robert W. *Babe: The Legend Comes to Life.* New York: Simon & Schuster, 1974.

Curran, William. *Big Sticks: The Batting Revolution of the Twenties.* New York: William Morrow, 1990.

Davids, L. Robert, ed., and Mike Cook. *Great Hitting Pitchers.* Phoenix: Society for American Baseball Research, 2012.

Di Salvatore, Bryan. *A Clever Base-Ballist: The Life and Times of John Montgomery Ward.* New York: Pantheon Books, 1999.

Dickson, Paul. *Baseball's Greatest Quotations.* New York: HarperCollins, 2008.

Dixon, Phil S. *Phil Dixon's American Baseball Chronicles, Great Teams: The 1905 Philadelphia Giants, Volume Three.* Charleston, SC: BookSurge, 2006.

Dixon, Phil S. *Wilber "Bullet" Rogan and the Kansas City Monarchs.* Jefferson, NC: McFarland, 2010.

Farrell, James T. *My Baseball Diary.* Carbondale: Southern Illinois University Press, 1998.

Figueredo, Jorge. *Cuban Baseball: A Statistical History, 1878-1961.* Jefferson, NC: McFarland, 2003.

Fletcher, Jeff. *SHO-TIME: The Inside Story of Shohei Ohtani and the Greatest Baseball Season Ever Played.* New York: Diversion Books, 2022.

Gilbert, Brother, C.F.X. *Young Babe Ruth.* Ed. Harry Rothberger. Jefferson, NC: McFarland, 1999.

Greenes, Steven R. *Negro Leaguers and the Hall of Fame.* Jefferson, NC: McFarland, 2020.

Gutman, Bill. *Giants of Baseball.* New York: Tempo Books, 1975.

Heaphy, Leslie A. *The Negro Leagues 1869-1960.* Jefferson, NC: McFarland, 2003.

Hogan, Lawrence D. *Shades of Glory: The Negro Leagues and the Story of African-American Baseball.* Washington, D.C.: National Geographic, 2006.

Holway, John. *The Complete Book of Baseball's Negro Leagues: The Other Half of Baseball History.* Roxbury, CT: Hastings House, 2001.

Holway, John B. *Black Giants.* Bloomington, IN: Xlibris, 2009.

Holway, John B. *Blackball Stars.* New York: Carroll & Graf, 1988.

Holway, John B. *Josh and Satch.* New York: Carroll & Graf, 1992.

Holway, John B. *Voices from the Great Black Baseball Leagues.* Boston: Da Capo Press, 1992.

Honig, Donald. *Baseball When the Grass Was Real: Baseball from the Twenties to the Forties Told by the Men Who Played It.* Lincoln: University of Nebraska Press, 1993.

Huhn, Rick. *The Chalmers Race: Ty Cobb, Napoleon Lajoie, and the Controversial 1910 Batting Title That Became a National Obsession.* Lincoln: University of Nebraska Press, 2014.

James, Bill. *The Bill James Handbook 2022.* Chicago: ACTA Sports, 2022.

James, Bill. *The New Bill James Historical Baseball Abstract.* New York: Free Press, 2003.

Jensen, Chris. *Baseball State by State.* Jefferson, NC: McFarland, 2012.

Jones, David, ed. *Deadball Stars of the American League.* Dulles, VA: Potomac Books, 2006.

Kelley, Brent. *Voices from the Negro Leagues: Conversations with 52 Baseball Standouts of the Period, 1924–1960.* Jefferson, NC: McFarland, 2005.

Lanctot, Neil. *Negro League Baseball: The Rise and Ruin of a Black Institution.* Philadelphia: University of Pennsylvania Press, 2004.

Leavy, Jane. *The Big Fella: Babe Ruth and the World He Created.* New York: Harper Collins, 2018.

Lee, Philip. *Black Stats Matter.* Jefferson, NC: McFarland, 2023.

Lester, Larry. *Baseball's First Colored World Series: The 1924 Meeting of the Hilldale Giants and Kansas City Monarchs.* Jefferson, NC: McFarland, 2006, 90.

Lester, Larry, and Wayne Stivers. *The Negro Leagues Book Volume 2: The Players, 1862–1960.* Kansas City, MO: Noir Tech Research, 2020.

McNeil, William F. *The California Winter League: America's First Integrated Professional Baseball League.* Jefferson, NC: McFarland, 2002.

Montville, Leigh. *The Big Bam: The Life and Times of Babe Ruth.* New York: Broadway Books, 2006.

Nemec, David. *Major League Baseball Profiles, 1871–1900, Volume 2.* Lincoln: University of Nebraska Press, 2011.

Nowlin, Bill, Len Levin, Dan Descrochers, and Maurice Bouchard, eds. *Opening Fenway Park with Style: The 1912 Champion Red Sox.* Phoenix: Society for American Baseball Research, 2012.

Okrent, Daniel, and Steve Wulf. *Baseball Anecdotes.* New York: Oxford University Press, 1989.

Peterson, Robert. *Only the Ball Was White.* New York: Gramercy Books, 1999.

Peterson, Todd, ed. *The Negro Leagues Were Major Leagues.* Jefferson, NC: McFarland, 2020.

Posnanski, Joe. *The Baseball 100.* New York: Avid Reader Press, 2021.

Posnanski, Joe. *Why We Love Baseball: A History in 50 Moments.* New York: Dutton, 2023.

Riley, James A. *All-Time All-Stars of Black Baseball.* Cocoa, FL: TK Publishers, 1983.

Riley, James A. *The Biographical Encyclopedia of the Negro Baseball Leagues.* New York: Carroll & Graf, 1994.

Riley, James A. *Dandy, Day, and the Devil.* Cocoa, FL: TK Publishers, 1987.

Riley, James A. *Of Monarchs and Black Barons.* Jefferson, NC: McFarland, 2012.

Ritter, Lawrence S. *The Glory of Their Times.* New York: Harper Perennial Modern Classics, 2010.

Ruth, George Herman. *Babe Ruth's Own Book of Baseball.* Lincoln: University of Nebraska Press, Bison Books, 1992.

Simon, Tom, ed. *Deadball Stars of the National League.* Dulles, VA: Brassey's, 2004.

Stevens, David. *Baseball's Radical For All Seasons: A Biography of John Montgomery Ward.* Lanham, MD: Scarecrow Press, 1998.

Stewart, Wayne, ed. *The Little Red Book of Baseball Wisdom.* New York: Skyhorse Publishing, 2012.

Thornley, Stew. *Baseball in Minnesota: The Definitive History.* St. Paul: Minnesota Historical Society, 2006.

Tye, Larry. *Satchel: The Life and Times of an American Legend.* New York: Random House, 2009.

Tygiel, Jules. *Past Time: Baseball as History.* New York: Oxford University Press, 2001.

Ward, Geoffrey C., and Ken Burns. *Baseball: An Illustrated History.* New York: Alfred A. Knopf, 1994.

Ward, John Montgomery. *Base-Ball: How to Become a Player.* Phoenix: The Society for American Baseball Research, 2014, p. 46.

Weintraub, Robert. *The House That Ruth Built.* New York: Little, Brown, 2011.

White, Sol. *History of Colored Base Ball.* Lincoln: University of Nebraska Press, 1995.

Williams, Peter. *When the Giants Were the Giants: Bill Terry and the Golden Age of New York Baseball.* Chapel Hill: Algonquin Books of Chapel Hill, 1994.

Index

Aaron, Hank 80, 154
Acuña, Ronald 232
Agee, Tommy 177
Aguila (CWL) 117
Alberto, Hanser 14
Alexander, Grover Cleveland "Pete" 32, 86, 106, 107, 109, 137, 172
Allen, Newt 104, 108
Almendares (CWL) 104, 138, 151–153, 156, 159, 163, 173
American Association (AA) 25, 26, 32, 35–39, 41, 42, 44, 45, 48, 50, 51, 53–55, 69, 102
American League (AL) 3, 15, 16, 34, 35, 43, 50, 56, 57, 59, 61, 64, 66, 67, 69–78, 84, 86, 90, 91, 94, 137, 194, 200, 205, 209, 222, 225–227, 230, 239, 240, 243–245
Angel Stadium 222, 225, 227
Ankiel, Rick 212–214, 227
Anson, Cap 53
Arenado, Nolan 228
Ashburn, Richie 185
Atlanta Black Crackers 173
Atlanta Braves 211, 232, 244
Azules de Veracruz 126–128, 180

Bacharach Giants 138, 145, 166
Ball, Walter 130
Baltimore Black Sox 146, 179
Baltimore Elite Giants 131, 181, 183
Baltimore Orioles 33, 40, 45, 63, 82, 83, 189, 190, 209
Bancroft, Dave 198
Bancroft, Frank 46
Bankhead, Dan 175
Banks, Ernie 99
Baró, Bernardo 122
Barrow, Ed 4, 86–88, 90
Bauers, Russ 182
Bautista, José 215
Bell, David 214

Bell, James "Cool Papa" 121–125, 169, 175
Bell, William 105, 106, 125, 126, 151, 180, 236
Bender, Charles 53
Bentley, Jack 189–191; Triple Crown 190
Berra, Yogi 218
Betts, Mookie 228
Billingham, Jack 89
Birmingham Black Barons 129, 144, 155, 157, 174, 209
Bismarck Churchills 128, 160, 173
Black, Joe 177
Black Sox/Black Sox scandal 39–40, 58, 90, 186, 192
Blackwell, Ewell 182
Bonds, Barry 80, 91, 97, 217
Boston Americans 69, 70, 76
Boston Beaneaters 52, 53
Boston Bees 197
Boston Braves 95, 196–198, 201, 244
Boston Red Sox 4, 11, 17, 60, 73–75, 80, 81, 83–91, 93–95, 195, 201, 205, 211, 237, 238, 240–243
Bradley, George 20, 31–33
Bragaña, Ramón 117, 126, 127, 180; "El Professor" 126
Brame, Erv 235–237
Branca, Ralph 207
Braun, Steve 199
Brecheen, Harry 89
Bressler, Rube 81, 191–193
Brett, Ken 6, 235
Brewer, Chet 105, 106, 108, 164, 173
Brewer, Sherwood 160
Bridges, Tommy 94
Brief, Bunny 102
Britt, George "Chippy" 127, 170
Brocail, Doug 215
Brooklyn Bridegrooms 25, 37, 39, 49, 50, 51
Brooklyn Dodgers 87, 156, 175, 197, 200, 202, 204–207, 241

Index

Brooklyn Eagles 129, 173, 179
Brooklyn Robins 85, 188, 195, 201, 245
Brooklyn Royal Giants 130, 137, 141, 145, 147, 164
Brooklyn Superbas 63
Brooklyn Ward's Wonders 26
Brotherhood of Professional Baseball Players 23, 24, 26
Brown, Barney "Brinquitos" 13, 116, 120, 128, 180
Brown, Dave 101, 109, 152
Brown, Ray 10, 13, 15, 120, 128–130, 164, 174, 236; pitcher's Triple Crown 129
Brown, Mordecai "Three Finger" 142
Brown, Willard 175, 182, 183
Browning, Pete 42
Brown's Tennessee Rats 136
Bubic, Kris 225
Buckner, Harry "Green River" 130
Buffinton, Charlie 33, 34
Bumgarner, Madison 89, 234
Bunning, Jim 21
Burgess, Smoky 199
Burns, Thomas "Oyster" 51
Bush, Bullet Joe 101, 247
Bush, Guy 95
Bush, Matt 215, 216
Bushong, Doc 51
Byrd, Bill 15, 130, 131, 144, 180, 236
Byrne, Charles 39

Caglianone, Jac 7
Caldwell, Ray 58–61, 102; "Slim" 59–61
California Winter League (CWL) 100, 107, 123, 137, 141, 143, 145, 149, 150, 239
Callahan, Jimmy "Nixey" 10, 15, 34–35, 67, 235
Camden Yards 184
Campanella, Roy 119, 131, 147, 181
Campos, Tatica 131, 132
Cannady, Walter "Rev" 132
Carey, Max 68, 107
Caribbean Baseball Hall of Fame 140
Carr, George 108
Carrigan, Bill 84
Caruthers, Bob 1, 9, 10, 11, 12, 13, 14, 35–39, 50, 51, 226, 236
Cash, Bill 183
Cavarretta, Phil 207
Cease, Dylan 228
Chacón, Pelayo 113
Chalmers, Harry 64
Chance, Frank 59, 137
Chapman, Ben 199, 200; "The Alabama Flash" 200
Chapman, Ray 186

Charleston, Oscar 109, 112–115, 118–120, 123, 124, 133, 134, 137, 163, 170, 171, 196
Chase, Hal 193
Chesbro, Jack 53, 59, 63, 66, 69
Chicago American Giants 100, 101, 103, 105, 108, 125, 129, 136, 137, 139, 141, 147, 152, 154, 157, 158, 160, 163, 169, 170, 172–176
Chicago Colts/Orphans 34, 35, 51, 52, 78
Chicago Cubs 72, 79, 89, 198, 207, 210, 211, 246
Chicago Leland Giants 140
Chicago White Sox 34, 35, 66, 67, 70–72, 74, 85, 137, 154, 212, 230, 241, 245
Chicago White Stockings 24, 31, 38, 52, 53
Chirban, Lou 176
Cijntje, Jurrangelo 7
Cincinnati Cuban Stars 122, 142
Cincinnati Reds 19, 45, 48, 69, 79, 129, 151, 188, 192, 198, 202, 208, 210, 214, 232, 239
Cincinnati Tigers 173
Clarizio, Louis 176
Clark, Bob 51
Clarkson, John 45, 47
Clemens, Roger 45
Clemente, Roberto 115
Cleveland Blues 48
Cleveland Buckeyes 144, 161, 175
Cleveland Indians 60, 61, 71, 75, 76, 144, 177, 203, 240
Cleveland Naps 77
Cleveland Spiders 49
Cleveland Tate Stars 145, 151
Cloninger, Tony 235
Cobb, Ty 40, 57, 64, 120, 164, 186, 195, 218
Cockrell, Phil 134, 138, 146
Cohen, Syd 95
Cole, Bert 92
Coleman, Clarence "Pops" 169
Collins, Eddie 63
Collins, Hub 51
Colorado Rockies 225, 243
Columbus Blue Birds 172
Columbus Buckeyes 12
Combs, Earle 237
Comiskey, Charles 137
Comiskey Park 94, 114, 161, 174, 181
Concordia Eagles 118
Connor, Roger 24, 92
Coombs, Jack 76, 77; "Colby Jack" 76
Cooney, Johnny 15, 196, 197
Cooper, Andy 105, 131, 160
Cora, Alex 230
Corbett, Charles 235
Corkhill, John 51
Cornelius, Willie 236

Index

Corriden, Red 64
Coveleski, Stan 60, 97
Crandall, Doc 61–63, 74
Crandall, Karl 63
Crane, Ed 55
Cravath, Gavvy 91
Crawford, Sam 151
Cuban Baseball Hall of Fame 116, 122, 127, 138, 142, 150, 151, 153, 156, 159, 164
Cuban Giants 120
Cuban Stars East 113, 115, 122, 138
Cuban Stars of Havana 137, 151, 153, 154, 156
Cuban Stars West 122, 141, 156
Cuban Winter League (CWL) 105, 112, 115, 116, 119, 122, 123, 125, 126, 128–132, 134–136, 138, 140–142, 148, 149, 151–157, 159, 163, 164, 173
Cuban X-Giants 140, 148, 153
Cummings, Candy 32
Cunningham, George 77
Curry, Homer "Goose" 13, 15, 134, 135, 183, 236
Curry, Rube 151, 152

Dailey, Hugh 54
Daily, Ed 55
Dandridge, Ray 180
Danforth, Dave 84
Daniels, Harry 130, 138, 148
Darvish, Yu 228
Daubert, Jake 193
Dauvray, Helen 25
Dauvray Cup 25
Davis, Johnny "Cherokee" 135
Davis, Roosevelt 170
Davis, Walter "Steel Arm" 135, 136, 152
Day, John 22
Day, Leon 1–3, 6, 10, 121, 130, 131, 178–185; elected to Hall of Fame 185; G.I. World Series 182; Opening Day no-hitter 182, 183
Deadball Era 1, 2, 56–79, 156, 168, 186, 187, 238, 245
Dean, Lovill "Chubby" 203
Dean, Dizzy 34, 108
Dean, Nelson 105
DeGrom, Jacob 218
De La Cruz, Elly 232
Delahanty, Ed 52
DeMoss, Bingo 169
Detroit Senators 124
Detroit Stars 103, 106, 135, 142, 146, 151, 153, 158, 163, 169, 170, 172
Detroit Tigers 34, 43, 72, 74, 84, 94, 156, 202, 209, 214, 239, 240, 243

Detroit Wolverines 21
Dickey, Bill 237, 238
Dihigo, Martín 1–3, 6, 7, 9, 10, 13, 103, 104, 111–119, 123, 163, 180, 222; Cuban leagues 111–114, 119; "El Inmortal" 111, 116; "El Maestro" 111–114, 117–119; Mexican League 111–113, 117–119, 121; pitcher's Triple Crown 117
DiMaggio, Joe 4, 111, 187, 196, 205, 206
Dixon, Rap 118, 179
Doby, Larry 175, 178, 183, 184
Donaldson, John 12, 120, 136, 137, 151
Donohue, Pete 239
Donovan, Bill 59, 83
Dorgan, Mike 20
Dowling, Pete 34
Drake, Bill 151
Drysdale, Don 72, 77, 247
Dugan, Joe 61
Duncan, Frank 108
Dunn, Jack 82, 86, 190
Dusak, Erv 206
Dyll, Frank 176

Earle, Charles 137, 138
East-West All-Star Game 108, 114, 123, 124, 128–130, 135, 139, 143, 147, 149, 155, 157, 160, 161, 167, 173, 174, 179–181, 209
Eastern Colored League 103, 106, 113, 122, 127, 132, 139, 145, 165, 166
Egan, Ben 83
Ehmke, Howard 93
Elmwood Giants 176
Evans, Bill "Happy" 171

Fabré, Isidro 138
Farrell, Luther 13, 15, 138, 139, 164, 235, 236
Federal League 28, 62, 64, 83
Feller, Bob 74, 95, 108, 129, 175, 182
Fenway Park 57, 73, 74, 91
Ferguson, Charlie 55
Ferrell, Rick 240
Ferrell, Wes 48, 234, 235, 237, 239, 240
Fields, Wilmer "Red" 139, 140, 175
Fletcher, Art 74
Fohl, Lee 76
Forbes Field 95
Ford, Whitey 39, 89
Foster, Andrew "Rube" 101, 109, 130, 137, 140, 141, 147, 150, 163; "The Father of Black Baseball" 141
Foster, Bill "Willie" 15, 99, 105, 109, 124, 125, 152, 170
Foster, Rube 83, 85
Foutz, Dave 1, 10, 15, 38, 39, 51, 228, 236

Frazee, Harry 90, 91
Freeman, Buck 90
Freeman, Freddie 225
Frick, Ford 91

Galvin, Pud 45
Garcia, Manuel "Cocaína" 141, 142
Gardner, Jelly 115, 163
Garner, Horace 154
Gatewood, Bill 142
Gehrig, Lou 94, 198, 200, 237
Gehringer, Charlie 169
Gibson, Bob 4, 178, 243, 244
Gibson, Josh 112, 118, 119, 124, 133, 167, 170, 171, 175, 180
Giles, George 150
Gilkerson's Union Giants 169
Gisentaner, Willie "Three Finger" 13, 142
Glass, Carl "Butch" 143
Glavine, Tom 244
Gleason, Kid 10, 39, 40
Glenn, Joe 94
Goldschmidt, Paul 228
Gomber, Austin 225
Gomez, Gonzalo 118
Gomez, Juan Vincente 118
Gomez, Lefty 53
Grant, Mudcat 177
Green, Shawn 42
Greenlee, Gus 171
Greenlee Field 114, 125, 171
Griffith, Bob "Schoolboy" 143
Griffith, Clark 35, 59, 70
Griffith Stadium 88
Grimes, Burleigh 34, 245
Grove, Lefty 74, 97, 109, 171
Guidry, Ron 84

Habana (CWL) 104, 116, 125, 126, 141, 148, 154
Hack, Stan 207
Hairston, Harold 175
Hall, Dick 208, 209
Hamilton, Josh 6
Hampton, Lewis 15, 143, 144, 235, 236
Hampton, Mike 237, 243
Hanlon, Ned 45
Hanyzewski, Ed 175
Haren, Dan 236
Harlem Globetrotters 175
Harper, Tommy 210
Harris, Joe 76, 77
Harrisburg Giants 132, 142, 166
Hartford Dark Blues 32
Hartung, Clint "Honda Hurricane" 206, 207, 214

Hawkins, Lemuel 99
Hecker, Guy 10, 12, 14, 37, 40-42, 45, 235, 236, 239, 244
Heilmann, Harry 169
Hendrix, Claude 245, 246
Henry, Tommy 229
Hensley, Logan 170
Herbel, Ron 234
Herman, Babe 108
Hershiser, Orel 77, 236
Hess, Otto 77, 78
Hicks, Aaron 6
Hilldale Club 103-105, 114, 125, 132, 134, 146, 151, 162, 165, 166
Hilltop Park 70
Hoblitzell, Dick 88
Hoelskoetter, Art 12
Hoffman, Trevor 5
Hokkaido Nippon-Ham Fighters 219, 220
Holland, Bill 152
Homestead Grays 114, 123, 124, 127, 128, 132, 139, 142, 144, 149, 154, 156, 161, 164, 167, 169-175, 180, 181, 183
Hooper, Harry 87, 90, 95
Hornsby, Rogers 195, 196
Hoskins, Dave "Wahoo" 144
House of David 107, 108, 172
Houston Black Buffaloes 106
Howell, Dixie 235
Howell, Harry 15, 63, 64, 67; "Handsome Harry" 63
Hoyt, Waite 97
Hubbard, Jesse "Mountain" 12, 144, 145
Hubbell, Carl 21, 126
Huggins, Miller 93
Hughes, Mickey 51
Hughes, Sammy 132, 181
Hunter, Catfish 21

Indianapolis ABCs 122, 133, 137, 144, 145, 162, 227
Inks, Bert 237
International League 24, 83, 183, 188-190
Irvin, Monte 178, 183, 184
Israel, Al 154
Israel, Clarence "Half a Pint" 180

Jackson, Joe 196
Jackson, Reggie 26, 223
Jackson, Travis 197
Jacksonville Jays 154
James, Bill 5, 29, 52, 109, 115, 131, 150, 162-164, 166, 168, 180, 201, 239
Jamestown Red Sox 107, 128, 172
Jeffcoat, Hal 207, 208
Jeffries, Jim 12, 13

Jenkins, Ferguson 45
Jenkinson, Bill 87
Jeter, Derek 233
Jethroe, Sam 175
John, Tommy 45
Johnson, Ban 56, 59, 64
Johnson, Connie 183
Johnson, Judy 103, 124, 150, 171
Johnson, Oscar "Heavy" 99, 103, 104
Johnson, Walter 21, 56, 59, 73, 74, 77, 85, 86, 88, 96, 106, 111, 190, 193, 222, 238, 239
Johnston, Wade 12, 145
Jones, Fielder 72
Jones, Sam 92
Joseph, Newt 104
Joss, Addie 29, 34
Judge, Aaron 6, 217, 228, 232, 233

Kaat, Jim 34
Kansas City All Nations 100, 136, 137, 151
Kansas City Blues 99, 102
Kansas City Giants 99, 100
Kansas City Monarchs 98, 100–108, 110, 121, 125, 137, 142, 146, 150, 151, 160, 161, 164, 165, 169, 171, 174, 175, 181, 183, 227, 234
Kansas City Royals 225, 227, 229
Kansas City Stars 124
Kelly, King 53
Kendrick, Bob 3, 7, 117
Kenyon, Harry 11, 12, 13, 14, 145, 146, 227
Kershaw, Clayton 28
Kieschnick, Brooks "Toolshed" 211, 212
Kimbrough, Larry 23
Kimsey, Chad 236
Konetchy, Ed 188

Lajoie, Nap 56, 64, 77
Lane, Isaac 12
Lannin, Joe 83
Lardner, Ring 73
Larsen, Don 246, 247
LaRussa, Tony 213
Lasorda, Tommy 201
Latino Baseball Hall of Fame 127
Law, Vern 245
Lazzeri, Tony 237
League Park 60
Lee, Holsey "Script" 115, 146, 151
Lee, Wyatt 14, 78
Leland Giants 140
Lelivelt, Bill 156
Lemon, Bob 5, 53, 240
Leonard, Buck 111, 113, 119, 147, 175, 179, 181
Leonard, Dutch 83, 188

Lester, Larry 6
Lewis, Duffy 74
Lindell, Johnny 204, 205
Lindsay, Bill "The Kansas Cyclone" 146, 147
Lindstrom, Freddie 190
Live Ball Era 2, 17, 90, 168, 186–216
Lloyd, Pop 132
LoanDepot Park 228
Lobert, Hans 83
Lorenzen, Michael 92, 214
Los Angeles Angels 12, 17, 62, 209, 210, 218, 221–230
Los Angeles Dodgers 3, 14, 72, 220, 225, 231, 232, 247
Los Angeles White Sox 100
Louisville Eclipse/Colonels 40, 42, 44, 51
Lovett, Tom 51
Lucas, Red 95, 198, 199, 234, 239; Cincinnati Reds Hall of Fame 199; "The Nashville Narcissus" 199
Lundy, Dick 132
Luque, Dolf 239
Lush, Johnny 1, 65
Lyons, Jimmie 163

Mack, Connie 76, 77, 83, 91, 203
Mackey, Biz 103
Macon, Max 204
Maddon, Joe 224, 225
Maddux, Greg 213, 217
Magee, Sherry 83
Mahay, Ron 211
Major League Baseball (MLB) 5, 6, 7, 18, 24, 26, 29, 30, 44, 47, 89, 120, 121, 186, 215, 217, 221, 222, 224–226, 231, 233
Malarcher, Dave 152
Mamaux, Al 87
Manley, Effa 184
Mantilla, Felix 154
Mantle, Mickey 206, 233
Manush, Heinie 169
Marianao (CWL) 116, 128
Maris, Roger 94, 233
Markakis, Nick 6
Markham, Johnny 155
Marquard, Rube 74
Martin, Dr. W.S. 173
Mathews, Bobby 19–20, 45
Mathewson, Christy 28, 32, 33, 60, 74, 194, 245, 246
Mathis, Verdell "Lefty" 147, 148
Matlock, Leroy 170
Matsui, Hideki 232
Matthews, Wid 207
Maul, Al 55

Mays, Carl 242, 243
Mays, Willie 134, 241
McCarthy, Joe 205
McClellan, Dan 130, 148
McCovey, Willie 210
McDuffie, Terris 13, 149, 180
McGinnity, Joe 56, 79
McGraw, John 35, 40, 61–63, 74, 111, 113, 137, 163, 164
McGunnigle, Bill 51
McGwire, Mark 221
McHenry, Henry "Cream" 149, 183, 236
McInnis, Stuffy 90
McNair, Hurley 104, 109, 150
McNally, Dave 235
McNeely, Earl 190
McNeil, Jeff 228
Meekin, Jouett 235
Melvin, Doug 212
Memphis Red Sox 135, 143, 147, 157, 173, 174
Méndez, José "The Black Diamond" 103, 104, 138, 150–152
Menefee, John "Jock" 15, 78
Mercer, Win 42–44, 236
Mesa, Pablo 122
Meusel, Bob 107
Mexican League 103, 117, 118, 123, 126–128, 141, 143, 147, 149, 157, 159, 161, 208
Mexican Professional Baseball Hall of Fame 118, 127, 159
Miarka, Stanley 176
Miller, Cyclone 46
Miller, Eddie "Buck" 152
Miller, Marvin 24
Milwaukee Braves 247
Milwaukee Brewers 211
Minasian, Perry 224
Minneapolis Millers 68
Miñoso, Minnie 117
Mitchell, Clarence 187–189
Mitchell, George 152, 153
Mize, Johnny 111, 118
Mizuhara, Ippei 231
Mobile Black Bears 168
Mohawk Giants 135
Monroe Monarchs 135, 155, 172
Monteagudo, René 12, 203
Montreal Royals 156
Moore, Dobie 99, 105
Moore, Red 167
Morgan, Jack 86
Morrill, John 34
Morris, Ed 38
Morris, Hal "Yellow Horse" 104
Morris, Jack 53

Muehlebach Field 7, 103
Mueller, Don 207
Mullane, Tony 14, 23, 41, 44, 45; "Apollo in the Box" 45
Mullin, George 238, 239
Mungo, Van Lingle 197
Muñoz, José 153
Musial, Stan 5

Nashville Sounds 207
National Baseball Hall of Fame 27, 29, 44, 45, 48, 53, 68, 99, 101, 106, 113, 123, 124, 125, 128, 133, 140, 141, 148, 150, 156, 159, 162–164, 167, 177, 184, 185, 194, 195, 240, 241, 245
National League (NL) 5, 19–24, 26–28, 30–32, 36, 37, 40, 42, 43, 45, 48–50, 52–54, 56, 57, 61, 63, 65, 66, 69, 78, 79, 190, 191, 195, 197, 199, 201, 202, 212, 234, 239, 241, 243–245, 247
Navin Field 92, 94
Negro American League 108, 128, 147, 149, 154, 157, 160, 173, 174, 181
Negro Leagues Baseball Museum 3, 112, 178
Negro National League (NNL) 98–101, 103, 106, 109, 114, 122, 123, 128, 131, 132, 134, 135, 140, 142, 143, 145, 148–150, 154, 155, 158, 163, 168, 170, 179, 181, 183, 186
Negro Southern League 136, 155, 172
Negro World Series 99, 125, 129, 132, 136, 139, 144–146, 150, 152, 154, 155, 157, 165, 166, 181, 183
Nevin, Phil 230
New York Black Yankees 158, 172
New York Cubans 114, 115, 158, 159, 183
New York Giants 22, 23, 24, 25, 27, 28, 40, 43, 54, 61, 62, 74, 90, 92, 93, 163, 189, 190, 195, 206, 207
New York Highlanders 58, 59, 63, 66, 69, 72
New York Lincoln Giants 142, 158, 164
New York Mets 209, 213, 243
New York Yankees 4, 59, 60, 61, 63, 66, 70, 81, 83, 87, 90–96, 98, 101, 186, 190, 195, 197, 200, 203–205, 225, 237, 238, 240, 242, 247; Bronx Bombers 92, 94, 237
Newark Eagles 135, 179–181, 183, 184
Newark Little Giants 24
Newcombe, Don 184, 237, 241, 242, 247
Nichols, Kid 49

Oakland A's 222
O'Brien, Darby 51
O'Connor, Jack 64
Odor, Rougned 215

O'Doul, Lefty 195, 196; Nippon Professional Baseball League 196
Ohtani, Shohei 1–7, 9, 10, 11, 12, 13, 15, 16, 17, 89, 121, 187, 209, 213, 214, 217–234; "Babe Ruth of Japan" 219; Commissioner's Historic Achievement Award 226; Fifty-fifty club 232; Los Angeles Angels 218, 221–230; Los Angeles Dodgers 231–233; MVP Award 217, 220, 221; Nippon Professional Baseball 219–21; Rookie of the Year 223; World Baseball Classic 228, 229
Olerud, John 6
Oliva, Tony 115
Oms, Alejandro 122
O'Neil, Buck 99, 108, 134, 161, 177, 183, 184
Oracle Park 196
O'Rourke, Jim 24, 52
Orth, Al 65–67; "Curveless Wonder" 65; "Smiling Al" 66
Owens, Brick 86
Owings, Micah 236, 237

Padrón, Juan 154
Padrón, Luis "El Mulo" 10, 137, 153, 154
Page, Ted 115, 170, 171
Paige, Satchel 15, 108, 109, 117–119, 124, 128, 129, 142, 147, 149, 160, 164, 165, 167, 168, 171–173, 176, 178, 181, 183
Parker, Tom "Big Train" 154
Parnell, Roy "Red" 155
Partlow, Roy 155, 156
Pedroso, Eustaquio "Bombin" 10, 12, 156
Pennock, Herb 34, 97
Perry, Alonzo 157, 175
Perry, Gaylord 243
Peters, Gary 245
Pettitte, Andy 34
Philadelphia Athletics 19, 33, 37, 53, 55, 72, 76, 77, 83, 87, 151, 152, 192, 203
Philadelphia Giants 140, 141, 148
Philadelphia Phillies 19, 33, 34, 40, 65, 70, 71, 75, 83, 94, 188, 189, 191, 195, 199, 201, 203, 205, 214, 242
Philadelphia Stars 149, 155, 156, 182, 183
Phillippe, Deacon 69
Pinkney, George 51
Pinson, Vada 210
Pittsburgh Crawfords 124, 125, 167, 171, 173
Pittsburgh Pirates 68, 69, 78, 95, 172, 193, 202, 205, 208, 237, 245, 246
Plank, Eddie 151, 192
Players' National League of Professional Base Ball Clubs 26, 40, 48
Plitt, Norman 86
Pollock's Cuban Stars 128

Polo Grounds 22, 75, 87, 91, 97, 197
Pompez, Alex 113
Posey, Cum 109, 112, 119, 128, 132, 142, 170, 171, 175, 181
Powell, Willie 157
Progressive Field 61
Providence Grays 19, 20, 21, 32, 46, 48, 54, 83, 188, 243
Puerto Rican Baseball Hall of Fame 184
Puerto Rico Winter League 128, 135, 139, 180, 181
Pujols, Albert 221

Queen, Mel 210

Radbourn, Charles "Old Hoss" 21, 22, 46–48
Radcliffe, Alex 168, 172, 174
Radcliffe, Ted "Double Duty" 1–3, 6, 12, 121, 153, 167–177, 180
Rector, Connie "Broadway" 157, 158
Redding, Dick 145
Redus, Frog 123
Reed, Jeremy 218
Reedy, Buddy 154
Reis, Bobby 200, 201
Rice, Grantland 29, 93, 199
Richmond, Lee 21
Richmond Colts 200
Rickey, Branch 59, 137, 193, 200, 204, 208, 245
Rigney, Bill 210
Rile, Ed "Huck" 10, 11, 12, 13, 15, 158, 235, 236
Rivera, Mariano 28
Roberts, Dave 231
Robinson, Bobby 168
Robinson, Frank 210
Robinson, Jackie 3, 113, 125, 147, 148, 156, 174, 175, 183, 199, 241
Rogan, Wilber "Bullet" 1–4, 6, 7, 9, 10, 11, 12, 13, 14, 15, 98–110, 121, 125, 145, 151, 166, 176, 222, 227, 233–236; compared to Satchel Paige 108, 109; 25th Infantry Wreckers 99, 100
Rooker, Jim 237
Rosen, Lon 233
Ross, William 236
Roush, Edd 193
Rowe, Schoolboy 74, 242
Rowland, Pants 67, 85
Royer, Carlos 109
Ruffing, Red 203, 234, 237, 238
Runyon, Damon 167
Ruppert, Jacob 59, 87, 93
Ruppert Stadium 183

Rusch, Glendon 212
Rusie, Amos 48
Russell, Johnny 123
Russell, Reb 67–69
Ruth, Babe 1–5, 7, 9–17, 36, 42, 58, 60, 69, 73, 80–98, 111, 120, 121, 126, 163, 186, 190, 194, 198–200, 203, 207, 213, 214, 217, 219, 225, 226, 230, 233, 237, 242, 243, 246, 247; "Bambino" 1, 4, 80, 88, 91–94, 97, 109, 112, 127, 237; Brother Gilbert Cairnes 82, 85; Brother Matthias Boutlier 81, 82, 91; Hot Springs, Arkansas 86, 87; St. Mary's Industrial School for Boys 81, 82, 84, 85, 91; "Sultan of Swat" 58, 80, 91, 93; The House That Ruth Built 93, 95
Ryan, Nolan 45, 217
Ryan, Red 146

St. Louis Brown Stockings 32
St. Louis Browns 31, 36–39, 48–50, 59, 63, 64, 72, 74, 83, 88, 184, 193, 237, 239, 246, 247
St. Louis Cardinals 62, 65, 94, 189, 197, 199, 204–206, 208, 212, 227, 243, 244
St. Louis Giants 134, 142, 162
St. Louis Maroons 54, 55
St. Louis Stars 105, 106, 123, 124, 161, 167, 169–171
St. Louis Terriers 62
St. Paul Gophers 174
Salazar, Lázaro "Cuban Peach" 9, 10, 159
San Diego Padres 215
San Francisco Giants 234
San Francisco Seals 195
Santa Clara (CWL) 116, 129, 152, 159
Saperstein, Abe 175
Scales, George "Tubby" 158, 170
Schmidt, Mike 185
Schwarber, Kyle 228
Seay, Dick 180
Sewell, Rip 202
Seybold, Socks 57, 77
Seymour, Cy 54
Shaw, "Grunting Jim" 222
Shawkey, Bob 237
Shibe Park 57
Shore, Ernie 83, 86
Simmons, Al 107
Sisler, George 193–195
Smith, Bob 197, 198
Smith, Chino 158
Smith, Elmer 53, 76
Smith, Germany 51
Smith, Hilton 15, 115, 120, 129, 131, 159–161, 172, 173, 183, 236

Smith, Theolic "Fireball" 161
Smith, Willie 1, 12, 15, 209, 210
Smoltz, John 218
Snider, Duke 187, 241
Soto, Juan 232
South Atlantic League 154
South Bend Studebakers 175, 176
Spahn, Warren 242
Spalding, Al 32, 237
Speaker, Tris 60, 74, 75
spitball usage 58, 60, 61, 66, 71, 142, 143, 188
Staley, Harry 235
Stearnes, Turkey 109, 115, 153, 169, 170, 179
Stengel, Casey 108, 125, 196, 197
Stephens, Jake 103, 171
Stivetts, Jack 14, 48, 49, 235, 237; "Happy Jack" 48
Stovey, George 24
Stratton, Scott 19, 54, 236, 237
Streeter, Sam 236
Stroman, Marcus 230
Strong, Joe 161, 162, 236
Strong, Ted 183
Sullivan, Ted 47
Summers, Ed 21
Suttles, Mule 114, 169, 179, 180
Suzuki, Ichiro 194, 218
Sweeney, Charlie 46, 54

T-Mobile Park 225
Talcott, E.B. 28
Tampa Bay Rays 215
Tannehill, Jesse 69, 70
Tannehill, Lee 70
Tatis, Fernando, Jr. 224
Taylor, Ben 10, 11, 13, 162
Taylor, Billy 54, 55
Taylor, Candy Jim 162
Taylor, C.I. 137, 145, 162
Taylor, Jack 78, 79
Taylor, Schoolboy 173
Taylor, Steel Arm Johnny 162
Terry, Adonis 36, 49–52
Terry, Bill 126, 195
Texas Rangers 211, 215, 216
Thomas, Ira 152
Thomson, Bobby 207
Thormahlen, Herb 90
Thorn, John 26, 29
Tiant, Luis 225
Tobin, Jim 42, 244
Toledo Blue Stockings 45
Tommy John surgery 215, 218, 222, 224, 230
Toronto Blue Jays 215

Torriente, Cristóbal 104, 105, 109, 125, 153, 163, 164, 169
Trent, Ted 170
Trouppe, Quincy 128
Trout, Mike 7, 223, 225, 228, 229
Turner, Trea 228

Uhle, George 235, 237, 241
Union Association 46, 55

Vance, Dazzy 109
Vander Meer, Johnny 202
Van Haltren, George 54
Venditte, Pat 7
Venezuelan Professional Baseball League 111, 118, 126, 139
Visner, Joe 51

Wagner, Honus 141
Walker, Edsall 235, 236
Walker, Fleet 24
Walker, Harry 182
Walsh, Ed 58, 72, 73, 77
Walsh, Jared 227
Walters, Bucky 14, 201–203, 237; pitcher's Triple Crown 202
Wambsganss, Bill 187, 188
Ward, John Montgomery 1–4, 9, 10, 13, 14, 18–29, 32, 33, 47
Warneke, Lon 242
Washington Nationals 86, 88, 238
Washington Senators 43, 59, 66, 74, 78, 95, 189, 203, 222, 240

Weimer, Jake 79
Welch, Mickey 45, 54
Wells, Jake 69
Wells, Willie 169, 180
Weyhing, Gus 43
White, Doc 14, 15, 70–73
White, Sol 140
Whitney, Jim "Grasshopper" 14, 47, 52, 53
Whittington Park 86
Wicker, Bob 79
Wiedman, George "Stump" 21
Wilkinson, J.L. 100, 106, 110, 136, 151
Williams, John 12
Williams, Lefty 170
Williams, Smokey Joe 120, 145, 164, 165, 170; "Cyclone Joe" 164
Williams, Ted 97, 175, 187, 206, 218
Wills, Maury 29
Wilson, Earl 243
Wilson, Jud 170, 171, 196
Wilson, W. Rollo 134
Wiltse, Snake 36
Winfield, Dave 6, 218
Winters, Nip 103, 109, 146, 165, 166, 235, 236
Wise, Rick 235
Wood, Smoky Joe 5, 10, 15, 73–76, 83, 238
Wright, Wild Bill 181
Wrigley Field/Weeghman Park 57
Wynn, Early 241

Yankee Stadium 93, 95–97, 131, 167
Young, Cy 49, 56

www.ingramcontent.com/pod-product-compliance
Lightning Source LLC
Chambersburg PA
CBHW032034300426
44117CB00009B/1052